ZAGAT
2013

Washington, DC
Baltimore
Restaurants

LOCAL EDITORS
Olga Boikess and Martha Thomas
with Dina Gan

SENIOR CONSULTING EDITOR
Marty Katz

STAFF EDITOR
Josh Rogers

Published and distributed by
Zagat Survey, LLC
76 Ninth Avenue
New York, NY 10011
T: 212.977.6000
E: washbalt@zagat.com
plus.google.com/local

ACKNOWLEDGMENTS

We're grateful to our local editors, Olga Boikess, a Washington lawyer and avid diner who has edited this Survey since 1987; Martha Thomas, a Baltimore-based freelance writer who writes for food and national publications; and Marty Katz, a Baltimore writer, photographer and barbecue researcher who has worked with us since 1995. We also sincerely thank the thousands of people who participated in this survey – this guide is really "theirs."

We thank Julie Alvin, American Institute of Wine and Food–DC Chapter, Jennifer Barger, Erin Behan, Dan Boward, Jody Brady, Kathyrn Carroll, Elizabeth Daleske, Corrie Davidson, Mike Evitts, Bill and Lorraine Fitzsimmons, Kara Freewind, Danielle Harris, Barbara Johnson, Natasha Lesser, Miranda Levenstein, Mike Lima, Jamie Selzer, Hilary Sims, Simon Spelling, Victoria Spencer, Stefanie Tuder, Alice Urmey and Samantha Zalaznick, as well as the following members of our staff: Aynsley Karps (editor), Brian Albert, Sean Beachell, Maryanne Bertollo, Danielle Borovoy, Reni Chin, Larry Cohn, Nicole Diaz, Kelly Dobkin, Jeff Freier, Alison Gainor, Matthew Hamm, Justin Hartung, Marc Henson, Ryutaro Ishikane, Natalie Lebert, Mike Liao, Vivian Ma, James Mulcahy, Polina Paley, Emily Rothschild, Amanda Spurlock, Chris Walsh, Jacqueline Wasilczyk, Sharon Yates, Anna Zappia and Kyle Zolner.

ABOUT ZAGAT

In 1979, we asked friends to rate and review restaurants purely for fun. The term "user-generated content" had yet to be coined. That hobby grew into Zagat Survey; 33 years later, we have loyal surveyors around the globe and our content now includes nightlife, shopping, tourist attractions, golf and more. Along the way, we evolved from being a print publisher to a digital content provider. We also produce marketing tools for a wide range of corporate clients, and you can find us on Google+ and just about any other social media network.

Our reviews are based on public opinion surveys. The ratings reflect the average scores given by the survey participants who voted on each establishment. The text is based on quotes from, or paraphrasings of, the surveyors' comments. Phone numbers, addresses and other factual data were correct to the best of our knowledge when published in this guide.

JOIN IN: To improve our guides, we solicit your comments – positive or negative; it's vital that we hear your opinions. Just contact us at **nina-tim@zagat.com**. We also invite you to share your opinions at plus.google.com/local.

© 2012 Zagat Survey, LLC
ISBN-13: 978-1-60478-511-1
ISBN-10: 1-60478-511-x
Printed in the
United States of America

Contents

Ratings & Symbols

Zagat Top Spot	Name	Symbols		Cuisine	Zagat Ratings			
					FOOD	DECOR	SERVICE	COST

Area, Address & Contact

Z Tim & Nina's ● *Steak* ▽ 23 | 9 | 13 | $15

Capitol Hill | 1600 J St. NW (Statesmen's Way | 202-555-6000 | www.zagat.com

Review, surveyor comments in quotes

This "meat-and-greet mecca" boasts the ultimate "see-or-avoid-being-seen" experience, with one-way glass booths ("you can look out but others can't look in") and a "hot line to the family quarters at the White House"; in the absence of waiters, you "pick your own salad" from the hydroponic planters, but the "real attraction" is the low price since "lobbyists pay for most meals."

Ratings   **Food, Decor** & **Service** are rated on a 30-point scale.

26 - 30 extraordinary to perfection

21 - 25 very good to excellent

16 - 20 good to very good

11 - 15 fair to good

0 - 10 poor to fair

▽ low response | less reliable

Cost   The price of dinner with a drink and tip; lunch is usually 25% to 30% less. For unrated **newcomers** or **write-ins,** the price range is as follows:

I $25 and below   E $41 to $65

M $26 to $40   VE $66 or above

Symbols   **Z** highest ratings, popularity and importance

● serves after 11 PM

Z M closed on Sunday or Monday

⊄ no credit cards accepted

Maps   Index maps show the restaurants with the highest Food ratings in those areas.

About This Survey

- 1,472 restaurants covered
- 16,363 surveyors
- 88 notable openings
- DC Area's Top Rated: **Inn at Little Washington** (Food, Decor, Service), **Clyde's** (Most Popular), **Buzz** (Bang for the Buck), **Little Serow** (Newcomer)
- Baltimore's Top Rated: **Charleston** (Food, Decor, Service), **Woodberry Kitchen** (Most Popular), **Broom's Bloom Dairy** (Bang for the Buck), **Wit & Wisdom** (Newcomer)

SURVEY STATS: DC Area surveyors report an average of 2.8 meals out per week, vs. 3.1 nationally . . . Despite service being the top complaint (61%), the average tip is 19.3% . . . 57% say they're eating out as often as they were a year ago, 24% more, 19% less . . . 61% think DC's dining scene is about the same as it was a year ago, while 37% claim it's better (for Baltimore, 73% say it's the same, 24% say better) . . . Favorite cuisines: Italian (25%), American (18%), French (13%), Japanese (9%) . . . 68% feel it's important that their food be 'green,' while 58% are willing to pay more for it . . . 76% want letter grades reflecting health-inspection results posted at all eateries . . . 39% say they're more likely to dine at a restaurant associated with a celebrity chef, while that has no effect on 57% (4% are actually less likely to go).

TECHNICAL DETAILS: At no-reservations places, 67% of customers say that they are willing to wait up to 30 minutes to be seated, however, 15% avoid such places altogether . . . A whopping 85% of respondents say taking pictures of dining companions or food is acceptable, but 53% still consider it rude to talk, text or e-mail on a mobile device while dining.

DC DEBUTS: Notable local toques' new openings include Cathal Armstrong's **Society Fair,** Jeff Black's **Pearl Dive Oyster Palace,** Enzo Fargione's **Elisir,** Scot Harlan's **Green Pig,** Cedric Maupillier's **Mintwood Place,** Johnny Monis' Little Serow, Bryan Voltaggio's **Family Meal** and **Lunchbox;** small-plates purveyors are big (**Boqueria, Sugo Cicchetti,** Mike Isabella's **Bandolero** and **Graffiato**); fast-casual options are multiplying: **Bobby's Burger Palace** and **Burger, Tap & Shake** (burgers), **Fishnet** (grilled fish sandwiches), **Mellow Mushroom** (pizza), **Shophouse Southeast Asian Kitchen** (Southeast Asian).

BALTIMORE BUZZ: Newcomers range in style from urban sophistication (**Museum, Silo.5% Wine Bar, Pabu** and Wit & Wisdom – the latter two from celeb chef Michael Mina) to homespun and rootsy (**Artifact Coffee, Food Market, Fork & Wrench, Hersh's Pizza, Of Love & Regret, Plug Ugly's Publick House**) to lively drinking spots (**Bond Street Social; Earth, Wood & Fire; Heavy Seas Alehouse; Kettle Hill; Townhouse Kitchen & Bar**).

New York, NY
September 5, 2012

Nina and Tim Zagat

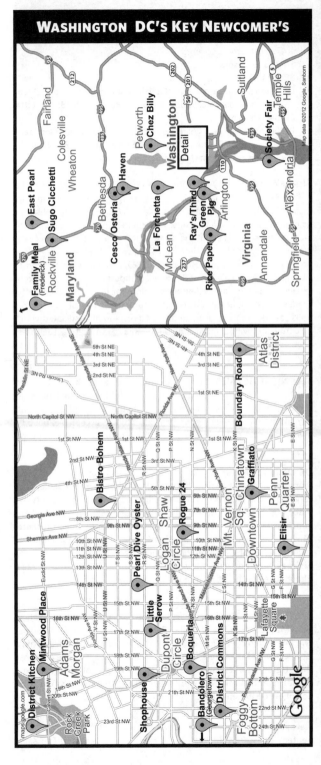

WASHINGTON DC'S KEY NEWCOMER'S

Map data ©2012 Google, Sanborn

East Pearl

Family Meal (Frederick)

Sugo Cicchetti

Haven

Cesco Osteria

La Forchetta

Chez Billy

Petworth

Washington

Detail

Society Fair

Temple Hills

Suitland

Alexandria

Virginia

Ray's/Third

Green Pig

Rice Paper

Fairland

Colesville

Wheaton

Bethesda

McLean

Arlington

Annandale

Springfield

Rockville

Maryland

Atlas District

Boundary Road

Bistro Bohem

Graffiato

Chinatown

Penn Quarter

Elisir

Downtown

Mt. Vernon Sq.

Rogue 24

Pearl Dive Oyster

Shaw

Logan Circle

Little Serow

Dupont Circle

Boqueria

District Commons

Lafayette Square

Mintwood Place

District Kitchen

Adams Morgan

Shophouse

Bandolero (Georgetown)

District Commons

Foggy Bottom

Rock Creek Park

maps.google.com

Google

Key Newcomers

Our editors' picks among this year's arrivals. See full list at p. 26.

Bandolero | *Mexican* | Mike Isabella's Mexican remix in Georgetown

Bistro Bohem | *European* | Modern Prague arrives in Shaw

Boqueria | *Spanish* | NYC's tapas star glimmers below Dupont Circle

Boundary Road | *Eclectic* | H Street gastropub attracts pols and foodies

Cesco Osteria | *Italian* | Francesco Ricchi in spacious Bethesda digs

Chez Billy | *French* | African-American landmark reinvented in Petworth

District Commons | *American* | Foggy Bottom's high-end, haute tavern

District Kitchen | *American* | Woodley Park rusticity backs regional updates

East Pearl | *Chinese* | Authentic noodles and fancy digs in Rockville

Elisir | *Italian* | Enzo Fargione's luxe Penn Quarter showroom

Family Meal | *American* | Bryan Voltaggio's everyman eatery in Frederick

Graffiato | *Italian* | Mike Isabella mines his Jersey roots in Chinatown

Green Pig | *American* | Snout-to-tail cooking in Clarendon neo-rusticity

Haven | *Pizza* | Bethesda flips for New Haven–style pies

La Forchetta | *Italian* | Roberto Donna slings pasta and pizza in Upper NW

Little Serow | *Thai* | Family-style Issan fare next door to cousin Komi

Mintwood Place | *American* | Cedric Maupillier heats up Adams Morgan

Pearl Dive | *Seafood* | Jumping 14th Street NW fish palace from Jeff Black

Ray's to the Third | *Steak* | Steak-frites fix near Courthouse

Rice Paper | *Vietnamese* | Eden Center gets a glitzy Vietnamese venue

Rogue 24 | *American* | RJ Cooper's multicourse marathon in Mt. Vernon Sq.

Shophouse | *SE Asian* | Chipotle's latest concept colonizes Dupont

Society Fair | *American* | Old Town epicurean emporium via Cathal Armstrong

Sugo Cicchetti | *Italian* | Small plates and pizza in Potomac from Cava & co.

ON TAP: This fall, Bryan Voltaggio (**Volt**) will open **Range,** a combo restaurant/coffeehouse/bakery/wine shop in Chevy Chase. Jeff Buben (**Bistro Bis, Vidalia**) will launch **Woodward Table** in the Woodward Building. Also, Merrifield's blockbuster Mosaic development will get branches of **Cava Mezze Grill, Matchbox, Sweetgreen** and **Taylor Gourmet,** plus **Empire Oyster House** from **Black Restaurant Group.**

Fourteenth Street NW will heat up with concepts from Mike Isabella (of **Bandolero** and **Graffiato**), who'll go Greek with **Kapnos.** The **Proof/Estadio** team will explore Southeast Asia. Edan MacQuaid (**Local 16**) will spin Neapolitan pies at his own pizzeria. And Nationals Park will get an **Osteria Morini** from NYC's Michael White in 2013.

Washington, DC's Most Popular

This list is plotted on the map at the back of this book.

1 Clyde's | *American*

2 2 Amys | *Pizza*

3 Zaytinya | *Med./Mideast.*

4 Rasika | *Indian*

5 1789 | *American*

6 Jaleo | *Spanish*

7 Inn at Little Washington | *Amer.*

8 Founding Farmers | *American*

9 2941 Restaurant | *American*

10 Blue Duck Tavern | *American*

11 Old Ebbitt Grill | *American*

12 Busboys/Poets | *Amer./Eclectic*

13 L'Auberge François* | *French*

14 Matchbox | *American*

15 Sweetwater Tavern | *SW*

16 Volt | *American*

17 Central Michel | *Amer./French*

18 Dogfish Head | *Pub Food*

19 Coastal Flats | *Seafood*

20 Acadiana | *Contemp. Louisiana*

21 Artie's | *American*

22 Kinkead's | *Seafood*

23 Brasserie Beck | *Belgian/French*

24 Mike's "American"* | *American*

25 100° C Chinese | *Chinese*

26 Chef Geoff's | *American*

27 Ben's Chili Bowl | *Diner*

28 Carlyle | *American*

29 Komi | *American/Mediterranean*

30 8407 Kitchen Bar | *American*

31 Ray's The Steaks | *Steak*

32 BlackSalt | *American/Seafood*

33 Lebanese Taverna | *Lebanese*

34 Oyamel | *Mexican*

35 CityZen | *American*

36 Marcel's | *Belgian/French*

37 La Tasca | *Spanish*

38 Dutch's Daughter | *American*

39 Austin Grill | *Tex-Mex*

40 Mon Ambi Gabi* | *Fr.*

MOST POPULAR CHAINS

1 Five Guys | *Burgers*

2 Cheesecake Factory | *American*

3 Capital Grille | *Steak*

4 Ledo Pizza | *Pizza*

5 Uncle Julio's | *Tex-Mex*

6 Ruth's Chris | *Steak*

7 Maggiano's Little Italy | *Italian*

8 Legal Sea Foods | *Seafood*

9 P.F. Chang's | *Chinese*

10 McCormick/Schmick | *Seafood*

Many of the above restaurants are among the Washington, DC, area's most expensive, but if popularity were calibrated to price, a number of other restaurants would surely join their ranks. To illustrate this, we have added two pages of Best Buys starting on page 14.

---

* Indicates a tie with restaurant above

Top Food

29 Inn at Little Washington | *Amer.*

28 Rasika | *Indian*
L'Auberge François | *French*
Komi | *Amer./Med.*
Marcel's | *Belgian/French*
Prime Rib | *Steak*
Volt | *American*
Corduroy | *American*
Lucky Corner | *Vietnamese*
Minibar | *Eclectic*
Obelisk | *Italian*
Little Serow | *Thai*
Monocacy Crossing | *American*
Peking Duck Rest.* | *Chinese*

27 CityZen | *American*
Tasting Room | *American*
Eve | *American*
Makoto | *Japanese*
Russia House Rest. | *Russian*
Foti's | *American*

Palena | *American*
Ray's The Steaks | *Steak*
Blue Duck Tavern | *American*
Ashby Inn | *American*
Tosca | *Italian*
BlackSalt | *American/Seafood*
Fiola | *Italian*
Ruan Thai | *Thai*
2941 Restaurant | *American*
Fogo de Chão | *Braz./Steak*
Hong Kong Palace | *Chinese*
Il Pizzico | *Italian*
Source | *Asian*

26 Thai Square | *Thai*
Capital Grille | *Steak*
Niwano Hana | *Japanese*
Pasta Mia* | *Italian*
Sushi Taro | *Japanese*
Bistro Provence | *French*
Pupatella Pizzeria | *Pizza*

BY CUISINE

AMERICAN (NEW)
29 Inn at Little Washington
28 Komi
Volt
Corduroy
Monocacy Crossing
27 CityZen
Tasting Room
Eve
Foti's
Palena
Blue Duck Tavern

AMERICAN (TRAD.)
26 Mike's "American"
25 Dutch's Daughter
Ray's/Third
Artie's
24 Majestic

BURGERS
26 Ray's Hell Burger
25 Black & Orange
24 Five Guys
Thunder Burger & Bar
23 Good Stuff Eatery

CHINESE
28 Peking Duck Rest.
27 Hong Kong Palace
25 China Jade
Peking Gourmet
Mark's Duck Hse.

FRENCH (BISTRO)
26 Bistro L'Hermitage
Central Michel
Le Refuge
25 Yves Bistro
Montmartre

FRENCH (CLASSIC)
28 L'Auberge Chez François
26 La Bergerie
Brabo by Robert Wiedmaier
La Chaumière
25 Et Voila

FRENCH (NEW)
28 Marcel's
26 Bistro Provence
Adour
Bistro Bis
24 Bezu

---

* Excludes places with low votes, unless otherwise indicated

GREEK/MED.

28 Komi
26 Zaytinya
Nostos
Athens Grill
Vaso's Kit.

INDIAN

28 Rasika
26 Bombay Tandoor
25 Masala Art
Jaipur
Bombay Club

ITALIAN

28 Obelisk
27 Tosca
Fiola
Il Pizzico
26 Pasta Mia

JAPANESE

27 Makoto
26 Niwano Hana
Sushi Taro
25 Kaz Sushi
Kotobuki

MEXICAN

25 Oyamel
24 Cacique
Azucar
23 Rosa Mexicano
22 Taqueria Poblano

MIDDLE EASTERN

26 Zaytinya
Kabob Palace
Bamian
25 Afghan Kabob Rest.
Kabob Bazaar

PAN-ASIAN

27 Source
25 Sweet Ginger
23 Asian Spice
Raku
22 Batik

PIZZA

26 Pupatella Pizzeria
25 2 Amys
Seventh Hill Pizza
Mia's Pizzas
Mellow Mushroom

SEAFOOD

27 BlackSalt
26 Pesce
PassionFish
Ford's Fish Shack
Pearl Dive Oyster

SOUTH AMERICAN

27 Fogo de Chão
26 Chima
24 Grill/Ipanema
23 La Canela
22 El Chalan

SOUTHERN

26 Vidalia
25 Carolina Kitchen
24 Acadiana
23 Evening Star
Art & Soul

SPANISH

26 Isabella's
La Taberna del Alabardero
25 Estadio
24 Cacique
Jaleo

STEAKHOUSES

28 Prime Rib
27 Ray's The Steaks
26 Capital Grille
Ruth's Chris
Morton's

TEX-MEX

25 El Mariachi
22 Mi Rancho
Guapo's
Calif. Tortilla
21 Uncle Julio's

THAI

28 Little Serow
27 Ruan Thai
26 Thai Square
Thai Basil
Nava Thai

VIETNAMESE

28 Lucky Corner Vietnamese
26 Present
25 Pho 14
Huong Viet
Four Sisters

BY SPECIAL FEATURE

BREAKFAST

- 24 Pho 75
- 23 Bread Line
- 22 Bayou Bakery
- 21 Johnny's Half Shell
- Café du Parc

BRUNCH

- 27 Palena
- Blue Duck Tavern
- BlackSalt
- 26 Mike's "American"
- Pearl Dive Oyster

CHILD-FRIENDLY

- 25 2 Amys
- 24 Majestic
- 22 Pete's Apizza
- 21 Cactus Cantina
- 20 Comet Ping Pong

DINING ALONE

- 27 Palena
- 26 Pesce
- Zaytinya
- Central Michel
- Vidalia

HOTEL DINING

- 29 Inn at Little Washington
- 27 CityZen (Mandarin Oriental)
- Blue Duck (Park Hyatt)
- 26 Adour (St. Regis)
- Plume (The Jefferson)

MEET FOR A DRINK

- 28 Rasika
- 26 Central Michel
- Vidalia
- Plume
- 21 Johnny's Half Shell

NEWCOMERS (RATED)

- 28 Little Serow
- 26 Pearl Dive Oyster
- 25 Ray's/Third
- Mellow Mushroom
- 24 Graffiato

POWER SCENES

- 27 Tosca
- 26 Capital Grille
- Charlie Palmer Steak
- Central Michel
- Bistro Bis

PRIVATE ROOMS

- 28 Rasika
- Marcel's
- Corduroy
- 27 CityZen
- Fiola

SMALL PLATES/TAPAS

- 28 Rasika
- 27 Fiola
- Source
- 26 Zaytinya
- La Taberna del Alabardero

TRENDY

- 28 Rasika
- Komi
- 27 Fiola
- 26 Zaytinya
- Pearl Dive Oyster

WORTH A TRIP

- 29 Inn at Little Washington (VA)
- 28 Volt (Frederick, MD)
- 27 Foti's (Culpeper, VA)
- Ashby Inn (Paris, VA)
- 26 Isabella's (Frederick, MD)

BY LOCATION

ADAMS MORGAN

- 26 Pasta Mia
- 25 Amsterdam Falafel
- Cashion's Eat Place
- Mellow Mushroom
- 24 Grill from Ipanema

ALEXANDRIA (OLD TOWN)

- 27 Eve
- 26 La Bergerie
- Le Refuge
- Vaso's Kitchen
- Brabo by Robert Wiedmaier

ATLAS DISTRICT

- 26 Toki Underground
- 25 Atlas Room
- 24 Granville Moore's
- Ethiopic
- 23 Sticky Rice

BETHESDA

- 26 Bistro Provence
- 25 Kabob Bazaar
- Persimmon
- Mia's Pizzas
- 24 Faryab

CAPITOL HILL

26 Charlie Palmer Steak
Bistro Bis
25 Montmartre
Belga Café
Seventh Hill Pizza*

CLARENDON

25 Kabob Bazaar
Cava Mezze
24 Pho 75
Delhi Club
Lyon Hall

CLEVELAND PARK/ WOODLEY PARK

27 Palena
25 2 Amys
24 Dino
23 Ripple
Indique

DOWNTOWN

26 Adour
Plume
Mio
25 Bibiana Osteria
Brasserie Beck

DUPONT CIRCLE

28 Komi
Obelisk
Little Serow
26 Sushi Taro
Pesce

FALLS CHURCH

27 2941 Restaurant
Hong Kong Palace
26 Present Restaurant
Bamian
Elephant Jumps

FREDERICK

28 Volt
Lucky Corner Vietnamese
Monocacy Crossing
27 Tasting Room
26 Firestone's

GEORGETOWN

26 1789
La Chaumière
25 Bourbon Steak
24 Filomena Ristorante
Neyla

GOLDEN TRIANGLE

28 Prime Rib
26 Morton's
Vidalia
Oval Room
25 BLT Steak

LOGAN CIRCLE

26 Pearl Dive Oyster
25 Cork
Estadio
24 Birch & Barley
23 Posto

PENN QUARTER

28 Rasika
Minibar
27 Tosca
Fiola
Fogo de Chão

ROCKVILLE

27 Il Pizzico
26 Niwano Hana
25 China Jade
Sushi Damo
Yuan Fu

SILVER SPRING

25 Ray's The Classics
24 Samantha's
Crisp & Juicy
8407 Kitchen Bar
Thai at Silver Spring

TYSONS CORNER

26 Capital Grille
Nostos
Bombay Tandoor
Chima*
25 Palm

U STREET CORRIDOR

25 Black & Orange
24 Etete
Dukem
Negril*
23 Al Crostino

WEST END

28 Rasika
Marcel's
27 Blue Duck Tavern
25 Ris
22 Westend Bistro by Eric Ripert

Top Decor

29	Inn at Little Washington	Bourbon Steak
28	Plume	Sei
	Grace's Mandarin	Chart House
27	Lightfoot	Blue Duck Tavern
	L'Auberge/François	Capital Grille
	Oya	1789
	Magnolias at the Mill	La Ferme
	CityZen	Fiola
	Adour	Corduroy
	2941 Restaurant	Sea Pearl
26	Marrakesh	Eve
	Cafe Renaissance	Tuscarora Mill*
	Prime Rib*	Gadsby's
	Marcel's	Rasika
	Volt	Caucus Room
	Charlie Palmer Steak	The Hamilton
	Eventide	Rogue 24
	Bistro L'Hermitage	Ashby Inn
	Trummer's On Main	
25	Bombay Club	24 La Taberna del Alabardero
		Dutch's Daughter

OUTDOORS

Addie's	L'Auberge/François
Bistro Provence	Old Angler's
Blue Duck Tavern	Poste Moderne
Bourbon Steak	701
Café du Parc	Standard
Johnny's Half Shell	Tabard Inn

ROMANCE

Bezu	Marvin
Birch & Barley	1905
Co Co. Sala	Nora
Cork	Rasika
Eventide	Tabard Inn
Firefly	Vermilion

ROOMS

Adour	Fiola
Birch & Barley	Marcel's
Central Michel	Rasika (West End)
CityZen	Plume
Clyde's	Taberna del Alabardero
Elisir	2941 Restaurant

VIEWS

Bond 45	1905
Charlie Palmer Steak	Perrys
El Centro D.F.	Sequoia
Jack Rose	Source
J&G Steakhouse	Tabaq Bistro
Masa 14	2941 Restaurant

Top Service

29 Inn at Little Washington	Ruth's Chris
Plume	Rasika
28 Komi	1789
Cafe Renaissance	Mike's "American"
L'Auberge/François	2941 Restaurant
Prime Rib	Morton's
Marcel's	Monocacy Crossing
Volt	Fiola
27 Minibar	Blue Duck Tavern
CityZen	**25** Rogue 24
Little Serow	Adour
Bistro L'Hermitage	La Taberna del Alabardero
Fogo de Chão	Chima
26 Obelisk	Bourbon Steak
Eve	Villa Mozart
Tasting Room	Vidalia
Corduroy	Oval Room
Ashby Inn	Charlie Palmer Steak
Tosca	Artie's
Capital Grille	Tuscarora Mill

Best Buys

BAR MENU LUNCHES

27 Eve ($15)
26 Elisir▽ ($19)
25 Bourbon Steak ($21)
Bibiana Osteria ($15)
24 Proof ($12)

CHICKEN ROASTERS

26 El Pollo Rico
24 Crisp & Juicy
Chicken on the Run
23 La Limeña
Don Pollo

DINERS

22 Ben's Chili Bowl
Florida Ave. Grill
21 Open City
Diner
20 Double T Diner

NOODLE SHOPS

26 Toki Underground
25 Full Key
23 DC Noodles
21 Nooshi
– Sakuramen

PRE-THEATER MENUS

28 Rasika ($35)
27 Tosca ($38)
26 Oval Room ($35)
24 J&G Steakhouse ($39)
23 701 ($30)

PUB FOOD

24 Liberty Tavern
23 Royal Mile Pub
22 Brewer's Alley
Clyde's
21 Dogfish Head

QUICK BITES

25 Ravi Kabob
24 C.F. Folks
Fishnet▽
23 Juice Joint Cafe
22 Cava Mezze Grill

SANDWICHES

23 Bread Line
Chutzpah
22 Paul
Buzz
Taylor Gourmet

BEST BUYS: BANG FOR THE BUCK

In order of rating.

1. Buzz
2. CapMac
3. Lunchbox
4. Calif. Tortilla
5. Five Guys
6. Banh Mi DC
7. Amsterdam Falafel
8. DC-3
9. Shophouse
10. Black & Orange
11. El Pollo Rico
12. Chop't Creative Salad
13. Roti Mediterranean
14. Pollo Campero
15. Elevation Burger
16. Sweetgreen
17. Pho 14
18. Horace & Dickie's Seafood
19. Ben's Chili Bowl
20. Crisp & Juicy
21. Chicken on the Run
22. Negril
23. Taylor Gourmet
24. Bobby's Burger Palace
25. Bob & Edith's Diner
26. Tryst
27. Pho 75
28. Good Stuff Eatery
29. Food Corner Kabob House
30. Cava Mezze Grill
31. Burger, Tap & Shake
32. Sunflower Vegetarian
33. Northside Social
34. BGR, The Burger Joint
35. Bread Line
36. Shake Shack
37. Pret A Manger
38. Nando's Peri-Peri
39. Dangerously Delicious Pies
40. Moby Dick

BEST BUYS: OTHER GOOD VALUES

Amerian Ice Co.
Amma Vegetarian
Athens Grill
Bandolero
Bangkok Golden
Bar Pilar
Bayou Bakery
Burma Road
Carolina Kitchen
Don Pollo
Eamonn's
Eatonville
Ethiopic
Family Meal
Fast Gourmet
Fishnet
Florida Ave.
Four Sisters
Hard Times Cafe
Haven
Honey Pig
India Palace
Java Green
Juice Joint Cafe
Kabob Bazaar

Kabob Palace
Kangaroo Boxing Club
Lost Dog Cafe
Luke's Lobster
Medium Rare
Merzi
Oohs & Aahs
Original Ledo
Palena
Pete's A Pizza
Pizzeria Paradiso
Pupatella Pizzeria
Ray's Hell Burger
Ray's/Third
Ren's Ramen
Room 11
Ruan Thai
Seventh Hill Pizza
Standard
Surfside
Taqueria Distrito Federal
Taqueria National
Ted's Bulletin
Toki Underground
We the Pizza

Latest openings, menus, photos and more on plus.google.com/local

WASHINGTON, DC
OTHER USEFUL LISTS*

LOCATION MAPS

---

* These lists include low vote places that do not qualify for top lists.

Special Features

Listings cover the best in each category and include names, locations and Food ratings. Multi-location restaurants' features may vary by branch.

BREAKFAST

(See also Hotel Dining)

Pho 75	**multi.**	24
Bread Line	**World Bank**	23
Mosaic Cuisine	**White Flint**	23
Dean & DeLuca	**Georgetown**	23
McCormick/Schmick	**multi.**	23
Old Ebbitt	**D'town**	23
Paul	**Penn Qtr**	22
Ben's Chili	**U St**	22
Parkway Deli	**Silver Spring**	22
Northside	**Clarendon**	22
Florida Ave. Grill	**Shaw**	22
Bayou Bakery	**Arlington**	22
Open City	**Woodley Pk**	21
Diner	**Adams Mor**	21
Johnny's	**Cap Hill**	21
Le Pain Quotidien	**multi.**	21
Mark's Kit.	**Takoma Pk**	21
NEW Hamilton	**D'town**	20
Teaism	**multi.**	20
Double T	**Frederick**	20
Bob & Edith's	**Arlington**	20
NEW Family Meal	**Frederick**	–

BRUNCH

Palena	**Cleve Pk**	27
Blue Duck	**West End**	27
BlackSalt	**Palisades**	27
Source	**Penn Qtr**	27
Mike's	**Springfield**	26
Firestone's	**Frederick**	26
Black Mkt.	**Garrett Pk**	26
NEW Pearl Dive	**Logan Cir**	26
Bistro Bis	**Cap Hill**	26
Room 11	**Columbia Hts**	26
Cork	**Logan Cir**	25
Dutch's Daughter	**Frederick**	25
Cashion's Eat	**Adams Mor**	25
Estadio	**Logan Cir**	25
Magnolias/Mill	**Purcellville**	25
Bombay Club	**Gldn Triangle**	25
Ris	**West End**	25
Tabard Inn	**Dupont Cir**	25
Et Voila	**Palisades**	25
Carlyle	**Arlington**	25
J&G Steak	**D'town**	24
Acacia Bistro	**Frederick**	24
Filomena	**Georgetown**	24

NEW Graffiato	**Chinatown**	24
Birch/Barley	**Logan Cir**	24
Napoleon Bistro	**Adams Mor**	24
Hank's Oyster	**Dupont Cir**	24
Liberty Tav.	**Clarendon**	24
Founding Farmers	**multi.**	24
Co Co. Sala	**Penn Qtr**	24
Evening Star	**Alexandria**	23
Praline	**Bethesda**	23
Matchbox	**multi.**	23
Jackie's	**Silver Spring**	23
Old Ebbitt	**D'town**	23
Eventide	**Clarendon**	23
Café Bonaparte	**Georgetown**	23
Masa 14	**Logan Cir**	23
Kellari Taverna	**Gldn Triangle**	23
Leopold's Kafe	**Georgetown**	23
Eatonville	**U St**	23
Matisse	**Upper NW**	23
Perrys	**Adams Mor**	22
Fortune	**Falls Ch**	22
B. Smith	**NE**	22
Clyde's	**multi.**	22
Georgia Brown	**D'town**	22
Ardeo/Bardeo	**Cleve Pk**	22
Medium Rare	**Cleve Pk**	22
Open City	**Woodley Pk**	21
Crème	**U St**	21
Chef Geoff's	**multi.**	21
Ping Pong	**multi.**	21
Nage	**Scott Cir**	21
Old Angler's	**Potomac**	20
Blvd. Woodgrill	**Clarendon**	20
Poste Moderne	**Penn Qtr**	20
Cafe Deluxe	**multi.**	20
Café Saint-Ex	**Logan Cir**	20
Sequoia	**Georgetown**	17
Roof Terr.	**Foggy Bottom**	16
NEW Green Pig	**Clarendon**	–
NEW Howard Theatre	**Shaw**	–
NEW La Forchetta	**Upper NW**	–
NEW Mintwood	**Adams Mor**	–

BUSINESS DINING

Rasika	**West End**	28
Marcel's	**West End**	28
Prime Rib	**Gldn Triangle**	28
Corduroy	**Mt. Vernon Sq**	28
CityZen	**SW**	27

Sergio Rist. | **Silver Spring**	27	Carlyle | **Arlington**	25
Eve | **Alexandria**	27	Il Fornaio | **Reston**	25
Lafayette Rm. | **Gldn Triangle**	27	Oceanaire | **D'town**	24
Foti's | **Culpeper**	27	Proof | **Penn Qtr**	24
Palena | **Cleve Pk**	27	J&G Steak | **D'town**	24
Ray's/Steaks | **Arlington**	27	Juniper | **West End**	24
Blue Duck | **West End**	27	2100 Prime | **Dupont Cir**	24
Tosca | **Penn Qtr**	27	Willow | **Arlington**	24
BlackSalt | **Palisades**	27	El Manantial | **Reston**	24
Fiola | **Penn Qtr**	27	I Ricchi | **Dupont Cir**	24
2941 | **Falls Ch**	27	8407 Kit. | **Silver Spring**	24
Fogo de Chão | **Penn Qtr**	27	La Ferme | **Chevy Chase**	24
Source | **Penn Qtr**	27	Ceiba | **D'town**	24
Capital Grille | **multi.**	26	C.F. Folks | **Dupont Cir**	24
Ruth's Chris | **multi.**	26	Acqua al 2 | **Cap Hill**	24
Mike's | **Springfield**	26	Ozzie's Corner | **Fairfax**	24
Morton's | **multi.**	26	Acadiana | **Mt. Vernon Sq**	24
Zaytinya | **Penn Qtr**	26	Founding Farmers | **multi.**	24
PassionFish | **Reston**	26	Black's Bar | **Bethesda**	24
Charlie Palmer | **Cap Hill**	26	Jackson's | **Reston**	23
Central Michel | **Penn Qtr**	26	701 | **Penn Qtr**	23
Vidalia | **Gldn Triangle**	26	Konami | **Vienna**	23
Thai Basil | **Chantilly**	26	Matchbox | **Rockville**	23
Bazin's/Church | **Vienna**	26	Posto | **Logan Cir**	23
Nostos | **Vienna**	26	Watershed | **NoMa**	23
Adour/St. Regis | **D'town**	26	DC Coast | **D'town**	23
Plume | **D'town**	26	PS 7's | **Penn Qtr**	23
Oval Rm. | **Gldn Triangle**	26	McCormick/Schmick | **multi.**	23
Bamian | **Falls Ch**	26	Rosa Mexicano | **multi.**	23
Mio | **D'town**	26	Old Ebbitt | **D'town**	23
Chima | **Vienna**	26	Woo Lae Oak | **Vienna**	23
Bistro Bis | **Cap Hill**	26	Caucus Rm. | **Penn Qtr**	23
La Taberna | **World Bank**	26	Kellari Taverna | **Gldn Triangle**	23
NEW Elisir | **Penn Qtr**	26	Vinifera | **Reston**	23
Kaz Sushi | **World Bank**	25	Assaggi | **McLean**	23
Kinkead's | **Foggy Bottom**	25	Härth | **McLean**	23
BLT Steak | **Gldn Triangle**	25	Occidental | **D'town**	23
Palm | **multi.**	25	Bobby Van's | **D'town**	23
Kazan | **McLean**	25	Westend Bistro | **West End**	22
Artie's | **Fairfax**	25	**NEW** District Commons |	22
Equinox | **Gldn Triangle**	25	**Foggy Bottom**	
Bourbon Steak | **Georgetown**	25	Busara | **multi.**	22
Addie's | **White Flint**	25	Wildfire | **McLean**	22
Bibiana | **D'town**	25	B. Smith | **NE**	22
Magnolias/Mill | **Purcellville**	25	Bond 45 | **Nat'l Harbor**	22
Bombay Club | **Gldn Triangle**	25	Degrees | **Georgetown**	22
Ris | **West End**	25	Clyde's | **multi.**	22
Tabard Inn | **Dupont Cir**	25	Cafe Milano | **Georgetown**	22
Persimmon | **Bethesda**	25	Georgia Brown | **D'town**	22
Landini Bros. | **Alexandria**	25	Zentan | **D'town**	22
Oyamel | **Penn Qtr**	25	15 Ria | **Scott Cir**	22
Smith/Wollensky |	25	Monocle | **Cap Hill**	21
Gldn Triangle		Hill Country | **Penn Qtr**	21
Brass. Beck | **D'town**	25	Café Dupont | **Dupont Cir**	21

Chef Geoff's | **multi.**	21
Johnny's | **Cap Hill**	21
Sou'Wester | **SW**	21
Sonoma | **Cap Hill**	21
Extra Virgin | **Arlington**	21
Café du Parc | **D'town**	21
Urbana | **Dupont Cir**	21
Jackson 20 | **Alexandria**	21
Nage | **Scott Cir**	21
Lia's | **Chevy Chase**	21
Harry's | **Arlington**	21
NEW Hamilton | **D'town**	20
Poste Moderne | **Penn Qtr**	20
Againn | **D'town**	20
Carmine's | **Penn Qtr**	20
Circle Bistro | **West End**	20
NEW Cesco Osteria | **Bethesda**	19
Primi Piatti | **Foggy Bottom**	19
Redwood | **Bethesda**	19
P.J. Clarke's | **D'town**	18
NEW Del Frisco's | **D'town**	-
NEW Family Meal | **Frederick**	-
Maple Ave | **Vienna**	-
NEW Unum | **Georgetown**	-

CELEBRITY CHEFS

José Andrés

Zaytinya | **Penn Qtr**	26
Oyamel | **Penn Qtr**	25
Jaleo | **multi.**	24

Cathal Armstrong

Eve | **Alexandria**	27
Majestic | **Alexandria**	24
NEW Society Fair | **Alexandria**	24
Eamonn's | **Alexandria**	23
Virtue | **Alexandria**	19

Yannick Cam

Bistro Provence | **Bethesda**	26

RJ Cooper

NEW Rogue 24 | **Mt. Vernon Sq**	23

Roberto Donna

NEW La Forchetta | **Upper NW**	-

Alain Ducasse

Adour/St. Regis | **D'town**	26

Bobby Flay

NEW Bobby's Burger | **multi.**	22

Todd Gray

Equinox | **Gldn Triangle**	25
Watershed | **NoMa**	23

Mike Isabella

NEW Graffiato | **Chinatown**	24
NEW Bandolero | **Georgetown**	-

Bob Kinkead

Kinkead's | **Foggy Bottom**	25

Ris Lacoste

Ris | **West End**	25

Susur Lee

Zentan | **D'town**	22

Spike Mendelsohn

Good Stuff | **multi.**	23
We The Pizza | **Cap Hill**	22

Michael Mina

Bourbon Steak | **Georgetown**	25

Johnny Monis

Komi | **Dupont Cir**	28
Little Serow | **Dupont Cir**	28

Guillermo Pernot

Cuba Libre | **Penn Qtr**	20

Nora Pouillon

Nora | **Dupont Cir**	26

Wolfgang Puck

Source | **Penn Qtr**	27

Francesco Ricchi

NEW Cesco Osteria | **Bethesda**	19

Michel Richard

Central Michel | **Penn Qtr**	26

Eric Ripert

Westend Bistro | **West End**	22

Frank Ruta

Palena | **Cleve Pk**	27

Richard Sandoval

Masa 14 | **Logan Cir**	23
Zengo | **Chinatown**	22
El Centro | **Logan Cir**	21

Art Smith

Art & Soul | **Cap Hill**	23

Fabio Trabocchi

Fiola | **Penn Qtr**	27

Mark Vidal

NEW Boqueria | **Dupont Cir**	-

Bryan Voltaggio

Volt | **Frederick**	28
NEW Lunchbox | **Frederick**	24
NEW Family Meal | **Frederick**	-

Jean-Georges Vongerichten

J&G Steak | **D'town**	24

Antoine Westermann

Café du Parc | **D'town**	21

Robert Wiedmaier

Marcel's | **West End**	28
Brabo | **Alexandria**	26
Brass. Beck | **D'town**	25
Mussel Bar | **Bethesda**	20

Eric Ziebold

CityZen | **SW**	27

CHILD-FRIENDLY

(Alternatives to the usual fast-food places; * children's menu available)

Mike's* | **Springfield**	26
Kabob Palace | **Arlington**	26
Black Mkt.* | **Garrett Pk**	26
Sweetwater Tav.* | **multi.**	26
2 Amys | **Cleve Pk**	25
Artie's* | **Fairfax**	25
Rabieng | **Falls Ch**	25
Carlyle* | **Arlington**	25
Cafe Pizzaiolo* | **multi.**	24
Majestic* | **Alexandria**	24
Filomena | **Georgetown**	24
Samantha's | **Silver Spring**	24
Five Guys* | **multi.**	24
Jaleo | **multi.**	24
Coastal Flats* | **Fairfax**	24
Founding Farmers | **Potomac**	24
Minerva | **multi.**	23
Maggiano's* | **multi.**	23
Pizzeria Paradiso | **multi.**	23
Matchbox* | **multi.**	23
Lebanese Tav.* | **multi.**	23
Eamonn's* | **Alexandria**	23
El Golfo* | **Silver Spring**	23
Firefly* | **Dupont Cir**	23
Guardado's* | **Bethesda**	23
Legal Sea Foods* | **multi.**	23
P.F. Chang's | **multi.**	23
Taste/Saigon | **multi.**	22
Taqueria Poblano* | **multi.**	22
Pizzeria Orso* | **Falls Ch**	22
Buzz | **Alexandria**	22
Mi Rancho | **multi.**	22
Red Hot/Blue* | **multi.**	22
Pete's New Haven* | **multi.**	22
Clyde's* | **multi.**	22
Calif. Tortilla* | **multi.**	22
Wild Tomato | **Potomac**	22
Ella's Pizza | **Penn Qtr**	21
Open City* | **Woodley Pk**	21
Uncle Julio's* | **multi.**	21
Serendipity 3 | **Georgetown**	21
Chef Geoff's* | **multi.**	21
Elevation Burger | **Falls Ch**	21
Lia's* | **Chevy Chase**	21
Cactus Cantina* | **Cleve Pk**	21
Surfside* | **Glover Pk**	21
Mark's Kit.* | **Takoma Pk**	21
Tara Thai* | **multi.**	20
Double T* | **Frederick**	20
Arucola* | **Chevy Chase**	20
Comet Ping Pong | **Upper NW**	20

Carmine's* | **Penn Qtr**	20
Cafe Deluxe* | **multi.**	20
Old Glory | **Georgetown**	19
Virtue | **Alexandria**	19
Austin Grill* | **multi.**	18
NEW Haven | **Bethesda**	-
NEW Sugo Cicchetti | **Potomac**	-

DESSERT SPECIALISTS

Inn/Little Washington | **Washington**	29
L'Aub./François | **Grt Falls**	28
Marcel's | **West End**	28
Obelisk | **Dupont Cir**	28
CityZen | **SW**	27
Eve | **Alexandria**	27
Palena | **Cleve Pk**	27
Blue Duck | **West End**	27
BlackSalt | **Palisades**	27
Fiola | **Penn Qtr**	27
2941 | **Falls Ch**	27
Zaytinya | **Penn Qtr**	26
1789 | **Georgetown**	26
Central Michel | **Penn Qtr**	26
Adour/St. Regis | **D'town**	26
Black Mkt. | **Garrett Pk**	26
2 Amys | **Cleve Pk**	25
Kinkead's | **Foggy Bottom**	25
Al Tiramisu | **Dupont Cir**	25
Equinox | **Gldn Triangle**	25
Ris | **West End**	25
Tabard Inn | **Dupont Cir**	25
Et Voila | **Palisades**	25
Carlyle | **Arlington**	25
J&G Steak | **D'town**	24
Juniper | **West End**	24
Majestic | **Alexandria**	24
Willow | **Arlington**	24
Birch/Barley | **Logan Cir**	24
Napoleon Bistro | **Adams Mor**	24
NEW Society Fair | **Alexandria**	24
Jaleo | **multi.**	24
Liberty Tav. | **Clarendon**	24
Acadiana | **Mt. Vernon Sq**	24
Cheesecake | **multi.**	24
Co Co. Sala | **Penn Qtr**	24
Bastille | **Alexandria**	24
Praline | **Bethesda**	23
Ted's Bulletin | **Cap Hill**	23
Bread Line | **World Bank**	23
Good Stuff | **Cap Hill**	23
Ripple | **Cleve Pk**	23
Café Bonaparte | **Georgetown**	23
Leopold's Kafe | **Georgetown**	23

Paul | **Penn Qtr**	22
Buzz | **multi.**	22
NEW District Commons | **Foggy Bottom**	22
Sweetgreen | **multi.**	22
Northside | **Clarendon**	22
Bayou Bakery | **Arlington**	22
Serendipity 3 | **Georgetown**	21
Johnny's | **Cap Hill**	21
Dangerously Delicious | **multi.**	21
Le Pain Quotidien | **multi.**	21
Café Saint-Ex | **Logan Cir**	20
NEW Green Pig | **Clarendon**	–
NEW Haven | **Bethesda**	–

ENTERTAINMENT

(Call for days and times of performances)

Bombay Club | piano | **Gldn Triangle**	25
Napoleon Bistro | DJs | **Adams Mor**	24
Marrakesh | belly dancing | **Shaw**	24
Neyla | belly dancing | **Georgetown**	24
Dukem | Ethiopian music | **U St**	24
Las Tapas | flamenco | **Alexandria**	24
Evening Star | live music | **Alexandria**	23
701 | jazz trio | **Penn Qtr**	23
Sticky Rice | varies | **Atlas Dist**	23
Taste/Morocco | belly dancing | **Clarendon**	23
Perrys | drag performers | **Adams Mor**	22
Georgia Brown | jazz | **D'town**	22
Hill Country | live music | **Penn Qtr**	21
NEW Hamilton | live music | **D'town**	20
Bayou | jazz/zydeco | **West End**	20
Comet Ping Pong | live music | **Upper NW**	20
Caribbean Breeze | varies | **Arlington**	20
Café Saint-Ex | DJs | **Logan Cir**	20
Banana Café | piano | **Cap Hill**	19
NEW Howard Theatre | varies | **Shaw**	–

FIREPLACES

Inn/Little Washington | **Washington**	29
L'Aub./François | **Grt Falls**	28
Eve | **Alexandria**	27

Foti's | **Culpeper**	27
2941 | **Falls Ch**	27
Fogo de Chão | **Penn Qtr**	27
L'Auberge Provençale | **Boyce**	26
Zaytinya | **Penn Qtr**	26
1789 | **Georgetown**	26
Plume | **D'town**	26
Wine Kit. | **Frederick**	26
Lightfoot | **Leesburg**	26
Isabella's | **Frederick**	26
La Chaumière | **Georgetown**	26
Bistro Bis | **Cap Hill**	26
Tuscarora Mill | **Leesburg**	25
Dutch's Daughter | **Frederick**	25
Al Tiramisu | **Dupont Cir**	25
Equinox | **Gldn Triangle**	25
Magnolias/Mill | **Purcellville**	25
Tabard Inn | **Dupont Cir**	25
Geranio | **Alexandria**	25
Grace's | **Nat'l Harbor**	25
Il Fornaio | **Reston**	25
Tavira | **Chevy Chase**	25
Trummer's | **Clifton**	24
Oya | **Penn Qtr**	24
I Ricchi | **Dupont Cir**	24
Blue Rock | **Sperryville**	24
La Ferme | **Chevy Chase**	24
Fyve | **Arlington**	24
Thunder Burger | **Georgetown**	24
Morrison-Clark | **D'town**	24
Bastille | **Alexandria**	24
Chart House | **Alexandria**	23
Eamonn's | **Alexandria**	23
Sea Catch | **Georgetown**	23
Bodega | **Georgetown**	23
Bistro D'Oc | **Penn Qtr**	23
Woo Lae Oak | **Vienna**	23
Mrs. K's | **Silver Spring**	23
Little Fountain | **Adams Mor**	23
Hunter's Head | **Upperville**	23
Matisse | **Upper NW**	23
Columbia Firehse. | **Alexandria**	23
Petits Plats | **Woodley Pk**	22
Clyde's | **multi.**	22
Rustico | **Alexandria**	22
Rolls 'N Rice | **Rockville**	22
15 Ria | **Scott Cir**	22
Uncle Julio's | **Woodbridge**	21
Chef Geoff's | **Vienna**	21
Station 4 | **SW Waterfront**	21
Lia's | **Chevy Chase**	21
Surfside | **Glover Pk**	21
Paolo's | **Georgetown**	21
Comus Inn | **Dickerson**	20

Old Angler's | **Potomac**	20
Daniel O'Connell's | **Alexandria**	20
NEW William Jeffrey's | **Arlington**	20
Circle Bistro | **West End**	20
Vapiano | **multi.**	20
Redwood | **Bethesda**	19
NEW Brixton | **U St**	-
NEW Irish Whiskey | **Dupont Cir**	-

FOOD TRUCKS

Red Hook | **Location Varies**	25
CapMac | **Location Varies**	23
Dangerously Delicious | **Location Varies**	21
Kangaroo/PORC | **Location Varies**	-

HISTORIC PLACES

(Year opened; * building)

1750 | Hunter's Head* | **Upperville**	23
1753 | L'Auberge Provençale* | **Boyce**	26
1786 | Virtue* | **Alexandria**	19
1800 | Corduroy* | **Mt. Vernon Sq**	28
1800 | Eve* | **Alexandria**	27
1800 | Black Mkt.* | **Garrett Pk**	26
1829 | Ashby Inn* | **Paris**	27
1841 | Poste Moderne* | **Penn Qtr**	20
1860 | Old Angler's* | **Potomac**	20
1862 | Comus Inn* | **Dickerson**	20
1864 | Morrison-Clark* | **D'town**	24
1869 | Trummer's* | **Clifton**	24
1872 | Brewer's Alley* | **Frederick**	22
1876 | District ChopHse.* | **Penn Qtr**	21
1883 | Columbia Firehse.* | **Alexandria**	23
1885 | Monocle* | **Cap Hill**	21
1887 | Tabard Inn* | **Dupont Cir**	25
1888 | Lightfoot* | **Leesburg**	26
1890 | Inn/Little Washington* | **Washington**	29
1890 | Volt* | **Frederick**	28
1890 | La Bergerie* | **Alexandria**	26
1890 | Nora* | **Dupont Cir**	26
1897 | Irish Inn/Glen Echo* | **Glen Echo**	20
1900 | Standard* | **Logan Cir**	-
1904 | Occidental* | **D'town**	23

1905 | Magnolias/Mill* | **Purcellville**	25
1907 | Liberty Tav.* | **Clarendon**	24
1908 | B. Smith* | **NE**	22
1909 | Ben's Chili* | **U St**	22
1912 | Zeffirelli Rist.* | **Herndon**	24
1913 | Boundary Stone* | **Bloomingdale**	24
1920 | Matchbox* | **Cap Hill**	23
1921 | Firestone's* | **Frederick**	26
1925 | Eventide* | **Clarendon**	23
1930 | Mrs. K's* | **Silver Spring**	23
1932 | Majestic* | **Alexandria**	24
1932 | Degrees* | **Georgetown**	22
1933 | Martin's Tav. | **Georgetown**	20
1940 | Graffiato* | **Chinatown**	24
1944 | Florida Ave. Grill | **Shaw**	22
1946 | Lyon Hall* | **Clarendon**	24
1950 | Lost Dog* | **Arlington**	23
1962 | 1789 | **Georgetown**	26

HOTEL DINING

Ashby Inn	
Ashby Inn | **Paris**	27
Blue Rock Inn	
Blue Rock | **Sperryville**	24
Donovan Hse.	
Zentan | **D'town**	22
DoubleTree DC	
15 Ria | **Scott Cir**	22
DoubleTree Silver Spring	
Sergio Rist. | **Silver Spring**	27
Dupont Circle Hotel	
Café Dupont | **Dupont Cir**	21
Fairfax at Embassy Row	
2100 Prime | **Dupont Cir**	24
Fairmont Hotel	
Juniper | **West End**	24
Four Seasons Hotel DC	
Bourbon Steak | **Georgetown**	25
Gaylord National Hotel	
Old Hickory | **Nat'l Harbor**	26
George, Hotel	
Bistro Bis | **Cap Hill**	26
Georgetown Hill Inn	
Cafe Divan | **Glover Pk**	24
George Washington Univ. Inn	
Notti Bianche | **Foggy Bottom**	22
Hay-Adams	
Lafayette Rm. | **Gldn Triangle**	27
Hilton Garden Inn	
Watershed | **NoMa**	23

Hilton McLean Tysons Corner	
Härth | **McLean**	23
Hyatt Regency	
Morton's | **Bethesda**	26
Inn at Little Washington	
Inn/Little Washington | **Washington**	29
Jefferson	
Plume | **D'town**	26
L'Auberge Provençale	
L'Auberge Provençale | **Boyce**	26
Liaison Capitol Hill	
Art & Soul | **Cap Hill**	23
Lorien Hotel & Spa	
Brabo | **Alexandria**	26
Mandarin Oriental	
CityZen | **SW**	27
Sou'Wester | **SW**	21
Marriott Embassy Row	
Nage | **Scott Cir**	21
Marriott Tysons Corner	
Shula's | **Vienna**	22
Monaco, Hotel	
Jackson 20 | **Alexandria**	21
Poste Moderne | **Penn Qtr**	20
Morrison-Clark Inn	
Morrison-Clark | **D'town**	24
Morrison Hse.	
Grille | **Alexandria**	25
One Washington Circle Hotel	
Circle Bistro | **West End**	20
Palomar, Hotel	
Urbana | **Dupont Cir**	21
Park Hyatt	
Blue Duck | **West End**	27
Ritz-Carlton DC	
Westend Bistro | **West End**	22
Ritz-Carlton Georgetown	
Degrees | **Georgetown**	22
Ritz-Carlton Pentagon City	
Fyve | **Arlington**	24
River Inn	
Dish/Drinks | **Foggy Bottom**	21
St. Regis	
Adour/St. Regis | **D'town**	26
Tabard Inn	
Tabard Inn | **Dupont Cir**	25
Westin Reston Heights	
Vinifera | **Reston**	23
W Hotel	
J&G Steak | **D'town**	24
Willard InterContinental Hotel	
Café du Parc | **D'town**	21

LATE DINING

(Weekday closing hour)

Kabob N Karahi | 12 AM | **Silver Spring**	26
BonChon | 12 AM | **multi.**	26
New Kam | 12 AM | **Wheaton**	25
Amsterdam Falafel | varies | **Adams Mor**	25
Black & Orange | 5 AM | **multi.**	25
Ravi Kabob | 1 AM | **Arlington**	25
Mezè | 1:30 AM | **Adams Mor**	24
NEW Graffiato | varies | **Chinatown**	24
Lyon Hall | 2 AM | **Clarendon**	24
Cafe Nola | varies | **Frederick**	24
Dukem | 1 AM | **U St**	24
Thunder Burger | varies | **Georgetown**	24
X.O. Taste | 2 AM | **Falls Ch**	24
Founding Farmers | 12 AM | **Potomac**	24
Layalina | 12 AM | **Arlington**	24
Co Co. Sala | varies | **Penn Qtr**	24
Full Kee (DC) | varies | **Chinatown**	23
Old Ebbitt | 1 AM | **D'town**	23
Mandu | 1:30 AM | **Mt. Vernon Sq**	23
New Fortune | 1 AM | **Gaith'burg**	23
Masa 14 | 1 AM | **Logan Cir**	23
Honey Pig | 24 hrs. | **multi.**	23
Ben's Chili | 2 AM | **U St**	22
Yechon | 24 hrs. | **Annandale**	22
Bistrot du Coin | 12 AM | **Dupont Cir**	22
Hard Times | varies | **multi.**	22
Clyde's | varies | **multi.**	22
Full Kee (VA) | varies | **Falls Ch**	22
Busboys/Poets | 12 AM | **multi.**	22
Eat First | 2 AM | **Chinatown**	22
Open City | 1:30 AM | **Woodley Pk**	21
Diner | 24 hrs. | **Adams Mor**	21
Bistro La Bonne | 12 AM | **U St**	21
Tryst | 1:30 AM | **Adams Mor**	21
Bistro Français | 3 AM | **Georgetown**	21
RedRocks | 12 AM | **multi.**	21
Dangerously Delicious | varies | **Atlas Dist**	21
El Tamarindo | 2 AM | **Adams Mor**	21
NEW Hamilton | 24 hrs. | **D'town**	20
Woomi Gdn. | 4 AM | **Wheaton**	20
Circa | varies | **multi.**	20

Daniel O'Connell's | 1 AM | **Alexandria** — 20

Tabaq Bistro | 12 AM | **U St** — 20

NEW William Jeffrey's | 1 AM | **Arlington** — 20

Meridian | 12 AM | **Columbia Hts** — 20

Kramerbooks | 1:30 AM | **Dupont Cir** — 19

Star/Shamrock | 12 AM | **Atlas Dist** — 19

Hudson | 12 AM | **West End** — 18

Austin Grill | varies | **Silver Spring** — 18

Blackfinn Amer. | 1 AM | **Bethesda** — 18

Stoney's Lounge | 12:45 AM | **Logan Cir** — 18

P.J. Clarke's | 1 AM | **D'town** — 18

Tonic | 12 AM | **Mt. Pleasant** — 17

Biergarten Haus | 12 AM | **Atlas Dist** — 17

NEW Bistro Bohem | 12 AM | **Shaw** — –

NEW Boundary Rd. | 2 AM | **Atlas Dist** — –

NEW Brixton | 1:30 AM | **U St** — –

NEW Del Frisco's | 12 AM | **D'town** — –

NEW El Chucho | 3 AM | **Columbia Hts** — –

NEW Fujimar | varies | **D'town** — –

NEW Irish Whiskey | 2 AM | **Dupont Cir** — –

NEW Kangaroo Boxing/PORC | 2 AM | **Columbia Hts** — –

NEW Majestic B&G | 1 AM | **Bethesda** — –

NEW Maple | 12 AM | **Columbia Hts** — –

Standard | 1 AM | **Logan Cir** — –

NEW Tel'Veh | 12 AM | **Mt. Vernon Sq** — –

MEET FOR A DRINK

Rasika | **multi.** — 28

CityZen | **SW** — 27

Tasting Rm. | **Frederick** — 27

Eve | **Alexandria** — 27

Blue Duck | **West End** — 27

Fiola | **Penn Qtr** — 27

Source | **Penn Qtr** — 27

Capital Grille | **multi.** — 26

Mike's | **Springfield** — 26

Zaytinya | **Penn Qtr** — 26

Central Michel | **Penn Qtr** — 26

Vidalia | **Gldn Triangle** — 26

Bazin's/Church | **Vienna** — 26

Sei | **Penn Qtr** — 26

Adour/St. Regis | **D'town** — 26

Plume | **D'town** — 26

NEW Pearl Dive | **Logan Cir** — 26

Mio | **D'town** — 26

Vermilion | **Alexandria** — 26

La Taberna | **World Bank** — 26

NEW Elisir | **Penn Qtr** — 26

Room 11 | **Columbia Hts** — 26

2 Amys | **Cleve Pk** — 25

BLT Steak | **Gldn Triangle** — 25

Sushi Damo | **Rockville** — 25

Tuscarora Mill | **Leesburg** — 25

Cork | **Logan Cir** — 25

Artie's | **Fairfax** — 25

Belga Café | **Cap Hill** — 25

Bourbon Steak | **Georgetown** — 25

Bibiana | **D'town** — 25

Kushi | **Mt. Vernon Sq** — 25

Estadio | **Logan Cir** — 25

Ris | **West End** — 25

Tabard Inn | **Dupont Cir** — 25

Landini Bros. | **Alexandria** — 25

Oyamel | **Penn Qtr** — 25

Brass. Beck | **D'town** — 25

Carlyle | **Arlington** — 25

Bezu | **Potomac** — 24

Proof | **Penn Qtr** — 24

Granville Moore's | **Atlas Dist** — 24

J&G Steak | **D'town** — 24

Oya | **Penn Qtr** — 24

Majestic | **Alexandria** — 24

Willow | **Arlington** — 24

Acacia Bistro | **Frederick** — 24

Mezè | **Adams Mor** — 24

NEW Graffiato | **Chinatown** — 24

Birch/Barley | **Logan Cir** — 24

8407 Kit. | **Silver Spring** — 24

Lyon Hall | **Clarendon** — 24

Jaleo | **multi.** — 24

Ceiba | **D'town** — 24

Tallula/EatBar | **Clarendon** — 24

Hank's Oyster | **multi.** — 24

Liberty Tav. | **Clarendon** — 24

Acadiana | **Mt. Vernon Sq** — 24

Fire Works | **multi.** — 24

Founding Farmers | **multi.** — 24

Black's Bar | **Bethesda** — 24

NEW Boundary Stone | **Bloomingdale** — 24

Co Co. Sala | **Penn Qtr** — 24

Tandoori Nights | **multi.** — 24

Bastille | **Alexandria** — 24

Evening Star | **Alexandria** — 23

Jackson's | **Reston**	23
701 | **Penn Qtr**	23
Matchbox | **multi.**	23
Art & Soul | **Cap Hill**	23
Watershed | **NoMa**	23
DC Coast | **D'town**	23
Rosa Mexicano | **multi.**	23
Jackie's | **Silver Spring**	23
Ripple | **Cleve Pk**	23
Old Ebbitt | **D'town**	23
Mandu | **multi.**	23
Eventide | **Clarendon**	23
Masa 14 | **Logan Cir**	23
Kellari Taverna | **Gldn Triangle**	23
Vinifera | **Reston**	23
Härth | **McLean**	23
Eatonville | **U St**	23
Columbia Firehse. | **Alexandria**	23
Firefly | **Dupont Cir**	23
Bar Pilar | **U St**	23
Rustik Tav. | **Bloomingdale**	23
Zengo | **Chinatown**	22
Perrys | **Adams Mor**	22
Westend Bistro | **West End**	22
Bistrot du Coin | **Dupont Cir**	22
Buzz | **Arlington**	22
Evo Bistro | **McLean**	22
Wildfire | **McLean**	22
Clyde's | **multi.**	22
Zentan | **D'town**	22
Ardeo/Bardeo | **Cleve Pk**	22
Rustico | **multi.**	22
Northside | **Clarendon**	22
Policy | **U St**	22
New Heights | **Woodley Pk**	22
Busboys/Poets | **multi.**	22
Smith Commons | **Atlas Dist**	22
Dogfish Head | **Falls Ch**	21
Monocle | **Cap Hill**	21
Russia Hse. | **Dupont Cir**	21
Hill Country | **Penn Qtr**	21
Lauriol Plaza | **Dupont Cir**	21
1905 | **Mt. Vernon Sq**	21
Chef Geoff's | **multi.**	21
Tryst | **Adams Mor**	21
Johnny's | **Cap Hill**	21
El Centro | **Logan Cir**	21
Ping Pong | **multi.**	21
Jackson 20 | **Alexandria**	21
Nage | **Scott Cir**	21
Lia's | **Chevy Chase**	21
Dickson Wine | **U St**	21
Harry's | **Arlington**	21
NEW Hamilton | **D'town**	20

Mad Fox Brew | **Falls Ch**	20
Poste Moderne | **Penn Qtr**	20
Lincoln | **D'town**	20
Bayou | **West End**	20
Againn | **D'town**	20
Jack Rose | **Adams Mor**	20
Twisted Vines | **Arlington**	20
Martin's Tav. | **Georgetown**	20
Café Saint-Ex | **Logan Cir**	20
Virtue | **Alexandria**	19
Biergarten Haus | **Atlas Dist**	17
NEW Bandolero | **Georgetown**	-
Big Bear Cafe | **Bloomingdale**	-
NEW Bistro Bohem | **Shaw**	-
NEW Boqueria | **Dupont Cir**	-
NEW Boundary Rd. | **Atlas Dist**	-
NEW Brixton | **U St**	-
NEW Chasin' Tails | **Arlington**	-
NEW Chez Billy | **Petworth**	-
NEW El Chucho | **Columbia Hts**	-
NEW Kangaroo Boxing/PORC | **Columbia Hts**	-
NEW Maple | **Columbia Hts**	-
NEW Quench | **Rockville**	-
NEW Unum | **Georgetown**	-

NEWCOMERS

Little Serow | **Dupont Cir**	28
Pearl Dive | **Logan Cir**	26
Elisir | **Penn Qtr**	26
Ray's/Third | **Arlington**	25
Mellow Mushroom | **Adams Mor**	25
Graffiato | **Chinatown**	24
Society Fair | **Alexandria**	24
District Kit. | **Woodley Pk**	24
Fishnet | **College Pk**	24
Lunchbox | **Frederick**	24
Boundary Stone | **Bloomingdale**	24
100° C | **Fairfax**	24
Rogue 24 | **Mt. Vernon Sq**	23
Pacci's Tratt. | **Silver Spring**	23
Bobby's Burger | **multi.**	22
District Commons | **Foggy Bottom**	22
Grillmarx | **Olney**	22
Shophouse | **Dupont Cir**	22
Le Zinc | **Cleve Pk**	22
Burger/Tap/Shake | **Foggy Bottom**	21
Boxcar Tav. | **Cap Hill**	21
Hamilton | **D'town**	20
Smoke/Barrel | **Adams Mor**	20
William Jeffrey's | **Arlington**	20
Cesco Osteria | **Bethesda**	19

Pork Barrel	**Alexandria**	19
Lost Society	**U St**	18
Bandolero	**Georgetown**	_
Bistro Bohem	**Shaw**	_
Bistro Vivant	**McLean**	_
Boqueria	**Dupont Cir**	_
Boundary Rd.	**Atlas Dist**	_
Brixton	**U St**	_
Chasin' Tails	**Arlington**	_
Chez Billy	**Petworth**	_
Curious Grape	**Arlington**	_
Del Frisco's	**D'town**	_
Dolce Veloce	**Fairfax**	_
East Pearl	**Rockville**	_
El Chucho	**Columbia Hts**	_
Family Meal	**Frederick**	_
Fuel Pizza	**multi.**	_
Fujimar	**D'town**	_
Green Pig	**Clarendon**	_
Haven	**Bethesda**	_
Howard Theatre	**Shaw**	_
Irish Whiskey	**Dupont Cir**	_
Kangaroo Boxing/PORC	**Columbia Hts**	_
LacoMelza	**Silver Spring**	_
La Forchetta	**Upper NW**	_
Majestic B&G	**Bethesda**	_
Maple	**Columbia Hts**	_
Mayfair & Pine	**Glover Pk**	_
Menomale	**NE**	_
Mintwood	**Adams Mor**	_
Pig	**Logan Cir**	_
Pulpo	**Cleve Pk**	_
Quench	**Rockville**	_
Rice Paper	**Falls Ch**	_
River Falls Tav.	**Potomac**	_
Sakuramen	**Adams Mor**	_
Sugo Cicchetti	**Potomac**	_
Tel'Veh	**Mt. Vernon Sq**	_
Unum	**Georgetown**	_

OUTDOOR DINING

L'Aub./François	**Grt Falls**	28
Marcel's	**West End**	28
Lucky Corner	**Frederick**	28
Monocacy Cross.	**Frederick**	28
Palena	**Cleve Pk**	27
Blue Duck	**West End**	27
Ashby Inn	**Paris**	27
Source	**Penn Qtr**	27
L'Auberge Provençale	**Boyce**	26
Bistro Provence	**Bethesda**	26
Zaytinya	**Penn Qtr**	26
Oval Rm.	**Gldn Triangle**	26

Bistro Bis	**Cap Hill**	26
La Taberna	**World Bank**	26
Room 11	**Columbia Hts**	26
2 Amys	**Cleve Pk**	25
Cashion's Eat	**Adams Mor**	25
Equinox	**Gldn Triangle**	25
Bourbon Steak	**Georgetown**	25
Addie's	**White Flint**	25
Magnolias/Mill	**Purcellville**	25
Bombay Club	**Gldn Triangle**	25
Ris	**West End**	25
Tabard Inn	**Dupont Cir**	25
Cava Mezze	**Cap Hill**	25
Proof	**Penn Qtr**	24
J&G Steak	**D'town**	24
Siroc	**D'town**	24
Juniper	**West End**	24
Mezè	**Adams Mor**	24
Jaleo	**Bethesda**	24
Neyla	**Georgetown**	24
Hank's Oyster	**Dupont Cir**	24
Bastille	**Alexandria**	24
Evening Star	**Alexandria**	23
Praline	**Bethesda**	23
Bread Line	**World Bank**	23
701	**Penn Qtr**	23
Dean & DeLuca	**Georgetown**	23
Chart House	**Alexandria**	23
Konami	**Vienna**	23
Pizzeria Paradiso	**Dupont Cir**	23
Sea Catch	**Georgetown**	23
Rail Stop	**Plains**	23
La Fourchette	**Adams Mor**	23
McCormick/Schmick	**multi.**	23
Raku	**multi.**	23
Mrs. K's	**Silver Spring**	23
Masa 14	**Logan Cir**	23
Leopold's Kafe	**Georgetown**	23
Marvin	**U St**	23
Indique	**Chevy Chase**	23
Occidental	**D'town**	23
Perrys	**Adams Mor**	22
Westend Bistro	**West End**	22
Renato/River Falls	**Potomac**	22
Cafe Milano	**Georgetown**	22
Medium Rare	**Cleve Pk**	22
Mon Ami Gabi	**Bethesda**	22
15 Ria	**Scott Cir**	22
Lauriol Plaza	**Dupont Cir**	21
Open City	**Woodley Pk**	21
Uncle Julio's	**multi.**	21
Chef Geoff's	**multi.**	21
Johnny's	**Cap Hill**	21
El Centro	**Logan Cir**	21

Sou'Wester	SW	21
Café du Parc	D'town	21
Ping Pong	Dupont Cir	21
Sette Osteria	Dupont Cir	21
Oro Pomodoro	Rockville	21
Levante's	Dupont Cir	21
Paolo's	multi.	21
Comus Inn	Dickerson	20
Old Angler's	Potomac	20
Poste Moderne	Penn Qtr	20
Café Olé	Upper NW	20
Chesapeake Rm.	Cap Hill	20
Arucola	Chevy Chase	20
Cafe Deluxe	multi.	20
Irish Inn/Glen Echo	Glen Echo	20
Circle Bistro	West End	20
Café Saint-Ex	Logan Cir	20
Redwood	Bethesda	19
American Ice	U St	19
Austin Grill	multi.	18
Local 16	U St	17
Sequoia	Georgetown	17
Biergarten Haus	Atlas Dist	17
NEW Mintwood	Adams Mor	-1
Standard	Logan Cir	-1

PEOPLE-WATCHING

Rasika	West End	28
Marcel's	West End	28
Lafayette Rm.	Gldn Triangle	27
BlackSalt	Palisades	27
Fiola	Penn Qtr	27
Source	Penn Qtr	27
Mike's	Springfield	26
Zaytinya	Penn Qtr	26
Charlie Palmer	Cap Hill	26
Central Michel	Penn Qtr	26
Vidalia	Gldn Triangle	26
Nora	Dupont Cir	26
Oval Rm.	Gldn Triangle	26
Bistro Bis	Cap Hill	26
NEW Elisir	Penn Qtr	26
Kinkead's	Foggy Bottom	25
BLT Steak	Gldn Triangle	25
Palm	multi.	25
Cork	Logan Cir	25
Equinox	Gldn Triangle	25
Bourbon Steak	Georgetown	25
Bibiana	D'town	25
Estadio	Logan Cir	25
Landini Bros.	Alexandria	25
Oyamel	Penn Qtr	25
Brass. Beck	D'town	25
Carlyle	Arlington	25

J&G Steak	D'town	24
NEW Graffiato	Chinatown	24
Jaleo	multi.	24
Black's Bar	Bethesda	24
Co Co. Sala	Penn Qtr	24
Bistrot Lepic	Georgetown	24
Bread Line	World Bank	23
Caucus Rm.	Penn Qtr	23
Monocle	Cap Hill	21
Hill Country	Penn Qtr	21
Lauriol Plaza	Dupont Cir	21
Tryst	Adams Mor	21
Johnny's	Cap Hill	21
Sonoma	Cap Hill	21
Blvd. Woodgrill	Clarendon	20
Mussel Bar	Bethesda	20
Poste Moderne	Penn Qtr	20
Lincoln	D'town	20
Circa	multi.	20
Jack Rose	Adams Mor	20
Carmine's	Penn Qtr	20
Martin's Tav.	Georgetown	20
Café Saint-Ex	Logan Cir	20
Commissary	Logan Cir	19
Sequoia	Georgetown	17
NEW Bandolero	Georgetown	-1
Big Bear Cafe	Bloomingdale	-1
NEW Boqueria	Dupont Cir	-1
NEW Boundary Rd.	Atlas Dist	-1
NEW Brixton	U St	-1
NEW Chez Billy	Petworth	-1
NEW Del Frisco's	D'town	-1
NEW El Chucho	Columbia Hts	-1
NEW Kangaroo Boxing/PORC	Columbia Hts	-1
NEW Sakuramen	Adams Mor	-1
Standard	Logan Cir	-1
NEW Sugo Cicchetti	Potomac	-1

POWER SCENES

Inn/Little Washington	Washington	29
Rasika	West End	28
Marcel's	West End	28
Prime Rib	Gldn Triangle	28
Volt	Frederick	28
Corduroy	Mt. Vernon Sq	28
CityZen	SW	27
Eve	Alexandria	27
Lafayette Rm.	Gldn Triangle	27
Palena	Cleve Pk	27
Tosca	Penn Qtr	27
Fiola	Penn Qtr	27
2941	Falls Ch	27

Source	**Penn Qtr**	27
Capital Grille	**multi.**	26
Morton's	**multi.**	26
Zaytinya	**Penn Qtr**	26
Charlie Palmer	**Cap Hill**	26
1789	**Georgetown**	26
Central Michel	**Penn Qtr**	26
Vidalia	**Gldn Triangle**	26
Bazin's/Church	**Vienna**	26
Adour/St. Regis	**D'town**	26
Plume	**D'town**	26
Nora	**Dupont Cir**	26
Oval Rm.	**Gldn Triangle**	26
Bistro Bis	**Cap Hill**	26
La Taberna	**World Bank**	26
NEW Elisir	**Penn Qtr**	26
Kinkead's	**Foggy Bottom**	25
BLT Steak	**Gldn Triangle**	25
Tuscarora Mill	**Leesburg**	25
Peking Gourmet	**Falls Ch**	25
Palm	**multi.**	25
Equinox	**Gldn Triangle**	25
Bourbon Steak	**Georgetown**	25
Bibiana	**D'town**	25
Bombay Club	**Gldn Triangle**	25
Landini Bros.	**Alexandria**	25
Brass. Beck	**D'town**	25
Oceanaire	**D'town**	24
Proof	**Penn Qtr**	24
J&G Steak	**D'town**	24
Willow	**Arlington**	24
I Ricchi	**Dupont Cir**	24
C.F. Folks	**Dupont Cir**	24
Acqua al 2	**Cap Hill**	24
Fyve	**Arlington**	24
Acadiana	**Mt. Vernon Sq**	24
Founding Farmers	**World Bank**	24
701	**Penn Qtr**	23
Art & Soul	**Cap Hill**	23
DC Coast	**D'town**	23
Old Ebbitt	**D'town**	23
Caucus Rm.	**Penn Qtr**	23
Columbia Firehse.	**Alexandria**	23
Occidental	**D'town**	23
Bobby Van's	**D'town**	23
Ben's Chili	**U St**	22
Westend Bistro	**West End**	22
NEW District Commons	**Foggy Bottom**	22
Evo Bistro	**McLean**	22
Renato/River Falls	**Potomac**	22
Clyde's	**multi.**	22
Cafe Milano	**Georgetown**	22

Georgia Brown	**D'town**	22
Ardeo/Bardeo	**Cleve Pk**	22
Monocle	**Cap Hill**	21
Hill Country	**Penn Qtr**	21
Chef Geoff's	**multi.**	21
Johnny's	**Cap Hill**	21
Sonoma	**Cap Hill**	21
NEW Hamilton	**D'town**	20
Hunan Dynasty	**Cap Hill**	20
Martin's Tav.	**Georgetown**	20
NEW Del Frisco's	**D'town**	-
NEW Mintwood	**Adams Mor**	-

PRIVATE ROOMS

(Restaurants charge less at off times; call for capacity)

Rasika	**Penn Qtr**	28
Marcel's	**West End**	28
Corduroy	**Mt. Vernon Sq**	28
CityZen	**SW**	27
Tosca	**Penn Qtr**	27
Fiola	**Penn Qtr**	27
2941	**Falls Ch**	27
Morton's	**multi.**	26
Charlie Palmer	**Cap Hill**	26
1789	**Georgetown**	26
Central Michel	**Penn Qtr**	26
Vidalia	**Gldn Triangle**	26
Adour/St. Regis	**D'town**	26
Lightfoot	**Leesburg**	26
Nora	**Dupont Cir**	26
Oval Rm.	**Gldn Triangle**	26
Chima	**Vienna**	26
Duangrat's	**Falls Ch**	26
La Chaumière	**Georgetown**	26
Bistro Bis	**Cap Hill**	26
La Taberna	**World Bank**	26
Palm	**multi.**	25
Dutch's Daughter	**Frederick**	25
Equinox	**Gldn Triangle**	25
Fleming's Steak	**McLean**	25
Geranio	**Alexandria**	25
Smith/Wollensky	**Gldn Triangle**	25
Brass. Beck	**D'town**	25
Oya	**Penn Qtr**	24
Birch/Barley	**Logan Cir**	24
La Ferme	**Chevy Chase**	24
Ceiba	**D'town**	24
Bistrot Lepic	**Georgetown**	24
Afghan	**Alexandria**	23
701	**Penn Qtr**	23
DC Coast	**D'town**	23
Pizzeria Da Marco	**Bethesda**	23
Bistro D'Oc	**Penn Qtr**	23

Woo Lae Oak	**Vienna**	23
Caucus Rm.	**Penn Qtr**	23
Matisse	**Upper NW**	23
Occidental	**D'town**	23
Zengo	**Chinatown**	22
Tragara	**Bethesda**	22
Wildfire	**McLean**	22
B. Smith	**NE**	22
Clyde's	**multi.**	22
Cafe Milano	**Georgetown**	22
Monocle	**Cap Hill**	21
Chef Geoff's	**multi.**	21
Johnny's	**Cap Hill**	21
Old Angler's	**Potomac**	20
Carmine's	**Penn Qtr**	20
Irish Inn/Glen Echo	**Glen Echo**	20
Sequoia	**Georgetown**	17

PRIX FIXE MENUS

(Call for prices and times)

Inn/Little Washington	**Washington**	29
L'Aub./François	**Grt Falls**	28
Marcel's	**West End**	28
Corduroy	**Mt. Vernon Sq**	28
Obelisk	**Dupont Cir**	28
Eve	**Alexandria**	27
Makoto	**Palisades**	27
Palena	**Cleve Pk**	27
Tosca	**Penn Qtr**	27
BlackSalt	**Palisades**	27
Source	**Penn Qtr**	27
La Bergerie	**Alexandria**	26
PassionFish	**Reston**	26
Charlie Palmer	**Cap Hill**	26
Nora	**Dupont Cir**	26
La Taberna	**World Bank**	26
Eola	**Dupont Cir**	25
Masala Art	**Upper NW**	25
Ray's/Classics	**Silver Spring**	25
Bombay Club	**Gldn Triangle**	25
J&G Steak	**D'town**	24
Me Jana	**Arlington**	24
Dino	**Cleve Pk**	24
Bastille	**Alexandria**	24
Bistrot Lafayette	**Alexandria**	23
NEW Rogue 24	**Mt. Vernon Sq**	23
Mannequin Pis	**Olney**	23
Matisse	**Upper NW**	23
Medium Rare	**Cleve Pk**	22
Chef Geoff's	**multi.**	21
Bistro Français	**Georgetown**	21
Lia's	**Chevy Chase**	21

QUIET CONVERSATION

Inn/Little Washington	**Washington**	29
Komi	**Dupont Cir**	28
Corduroy	**Mt. Vernon Sq**	28
Obelisk	**Dupont Cir**	28
CityZen	**SW**	27
Sergio Rist.	**Silver Spring**	27
Eve	**Alexandria**	27
Makoto	**Palisades**	27
Lafayette Rm.	**Gldn Triangle**	27
Russia House Rest.	**Herndon**	27
Palena	**Cleve Pk**	27
Ashby Inn	**Paris**	27
Tosca	**Penn Qtr**	27
Fiola	**Penn Qtr**	27
2941	**Falls Ch**	27
Source	**Penn Qtr**	27
Sushi Taro	**Dupont Cir**	26
L'Auberge Provençale	**Boyce**	26
Pesce	**Dupont Cir**	26
Bistro L'Hermitage	**Woodbridge**	26
Café Renaissance	**Vienna**	26
La Bergerie	**Alexandria**	26
1789	**Georgetown**	26
Adour/St. Regis	**D'town**	26
Plume	**D'town**	26
Nora	**Dupont Cir**	26
Oval Rm.	**Gldn Triangle**	26
Villa Mozart	**Fairfax**	26
La Chaumière	**Georgetown**	26
La Taberna	**World Bank**	26
NEW Elisir	**Penn Qtr**	26
Kinkead's	**Foggy Bottom**	25
Sweet Ginger	**Vienna**	25
Eola	**Dupont Cir**	25
Masala Art	**Upper NW**	25
Equinox	**Gldn Triangle**	25
Bourbon Steak	**Georgetown**	25
Bombay Club	**Gldn Triangle**	25
Ris	**West End**	25
Orchard	**Frederick**	25
Oceanaire	**D'town**	24
J&G Steak	**D'town**	24
Juniper	**West End**	24
2100 Prime	**Dupont Cir**	24
Minh's	**Arlington**	24
El Manantial	**Reston**	24
Blue Rock	**Sperryville**	24
La Ferme	**Chevy Chase**	24
Liberty Tav.	**Clarendon**	24
Passage to India	**Bethesda**	24
Bastille	**Alexandria**	24

701 | **Penn Qtr**	23
Benjarong | **Rockville**	23
Watershed | **NoMa**	23
Sea Catch | **Georgetown**	23
Woo Lae Oak | **Vienna**	23
Eventide | **Clarendon**	23
Caucus Rm. | **Penn Qtr**	23
Kellari Taverna | **Gldn Triangle**	23
Matisse | **Upper NW**	23
Indique | **multi.**	23
Guardado's | **Bethesda**	23
Heritage India | **Glover Pk**	22
Westend Bistro | **West End**	22
Il Canale | **Georgetown**	22
Degrees | **Georgetown**	22
Zentan | **D'town**	22
Newton's | **Bethesda**	22
New Heights | **Woodley Pk**	22
15 Ria | **Scott Cir**	22
Sou'Wester | **SW**	21
Ching Ching | **Georgetown**	20

ROMANTIC PLACES

Inn/Little Washington | **Washington**	29
Rasika | **multi.**	28
L'Aub./François | **Grt Falls**	28
Komi | **Dupont Cir**	28
Corduroy | **Mt. Vernon Sq**	28
Obelisk | **Dupont Cir**	28
Little Serow | **Dupont Cir**	28
CityZen | **SW**	27
Eve | **Alexandria**	27
Foti's | **Culpeper**	27
Palena | **Cleve Pk**	27
Ashby Inn | **Paris**	27
Fiola | **Penn Qtr**	27
2941 | **Falls Ch**	27
Source | **Penn Qtr**	27
L'Auberge Provençale | **Boyce**	26
Bistro Provence | **Bethesda**	26
Bistro L'Hermitage | **Woodbridge**	26
Café Renaissance | **Vienna**	26
La Bergerie | **Alexandria**	26
1789 | **Georgetown**	26
Le Refuge | **Alexandria**	26
Sei | **Penn Qtr**	26
Plume | **D'town**	26
Nora | **Dupont Cir**	26
Present | **Falls Ch**	26
Brabo | **Alexandria**	26
Vermilion | **Alexandria**	26
La Chaumière | **Georgetown**	26

La Taberna | **World Bank**	26
Room 11 | **Columbia Hts**	26
Dolce Vita | **Fairfax**	25
Cork | **Logan Cir**	25
Al Tiramisu | **Dupont Cir**	25
Montmartre | **Cap Hill**	25
Cashion's Eat | **Adams Mor**	25
Bangkok 54 | **Arlington**	25
Addie's | **White Flint**	25
Estadio | **Logan Cir**	25
Bombay Club | **Gldn Triangle**	25
Tabard Inn | **Dupont Cir**	25
Cava Mezze | **multi.**	25
Fontaine Caffe | **Alexandria**	25
Atlas Rm. | **Atlas Dist**	25
Trummer's | **Clifton**	24
Bezu | **Potomac**	24
Proof | **Penn Qtr**	24
J&G Steak | **D'town**	24
Oya | **Penn Qtr**	24
Juniper | **West End**	24
Floriana Rest. | **Dupont Cir**	24
Mezè | **Adams Mor**	24
Birch/Barley | **Logan Cir**	24
8407 Kit. | **Silver Spring**	24
Blue Rock | **Sperryville**	24
La Ferme | **Chevy Chase**	24
Neyla | **Georgetown**	24
Tallula/EatBar | **Clarendon**	24
Acqua al 2 | **Cap Hill**	24
NEW District Kit. | **Woodley Pk**	24
Co Co. Sala | **Penn Qtr**	24
Bistrot Lepic | **Georgetown**	24
Bistro Cacao | **Cap Hill**	24
701 | **Penn Qtr**	23
Marrakesh P | **Dupont Cir**	23
Bodega | **Georgetown**	23
La Canela | **Rockville**	23
Ripple | **Cleve Pk**	23
Little Fountain | **Adams Mor**	23
Agora | **Dupont Cir**	23
Eventide | **Clarendon**	23
Café Bonaparte | **Georgetown**	23
Grapeseed | **Bethesda**	23
Marvin | **U St**	23
Firefly | **Dupont Cir**	23
Indique | **multi.**	23
Bar Pilar | **U St**	23
Sea Pearl | **Merrifield**	23
Heritage India | **Glover Pk**	22
Paul | **Georgetown**	22
Il Canale | **Georgetown**	22
Busara | **McLean**	22
Ezmè | **Dupont Cir**	22

Casa Oaxaca | **Adams Mor**	22
Zentan | **D'town**	22
Rustico | **Arlington**	22
Newton's | **Bethesda**	22
New Heights | **Woodley Pk**	22
Busboys/Poets | **Arlington**	22
1905 | **Mt. Vernon Sq**	21
El Centro | **Logan Cir**	21
Himalayan Heritage | **Adams Mor**	21
Dickson Wine | **U St**	21
Comus Inn | **Dickerson**	20
Old Angler's | **Potomac**	20
Cuba Libre | **Penn Qtr**	20
Jack Rose | **Adams Mor**	20
Circle Bistro | **West End**	20
Redwood | **Bethesda**	19
Big Bear Cafe | **Bloomingdale**	-
NEW Bistro Bohem | **Shaw**	-
NEW Brixton | **U St**	-
NEW Chez Billy | **Petworth**	-
NEW Mintwood | **Adams Mor**	-
NEW Unum | **Georgetown**	-

SINGLES SCENES

Tasting Rm. | **Frederick**	27
Zaytinya | **Penn Qtr**	26
Central Michel | **Penn Qtr**	26
Mio | **D'town**	26
Room 11 | **Columbia Hts**	26
BLT Steak | **Gldn Triangle**	25
Oyamel | **Penn Qtr**	25
Brass. Beck | **D'town**	25
Oya | **Penn Qtr**	24
Birch/Barley | **Logan Cir**	24
Neyla | **Georgetown**	24
Liberty Tav. | **Clarendon**	24
Jackson's | **Reston**	23
PS 7's | **Penn Qtr**	23
Old Ebbitt | **D'town**	23
Masa 14 | **Logan Cir**	23
Marvin | **U St**	23
Columbia Firehse. | **Alexandria**	23
Indique | **Chevy Chase**	23
Bar Pilar | **U St**	23
Zengo | **Chinatown**	22
Perrys | **Adams Mor**	22
Clyde's | **multi.**	22
Cafe Milano | **Georgetown**	22
Rustico | **multi.**	22
Dogfish Head | **Falls Ch**	21
Chef Geoff's | **Vienna**	21
Asia Bistro/Zen | **Arlington**	21
Bourbon | **multi.**	21

Circa | **multi.**	20
Tabaq Bistro | **U St**	20
Cafe Deluxe | **multi.**	20
Café Saint-Ex | **Logan Cir**	20
Kramerbooks | **Dupont Cir**	19
Star/Shamrock | **Atlas Dist**	19
Austin Grill | **multi.**	18
Blackfinn Amer. | **Bethesda**	18
Madhatter | **Dupont Cir**	18
Local 16 | **U St**	17
Sequoia | **Georgetown**	17
Standard | **Logan Cir**	-

SLEEPERS

(Good food, but little known)

Sergio Rist. | **Silver Spring**	27
Fast Gourmet | **U St**	27
Lafayette Rm. | **Gldn Triangle**	27
Shamshiry | **Vienna**	27
Cosmopolitan Grill | **Alexandria**	27
L'Auberge Provençale | **Boyce**	26
Kabob N Karahi | **Silver Spring**	26
India Palace | **Germantown**	26
Village Bistro | **Arlington**	26
Old Hickory | **Nat'l Harbor**	26
Room 11 | **Columbia Hts**	26
Taste/Burma | **Sterling**	26
La Caraqueña | **Falls Ch**	25
New Kam | **Wheaton**	25
Toscana Café | **Cap Hill**	25
Panjshir | **Falls Ch**	25
Adam Express | **Mt. Pleasant**	25
Huong Viet | **Falls Ch**	25
Sweet Ginger | **Vienna**	25
Eola | **Dupont Cir**	25
Hama Sushi | **Herndon**	25
Ray's/East River | **NE**	25
Sichuan Jin River | **Rockville**	25
Grille | **Alexandria**	25
Fontaine Caffe | **Alexandria**	25
Las Canteras | **Adams Mor**	24
Rangoli | **S Riding**	24
Juniper | **West End**	24
Regent | **Dupont Cir**	24
Ren's Ramen | **Wheaton**	24
Pho DC | **Chinatown**	24
Blue Rock | **Sperryville**	24
Napoleon Bistro | **Adams Mor**	24
Fyve | **Arlington**	24
Senart's Oyster | **Cap Hill**	24
Morrison-Clark | **D'town**	24
Lighthouse/Vit Goel | **Rockville**	24
Myanmar | **Falls Ch**	24

TRANSPORTING EXPERIENCES

L'Aub./François | **Grt Falls**	28
Makoto | **Palisades**	27
Sushi Taro | **Dupont Cir**	26
La Taberna | **World Bank**	26
Kazan | **McLean**	25
Kushi | **Mt. Vernon Sq**	25
Bombay Club | **Gldn Triangle**	25
Brass. Beck | **D'town**	25
Oya | **Penn Qtr**	24
Neyla | **Georgetown**	24
Marrakesh P | **Dupont Cir**	23
Hunter's Head | **Upperville**	23
Honey Pig | **Annandale**	23
Heritage India | **Glover Pk**	22
Russia Hse. | **Dupont Cir**	21
Hill Country | **Penn Qtr**	21
Cuba Libre | **Penn Qtr**	20
Ching Ching | **Georgetown**	20
Martin's Tav. | **Georgetown**	20
Freddy's Lobster | **Bethesda**	19
Biergarten Haus | **Atlas Dist**	17

TRENDY

Rasika | **multi.**	28
Komi | **Dupont Cir**	28
Volt | **Frederick**	28
Little Serow | **Dupont Cir**	28
CityZen | **SW**	27
Fast Gourmet | **U St**	27
Eve | **Alexandria**	27
Palena | **Cleve Pk**	27
Fiola | **Penn Qtr**	27
Ruan Thai | **Wheaton**	27
Source | **Penn Qtr**	27
Pupatella Pizzeria | **Arlington**	26
Zaytinya | **Penn Qtr**	26
Toki | **Atlas Dist**	26
Central Michel | **Penn Qtr**	26
Sei | **Penn Qtr**	26
Ray's Hell Burger | **Arlington**	26
NEW Pearl Dive | **Logan Cir**	26
Mio | **D'town**	26
Vermilion | **Alexandria**	26
Bistro Bis | **Cap Hill**	26
Room 11 | **Columbia Hts**	26
Pho 14 | **Columbia Hts**	25
2 Amys | **Cleve Pk**	25
Red Hook | **Location Varies**	25
Sushi Damo | **Rockville**	25
Cork | **Logan Cir**	25
Cashion's Eat | **Adams Mor**	25
Bibiana | **D'town**	25

Kushi | **Mt. Vernon Sq**	25
Estadio | **Logan Cir**	25
Tabard Inn | **Dupont Cir**	25
Oyamel | **Penn Qtr**	25
Brass. Beck | **D'town**	25
Atlas Rm. | **Atlas Dist**	25
Proof | **Penn Qtr**	24
Granville Moore's | **Atlas Dist**	24
Ethiopic | **Atlas Dist**	24
J&G Steak | **D'town**	24
Oya | **Penn Qtr**	24
Ren's Ramen | **Wheaton**	24
NEW Graffiato | **Chinatown**	24
Birch/Barley | **Logan Cir**	24
NEW Society Fair | **Alexandria**	24
Jaleo | **multi.**	24
Tallula/EatBar | **Clarendon**	24
Hank's Oyster | **Dupont Cir**	24
Thunder Burger | **Georgetown**	24
Founding Farmers | **multi.**	24
Black's Bar | **Bethesda**	24
Co Co. Sala | **Penn Qtr**	24
Evening Star | **Alexandria**	23
Bread Line | **World Bank**	23
Good Stuff | **multi.**	23
Matchbox | **multi.**	23
Art & Soul | **Cap Hill**	23
NEW Rogue 24 | **Mt. Vernon Sq**	23
District of Pi | **Penn Qtr**	23
Jackie's | **Silver Spring**	23
Ripple | **Cleve Pk**	23
Mandu | **multi.**	23
Masa 14 | **Logan Cir**	23
Leopold's Kafe | **Georgetown**	23
Marvin | **U St**	23
Eatonville | **U St**	23
Honey Pig | **Annandale**	23
Zengo | **Chinatown**	22
Perrys | **Adams Mor**	22
Bistrot du Coin | **Dupont Cir**	22
Vinoteca | **U St**	22
Renato/River Falls | **Potomac**	22
Pete's New Haven | **multi.**	22
Cafe Milano | **Georgetown**	22
Zentan | **D'town**	22
We The Pizza | **Cap Hill**	22
Policy | **U St**	22
Busboys/Poets | **multi.**	22
Taylor Gourmet | **multi.**	22
Bayou Bakery | **Arlington**	22
Russia Hse. | **Dupont Cir**	21
Hill Country | **Penn Qtr**	21
Lauriol Plaza | **Dupont Cir**	21
1905 | **Mt. Vernon Sq**	21

Johnny's | **Cap Hill**	21
El Centro | **Logan Cir**	21
Dickson Wine | **U St**	21
Mussel Bar | **Bethesda**	20
Lincoln | **D'town**	20
Circa | **multi.**	20
Jack Rose | **Adams Mor**	20
Café Saint-Ex | **Logan Cir**	20
American Ice | **U St**	19
Stoney's Lounge | **Logan Cir**	18
Local 16 | **U St**	17
NEW Alegria | **Vienna**	–
NEW Bandolero | **Georgetown**	–
NEW Bistro Bohem | **Shaw**	–
NEW Boqueria | **Dupont Cir**	–
NEW Boundary Rd. | **Atlas Dist**	–
NEW Brixton | **U St**	–
NEW Chez Billy | **Petworth**	–
NEW Del Frisco's | **D'town**	–
NEW Family Meal | **Frederick**	–
NEW Fuel Pizza | **multi.**	–
NEW Fujimar | **D'town**	–
NEW Green Pig | **Clarendon**	–
NEW Haven | **Bethesda**	–
NEW Kangaroo Boxing/PORC | **Columbia Hts**	–
Standard | **Logan Cir**	–
NEW Sugo Cicchetti | **Potomac**	–

VALET PARKING

Inn/Little Washington | **Washington**	29
Rasika | **Penn Qtr**	28
Marcel's | **West End**	28
Prime Rib | **Gldn Triangle**	28
CityZen | **SW**	27
Lafayette Rm. | **Gldn Triangle**	27
Blue Duck | **West End**	27
Tosca | **Penn Qtr**	27
Fiola | **Penn Qtr**	27
2941 | **Falls Ch**	27
Fogo de Chão | **Penn Qtr**	27
Source | **Penn Qtr**	27
Thai Sq. | **Arlington**	26
Capital Grille | **multi.**	26
Ruth's Chris | **multi.**	26
Pesce | **Dupont Cir**	26
Morton's | **multi.**	26
Zaytinya | **Penn Qtr**	26
Charlie Palmer | **Cap Hill**	26
1789 | **Georgetown**	26
Central Michel | **Penn Qtr**	26
Vidalia | **Gldn Triangle**	26
Sei | **Penn Qtr**	26

Adour/St. Regis | **D'town**	26
Plume | **D'town**	26
Nora | **Dupont Cir**	26
Oval Rm. | **Gldn Triangle**	26
Mio | **D'town**	26
Brabo | **Alexandria**	26
Chima | **Vienna**	26
NEW Elisir | **Penn Qtr**	26
BLT Steak | **Gldn Triangle**	25
Palm | **multi.**	25
Al Tiramisu | **Dupont Cir**	25
Cashion's Eat | **Adams Mor**	25
Bourbon Steak | **Georgetown**	25
Bibiana | **D'town**	25
Estadio | **Logan Cir**	25
Bombay Club | **Gldn Triangle**	25
Fleming's Steak | **McLean**	25
Tabard Inn | **Dupont Cir**	25
Grille | **Alexandria**	25
Cava Mezze | **Cap Hill**	25
Smith/Wollensky | **Gldn Triangle**	25
Brass. Beck | **D'town**	25
Oceanaire | **D'town**	24
Proof | **Penn Qtr**	24
J&G Steak | **D'town**	24
Oya | **Penn Qtr**	24
Siroc | **D'town**	24
Juniper | **West End**	24
2100 Prime | **Dupont Cir**	24
Grill/Ipanema | **Adams Mor**	24
NEW Graffiato | **Chinatown**	24
I Ricchi | **Dupont Cir**	24
Lyon Hall | **Clarendon**	24
Ceiba | **D'town**	24
Neyla | **Georgetown**	24
Sushiko | **Glover Pk**	24
Acadiana | **Mt. Vernon Sq**	24
Cheesecake | **multi.**	24
Morrison-Clark | **D'town**	24
Co Co. Sala | **Penn Qtr**	24
Passage to India | **Bethesda**	24
Maggiano's | **McLean**	23
701 | **Penn Qtr**	23
Marrakesh P | **Dupont Cir**	23
Asian Spice | **Chinatown**	23
Matchbox | **multi.**	23
Art & Soul | **Cap Hill**	23
Watershed | **NoMa**	23
DC Coast | **D'town**	23
PS 7's | **Penn Qtr**	23
McCormick/Schmick | **multi.**	23
Rosa Mexicano | **multi.**	23
Old Ebbitt | **D'town**	23

Woo Lae Oak | **Vienna**	23	
Masa 14 | **Logan Cir**	23	
Kellari Taverna | **Gldn Triangle**	23	
Vinifera | **Reston**	23	
Grapeseed | **Bethesda**	23	
Hee Been | **Alexandria**	23	
Assaggi | **Bethesda**	23	
Härth | **McLean**	23	
Tutto Bene | **Arlington**	23	
Occidental | **D'town**	23	
Bobby Van's | **D'town**	23	
P.F. Chang's | **Sterling**	23	
Heritage India | **Glover Pk**	22	
Zengo | **Chinatown**	22	
Petits Plats | **Woodley Pk**	22	
Westend Bistro | **West End**	22	
Brass. Monte Carlo | **Bethesda**	22	
Tragara | **Bethesda**	22	
NEW District Commons | **Foggy Bottom**	22	
Wildfire | **McLean**	22	
Bond 45 | **Nat'l Harbor**	22	
Degrees | **Georgetown**	22	
Notti Bianche | **Foggy Bottom**	22	
Clyde's | **multi.**	22	
Georgia Brown | **D'town**	22	
Ardeo/Bardeo | **Cleve Pk**	22	
Newton's | **Bethesda**	22	
Mon Ami Gabi | **Bethesda**	22	
Policy | **U St**	22	
Calif. Tortilla | **Cleve Pk**	22	
New Heights | **Woodley Pk**	22	
M&S Grill | **D'town**	22	
15 Ria | **Scott Cir**	22	
Café Dupont | **Dupont Cir**	21	
Chef Geoff's | **multi.**	21	
Sou'Wester | **SW**	21	
Café du Parc | **D'town**	21	
Panache | **McLean**	21	
Sette Osteria | **Dupont Cir**	21	
Nage | **Scott Cir**	21	
Lia's | **Chevy Chase**	21	
District ChopHse. | **Penn Qtr**	21	
Acre 121 | **Columbia Hts**	21	
Dish/Drinks | **Foggy Bottom**	21	
Poste Moderne | **Penn Qtr**	20	
Cuba Libre | **Penn Qtr**	20	
Finemondo | **D'town**	20	
Ulah Bistro | **U St**	20	
Tabaq Bistro | **U St**	20	
Carmine's | **Penn Qtr**	20	
Irish Inn/Glen Echo | **Glen Echo**	20	
Circle Bistro | **West End**	20	
Caribbean Breeze | **Arlington**	20	

NEW Cesco Osteria | **Bethesda**	19
Primi Piatti | **Foggy Bottom**	19
P.J. Clarke's | **D'town**	18
Local 16 | **U St**	17
Biergarten Haus | **Atlas Dist**	17
NEW Howard Theatre | **Shaw**	-
NEW Mintwood | **Adams Mor**	-

VIEWS

Inn/Little Washington | **Washington**	29
L'Aub./François | **Grt Falls**	28
Lafayette Rm. | **Gldn Triangle**	27
Ashby Inn | **Paris**	27
2941 | **Falls Ch**	27
Source | **Penn Qtr**	27
Ruth's Chris | **Arlington**	26
Charlie Palmer | **Cap Hill**	26
J&G Steak | **D'town**	24
Blue Rock | **Sperryville**	24
701 | **Penn Qtr**	23
Sea Catch | **Georgetown**	23
Rosa Mexicano | **Nat'l Harbor**	23
Mai Thai | **Alexandria**	23
Masa 14 | **Logan Cir**	23
Perrys | **Adams Mor**	22
Roti Med. | **World Bank**	22
NEW District Commons | **Foggy Bottom**	22
Bond 45 | **Nat'l Harbor**	22
Clyde's | **Rockville**	22
Guapo's | **Gaith'burg**	22
New Heights | **Woodley Pk**	22
1905 | **Mt. Vernon Sq**	21
El Centro | **Logan Cir**	21
Sou'Wester | **SW**	21
Café du Parc | **D'town**	21
NEW Boxcar Tav. | **Cap Hill**	21
Acre 121 | **Columbia Hts**	21
Old Angler's | **Potomac**	20
Jack Rose | **Adams Mor**	20
Tabaq Bistro | **U St**	20
Phillips | **SW**	20
Virtue | **Alexandria**	19
Sequoia | **Georgetown**	17
Roof Terr. | **Foggy Bottom**	16

WINE BARS

Vidalia | **Gldn Triangle**	26
Bazin's/Church | **Vienna**	26
Wine Kit. | **multi.**	26
NEW Pearl Dive | **Logan Cir**	26
Room 11 | **Columbia Hts**	26
Cork | **Logan Cir**	25

Estadio | **Logan Cir**	25
Iron Bridge Wine | **Warrenton**	25
Fleming's Steak | **McLean**	25
Cava Mezze | **Rockville**	25
Proof | **Penn Qtr**	24
Bistrot Lepic | **Georgetown**	24
Bastille | **Alexandria**	24
A La Lucia | **Alexandria**	23
Bistro Cacao | **Cap Hill**	23
701 | **Penn Qtr**	23
Posto | **Logan Cir**	23
Al Crostino | **U St**	23
Ripple | **Cleve Pk**	23
Mrs. K's | **Silver Spring**	23
Vinifera | **Reston**	23
Grapeseed | **Bethesda**	23
Evo Bistro | **McLean**	22
Vinoteca | **U St**	22
Ezmè | **Dupont Cir**	22
Ardeo/Bardeo | **Cleve Pk**	22
Northside | **Clarendon**	22
Sonoma | **Cap Hill**	21
Asia Bistro/Zen | **Arlington**	21
Urbana | **Dupont Cir**	21
Oakville Grille | **Bethesda**	21
Dickson Wine | **U St**	21
Acacia Bistro | **Upper NW**	20
Circa | **Dupont Cir**	20
Twisted Vines | **Arlington**	20
Redwood | **Bethesda**	19
NEW Curious Grape | **Arlington**	-
NEW Dolce Veloce | **Fairfax**	-
NEW Maple | **Columbia Hts**	-

WINNING WINE LISTS

Inn/Little Washington | **Washington**	29
Rasika | **multi.**	28
L'Aub./François | **Grt Falls**	28
Komi | **Dupont Cir**	28
Marcel's | **West End**	28
Prime Rib | **Gldn Triangle**	28
Volt | **Frederick**	28
Corduroy | **Mt. Vernon Sq**	28
Obelisk | **Dupont Cir**	28
Little Serow | **Dupont Cir**	28
CityZen | **SW**	27
Tasting Rm. | **Frederick**	27
Eve | **Alexandria**	27
Foti's | **Culpeper**	27
Palena | **Cleve Pk**	27
Ray's/Steaks | **Arlington**	27
Blue Duck | **West End**	27

Ashby Inn | **Paris**	27
Tosca | **Penn Qtr**	27
BlackSalt | **Palisades**	27
Fiola | **Penn Qtr**	27
2941 | **Falls Ch**	27
Il Pizzico | **Rockville**	27
Source | **Penn Qtr**	27
Capital Grille | **multi.**	26
L'Auberge Provençale | **Boyce**	26
Bistro Provence | **Bethesda**	26
Pesce | **Dupont Cir**	26
Bistro L'Hermitage | **Woodbridge**	26
Café Renaissance | **Vienna**	26
Zaytinya | **Penn Qtr**	26
PassionFish | **Reston**	26
Charlie Palmer | **Cap Hill**	26
Central Michel | **Penn Qtr**	26
Vidalia | **Gldn Triangle**	26
Nostos | **Vienna**	26
Adour/St. Regis | **D'town**	26
Plume | **D'town**	26
Nora | **Dupont Cir**	26
Oval Rm. | **Gldn Triangle**	26
Brabo | **Alexandria**	26
Sabai | **Germantown**	26
La Chaumière | **Georgetown**	26
Bistro Bis | **Cap Hill**	26
La Taberna | **World Bank**	26
NEW Elisir | **Penn Qtr**	26
Room 11 | **Columbia Hts**	26
Kaz Sushi | **World Bank**	25
Toscana Café | **Cap Hill**	25
2 Amys | **Cleve Pk**	25
Kinkead's | **Foggy Bottom**	25
BLT Steak | **Gldn Triangle**	25
Tuscarora Mill | **Leesburg**	25
Eola | **Dupont Cir**	25
Palm | **multi.**	25
Dolce Vita | **Fairfax**	25
Ray's/Classics | **Silver Spring**	25
Cork | **Logan Cir**	25
NEW Ray's/Third | **Arlington**	25
Al Tiramisu | **Dupont Cir**	25
Cashion's Eat | **Adams Mor**	25
Equinox | **Gldn Triangle**	25
Bourbon Steak | **Georgetown**	25
Bibiana | **D'town**	25
Kushi | **Mt. Vernon Sq**	25
Estadio | **Logan Cir**	25
Fleming's Steak | **McLean**	25
Ris | **West End**	25
Tabard Inn | **Dupont Cir**	25
Persimmon | **Bethesda**	25

Et Voila	**Palisades**	25
Landini Bros.	**Alexandria**	25
Smith/Wollensky	**Gldn Triangle**	25
Brass. Beck	**D'town**	25
Carlyle	**Arlington**	25
Tavira	**Chevy Chase**	25
Trummer's	**Clifton**	24
Proof	**Penn Qtr**	24
J&G Steak	**D'town**	24
Oya	**Penn Qtr**	24
2100 Prime	**Dupont Cir**	24
Willow	**Arlington**	24
Floriana Rest.	**Dupont Cir**	24
NEW Graffiato	**Chinatown**	24
Birch/Barley	**Logan Cir**	24
I Ricchi	**Dupont Cir**	24
NEW Society Fair	**Alexandria**	24
Jaleo	**multi.**	24
Tallula/EatBar	**Clarendon**	24
Acqua al 2	**Cap Hill**	24
NEW District Kit.	**Woodley Pk**	24
Sushiko	**multi.**	24
Dino	**Cleve Pk**	24
Bistrot Lepic	**Georgetown**	24
Bastille	**Alexandria**	24
Evening Star	**Alexandria**	23
NEW Rogue 24	**Mt. Vernon Sq**	23
Posto	**Logan Cir**	23
PS 7's	**Penn Qtr**	23
Pizzeria Da Marco	**Bethesda**	23
Ripple	**Cleve Pk**	23
Old Ebbitt	**D'town**	23
Mrs. K's	**Silver Spring**	23
Eventide	**Clarendon**	23
Caucus Rm.	**Penn Qtr**	23
Kellari Taverna	**Gldn Triangle**	23
Vinifera	**Reston**	23
Grapeseed	**Bethesda**	23
Ping	**Arlington**	23
Leopold's Kafe	**Georgetown**	23
Occidental	**D'town**	23
Westend Bistro	**West End**	22
Il Canale	**Georgetown**	22
NEW District Commons	**Foggy Bottom**	22
Evo Bistro	**McLean**	22
Vinoteca	**U St**	22
Sorriso	**Cleve Pk**	22
Wildfire	**McLean**	22
Bond 45	**Nat'l Harbor**	22
Cafe Milano	**Georgetown**	22

Medium Rare	**Cleve Pk**	22
Northside	**Clarendon**	22
Mon Ami Gabi	**multi.**	22
New Heights	**Woodley Pk**	22
Food Wine	**Bethesda**	22
Johnny's	**Cap Hill**	21
Sonoma	**Cap Hill**	21
Café du Parc	**D'town**	21
Jackson 20	**Alexandria**	21
Oakville Grille	**Bethesda**	21
Dickson Wine	**U St**	21
Harry's	**Arlington**	21
Blvd. Woodgrill	**Clarendon**	20
Mussel Bar	**Bethesda**	20
Circa	**Dupont Cir**	20
Buck's Fishing	**Upper NW**	20
Jack Rose	**Adams Mor**	20
Twisted Vines	**Arlington**	20
NEW Cesco Osteria	**Bethesda**	19
Redwood	**Bethesda**	19
NEW Boqueria	**Dupont Cir**	-
NEW Curious Grape	**Arlington**	-
NEW Irish Whiskey	**Dupont Cir**	-
NEW La Forchetta	**Upper NW**	-
NEW Maple	**Columbia Hts**	-
NEW Menomale	**NE**	-
NEW Mintwood	**Adams Mor**	-
NEW Tel'Veh	**Mt. Vernon Sq**	-

WORTH A TRIP

Boyce, VA	
L'Auberge Provençale	26
Clifton, VA	
Trummer's	24
Culpeper, VA	
Foti's	27
Dickerson, MD	
Comus Inn	20
Frederick, MD	
Volt	28
Firestone's	26
Wine Kit.	26
Isabella's	26
Paris, VA	
Ashby Inn	27
The Plains, VA	
Rail Stop	23
Warrenton, VA	
Iron Bridge Wine	25
Washington, VA	
Inn/Little Washington	29

Cuisines

Includes names, locations and Food ratings.

AFGHAN

Kabob Palace	**Arlington**	26
Bamian	**Falls Ch**	26
Afghan Kabob Rest.	**Springfield**	25
Panjshir	**Falls Ch**	25
Food Corner Kabob	**multi.**	25
Faryab	**Bethesda**	24
Afghan	**Alexandria**	23
Afghan Kabob Hse.	**Arlington**	23

AMERICAN

Inn/Little Washington	**Washington**	29
Komi	**Dupont Cir**	28
Volt	**Frederick**	28
Corduroy	**Mt. Vernon Sq**	28
Monocacy Cross.	**Frederick**	28
CityZen	**SW**	27
Tasting Rm.	**Frederick**	27
Eve	**Alexandria**	27
Lafayette Rm.	**Gldn Triangle**	27
Foti's	**Culpeper**	27
Palena	**Cleve Pk**	27
Ray's/Steaks	**Arlington**	27
Blue Duck	**West End**	27
Ashby Inn	**Paris**	27
BlackSalt	**Palisades**	27
2941	**Falls Ch**	27
Mike's	**Springfield**	26
PassionFish	**Reston**	26
1789	**Georgetown**	26
Central Michel	**Penn Qtr**	26
Firestone's	**Frederick**	26
Vidalia	**Gldn Triangle**	26
Bazin's/Church	**Vienna**	26
Adour/St. Regis	**D'town**	26
Plume	**D'town**	26
Black Mkt.	**Garrett Pk**	26
Wine Kit.	**multi.**	26
Lightfoot	**Leesburg**	26
Nora	**Dupont Cir**	26
Oval Rm.	**Gldn Triangle**	26
NEW Pearl Dive	**Logan Cir**	26
Vermilion	**Alexandria**	26
Tuscarora Mill	**Leesburg**	25
Eola	**Dupont Cir**	25
Cork	**Logan Cir**	25
Dutch's Daughter	**Frederick**	25
NEW Ray's/Third	**Arlington**	25
Artie's	**Fairfax**	25

Cashion's Eat	**Adams Mor**	25
Equinox	**Gldn Triangle**	25
Ray's/East River	**NE**	25
Addie's	**White Flint**	25
Magnolias/Mill	**Purcellville**	25
Iron Bridge Wine	**Warrenton**	25
Ris	**West End**	25
Tabard Inn	**Dupont Cir**	25
Persimmon	**Bethesda**	25
Grille	**Alexandria**	25
Carlyle	**Arlington**	25
Trummer's	**Clifton**	24
Blue Ridge	**multi.**	24
Bezu	**Potomac**	24
Proof	**Penn Qtr**	24
Granville Moore's	**Atlas Dist**	24
J&G Steak	**D'town**	24
Juniper	**West End**	24
2100 Prime	**Dupont Cir**	24
Majestic	**Alexandria**	24
Willow	**Arlington**	24
Acacia Bistro	**Frederick**	24
Birch/Barley	**Logan Cir**	24
8407 Kit.	**Silver Spring**	24
Blue Rock	**Sperryville**	24
Cafe Nola	**Frederick**	24
NEW Society Fair	**Alexandria**	24
Tallula/EatBar	**Clarendon**	24
NEW District Kit.	**Woodley Pk**	24
Fyve	**Arlington**	24
Hank's Oyster	**multi.**	24
Liberty Tav.	**Clarendon**	24
NEW Lunchbox	**Frederick**	24
Founding Farmers	**multi.**	24
Black's Bar	**Bethesda**	24
Cheesecake	**multi.**	24
Morrison-Clark	**D'town**	24
Co Co. Sala	**Penn Qtr**	24
Evening Star	**Alexandria**	23
Ted's Bulletin	**Cap Hill**	23
Jackson's	**Reston**	23
701	**Penn Qtr**	23
Liberty Tree	**Atlas Dist**	23
Town Hall	**Glover Pk**	23
Matchbox	**multi.**	23
Art & Soul	**Cap Hill**	23
NEW Rogue 24	**Mt. Vernon Sq**	23
Watershed	**NoMa**	23
Rail Stop	**Plains**	23

DC Coast	**D'town**	23
PS 7's	**Penn Qtr**	23
CapMac	**Location Varies**	23
Cedar Rest.	**Penn Qtr**	23
Jackie's	**Silver Spring**	23
Ripple	**Cleve Pk**	23
Old Ebbitt	**D'town**	23
Mrs. K's	**Silver Spring**	23
Eventide	**Clarendon**	23
Caucus Rm.	**Penn Qtr**	23
Vinifera	**Reston**	23
Grapeseed	**Bethesda**	23
Marvin	**U St**	23
Farrah Olivia	**Arlington**	23
Härth	**McLean**	23
Columbia Firehse.	**Alexandria**	23
Mitsitam	**SW**	23
Firefly	**Dupont Cir**	23
Bar Pilar	**U St**	23
Lost Dog	**multi.**	23
Rustik Tav.	**Bloomingdale**	23
Perrys	**Adams Mor**	22
Ben's Chili	**U St**	22
Westend Bistro	**West End**	22
Hard Times	**multi.**	22
NEW District Commons	**Foggy Bottom**	22
Clyde's	**multi.**	22
Ardeo/Bardeo	**Cleve Pk**	22
Rustico	**multi.**	22
Newton's	**Bethesda**	22
Peacock Cafe	**Georgetown**	22
901 Rest.	**Mt. Vernon Sq**	22
Policy	**U St**	22
New Heights	**Woodley Pk**	22
Busboys/Poets	**multi.**	22
M&S Grill	**multi.**	22
Smith Commons	**Atlas Dist**	22
Food Wine	**Bethesda**	22
Wild Tomato	**Potomac**	22
BGR	**multi.**	22
15 Ria	**Scott Cir**	22
Zest	**Cap Hill**	21
Monocle	**Cap Hill**	21
Counter	**Reston**	21
Open City	**Woodley Pk**	21
Eggspectation	**multi.**	21
Chop't	**multi.**	21
Serendipity 3	**Georgetown**	21
Gadsby's	**Alexandria**	21
Chef Geoff's	**multi.**	21
Johnny's	**Cap Hill**	21
Sou'Wester	**SW**	21
Sonoma	**Cap Hill**	21

Dangerously Delicious	**multi.**	21
Station 4	**SW Waterfront**	21
Jackson 20	**Alexandria**	21
Nage	**Scott Cir**	21
Lia's	**Chevy Chase**	21
Oakville Grille	**Bethesda**	21
NEW Boxcar Tav.	**Cap Hill**	21
Dish/Drinks	**Foggy Bottom**	21
Comus Inn	**Dickerson**	20
NEW Hamilton	**D'town**	20
Mad Fox Brew	**Falls Ch**	20
Old Angler's	**Potomac**	20
Blvd. Woodgrill	**Clarendon**	20
Poste Moderne	**Penn Qtr**	20
Lincoln	**D'town**	20
Chesapeake Rm.	**Cap Hill**	20
Ulah Bistro	**U St**	20
Againn	**D'town**	20
Circa	**multi.**	20
Buck's Fishing	**Upper NW**	20
Jack Rose	**Adams Mor**	20
NEW William Jeffrey's	**Arlington**	20
Cafe Deluxe	**multi.**	20
Irish Inn/Glen Echo	**Glen Echo**	20
Logan Tav.	**Logan Cir**	20
Meridian	**Columbia Hts**	20
Circle Bistro	**West End**	20
Martin's Tav.	**Georgetown**	20
Scion Rest.	**Dupont Cir**	19
Kramerbooks	**Dupont Cir**	19
Redwood	**Bethesda**	19
Virtue	**Alexandria**	19
Commissary	**Logan Cir**	19
Hudson	**West End**	18
Blackfinn Amer.	**multi.**	18
DC-3	**Cap Hill**	18
NEW Lost Society	**U St**	18
Madhatter	**Dupont Cir**	18
P.J. Clarke's	**D'town**	18
Tonic	**multi.**	17
Local 16	**U St**	17
Sequoia	**Georgetown**	17
Roof Terr.	**Foggy Bottom**	16
Big Bear Cafe	**Bloomingdale**	−
NEW Del Frisco's	**D'town**	−
NEW Family Meal	**Frederick**	−
NEW Fuel Pizza	**multi.**	−
NEW Green Pig	**Clarendon**	−
NEW Majestic B&G	**Bethesda**	−
NEW Maple	**Columbia Hts**	−
NEW Mintwood	**Adams Mor**	−
NEW Pig	**Logan Cir**	−
NEW Quench	**Rockville**	−

NEW River Falls Tav. | Potomac ⌐|

NEW Unum | Georgetown ⌐|

ASIAN

Source	**Penn Qtr**	27
Sei	**Penn Qtr**	26
Adam Express	**Mt. Pleasant**	25
Sweet Ginger	**Vienna**	25
Sunflower Veg.	**multi.**	25
Asian Bistro	**multi.**	25
Grace's	**Nat'l Harbor**	25
Oya	**Penn Qtr**	24
Asian Spice	**Chinatown**	23
Sticky Rice	**Atlas Dist**	23
Raku	**multi.**	23
Masa 14	**Logan Cir**	23
Zengo	**Chinatown**	22
Batik	**Gaith'burg**	22
NEW Shophouse	**Dupont Cir**	22
Zentan	**D'town**	22
Red Curry	**Alexandria**	22
901 Rest.	**Mt. Vernon Sq**	22
Asia Bistro/Zen	**Arlington**	21
Cafe Asia	**multi.**	21
Teaism	**multi.**	20
Ching Ching	**Georgetown**	20
Banana Leaves	**Dupont Cir**	⌐|
NEW Fujimar	**D'town**	⌐|

AUSTRIAN

Leopold's Kafe	**Georgetown**	23

BAKERIES

Il Fornaio	**Reston**	25
Praline	**Bethesda**	23
Bread Line	**World Bank**	23
Leopold's Kafe	**Georgetown**	23
Paul	**multi.**	22
Buzz	**multi.**	22
Dangerously Delicious	**multi.**	21
Le Pain Quotidien	**multi.**	21

BARBECUE

Urban BBQ	**multi.**	24
Rocklands	**multi.**	22
Red Hot/Blue	**multi.**	22
Hill Country	**Penn Qtr**	21
Acre 121	**Columbia Hts**	21
Harry's	**Arlington**	21
NEW Smoke/Barrel	**Adams Mor**	20
NEW Pork Barrel	**Alexandria**	19
Old Glory	**Georgetown**	19

American Ice | **U St** — 19

NEW Kangaroo Boxing/PORC | **multi.** ⌐|

Standard | **Logan Cir** ⌐|

BELGIAN

Marcel's	**West End**	28
Brabo	**Alexandria**	26
Belga Café	**Cap Hill**	25
Et Voila	**Palisades**	25
Brass. Beck	**D'town**	25
Granville Moore's	**Atlas Dist**	24
Mannequin Pis	**Olney**	23
Marvin	**U St**	23
Le Pain Quotidien	**multi.**	21
Mussel Bar	**Bethesda**	20

BRAZILIAN

Fogo de Chão	**Penn Qtr**	27
Chima	**Vienna**	26
Grill/Ipanema	**Adams Mor**	24

BRITISH

Queen Vic	**Atlas Dist**	23
Hunter's Head	**Upperville**	23
NEW Brixton	**U St**	⌐|
NEW Mayfair & Pine	**Glover Pk**	⌐|

BURGERS

Palena	**Cleve Pk**	27
Ray's Hell Burger	**Arlington**	26
Black & Orange	**multi.**	25
Ray's/East River	**NE**	25
Five Guys	**multi.**	24
Thunder Burger	**Georgetown**	24
Good Stuff	**multi.**	23
Matchbox	**multi.**	23
Old Ebbitt	**D'town**	23
NEW Bobby's Burger	**multi.**	22
Clyde's	**multi.**	22
BGR	**multi.**	22
Counter	**Reston**	21
Shake Shack	**multi.**	21
Elevation Burger	**multi.**	21
NEW Burger/Tap/Shake	**Foggy Bottom**	21
Harry's	**Arlington**	21

BURMESE

Taste/Burma	**Sterling**	26
Myanmar	**Falls Ch**	24
Mandalay	**Silver Spring**	23
Burma	**Chinatown**	22
Burma Rd.	**Gaith'burg**	22

CAJUN

RT's | **Alexandria**	26
Acadiana | **Mt. Vernon Sq**	24
Cajun Experience | **Leesburg**	23
Bayou | **West End**	20
Hot 'N Juicy | **Woodley Pk**	20
NEW Chasin' Tails | **Arlington**	–

CALIFORNIAN

Sea Pearl | **Merrifield**	23
Surfside | **Glover Pk**	21
Paolo's | **multi.**	21

CENTRAL AMERICAN

Pollo Campero | **multi.**	19

CHICKEN

El Pollo | **multi.**	26
Wings To Go | **NE**	25
Crisp/Juicy | **multi.**	24
Chicken/ Run | **Bethesda**	24
La Limeña | **Rockville**	23
Don Pollo | **multi.**	23
Nando's | **multi.**	22
Pollo Campero | **multi.**	19

CHINESE

(* dim sum specialist)

Peking Duck | **Alexandria**	28
Hong Kong Palace | **Falls Ch**	27
China Jade | **Rockville**	25
New Kam | **Wheaton**	25
Peking Gourmet | **Falls Ch**	25
Mark's Duck Hse.* | **Falls Ch**	25
Sichuan Jin River | **Rockville**	25
Yuan Fu | **Rockville**	25
Full Key | **Wheaton**	25
A&J* | **multi.**	25
China Bistro | **Rockville**	24
China Star | **Fairfax**	24
Hollywood E.* | **Wheaton**	24
X.O. Taste | **multi.**	24
Vegetable Gdn. | **White Flint**	24
NEW 100° C | **Fairfax**	24
Chinatown Express | **Chinatown**	23
Oriental E.* | **Silver Spring**	23
Joe's Noodle Hse. | **Rockville**	23
Full Kee (DC) | **Chinatown**	23
New Fortune* | **Gaith'burg**	23
Ping | **Arlington**	23
P.F. Chang's | **multi.**	23
Fortune* | **Falls Ch**	22
Tony Cheng's* | **Chinatown**	22
Fu Shing | **Bethesda**	22
China Gdn.* | **Rosslyn**	22

Burma Rd. | **Gaith'burg**	22
Michael's Noodles | **Rockville**	22
Good Fortune* | **Wheaton**	22
Mala Tang | **Arlington**	22
Full Kee (VA) | **Falls Ch**	22
Seven Seas | **multi.**	22
Eat First | **Chinatown**	22
Meiwah | **multi.**	21
Ping Pong* | **multi.**	21
Hunan Dynasty | **Cap Hill**	20
City Lights | **multi.**	19
NEW East Pearl | **Rockville**	–

COFFEEHOUSES

Café Bonaparte | **Georgetown**	23
Buzz | **multi.**	22
Northside | **Clarendon**	22
Tryst | **Adams Mor**	21

CONTEMPORARY LOUISIANA

Acadiana | **Mt. Vernon Sq**	24

CONTINENTAL

Café Renaissance | **Vienna**	26

CREOLE

RT's | **Alexandria**	26
Acadiana | **Mt. Vernon Sq**	24
Cajun Experience | **Leesburg**	23
Bayou | **West End**	20

CUBAN

Cuba de Ayer | **Burtonsville**	25
La Limeña | **Rockville**	23
Cubano's | **Silver Spring**	23
Cuba Libre | **Penn Qtr**	20
Banana Café | **Cap Hill**	19

CZECH

NEW Bistro Bohem | **Shaw**	–

DELIS

Toscana Café | **Cap Hill**	25
Chutzpah | **Fairfax**	23
Parkway Deli | **Silver Spring**	22
Taylor Gourmet | **multi.**	22
Star/Shamrock | **Atlas Dist**	19

DINERS

Ben's Chili | **U St**	22
Florida Ave. Grill | **Shaw**	22
Open City | **Woodley Pk**	21
Diner | **Adams Mor**	21

Double T	**Frederick**	20
Bob & Edith's	**Arlington**	20
Luna Grill	**multi.**	19
🆕 Family Meal	**Frederick**	–

EASTERN EUROPEAN

Cosmopolitan Grill	**Alexandria**	27
Domku	**Petworth**	22

ECLECTIC

Minibar	**Penn Qtr**	28
Room 11	**Columbia Hts**	26
It's About Thyme	**Culpeper**	25
Orchard	**Frederick**	25
Atlas Rm.	**Atlas Dist**	25
C.F. Folks	**Dupont Cir**	24
Co Co. Sala	**Penn Qtr**	24
Dean & DeLuca	**Georgetown**	23
Sticky Rice	**Atlas Dist**	23
Little Fountain	**Adams Mor**	23
Rustik Tav.	**Bloomingdale**	23
Perrys	**Adams Mor**	22
Vinoteca	**U St**	22
Northside	**Clarendon**	22
Busboys/Poets	**multi.**	22
Dickson Wine	**U St**	21
Mark's Kit.	**Takoma Pk**	21
Twisted Vines	**Arlington**	20
Café Saint-Ex	**Logan Cir**	20
🆕 Boundary Rd.	**Atlas Dist**	–
🆕 Curious Grape	**Arlington**	–
🆕 Majestic B&G	**Bethesda**	–
Maple Ave	**Vienna**	–
🆕 Pig	**Logan Cir**	–

ETHIOPIAN

Ethiopic	**Atlas Dist**	24
Etete	**U St**	24
Dukem	**U St**	24
Meskerem	**Adams Mor**	22
🆕 LacoMelza	**Silver Spring**	–

EUROPEAN

Village Bistro	**Arlington**	26

FRENCH

L'Aub./François	**Grt Falls**	28
Marcel's	**West End**	28
Russia House Rest.	**Herndon**	27
L'Auberge Provençale	**Boyce**	26
Bistro Provence	**Bethesda**	26
La Bergerie	**Alexandria**	26
Adour/St. Regis	**D'town**	26
Brabo	**Alexandria**	26
La Chaumière	**Georgetown**	26

Bistro Bis	**Cap Hill**	26
Grille	**Alexandria**	25
Et Voila	**Palisades**	25
Bezu	**Potomac**	24
La Ferme	**Chevy Chase**	24
Tempo	**Alexandria**	24
La Fourchette	**Adams Mor**	23
Matisse	**Upper NW**	23
Lavandou	**Cleve Pk**	23
Paul	**multi.**	22
Brass. Monte Carlo	**Bethesda**	22
Degrees	**Georgetown**	22
Urbana	**Dupont Cir**	21
🆕 Chez Billy	**Petworth**	–
Citronelle	**Georgetown**	–

FRENCH (BISTRO)

Bistro L'Hermitage	**Woodbridge**	26
Central Michel	**Penn Qtr**	26
Le Refuge	**Alexandria**	26
Yves Bistro	**Alexandria**	25
Montmartre	**Cap Hill**	25
Fontaine Caffe	**Alexandria**	25
Brass. Beck	**D'town**	25
La Côte d'Or	**Arlington**	24
Lyon Hall	**Clarendon**	24
Napoleon Bistro	**Adams Mor**	24
Bistrot Lepic	**Georgetown**	24
Bastille	**Alexandria**	24
Praline	**Bethesda**	23
Bistro Cacao	**Cap Hill**	23
Bistrot Lafayette	**Alexandria**	23
Bistro D'Oc	**Penn Qtr**	23
Café Bonaparte	**Georgetown**	23
Petits Plats	**Woodley Pk**	22
Bistrot du Coin	**Dupont Cir**	22
🆕 Le Zinc	**Cleve Pk**	22
Mon Ami Gabi	**multi.**	22
1905	**Mt. Vernon Sq**	21
Café Dupont	**Dupont Cir**	21
Bistro La Bonne	**U St**	21
Bistro Français	**Georgetown**	21
Café du Parc	**D'town**	21
Le Chat Noir	**Upper NW**	20
🆕 Bistro Vivant	**McLean**	–

GASTROPUB

Granville Moore's	Amer./Belgian	**Atlas Dist**	24
Birch/Barley	Amer.	**Logan Cir**	24
Queen Vic	British	**Atlas Dist**	23
Bar Pilar	Amer.	**U St**	23
Mad Fox Brew	Amer.	**Falls Ch**	20

Againn | Amer. | **D'town** 20
Virtue | Amer. | **Alexandria** 19
NEW Boundary Rd. | Eclectic | -
Atlas Dist

GERMAN

Lyon Hall | **Clarendon** 24
Biergarten Haus | **Atlas Dist** 17

GREEK

Nostos | **Vienna** 26
Athens Grill | **Gaith'burg** 26
Vaso's Kit. | **Alexandria** 26
Mourayo | **Dupont Cir** 25
Cava Mezze | **multi.** 25
Plaka Grill | **Vienna** 24
Mykonos Grill | **Rockville** 23
Zorba's Cafe | **Dupont Cir** 23
Kellari Taverna | **Gldn Triangle** 23
Cava Mezze Grill | **multi.** 22

HEALTH FOOD

(See also Vegetarian)
Sweetgreen | **multi.** 22

HOT DOGS

Shake Shack | **multi.** 21
DC-3 | **Cap Hill** 18

INDIAN

Rasika | **multi.** 28
Kabob N Karahi | **Silver Spring** 26
India Palace | **Germantown** 26
Bombay Tandoor | **Vienna** 26
Masala Art | **Upper NW** 25
Jaipur | **Fairfax** 25
Bombay Club | **Gldn Triangle** 25
Rangoli | **S Riding** 24
Bombay Bistro | **Rockville** 24
Delhi Club | **Clarendon** 24
Haandi | **multi.** 24
Woodlands Rest. | **Hyattsville** 24
Passage to India | **Bethesda** 24
Tandoori Nights | **multi.** 24
Angeethi | **multi.** 23
Minerva | **multi.** 23
Curry Mantra | **Fairfax** 23
Aditi | **multi.** 23
Indique | **multi.** 23
Aroma Indian | **multi.** 23
Heritage India | **Glover Pk** 22
Amma Veg. | **Vienna** 22
Spice Xing | **Rockville** 22
Himalayan Heritage | 21
Adams Mor

Delhi Dhaba | **Arlington** 20
Merzi | **Penn Qtr** 20

IRISH

Eamonn's | **Alexandria** 23
Daniel O'Connell's | **Alexandria** 20
Irish Inn/Glen Echo | **Glen Echo** 20
Star/Shamrock | **Atlas Dist** 19
NEW Irish Whiskey | -
Dupont Cir

ITALIAN

(N=Northern; S=Southern)
Obelisk | **Dupont Cir** 28
Sergio Rist. | **Silver Spring** 27
Tosca | N | **Penn Qtr** 27
Fiola | **Penn Qtr** 27
Il Pizzico | **Rockville** 27
Pasta Mia | **Adams Mor** 26
Villa Mozart | N | **Fairfax** 26
NEW Elisir | **Penn Qtr** 26
Toscana Café | **Cap Hill** 25
2 Amys | **Cleve Pk** 25
Dolce Vita | **Fairfax** 25
Al Tiramisu | **Dupont Cir** 25
Bibiana | **D'town** 25
Geranio | N | **Alexandria** 25
Landini Bros. | N | **Alexandria** 25
Il Fornaio | **Reston** 25
Cafe Pizzaiolo | S | **multi.** 24
Siroc | **D'town** 24
Zeffirelli Rist. | **Herndon** 24
Il Porto | **Alexandria** 24
Floriana Rest. | **Dupont Cir** 24
Ricciuti's | **Olney** 24
Filomena | **Georgetown** 24
NEW Graffiato | **Chinatown** 24
I Ricchi | N | **Dupont Cir** 24
Olazzo | **multi.** 24
Acqua al 2 | **Cap Hill** 24
Ozzie's Corner | **Fairfax** 24
Dino | **Cleve Pk** 24
Ledo, Original | **College Pk** 24
Tempo | N | **Alexandria** 24
A La Lucia | **Alexandria** 23
La Strada | **Alexandria** 23
Maggiano's | **multi.** 23
Da Domenico | **McLean** 23
Capri | **McLean** 23
Posto | **Logan Cir** 23
Al Crostino | **U St** 23
NEW Pacci's Tratt. | 23
Silver Spring
Agrodolce | **Germantown** 23
Faccia Luna | **multi.** 23

Assaggi	multi.	23	Yama*	Vienna	25
Ledo Pizza	N	multi.	23	Tachibana*	McLean	24
Tutto Bene	N	Arlington	23	Tako Grill*	Bethesda	24
Coppi's Organic	N	U St	23	Sushiko*	multi.	24
Pizzeria Orso	Falls Ch	22	Konami*	Vienna	23
Il Canale	Georgetown	22	Sakana*	Dupont Cir	23
Tragara	N	Bethesda	22	Ping	Arlington	23
Sorriso	Cleve Pk	22	Matuba*	Bethesda	23
Bond 45	Nat'l Harbor	22	Murasaki*	Upper NW	23
Renato/River Falls	Potomac	22	Yechon	Annandale	22
Notti Bianche	Foggy Bottom	22	Tono Sushi*	Woodley Pk	22
Cafe Milano	Georgetown	22	Seven Seas	multi.	22
Mamma Lucia	multi.	22	Rolls 'N Rice*	Rockville	22
Taylor Gourmet	multi.	22	Spices*	Cleve Pk	21
Piola	Rosslyn	21	Yosaku*	Upper NW	21
RedRocks	multi.	21	Hinode*	multi.	20
Argia's	Falls Ch	21	Woomi Gdn.*	Wheaton	20
Extra Virgin	Arlington	21	Hooked*	Sterling	20

Amici Miei | Potomac | 21

Urbana | Dupont Cir | 21

JEWISH

Sette Osteria	Dupont Cir	21
Lia's	Chevy Chase	21
Oro Pomodoro	Rockville	21
Paolo's	multi.	21

Chutzpah	Fairfax	23
Parkway Deli	Silver Spring	22
Star/Shamrock	Atlas Dist	19

Fontina Grille	Rockville	20
Finemondo	D'town	20
Acacia Bistro	Upper NW	20
Arucola	Chevy Chase	20
Carmine's	S	Penn Qtr	20
Vapiano	multi.	20
NEW Cesco Osteria	Bethesda	19
Primi Piatti	Foggy Bottom	19
La Tomate	Dupont Cir	19
Kora	Arlington	17
NEW Dolce Veloce	Fairfax	–
NEW La Forchetta	Upper NW	–
NEW Maple	Columbia Hts	–
NEW Sugo Cicchetti	Potomac	–

KOREAN

(* barbecue specialist)

BonChon	multi.	26
Lighthouse/Vit Goel	Rockville	24
Woo Lae Oak*	Vienna	23
Mandu	multi.	23
Hee Been*	multi.	23
Honey Pig*	multi.	23
Yechon	Annandale	22
Woomi Gdn.*	Wheaton	20

LAOTIAN

Bangkok Golden	multi.	24

JAMAICAN

Negril	multi.	24

LEBANESE

Neyla	Georgetown	24
Me Jana	Arlington	24
Layalina	Arlington	24
Lebanese Tav.	multi.	23

JAPANESE

(* sushi specialist)

Makoto	Palisades	27
Kobe	Leesburg	27
Niwano Hana*	Rockville	26
Sushi Taro*	Dupont Cir	26
Kaz Sushi*	World Bank	25
Kotobuki*	Palisades	25
Yamazato*	Alexandria	25
Sushi Damo*	Rockville	25
Hama Sushi*	Herndon	25
Kushi*	Mt. Vernon Sq	25

MALAYSIAN

Malaysia Kopitiam	Dupont Cir	23

MEDITERRANEAN

Komi	Dupont Cir	28
Zaytinya	Penn Qtr	26
Cava Mezze	multi.	25
Tavira	Chevy Chase	25
El Manantial	Reston	24
Pasha Cafe	Arlington	23

Agora | **Dupont Cir** 23
Matisse | **Upper NW** 23
Brass. Monte Carlo | **Bethesda** 22
Roti Med. | **multi.** 22
Evo Bistro | **McLean** 22
Bistro LaZeez | **Bethesda** 22
Panache | **multi.** 21
Café Olé | **Upper NW** 20
Acacia Bistro | **Upper NW** 20
Tabaq Bistro | **U St** 20
🆕 Tel'Veh | **Mt. Vernon Sq** ⌐

MEXICAN

Oyamel | **Penn Qtr** 25
Cacique | **Frederick** 24
Azucar | **Silver Spring** 24
Taqueria Nacional | **Cap Hill** 23
Rosa Mexicano | **multi.** 23
Taqueria Poblano | **multi.** 22
Casa Oaxaca | **Adams Mor** 22
Taqueria Distrito | **multi.** 22
Lauriol Plaza | **Dupont Cir** 21
Guajillo | **Arlington** 21
El Centro | **Logan Cir** 21
Surfside | **Glover Pk** 21
El Tamarindo | **Adams Mor** 21
🆕 Alegria | **Vienna** ⌐
🆕 Bandolero | **Georgetown** ⌐
🆕 El Chucho | **Columbia Hts** ⌐

MIDDLE EASTERN

Zaytinya | **Penn Qtr** 26
Amsterdam Falafel | 25
  Adams Mor
Mezè | **Adams Mor** 24
Bistro LaZeez | **Bethesda** 22
Levante's | **Dupont Cir** 21

MONGOLIAN

Tony Cheng's | **Chinatown** 22

MOROCCAN

Marrakesh | **Shaw** 24
Marrakesh P | **Dupont Cir** 23
Taste/Morocco | **Clarendon** 23

NEPALESE

Kabob N Karahi | **Silver Spring** 26
Himalayan Heritage | 21
  Adams Mor

NEW ENGLAND

Ford's Fish | **Ashburn** 26
Red Hook | **Location Varies** 25
Freddy's Lobster | **Bethesda** 19

NEW ZEALAND

Cassatt's Café | **Arlington** 20

NOODLE SHOPS

Toki | **Atlas Dist** 26
Full Key | **Wheaton** 25
Pho 75 | **multi.** 24
Chinatown Express | **Chinatown** 23
DC Noodles | **U St** 23
Bob's Noodle | **Rockville** 22
Nooshi | **Gldn Triangle** 21
🆕 Sakuramen | **Adams Mor** ⌐

NUEVO LATINO

Mio | **D'town** 26
Ceiba | **D'town** 24
Caribbean Breeze | **Arlington** 20

PAKISTANI

Kabob N Karahi | **Silver Spring** 26
Kabob Palace | **Arlington** 26
Ravi Kabob | **Arlington** 25

PAN-LATIN

Fast Gourmet | **U St** 27
Samantha's | **Silver Spring** 24
Azucar | **Silver Spring** 24
El Golfo | **Silver Spring** 23
Masa 14 | **Logan Cir** 23
Guardado's | **Bethesda** 23
Zengo | **Chinatown** 22
🆕 Fujimar | **D'town** ⌐

PERSIAN

Shamshiry | **Vienna** 27
Kabob Bazaar | **multi.** 25
Moby Dick | **multi.** 23

PERUVIAN

El Pollo | **multi.** 26
Las Canteras | **Adams Mor** 24
Crisp/Juicy | **multi.** 24
Chicken/ Run | **Bethesda** 24
La Limeña | **Rockville** 23
Don Pollo | **multi.** 23
La Canela | **Rockville** 23
El Chalan | **Foggy Bottom** 22

PIZZA

Pupatella Pizzeria | **Arlington** 26
2 Amys | **Cleve Pk** 25
Dolce Vita | **Fairfax** 25
Seventh Hill | **Cap Hill** 25
Mia's Pizzas | **Bethesda** 25

NEW Mellow Mushroom | **Adams Mor**	25	
Cafe Pizzaiolo | **multi.**	24	
Ricciuti's | **Olney**	24	
NEW Graffiato | **Chinatown**	24	
Fire Works | **multi.**	24	
Ledo, Original | **College Pk**	24	
Liberty Tree | **Atlas Dist**	23	
Pizzeria Paradiso | **multi.**	23	
Matchbox | **multi.**	23	
District of Pi | **Penn Qtr**	23	
Posto | **Logan Cir**	23	
Agrodolce | **Germantown**	23	
Pizzeria Da Marco | **Bethesda**	23	
Faccia Luna | **multi.**	23	
Pie-Tanza | **multi.**	23	
Ledo Pizza | **multi.**	23	
Lost Dog | **multi.**	23	
Coppi's Organic | **U St**	23	
Pacci's Neapolitan | **Silver Spring**	23	
Rustik Tav. | **Bloomingdale**	23	
Pizzeria Orso | **Falls Ch**	22	
Il Canale | **Georgetown**	22	
Sorriso | **Cleve Pk**	22	
Coal Fire | **multi.**	22	
Pete's New Haven | **multi.**	22	
Rustico | **multi.**	22	
Mamma Lucia | **multi.**	22	
We The Pizza | **Cap Hill**	22	
Piola | **Rosslyn**	21	
Ella's Pizza | **Penn Qtr**	21	
RedRocks | **multi.**	21	
Sette Osteria | **Dupont Cir**	21	
Oro Pomodoro | **Rockville**	21	
Fontina Grille | **Rockville**	20	
Comet Ping Pong | **Upper NW**	20	
Vapiano | **multi.**	20	
Kora | **Arlington**	17	
Local 16 | **U St**	17	
NEW Fuel Pizza | **multi.**	–	
NEW Haven | **Bethesda**	–	
NEW La Forchetta | **Upper NW**	–	
NEW Menomale | **NE**	–	
NEW Sugo Cicchetti | **Potomac**	–	

PORTUGUESE

Tavira | **Chevy Chase**	25
Nando's | **multi.**	22

PUB FOOD

Liberty Tav. | **Clarendon**	24
NEW Boundary Stone | **Bloomingdale**	24
Royal Mile | **Wheaton**	23
Hunter's Head | **Upperville**	23
Lost Dog | **multi.**	23
Brewer's Alley | **Frederick**	22
Clyde's | **multi.**	22
Dogfish Head | **multi.**	21
Franklin's | **Hyattsville**	21
Bourbon | **multi.**	21
Daniel O'Connell's | **Alexandria**	20
Meridian | **Columbia Hts**	20
Star/Shamrock | **Atlas Dist**	19
Stoney's Lounge | **Logan Cir**	18
Madhatter | **Dupont Cir**	18
P.J. Clarke's | **D'town**	18
Biergarten Haus | **Atlas Dist**	17
NEW Brixton | **U St**	–

PUERTO RICAN

Banana Café | **Cap Hill**	19

RUSSIAN

Russia House Rest. | **Herndon**	27
Russia Hse. | **Dupont Cir**	21

SANDWICHES

(See also Delis)

Fast Gourmet | **U St**	27
C.F. Folks | **Dupont Cir**	24
NEW Lunchbox | **Frederick**	24
Bread Line | **World Bank**	23
Chutzpah | **Fairfax**	23
Buzz | **multi.**	22
Northside | **Clarendon**	22
Taylor Gourmet | **multi.**	22
Banh Mi DC | **Falls Ch**	21
Le Pain Quotidien | **multi.**	21
Pret A Manger | **multi.**	19

SCOTTISH

Royal Mile | **Wheaton**	23

SEAFOOD

(See also Crab Houses)

BlackSalt | **Palisades**	27
Pesce | **Dupont Cir**	26
PassionFish | **Reston**	26
Ford's Fish | **Ashburn**	26
NEW Pearl Dive | **Logan Cir**	26
Kinkead's | **Foggy Bottom**	25
Adam Express | **Mt. Pleasant**	25
Red Hook | **Location Varies**	25
Palm | **McLean**	25
Ray's/Classics | **Silver Spring**	25
Dutch's Daughter | **Frederick**	25
Oceanaire | **D'town**	24

Coastal Flats	**multi.**	24
Hank's Oyster	**multi.**	24
NEW Fishnet	**College Pk**	24
Senart's Oyster	**Cap Hill**	24
Black's Bar	**Bethesda**	24
Luke's Lobster	**multi.**	23
Jackson's	**Reston**	23
Watershed	**NoMa**	23
Sea Catch	**Georgetown**	23
DC Coast	**D'town**	23
McCormick/Schmick	**multi.**	23
Kellari Taverna	**Gldn Triangle**	23
Legal Sea Foods	**multi.**	23
Occidental	**D'town**	23
Perrys	**Adams Mor**	22
Wildfire	**McLean**	22
Horace/Dickie	**multi.**	22
Seven Seas	**Rockville**	22
M&S Grill	**multi.**	22
Johnny's	**Cap Hill**	21
Nage	**Scott Cir**	21
Surfside	**Glover Pk**	21
Grillfish	**West End**	20
Mussel Bar	**Bethesda**	20
Chesapeake Rm.	**Cap Hill**	20
Hooked	**Sterling**	20
Hot 'N Juicy	**Woodley Pk**	20
Phillips	**SW**	20
Freddy's Lobster	**Bethesda**	19
Tackle Box	**Georgetown**	18

SMALL PLATES

(See also Spanish tapas specialist)

Rasika	Indian	**multi.**	28
Fiola	Italian	**Penn Qtr**	27
2941	Amer.	**Falls Ch**	27
Source	Amer.	**Penn Qtr**	27
Zaytinya	Mideast.	**Penn Qtr**	26
Sei	Asian	**Penn Qtr**	26
Room 11	Eclectic	**Columbia Hts**	26
Kaz Sushi	Japanese	**World Bank**	25
Cork	Amer.	**Logan Cir**	25
Iron Bridge Wine	Amer.	**Warrenton**	25
Cava Mezze	Greek	**Cap Hill**	25
Oyamel	Mex.	**Penn Qtr**	25
Mezè	Turkish	**Adams Mor**	24
NEW Graffiato	Italian	**Chinatown**	24
Tallula/EatBar	Amer.	**Clarendon**	24
Sushiko	Japanese	**multi.**	24
Dino	Italian	**Cleve Pk**	24

Co Co. Sala	Eclectic	**Penn Qtr**	24
Tandoori Nights	Indian	**multi.**	24
Raku	Asian	**multi.**	23
Vinifera	Amer.	**Reston**	23
Indique	Indian	**multi.**	23
Bar Pilar	Amer.	**U St**	23
Zengo	Asian/Pan-Latin	**Chinatown**	22
Pizzeria Orso	Pizza	**Falls Ch**	22
Evo Bistro	Med.	**McLean**	22
Northside	Eclectic	**Clarendon**	22
901 Rest.	Amer./Asian	**Mt. Vernon Sq**	22
Policy	Amer.	**U St**	22
Asia Bistro/Zen	Asian	**Arlington**	21
Café du Parc	French	**D'town**	21
Dickson Wine	Eclectic	**U St**	21
Lincoln	Amer.	**D'town**	20
Café Olé	Med.	**Upper NW**	20
Acacia Bistro	Italian	**Upper NW**	20
Tabaq Bistro	Med.	**U St**	20
NEW Bandolero	Mex.	**Georgetown**	–
NEW Bistro Vivant	French	**McLean**	–
NEW La Forchetta	Italian	**Upper NW**	–
NEW Maple	Italian	**Columbia Hts**	–
NEW Mintwood	Amer.	**Adams Mor**	–
NEW Sugo Cicchetti	Italian	**Potomac**	–
NEW Tel'Veh	Med.	**Mt. Vernon Sq**	–

SOUTH AMERICAN

La Caraqueña	**Falls Ch**	25
El Mariachi	**Rockville**	25

SOUTHERN

Vidalia	**Gldn Triangle**	26
Carolina Kit.	**Hyattsville**	25
Evening Star	**Alexandria**	23
Oohhs & Aahhs	**U St**	23
Art & Soul	**Cap Hill**	23
Marvin	**U St**	23
Eatonville	**U St**	23
B. Smith	**NE**	22
Georgia Brown	**D'town**	22
Florida Ave. Grill	**Shaw**	22
Bayou Bakery	**Arlington**	22
Crème	**U St**	21
Sou'Wester	**SW**	21

Acre 121 | **Columbia Hts**	21
NEW Howard Theatre | **Shaw**	–

SOUTHWESTERN

Sweetwater Tav. | **multi.**	26

SPANISH

(* tapas specialist)

Isabella's* | **Frederick**	26
La Taberna* | **World Bank**	26
Estadio* | **Logan Cir**	25
Cacique | **Frederick**	24
Jaleo* | **multi.**	24
Las Tapas* | **Alexandria**	24
Bodega* | **Georgetown**	23
Guardado's* | **Bethesda**	23
La Tasca* | **multi.**	21
NEW Boqueria* | **Dupont Cir**	–
NEW Pulpo* | **Cleve Pk**	–

STEAKHOUSES

Prime Rib | **Gldn Triangle**	28
Ray's/Steaks | **Arlington**	27
Fogo de Chão | **Penn Qtr**	27
Capital Grille | **multi.**	26
Ruth's Chris | **multi.**	26
Morton's | **multi.**	26
Charlie Palmer | **Cap Hill**	26
Old Hickory | **Nat'l Harbor**	26
BLT Steak | **Gldn Triangle**	25
Palm | **multi.**	25
Ray's/Classics | **Silver Spring**	25
NEW Ray's/Third | **Arlington**	25
Ray's/East River | **NE**	25
Bourbon Steak | **Georgetown**	25
Fleming's Steak | **McLean**	25
Smith/Wollensky | **Gldn Triangle**	25
J&G Steak | **D'town**	24
Senart's Oyster | **Cap Hill**	24
Caucus Rm. | **Penn Qtr**	23
Occidental | **D'town**	23
Bobby Van's | **D'town**	23
NEW Grillmarx | **Olney**	22
Wildfire | **McLean**	22
Bond 45 | **Nat'l Harbor**	22
Shula's | **Vienna**	22
Medium Rare | **Cleve Pk**	22
M&S Grill | **multi.**	22
Nick's Chophse. | **Rockville**	21
District ChopHse. | **Penn Qtr**	21
NEW Lost Society | **U St**	18
NEW Del Frisco's | **D'town**	–

SYRIAN

Layalina | **Arlington**	24

TAIWANESE

Toki | **Atlas Dist**	26
Bob's Noodle | **Rockville**	22

TEAHOUSES

Teaism | **multi.**	20
Ching Ching | **Georgetown**	20

TEX-MEX

El Mariachi | **Rockville**	25
Mi Rancho | **multi.**	22
Guapo's | **multi.**	22
Calif. Tortilla | **multi.**	22
Uncle Julio's | **multi.**	21
Cactus Cantina | **Cleve Pk**	21
Austin Grill | **multi.**	18

THAI

Little Serow | **Dupont Cir**	28
Ruan Thai | **Wheaton**	27
Thai Sq. | **Arlington**	26
Thai Basil | **Chantilly**	26
Nava Thai | **Wheaton**	26
Elephant Jumps | **Falls Ch**	26
Sabai | **Germantown**	26
Duangrat's | **Falls Ch**	26
Rabieng | **Falls Ch**	25
Bangkok 54 | **Arlington**	25
T.H.A.I. | **Arlington**	25
Regent | **Dupont Cir**	24
Thai/Silver Spring | **Silver Spring**	24
Bangkok Golden | **multi.**	24
Crystal Thai | **Arlington**	23
Benjarong | **Rockville**	23
Bangkok Joe's | **Georgetown**	23
DC Noodles | **U St**	23
Mai Thai | **multi.**	23
Thai Tanic | **multi.**	23
Sakoontra | **Fairfax**	23
Rice | **Logan Cir**	22
Busara | **multi.**	22
Thaiphoon | **multi.**	21
Haad Thai | **D'town**	21
Neisha Thai | **multi.**	20
Tara Thai | **multi.**	20

TURKISH

Kazan | **McLean**	25
Cafe Divan | **Glover Pk**	24
Agora | **Dupont Cir**	23
Ezmè | **Dupont Cir**	22

VEGETARIAN

(* vegan)

Amsterdam Falafel | **Adams Mor**	25
Sunflower Veg. | **multi.**	25

Yuan Fu* | **Rockville**	25	
Woodlands Rest. | **Hyattsville**	24	
Vegetable Gdn.* | **White Flint**	24	
Juice Joint | **D'town**	23	
Mandalay | **Silver Spring**	23	
Amma Veg. | **Vienna**	22	
Java Green* | **Gldn Triangle**	22	
Mark's Kit. | **Takoma Pk**	21	
Luna Grill* | **multi.**	19	

VIETNAMESE

Lucky Corner | **Frederick**	28
Present | **Falls Ch**	26

Pho 14 | **Columbia Hts**	25
Huong Viet | **Falls Ch**	25
Four Sisters | **Merrifield**	25
Pho 75 | **multi.**	24
Minh's | **Arlington**	24
Pho DC | **Chinatown**	24
Taste/Saigon | **multi.**	22
Nam-Viet | **multi.**	21
Banh Mi DC | **Falls Ch**	21
NEW Rice Paper | **Falls Ch**	-

WASHINGTON, DC

CUISINES

Locations

Includes names, cuisines and Food ratings.

Washington, DC

ADAMS MORGAN

(See map on page 67)
Pasta Mia	*Italian*	26
Amsterdam Falafel	*Mideast.*	25
Cashion's Eat.	*Amer.*	25
NEW Mellow Mushroom	*Pizza*	25
Las Canteras	*Peruvian*	24
Grill/Ipanema	*Brazilian*	24
Mezè	*Mideast.*	24
Napoleon Bistro	*French*	24
La Fourchette	*French*	23
Little Fountain	*Eclectic*	23
Perrys	*Amer./Eclectic*	22
Meskerem	*Ethiopian*	22
Casa Oaxaca	*Mex.*	22
Diner	*Diner*	21
Tryst	*Coffee*	21
Himalayan Heritage	*Indian/Nepalese*	21
Bourbon	*Pub*	21
El Tamarindo	*Mex.*	21
Jack Rose	*Amer.*	20
NEW Smoke/Barrel	*Amer./BBQ*	20
NEW Mintwood	*Amer.*	-
NEW Sakuramen	*Noodle Shop*	-

ANACOSTIA

Negril	*Jamaican*	24

ATLAS DISTRICT

Toki	*Noodle Shop/Taiwanese*	26
Atlas Rm.	*Eclectic*	25
Granville Moore's	*Amer./Belgian*	24
Ethiopic	*Ethiopian*	24
Liberty Tree	*Amer./Pizza*	23
Sticky Rice	*Asian/Eclectic*	23
Queen Vic	*British*	23
Horace/Dickie	*Seafood*	22
Smith Commons	*Amer.*	22
Taylor Gourmet	*Deli/Italian*	22
Dangerously Delicious	*Amer./Bakery*	21
Star/Shamrock	*Deli/Pub*	19
Biergarten Haus	*German*	17
NEW Boundary Rd.	*Eclectic*	-

BLOOMINGDALE

NEW Boundary Stone	*Pub*	24
Rustik Tav.	*Amer./Eclectic*	23
Big Bear Cafe	*Amer.*	-

CAPITOL HILL

Charlie Palmer	*Steak*	26
Bistro Bis	*French*	26
Toscana Café	*Deli/Italian*	25
Montmartre	*French*	25
Belga Café	*Belgian*	25
Seventh Hill	*Pizza*	25
Cava Mezze	*Greek*	25
Acqua al 2	*Italian*	24
Hank's Oyster	*Amer./Seafood*	24
Senart's Oyster	*Seafood/Steak*	24
Bistro Cacao	*French*	23
Ted's Bulletin	*Amer.*	23
Good Stuff	*Burgers*	23
Matchbox	*Amer.*	23
Art & Soul	*Southern*	23
Taqueria Nacional	*Mex.*	23
Sweetgreen	*Health*	22
We The Pizza	*Pizza*	22
Zest	*Amer.*	21
Monocle	*Amer.*	21
Johnny's	*Amer./Seafood*	21
Sonoma	*Amer.*	21
Le Pain Quotidien	*Bakery/Belgian*	21
NEW Boxcar Tav.	*Amer.*	21
Hunan Dynasty	*Chinese*	20
Chesapeake Rm.	*Amer./Seafood*	20
Banana Café	*Cuban/Puerto Rican*	19
DC-3	*Hot Dogs*	18

CHEVY CHASE

Rosa Mexicano	*Mex.*	23
Arucola	*Italian*	20

CHINATOWN/ PENN QUARTER

(Including Gallery Place; see map on page 62)
Rasika	*Indian*	28
Minibar	*Eclectic*	28
Tosca	*Italian*	27
Fiola	*Italian*	27
Fogo de Chão	*Brazilian/Steak*	27
Source	*Asian*	27
Capital Grille	*Steak*	26
Ruth's Chris	*Steak*	26

Zaytinya	Med./Mideast.	26
Central Michel	Amer./French	26
Sei	Asian	26
NEW Elisir	Italian	26
Oyamel	Mex.	25
Proof	Amer.	24
Oya	Asian	24
NEW Graffiato	Italian/Pizza	24
Pho DC	Viet.	24
Five Guys	Burgers	24
Jaleo	Spanish	24
Co Co. Sala	Eclectic	24
Luke's Lobster	Seafood	23
Chinatown Express	Chinese	23
701	Amer.	23
Asian Spice	Asian	23
Matchbox	Amer.	23
District of Pi	Pizza	23
PS 7's	Amer.	23
McCormick/Schmick	Seafood	23
Rosa Mexicano	Mex.	23
Cedar Rest.	Amer.	23
Full Kee (DC)	Chinese	23
Bistro D'Oc	French	23
Caucus Rm.	Amer.	23
Legal Sea Foods	Seafood	23
Zengo	Asian/Pan-Latin	22
Paul	Bakery	22
Burma	Burmese	22
Tony Cheng's	Chinese	22
Clyde's	Amer.	22
Nando's	Chicken	22
Calif. Tortilla	Tex-Mex	22
Eat First	Chinese	22
Hill Country	BBQ	21
Ella's Pizza	Pizza	21
Chop't	Amer.	21
La Tasca	Spanish	21
Ping Pong	Asian	21
District ChopHse.	Steak	21
Teaism	Tea	20
Poste Moderne	Amer.	20
Cuba Libre	Cuban	20
Carmine's	Italian	20
Merzi	Indian	20
Vapiano	Italian	20
Pret A Manger	Sandwiches	19
Austin Grill	Tex-Mex	18
NEW Fuel Pizza	Amer./Pizza	–

CLEVELAND PARK/ WOODLEY PARK

Palena	Amer.	27
2 Amys	Pizza	25
NEW District Kit.	Amer.	24

Dino	Italian	24
Ripple	Amer.	23
Indique	Indian	23
Lavandou	French	23
Petits Plats	French	22
Sorriso	Italian	22
Tono Sushi	Japanese	22
NEW Le Zinc	French	22
Ardeo/Bardeo	Amer./Wine	22
Medium Rare	Steak	22
Calif. Tortilla	Tex-Mex	22
New Heights	Amer.	22
Nam-Viet	Viet.	21
Open City	Diner	21
Spices	Asian	21
Cactus Cantina	Tex-Mex	21
Hot 'N Juicy	Cajun/Creole	20
Cafe Deluxe	Amer.	20
NEW Pulpo	Spanish	–

DOWNTOWN

(See map on page 62)

Adour/St. Regis	Amer./French	26
Plume	Amer.	26
Mio	Nuevo Latino	26
Bibiana	Italian	25
Brass. Beck	Belgian/French	25
Oceanaire	Seafood	24
J&G Steak	Amer./Steak	24
Siroc	Italian	24
Ceiba	Nuevo Latino	24
Morrison-Clark	Amer.	24
Juice Joint	Health	23
DC Coast	Amer.	23
Old Ebbitt	Amer.	23
Occidental	Seafood/Steak	23
Bobby Van's	Steak	23
Roti Med.	Med.	22
Georgia Brown	Southern	22
Zentan	Asian	22
M&S Grill	Seafood/Steak	22
Chop't	Amer.	21
Chef Geoff's	Amer.	21
Café du Parc	French	21
Haad Thai	Thai	21
NEW Hamilton	Amer.	20
Lincoln	Amer.	20
Finemondo	Italian	20
Againn	British	20
Pret A Manger	Sandwiches	19
Blackfinn Amer.	Amer.	18
P.J. Clarke's	Pub	18
NEW Del Frisco's	Steak	–
NEW Fuel Pizza	Amer./Pizza	–
NEW Fujimar	Asian/Pan-Latin	–

DUPONT CIRCLE

(See map on page 67)

Komi | *Amer./Med.*	28
Obelisk | *Italian*	28
Little Serow | *Thai*	28
Sushi Taro | *Japanese*	26
Ruth's Chris | *Steak*	26
Pesce | *Seafood*	26
Nora | *Amer.*	26
Mourayo | *Greek*	25
Eola | *Amer.*	25
Palm | *Steak*	25
Al Tiramisu | *Italian*	25
Black & Orange | *Burgers*	25
Food Corner Kabob | *Afghan*	25
Tabard Inn | *Amer.*	25
Regent | *Thai*	24
2100 Prime | *Amer.*	24
Floriana Rest. | *Italian*	24
I Ricchi | *Italian*	24
C.F. Folks | *Eclectic*	24
Hank's Oyster | *Amer./Seafood*	24
Moby Dick | *Persian*	23
Malaysia Kopitiam | *Malaysian*	23
Marrakesh P | *Moroccan*	23
Pizzeria Paradiso | *Pizza*	23
Sakana | *Japanese*	23
Raku | *Asian*	23
Mai Thai | *Thai*	23
Mandu | *Korean*	23
Agora | *Turkish*	23
Zorba's Cafe | *Greek*	23
Firefly | *Amer.*	23
Bistrot du Coin | *French*	22
Ezmè | *Turkish*	22
Sweetgreen | *Health*	22
NEW Shophouse | *SE Asian*	22
Nando's | *Chicken*	22
Taylor Gourmet | *Deli/Italian*	22
BGR | *Burgers*	22
Russia Hse. | *Russian*	21
Lauriol Plaza | *Mex.*	21
Chop't | *Amer.*	21
Thaiphoon | *Thai*	21
Café Dupont | *French*	21
Shake Shack | *Burgers*	21
Ping Pong | *Asian*	21
Urbana | *French/Italian*	21
Sette Osteria | *Italian*	21
Le Pain Quotidien | *Bakery/Belgian*	21
Levante's | *Mideast.*	21
Teaism | *Tea*	20
Circa | *Amer.*	20
Scion Rest. | *Amer.*	19

Kramerbooks | *Amer.*	19
La Tomate | *Italian*	19
City Lights | *Chinese*	19
Luna Grill | *Diner/Veg.*	19
Madhatter | *Amer./Pub*	18
Banana Leaves | *Asian*	-
NEW Boqueria | *Spanish*	-
NEW Irish Whiskey | *Pub*	-

FARRAGUT

Paul | *Bakery*	22
Roti Med. | *Med.*	22
Chop't | *Amer.*	21
Pret A Manger | *Sandwiches*	19

FOGGY BOTTOM/ WORLD BANK

(See map on page 64)

La Taberna | *Spanish*	26
Kaz Sushi | *Japanese*	25
Kinkead's | *Seafood*	25
Founding Farmers | *Amer.*	24
Bread Line | *Bakery/Sandwiches*	23
Aroma Indian | *Indian*	23
El Chalan | *Peruvian*	22
Roti Med. | *Med.*	22
NEW District Commons | *Amer.*	22
Sweetgreen | *Health*	22
Notti Bianche | *Italian*	22
NEW Burger/Tap/Shake | *Burgers*	21
Dish/Drinks | *Amer.*	21
Circa | *Amer.*	20
Primi Piatti | *Italian*	19
Tonic | *Amer.*	17
Roof Terr. | *Amer.*	16

GEORGETOWN

(See map on page 66)

Morton's | *Steak*	26
1789 | *Amer.*	26
La Chaumière | *French*	26
Bourbon Steak | *Steak*	25
Filomena | *Italian*	24
Five Guys | *Burgers*	24
Neyla | *Lebanese*	24
Thunder Burger | *Burgers*	24
Bistrot Lepic | *French*	24
Moby Dick | *Persian*	23
Dean & DeLuca | *Eclectic*	23
Pizzeria Paradiso | *Pizza*	23
Bangkok Joe's | *Thai*	23
Sea Catch | *Seafood*	23
Bodega | *Spanish*	23
Mai Thai | *Thai*	23

Café Bonaparte	*French*	23
Leopold's Kafe	*Austrian*	23
Ledo Pizza	*Pizza*	23
Paul	*Bakery*	22
Il Canale	*Italian/Pizza*	22
Degrees	*French*	22
Sweetgreen	*Health*	22
Clyde's	*Amer.*	22
Cafe Milano	*Italian*	22
Peacock Cafe	*Amer.*	22
Serendipity 3	*Amer./Dessert*	21
Bistro Français	*French*	21
Le Pain Quotidien	*Bakery/Belgian*	21
Paolo's	*Cal./Italian*	21
Ching Ching	*Tea*	20
Martin's Tav.	*Amer.*	20
Old Glory	*BBQ*	19
Tackle Box	*Seafood*	18
Sequoia	*Amer.*	17
NEW Bandolero	*Mex.*	-
Citronelle	*French*	-
NEW Unum	*Amer.*	-

GLOVER PARK

Cafe Divan	*Turkish*	24
Sushiko	*Japanese*	24
Town Hall	*Amer.*	23
Heritage India	*Indian*	22
Rocklands	*BBQ*	22
Bourbon	*Pub*	21
Surfside	*Cal./Mex.*	21
NEW Mayfair & Pine	*British*	-

GOLDEN TRIANGLE

(See map on page 64)

Prime Rib	*Steak*	28
Lafayette Rm.	*Amer.*	27
Morton's	*Steak*	26
Vidalia	*Southern*	26
Oval Rm.	*Amer.*	26
BLT Steak	*Steak*	25
Equinox	*Amer.*	25
Bombay Club	*Indian*	25
Smith/Wollensky	*Steak*	25
McCormick/Schmick	*Seafood*	23
Kellari Taverna	*Greek*	23
Java Green	*Veg./Vegan*	22
Chop't	*Amer.*	21
Nooshi	*Asian*	21
Panache	*Med.*	21
Cafe Asia	*Asian*	21
Teaism	*Tea*	20
Vapiano	*Italian*	20
Pret A Manger	*Sandwiches*	19

MT. PLEASANT

Adam Express	*Asian/Seafood*	25
Tonic	*Amer.*	17

MT. VERNON SQUARE/ CONVENTION CENTER

Corduroy	*Amer.*	28
Kushi	*Japanese*	25
Acadiana	*Contemp. LA*	24
NEW Rogue 24	*Amer.*	23
Mandu	*Korean*	23
901 Rest.	*Amer./Asian*	22
Busboys/Poets	*Amer./Eclectic*	22
Taylor Gourmet	*Deli/Italian*	22
1905	*French*	21
NEW Tel'Veh	*Med.*	-

NOMA

Watershed	*Amer./Seafood*	23
Roti Med.	*Med.*	22

NORTHEAST

Wings To Go	*Chicken*	25
Ray's/East River	*Burgers/Steak*	25
Aditi	*Indian*	23
Ledo Pizza	*Pizza*	23
B. Smith	*Southern*	22
Chop't	*Amer.*	21
Pret A Manger	*Sandwiches*	19
NEW Menomale	*Pizza*	-

PALISADES

Makoto	*Japanese*	27
BlackSalt	*Amer./Seafood*	27
Kotobuki	*Japanese*	25
Et Voila	*Belgian/French*	25

PETWORTH/ BRIGHTWOOD/ COLUMBIA HEIGHTS

Room 11	*Eclectic*	26
Pho 14	*Viet.*	25
Thai Tanic	*Thai*	23
Domku	*E Euro./Scan.*	22
Cava Mezze Grill	*Greek*	22
Pete's New Haven	*Pizza*	22
Taqueria Distrito	*Mex.*	22
RedRocks	*Pizza*	21
Acre 121	*BBQ/Southern*	21
Meridian	*Pub*	20
Pollo Campero	*Central Amer.*	19
NEW Chez Billy	*French*	-
NEW El Chucho	*Mex.*	-

NEW Kangaroo Boxing/PORC | BBQ	⌐⌐
NEW Maple | Italian	⌐⌐

SCOTT CIRCLE/ LOGAN CIRCLE

NEW Pearl Dive | Seafood	26
Cork | Amer.	25
Estadio | Spanish	25
Birch/Barley | Amer.	24
Posto | Italian	23
Masa 14 | Asian/Pan-Latin	23
Thai Tanic | Thai	23
Rice | Thai	22
Sweetgreen | Health	22
Taylor Gourmet | Deli/Italian	22
15 Ria | Amer.	22
El Centro | Mex.	21
Nage | Amer./Seafood	21
Logan Tav. | Amer.	20
Café Saint-Ex | Eclectic	20
Commissary | Amer.	19
Stoney's Lounge | Pub	18
NEW Pig | Amer./Eclectic	⌐⌐
Standard | BBQ	⌐⌐

SHAW

Marrakesh | Moroccan	24
Florida Ave. Grill | Diner	22
NEW Bistro Bohem | Czech/Euro.	⌐⌐
NEW Howard Theatre | Southern	⌐⌐

SW/SW WATERFRONT

CityZen | Amer.	27
Mitsitam | Amer.	23
Roti Med. | Med.	22
Shake Shack | Burgers	21
Sou'Wester | Amer.	21
Station 4 | Amer.	21
Phillips | Seafood	20

TAKOMA

Horace/Dickie | Seafood	22

UPPER NW

Masala Art | Indian	25
Crisp/Juicy | Chicken/Peruvian	24
Cheesecake | Amer.	24
Maggiano's | Italian	23
Matisse | French/Med.	23
Murasaki | Japanese	23
Pete's New Haven | Pizza	22
Guapo's | Tex-Mex	22
Chef Geoff's | Amer.	21

Yosaku | Japanese	21
Le Pain Quotidien | Bakery/Belgian	21
Neisha Thai | Thai	20
Tara Thai | Thai	20
Café Olé | Med.	20
Le Chat Noir | French	20
Acacia Bistro | Med.	20
Comet Ping Pong | Pizza	20
Buck's Fishing | Amer.	20
NEW La Forchetta | Italian/Pizza	⌐⌐

U STREET CORRIDOR

Fast Gourmet | Pan-Latin	27
Black & Orange | Burgers	25
Etete | Ethiopian	24
Dukem | Ethiopian	24
Negril | Jamaican	24
Oohhs & Aahhs | Southern	23
Al Crostino | Italian	23
DC Noodles | Thai	23
Marvin | Amer./Belgian	23
Eatonville | Southern	23
Bar Pilar | Amer.	23
Coppi's Organic | Italian	23
Ben's Chili | Diner	22
Vinoteca | Eclectic	22
Policy | Amer.	22
Busboys/Poets | Amer./Eclectic	22
Crème | Southern	21
Bistro La Bonne | French	21
Dickson Wine | Eclectic	21
Ulah Bistro | Amer.	20
Tabaq Bistro | Med.	20
American Ice | BBQ	19
NEW Lost Society | Amer./Steak	18
Local 16 | Amer./Pizza	17
NEW Brixton | Pub	⌐⌐

WEST END

(See map on page 66)

Rasika | Indian	28
Marcel's | Belgian/French	28
Blue Duck | Amer.	27
Ris | Amer.	25
Juniper | Amer.	24
Westend Bistro | Amer.	22
NEW Bobby's Burger | Burgers	22
Meiwah | Chinese	21
Grillfish | Seafood	20
Bayou | Cajun/Creole	20
Circle Bistro | Amer.	20
Hudson | Amer.	18

Nearby Maryland

BETHESDA/ CHEVY CHASE

Capital Grille	*Steak*	26
Bistro Provence	*French*	26
Ruth's Chris	*Steak*	26
Morton's	*Steak*	26
Kabob Bazaar	*Persian*	25
Persimmon	*Amer.*	25
Mia's Pizzas	*Pizza*	25
Tavira	*Portug.*	25
Faryab	*Afghan*	24
Haandi	*Indian*	24
Five Guys	*Burgers*	24
Tako Grill	*Japanese*	24
Jaleo	*Spanish*	24
La Ferme	*French*	24
Olazzo	*Italian*	24
Sushiko	*Japanese*	24
Chicken/ Run	*Chicken/Peruvian*	24
Black's Bar	*Amer.*	24
Passage to India	*Indian*	24
Tandoori Nights	*Indian*	24
Luke's Lobster	*Seafood*	23
Praline	*Bakery/French*	23
Moby Dick	*Persian*	23
Lebanese Tav.	*Lebanese*	23
Don Pollo	*Chicken/Peruvian*	23
Pizzeria Da Marco	*Pizza*	23
Raku	*Asian*	23
Grapeseed	*Amer.*	23
Assaggi	*Italian*	23
Matuba	*Japanese*	23
Ledo Pizza	*Pizza*	23
Indique	*Indian*	23
Guardado's	*Pan-Latin/Spanish*	23
Legal Sea Foods	*Seafood*	23
P.F. Chang's	*Chinese*	23
Brass. Monte Carlo	*French/Med.*	22
Fu Shing	*Chinese*	22
Tragara	*Italian*	22
Hard Times	*Amer.*	22
Bistro LaZeez	*Mideast.*	22
Cava Mezze Grill	*Greek*	22
Sweetgreen	*Health*	22
Clyde's	*Amer.*	22
Newton's	*Amer.*	22
Mamma Lucia	*Italian*	22
Mon Ami Gabi	*French*	22
Nando's	*Chicken*	22
Guapo's	*Tex-Mex*	22

Calif. Tortilla	*Tex-Mex*	22
Taylor Gourmet	*Deli/Italian*	22
Food Wine	*Amer.*	22
BGR	*Burgers*	22
Uncle Julio's	*Tex-Mex*	21
Meiwah	*Chinese*	21
Lia's	*Amer./Italian*	21
Le Pain Quotidien	*Bakery/Belgian*	21
Oakville Grille	*Amer.*	21
Hinode	*Japanese*	20
Mussel Bar	*Belgian*	20
Tara Thai	*Thai*	20
Cafe Deluxe	*Amer.*	20
Vapiano	*Italian*	20
NEW Cesco Osteria	*Italian*	19
City Lights	*Chinese*	19
Freddy's Lobster	*Seafood*	19
Redwood	*Amer.*	19
Blackfinn Amer.	*Amer.*	18
NEW Haven	*Pizza*	-
NEW Majestic B&G	*Amer./Eclectic*	-

FREDERICK

Volt	*Amer.*	28
Lucky Corner	*Viet.*	28
Monocacy Cross.	*Amer.*	28
Tasting Rm.	*Amer.*	27
Firestone's	*Amer.*	26
Wine Kit.	*Amer.*	26
Isabella's	*Spanish*	26
Dutch's Daughter	*Amer.*	25
Orchard	*Eclectic*	25
Cacique	*Mex./Spanish*	24
Acacia Bistro	*Amer.*	24
Cafe Nola	*Amer.*	24
Five Guys	*Burgers*	24
NEW Lunchbox	*Amer.*	24
Brewer's Alley	*Pub*	22
Coal Fire	*Pizza*	22
Mamma Lucia	*Italian*	22
Hinode	*Japanese*	20
Double T	*Diner*	20
NEW Family Meal	*Amer./Diner*	-

GAITHERSBURG/ DICKERSON/ GERMANTOWN/ OLNEY/ SHADY GROVE

India Palace	*Indian*	26
Athens Grill	*Greek*	26
Sabai	*Thai*	26

Ricciuti's | *Italian*	24
Crisp/Juicy | *Chicken/Peruvian*	24
X.O. Taste | *Chinese*	24
Tandoori Nights | *Indian*	24
Minerva | *Indian*	23
Moby Dick | *Persian*	23
Agrodolce | *Italian*	23
Mannequin Pis | *Belgian*	23
New Fortune | *Chinese*	23
Batik | *Asian*	22
Hard Times | *Amer.*	22
NEW Grillmarx | *Steak*	22
Mi Rancho | *Tex-Mex*	22
Coal Fire | *Pizza*	22
Red Hot/Blue | *BBQ*	22
Burma Rd. | *Burmese/Chinese*	22
Mamma Lucia | *Italian*	22
Nando's | *Chicken*	22
Guapo's | *Tex-Mex*	22
Calif. Tortilla | *Tex-Mex*	22
Dogfish Head | *Pub*	21
Uncle Julio's | *Tex-Mex*	21
Comus Inn | *Amer.*	20
Tara Thai | *Thai*	20
Cafe Deluxe | *Amer.*	20
Pollo Campero | *Central Amer.*	19

NATIONAL HARBOR/ FORT WASHINGTON

Old Hickory | *Steak*	26
Grace's | *Asian*	25
Bangkok Golden | *Thai*	24
Rosa Mexicano | *Mex.*	23
Bond 45 | *Italian*	22
Nando's | *Chicken*	22
Elevation Burger | *Burgers*	21

POTOMAC/GLEN ECHO

Bezu | *Amer./French*	24
Founding Farmers | *Amer.*	24
Renato/River Falls | *Italian*	22
Calif. Tortilla | *Tex-Mex*	22
Wild Tomato | *Amer.*	22
Amici Miei | *Italian*	21
Old Angler's | *Amer.*	20
Irish Inn/Glen Echo | *Irish*	20
NEW River Falls Tav. | *Amer.*	-
NEW Sugo Cicchetti | *Italian/Pizza*	-

PRINCE GEORGE'S COUNTY

Carolina Kit. | *Southern*	25
Cuba de Ayer | *Cuban*	25

Pho 75 | *Viet.*	24
Woodlands Rest. | *Indian/Veg.*	24
NEW Fishnet | *Seafood*	24
Ledo, Original | *Italian/Pizza*	24
NEW Bobby's Burger | *Burgers*	22
Hard Times | *Amer.*	22
Mamma Lucia | *Italian*	22
Seven Seas | *Chinese/Japanese*	22
Busboys/Poets | *Amer./Eclectic*	22
Franklin's | *Pub*	21
Elevation Burger | *Burgers*	21
Tara Thai | *Thai*	20

ROCKVILLE/ GARRETT PARK/ WHITE FLINT

Il Pizzico | *Italian*	27
Niwano Hana | *Japanese*	26
Black Mkt. | *Amer.*	26
China Jade | *Chinese*	25
Sushi Damo | *Japanese*	25
Sichuan Jin River | *Chinese*	25
Yuan Fu | *Chinese/Veg.*	25
Addie's | *Amer.*	25
A&J | *Chinese*	25
Cava Mezze | *Greek*	25
El Mariachi | *S Amer./Tex-Mex*	25
China Bistro | *Chinese*	24
Pho 75 | *Viet.*	24
Bombay Bistro | *Indian*	24
Crisp/Juicy | *Chicken/Peruvian*	24
Vegetable Gdn. | *Chinese/Veg.*	24
Cheesecake | *Amer.*	24
Urban BBQ | *BBQ*	24
Lighthouse/Vit Goel | *Korean*	24
Mosaic Cuisine | *Eclectic*	23
Moby Dick | *Persian*	23
La Limeña | *Cuban/Peruvian*	23
Mykonos Grill | *Greek*	23
Matchbox | *Amer.*	23
Benjarong | *Thai*	23
Lebanese Tav. | *Lebanese*	23
Don Pollo | *Chicken/Peruvian*	23
Joe's Noodle Hse. | *Chinese*	23
La Canela | *Peruvian*	23
P.F. Chang's | *Chinese*	23
Taste/Saigon | *Viet.*	22
Rocklands | *BBQ*	22
Hard Times | *Amer.*	22
Mi Rancho | *Tex-Mex*	22
Michael's Noodles | *Chinese*	22
Bob's Noodle | *Taiwanese*	22
Spice Xing | *Indian*	22
Clyde's | *Amer.*	22

Mamma Lucia | *Italian*	22
Seven Seas | *Chinese/Japanese*	22
Calif. Tortilla | *Tex-Mex*	22
Rolls 'N Rice | *Japanese*	22
Nick's Chophse. | *Steak*	21
Elevation Burger | *Burgers*	21
La Tasca | *Spanish*	21
Oro Pomodoro | *Italian/Pizza*	21
Hinode | *Japanese*	20
Fontina Grille | *Italian*	20
Tara Thai | *Thai*	20
NEW East Pearl | *Chinese*	-
NEW Quench | *Amer.*	-

SANDY SPRINGS

Urban BBQ | *BBQ*	24

SILVER SPRING/ TAKOMA PARK/ WHEATON

Sergio Rist. | *Italian*	27
Ruan Thai | *Thai*	27
Kabob N Karahi | *Nepalese/Pakistani*	26
El Pollo | *Chicken/Peruvian*	26
Nava Thai | *Thai*	26
New Kam | *Chinese*	25
Ray's/Classics | *Steak*	25
Full Key | *Chinese*	25
Ren's Ramen | *Japanese/Noodle Shop*	24
Samantha's | *Pan-Latin*	24
Crisp/Juicy | *Chicken/Peruvian*	24
8407 Kit. | *Amer.*	24
Thai/Silver Spring | *Thai*	24
Hollywood E. | *Chinese*	24
Olazzo | *Italian*	24
Negril | *Jamaican*	24
Azucar | *Mex./Pan-Latin*	24
Urban BBQ | *BBQ*	24
Moby Dick | *Persian*	23
Cubano's | *Cuban*	23
Lebanese Tav. | *Lebanese*	23
El Golfo | *Pan-Latin*	23
NEW Pacci's Tratt. | *Italian*	23
Oriental E. | *Chinese*	23
Royal Mile | *Scottish*	23
Jackie's | *Amer.*	23
Mandalay | *Burmese*	23
Mrs. K's | *Amer.*	23
Ledo Pizza | *Pizza*	23
Pacci's Neapolitan | *Pizza*	23
Mi Rancho | *Tex-Mex*	22
Parkway Deli | *Deli*	22
Good Fortune | *Chinese*	22

Mamma Lucia | *Italian*	22
Nando's | *Chicken*	22
Calif. Tortilla | *Tex-Mex*	22
Eggspectation | *Amer.*	21
Mark's Kit. | *Eclectic*	21
Woomi Gdn. | *Korean*	20
Pollo Campero | *Central Amer.*	19
Austin Grill | *Tex-Mex*	18
NEW LacoMelza | *Ethiopian*	-

Nearby Virginia

ALEXANDRIA

Peking Duck | *Chinese*	28
Cosmopolitan Grill | *E Euro.*	27
RT's | *Cajun/Creole*	26
Yamazato | *Japanese*	25
Cafe Pizzaiolo | *Italian/Pizza*	24
Il Porto | *Italian*	24
Five Guys | *Burgers*	24
Tempo | *French/Italian*	24
Evening Star | *Southern*	23
Afghan | *Afghan*	23
La Strada | *Italian*	23
Aditi | *Indian*	23
Hee Been | *Korean*	23
Taqueria Poblano | *Mex.*	22
Rocklands | *BBQ*	22
Buzz | *Coffee*	22
Red Hot/Blue | *BBQ*	22
Clyde's | *Amer.*	22
Rustico | *Amer.*	22
Calif. Tortilla | *Tex-Mex*	22
Teaism | *Tea*	20
NEW Pork Barrel | *BBQ*	19

ALEXANDRIA (OLD TOWN)

Eve | *Amer.*	27
La Bergerie | *French*	26
Le Refuge | *French*	26
Vaso's Kit. | *Greek*	26
Brabo | *Belgian/French*	26
Vermilion | *Amer.*	26
Yves Bistro | *French*	25
Asian Bistro | *Asian*	25
Grille | *Amer./French*	25
Geranio | *Italian*	25
Landini Bros. | *Italian*	25
Fontaine Caffe | *French*	25
Majestic | *Amer.*	24
NEW Society Fair | *Amer.*	24
Five Guys | *Burgers*	24
Hank's Oyster | *Amer./Seafood*	24

Las Tapas	*Spanish*	24
Bastille	*French*	24
A La Lucia	*Italian*	23
Chart House	*Seafood*	23
Bistrot Lafayette	*French*	23
Pizzeria Paradiso	*Pizza*	23
Eamonn's	*Irish*	23
Faccia Luna	*Pizza*	23
Mai Thai	*Thai*	23
Columbia Firehse.	*Amer.*	23
Hard Times	*Amer.*	22
Red Curry	*Asian*	22
BGR	*Burgers*	22
Gadsby's	*Amer.*	21
RedRocks	*Pizza*	21
La Tasca	*Spanish*	21
Jackson 20	*Amer.*	21
Le Pain Quotidien	*Bakery/Belgian*	21
Daniel O'Connell's	*Pub*	20
Virtue	*Amer.*	19
Austin Grill	*Tex-Mex*	18

ARLINGTON

Ray's/Steaks	*Steak*	27
Thai Sq.	*Thai*	26
Pupatella Pizzeria	*Pizza*	26
Ruth's Chris	*Steak*	26
Morton's	*Steak*	26
El Pollo	*Chicken/Peruvian*	26
Kabob Palace	*Mideast.*	26
Ray's Hell Burger	*Burgers*	26
Village Bistro	*Euro.*	26
NEW Ray's/Third	*Amer./Steak*	25
Bangkok 54	*Thai*	25
Ravi Kabob	*Pakistani*	25
T.H.A.I.	*Thai*	25
Carlyle	*Amer.*	25
Cafe Pizzaiolo	*Italian/Pizza*	24
La Côte d'Or	*French*	24
Minh's	*Viet.*	24
Willow	*Amer.*	24
Crisp/Juicy	*Chicken/Peruvian*	24
Jaleo	*Spanish*	24
Fyve	*Amer.*	24
Me Jana	*Lebanese*	24
Fire Works	*Pizza*	24
Layalina	*Lebanese/Syrian*	24
Crystal Thai	*Thai*	23
Good Stuff	*Burgers*	23
Moby Dick	*Persian*	23
Pasha Cafe	*Med.*	23
Lebanese Tav.	*Lebanese*	23
McCormick/Schmick	*Seafood*	23

Afghan Kabob Hse.	*Afghan*	23
Pie-Tanza	*Pizza*	23
Ping	*Asian*	23
Hee Been	*Korean*	23
Ledo Pizza	*Pizza*	23
Farrah Olivia	*Amer.*	23
Tutto Bene	*Italian/S Amer.*	23
Lost Dog	*Pub*	23
Legal Sea Foods	*Seafood*	23
P.F. Chang's	*Chinese*	23
Aroma Indian	*Indian*	23
Taqueria Poblano	*Mex.*	22
Rocklands	*BBQ*	22
Roti Med.	*Med.*	22
China Gdn.	*Chinese*	22
Buzz	*Coffee*	22
Red Hot/Blue	*BBQ*	22
Sweetgreen	*Health*	22
Mala Tang	*Chinese*	22
Rustico	*Amer.*	22
Nando's	*Chicken*	22
Guapo's	*Tex-Mex*	22
Calif. Tortilla	*Tex-Mex*	22
Busboys/Poets	*Amer./Eclectic*	22
BGR	*Burgers*	22
Bayou Bakery	*Southern*	22
Piola	*Italian/Pizza*	21
Uncle Julio's	*Tex-Mex*	21
Chop't	*Amer.*	21
Thaiphoon	*Thai*	21
Guajillo	*Mex.*	21
Elevation Burger	*Burgers*	21
Asia Bistro/Zen	*Asian*	21
Extra Virgin	*Italian*	21
Cafe Asia	*Asian*	21
Harry's	*BBQ/Burgers*	21
Cassatt's Café	*New Zealand*	20
Delhi Dhaba	*Indian*	20
Twisted Vines	*Eclectic*	20
NEW William Jeffrey's	*Amer.*	20
Caribbean Breeze	*Nuevo Latino*	20
Vapiano	*Italian*	20
Bob & Edith's	*Diner*	20
Luna Grill	*Diner/Veg.*	19
Kora	*Italian*	17
NEW Chasin' Tails	*Cajun/Creole*	-
NEW Curious Grape	*Eclectic*	-

CLARENDON

Kabob Bazaar	*Persian*	25
Cava Mezze	*Greek*	25
Pho 75	*Viet.*	24
Delhi Club	*Indian*	24

Lyon Hall	*French/German*	24
Tallula/EatBar	*Amer.*	24
Liberty Tav.	*Amer.*	24
Cheesecake	*Amer.*	24
Tandoori Nights	*Indian*	24
Taste/Morocco	*Moroccan*	23
Faccia Luna	*Pizza*	23
Eventide	*Amer.*	23
Hard Times	*Amer.*	22
Pete's New Haven	*Pizza*	22
Northside	*Coffee*	22
BGR	*Burgers*	22
Nam-Viet	*Viet.*	21
La Tasca	*Spanish*	21
Le Pain Quotidien	*Bakery/Belgian*	21
Blvd. Woodgrill	*Amer.*	20
Circa	*Amer.*	20
NEW Green Pig	*Amer.*	–

FAIRFAX

Ruth's Chris	*Steak*	26
BonChon	*Korean*	26
Villa Mozart	*Italian*	26
Dolce Vita	*Italian*	25
Artie's	*Amer.*	25
Jaipur	*Indian*	25
Asian Bistro	*Asian*	25
China Star	*Chinese*	24
Coastal Flats	*Seafood*	24
Ozzie's Corner	*Italian*	24
Bangkok Golden	*Thai*	24
Cheesecake	*Amer.*	24
NEW 100° C	*Chinese*	24
Minerva	*Indian*	23
Moby Dick	*Persian*	23
Curry Mantra	*Indian*	23
Sakoontra	*Thai*	23
Chutzpah	*Deli*	23
P.F. Chang's	*Chinese*	23
Hard Times	*Amer.*	22
Red Hot/Blue	*BBQ*	22
Guapo's	*Tex-Mex*	22
Calif. Tortilla	*Tex-Mex*	22
Dogfish Head	*Pub*	21
Uncle Julio's	*Tex-Mex*	21
NEW Dolce Veloce	*Italian*	–

FALLS CHURCH

2941	*Amer.*	27
Hong Kong Palace	*Chinese*	27
Present	*Viet.*	26
Bamian	*Afghan*	26
Elephant Jumps	*Thai*	26

Duangrat's	*Thai*	26
La Caraqueña	*S Amer.*	25
Panjshir	*Afghan*	25
Huong Viet	*Viet.*	25
Peking Gourmet	*Chinese*	25
Mark's Duck Hse.	*Chinese*	25
Rabieng	*Thai*	25
Sunflower Veg.	*Asian/Veg.*	25
Pho 75	*Viet.*	24
Crisp/Juicy	*Chicken/Peruvian*	24
Haandi	*Indian*	24
Bangkok Golden	*Thai*	24
X.O. Taste	*Chinese*	24
Myanmar	*Burmese*	24
Pie-Tanza	*Pizza*	23
Ledo Pizza	*Pizza*	23
Pizzeria Orso	*Pizza*	22
Fortune	*Chinese*	22
Red Hot/Blue	*BBQ*	22
Full Kee (VA)	*Chinese*	22
Dogfish Head	*Pub*	21
Elevation Burger	*Burgers*	21
Banh Mi DC	*Viet.*	21
Argia's	*Italian*	21
Mad Fox Brew	*Amer.*	20
Tara Thai	*Thai*	20
Pollo Campero	*Central Amer.*	19
NEW Rice Paper	*Viet.*	–

GREAT FALLS

L'Aub./François	*French*	28

MCLEAN

Kazan	*Turkish*	25
Tachibana	*Japanese*	24
Moby Dick	*Persian*	23
Capri	*Italian*	23
Assaggi	*Italian*	23
Lost Dog	*Pub*	23
Evo Bistro	*Med.*	22
NEW Bistro Vivant	*French*	–

RESTON/HERNDON

Russia House Rest.	*Russian*	27
Morton's	*Steak*	26
PassionFish	*Amer./Seafood*	26
Hama Sushi	*Japanese*	25
Il Fornaio	*Italian*	25
Pho 75	*Viet.*	24
Zeffirelli Rist.	*Italian*	24
El Manantial	*Med.*	24
Five Guys	*Burgers*	24
Angeethi	*Indian*	23
Minerva	*Indian*	23

Jackson's | *Amer./Seafood* 23
McCormick/Schmick | *Seafood* 23
Vinifera | *Amer.* 23
Ledo Pizza | *Pizza* 23
Busara | *Thai* 22
Red Hot/Blue | *BBQ* 22
Sweetgreen | *Health* 22
Clyde's | *Amer.* 22
Mamma Lucia | *Italian* 22
Mon Ami Gabi | *French* 22
M&S Grill | *Seafood/Steak* 22
Counter | *Burgers* 21
Uncle Julio's | *Tex-Mex* 21
Paolo's | *Cal./Italian* 21
Tara Thai | *Thai* 20
Vapiano | *Italian* 20
Pollo Campero | *Central Amer.* 19

SPRINGFIELD/ ANNANDALE

Mike's | *Amer.* 26
BonChon | *Korean* 26
Afghan Kabob Rest. | *Afghan* 25
A&J | *Chinese* 25
Food Corner Kabob | *Afghan* 25
Five Guys | *Burgers* 24
Honey Pig | *Korean* 23
Yechon | *Japanese/Korean* 22
Hard Times | *Amer.* 22
BGR | *Burgers* 22
Austin Grill | *Tex-Mex* 18

TYSONS CORNER

Shamshiry | *Persian* 27
Capital Grille | *Steak* 26
Nostos | *Greek* 26
Bombay Tandoor | *Indian* 26
Chima | *Brazilian* 26
Palm | *Steak* 25
Food Corner Kabob | *Afghan* 25
Fleming's Steak | *Steak* 25
Coastal Flats | *Seafood* 24
Cheesecake | *Amer.* 24
Maggiano's | *Italian* 23
Konami | *Japanese* 23
Da Domenico | *Italian* 23
Lebanese Tav. | *Lebanese* 23
McCormick/Schmick | *Seafood* 23
Woo Lae Oak | *Korean* 23
Härth | *Amer.* 23
Legal Sea Foods | *Seafood* 23
P.F. Chang's | *Chinese* 23
Taste/Saigon | *Viet.* 22

Busara | *Thai* 22
Cava Mezze Grill | *Greek* 22
Wildfire | *Seafood/Steak* 22
Clyde's | *Amer.* 22
Shula's | *Steak* 22
Chef Geoff's | *Amer.* 21
Panache | *Med.* 21
Neisha Thai | *Thai* 20
Cafe Deluxe | *Amer.* 20

VIENNA/OAKTON/ MERRIFIELD

Ruth's Chris | *Steak* 26
Café Renaissance | *Continental* 26
Bazin's/Church | *Amer.* 26
Sweetwater Tav. | *SW* 26
Sweet Ginger | *Asian* 25
Sunflower Veg. | *Asian/Veg.* 25
Four Sisters | *Viet.* 25
Yama | *Japanese* 25
Plaka Grill | *Greek* 24
Sea Pearl | *Amer./Cal.* 23
Amma Veg. | *Indian* 22
Tara Thai | *Thai* 20
NEW Alegria | *Mex.* -
Maple Ave | *Eclectic* -

Exurban Virginia

BROADLANDS

Clyde's | *Amer.* 22

CENTREVILLE/ MANASSAS/PRINCE WILLIAM COUNTY

Bistro L'Hermitage | *French* 26
El Pollo | *Chicken/Peruvian* 26
BonChon | *Korean* 26
Sweetwater Tav. | *SW* 26
Food Corner Kabob | *Afghan* 25
Five Guys | *Burgers* 24
Honey Pig | *Korean* 23
Hard Times | *Amer.* 22
Red Hot/Blue | *BBQ* 22
Uncle Julio's | *Tex-Mex* 21
Pollo Campero | *Central Amer.* 19

CHANTILLY

Thai Basil | *Thai* 26
Minerva | *Indian* 23
Eggspectation | *Amer.* 21

CLIFTON

Trummer's | *Amer.* 24

LEESBURG/ LANSDOWNE

Kobe | *Japanese* 27
Wine Kit. | *Amer.* 26
Lightfoot | *Amer.* 26
Tuscarora Mill | *Amer.* 25
Blue Ridge | *Amer.* 24
Fire Works | *Pizza* 24
Angeethi | *Indian* 23
Cajun Experience | *Cajun/Creole* 23
Red Hot/Blue | *BBQ* 22
Eggspectation | *Amer.* 21

PURCELLVILLE

Magnolias/Mill | *Amer.* 25

STERLING/ASHBURN/ SOUTH RIDING

Ford's Fish | *New Eng./Seafood* 26
Sweetwater Tav. | *SW* 26

Taste/Burma | *Burmese* 26
Blue Ridge | *Amer.* 24
Rangoli | *Indian* 24
Cheesecake | *Amer.* 24
Urban BBQ | *BBQ* 24
P.F. Chang's | *Chinese* 23
Hooked | *Seafood* 20
Vapiano | *Italian* 20

Virginia Countryside

Inn/Little Washington | *Amer.* 29
Foti's | *Amer.* 27
Ashby Inn | *Amer.* 27
L'Auberge Provençale | *French* 26
It's About Thyme | *Eclectic* 25
Iron Bridge Wine | *Amer.* 25
Blue Rock | *Amer.* 24
Rail Stop | *Amer.* 23
Hunter's Head | *British* 23

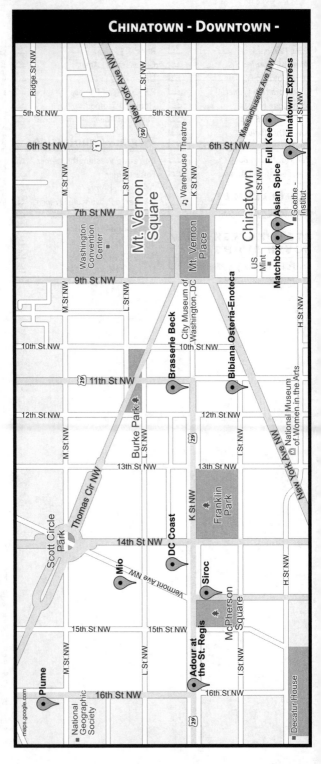

CHINATOWN - DOWNTOWN -

Ridge St NW

New York Ave NW

L St NW

Massachusetts Ave NW

Chinatown Express

5th St NW

5th St NW

Full Kee

6th St NW

6th St NW

Warehouse Theatre

Asian Spice

Chinatown

Goethe - Institut

7th St NW

Mt. Vernon Square

Matchbox

Washington Convention Center

Mt. Vernon Place

US Mint

9th St NW

City Museum of Washington, DC

Bibiana Osteria-Enoteca

National Museum of Women in the Arts

Brasserie Beck

10th St NW

10th St NW

Burke Park

11th St NW

12th St NW

12th St NW

13th St NW

13th St NW

Thomas Cir NW

Franklin Park

Scott Circle Park

DC Coast

14th St NW

Mio

Vermont Ave NW

Siroc

15th St NW

15th St NW

McPherson Square

Adour at the St. Regis

Decatur House

Plume

16th St NW

16th St NW

National Geographic Society

maps.google.com

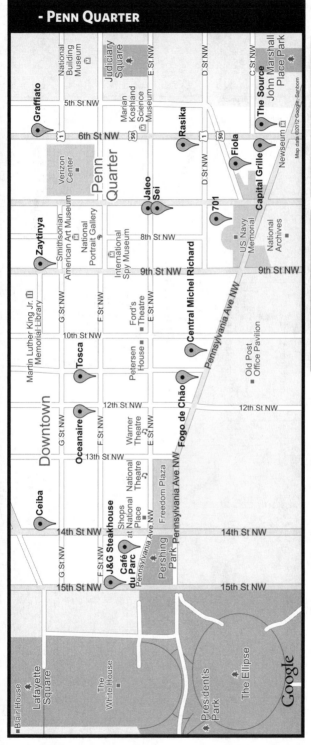

FOGGY BOTTOM - GOLDEN

Scott Circle

B'nai B'rith Klutznick National Jewish Museum

National Geographic Society

L St NW

N St NW

Rhode Island Ave NW

M St NW

Morton's

Connecticut Ave NW

Connecticut Ave NW

Golden Triangle

Malaysia Kopitiam

Jefferson Pl NW

C.F. Folks
The Palm

Vidalia

Smith & Wollensky

Historical Society of Washington, DC

N St NW

Mai Thai

M St NW

19th St NW

L St NW

20th St NW

N St NW

20th St NW

21st St NW

N St NW

New Hampshire Ave NW

21st St NW

22nd St NW

N St NW

22nd St NW

Rock Creek Park

maps.google.com

23rd St NW

N St NW

M St NW

23rd St NW

L St NW

Columbia Hospital for Women

24th St NW

H

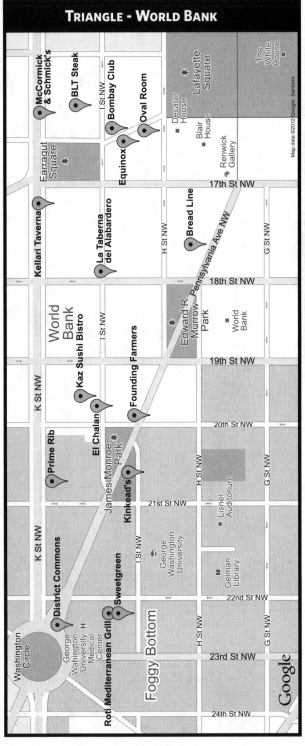

TRIANGLE - WORLD BANK

WASHINGTON, DC

MAPS

McCormick & Schmick's

BLT Steak

Bombay Club

Oval Room

Lafayette Square

The White House

Decatur House

Blair House

Renwick Gallery

Map data ©2012 Google, Sanborn

Equinox

Farragut Square

17th St NW

Kellari Taverna

La Taberna del Alabardero

Bread Line

H St NW

G St NW

Pennsylvania Ave NW

18th St NW

World Bank

Kaz Sushi Bistro

Edward R. Murrow Park

World Bank

19th St NW

Founding Farmers

K St NW

El Chalan

James Monroe Park

20th St NW

H St NW

G St NW

Prime Rib

Kinkead's

Lisner Auditorium

21st St NW

George Washington University

Gelman Library

District Commons

George Wahington University Medical Center

Sweetgreen

H St NW

G St NW

22nd St NW

Roti Mediterranean Grill

Washington Circle

Foggy Bottom

23rd St NW

Google

24th St NW

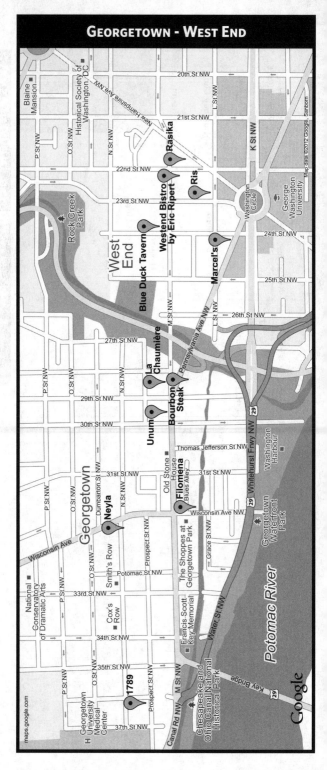

GEORGETOWN - WEST END

Latest openings, menus, photos and more on plus.google.com/local

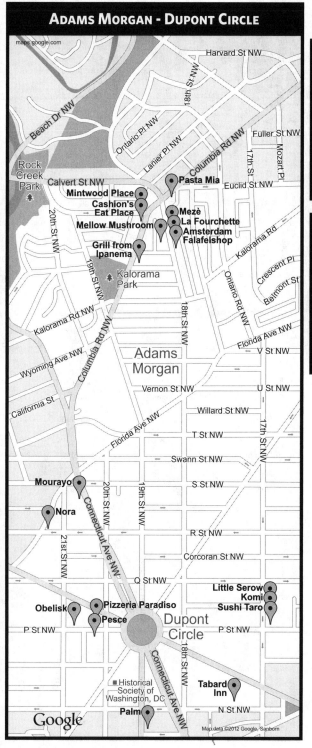

ADAMS MORGAN - DUPONT CIRCLE

maps.google.com

WASHINGTON, DC

MAPS

Harvard St NW

Beach Dr NW

Rock Creek Park

Calvert St NW

Mintwood Place

Cashion's Eat Place

Mellow Mushroom

Grill from Ipanema

Kalorama Park

Ontario Pl NW

Lanier Pl NW

18th St NW

Columbia Rd NW

Fuller St NW

Mozart Pl

17th St

Euclid St NW

Pasta Mia

Mezè

La Fourchette

Amsterdam Falafelshop

Kalorama Rd

Crescent Pl

Belmont St

20th St NW

19th St NW

Kalorama Rd NW

Columbia Rd NW

Wyoming Ave NW

California St

Adams Morgan

18th St NW

Ontario Rd NW

Florida Ave NW

V St NW

Vernon St NW

U St NW

Willard St NW

17th St NW

Florida Ave NW

T St NW

Swann St NW

Mourayo

Nora

20th St NW

19th St NW

Connecticut Ave NW

S St NW

R St NW

Corcoran St NW

Q St NW

Little Serow

Komi

Sushi Taro

Obelisk

21st St NW

Pizzeria Paradiso

Pesce

Dupont Circle

18th St NW

P St NW

P St NW

Historical Society of Washington, DC

Tabard Inn

Google

Palm

Connecticut Ave NW

N St NW

Map data ©2012 Google, Sanborn

Share your reviews on plus.google.com/local

67

OLD TOWN ALEXANDRIA

Potomac River

Founders Park

Bastille

Waterfront Park

The Strand

N. Union St

King St

S. Union St

Landini Bros.

Vaso's Kitchen

N. Lee St

S. Lee St

Thompsons Alley

La Bergerie

N. Fairfax St

Wales Alley

S. Fairfax St

Prince St

Duke St

Market Square

N. Royal St

S. Royal St

Princess St

Queen St

N. Pitt St

Eve

S. Pitt St

Wolfe St

Cameron St

King St

Prince St

N. St. Asaph St

S. St. Asaph St

Le Refuge

N. Washington St

Geranio

S. Washington St

N. Columbus St

S. Columbus St

Society Fair

Majestic

Cameron St

King St

S. Alfred St

Duke St

N. Patrick St

S. Patrick St

N. Henry St

S. Henry St

Vermilion

N. Fayette St

S. Fayette St

Five Guys

N. Payne St

S. Payne St

Commerce St

N. West St

S. West St

Cameron St

Prince St

Brabo by Robert Wiedmaier

S. Payton St

Duke St

King St

Daingerfield Rd

Jamieson St

Yves Bistro LLC

Google

Boyle St

Buchanan St

Mt. Vernon Ave

Service Alley

maps.google.com

Map data ©2012 Google, Sanborn

WASHINGTON, DC
RESTAURANT
DIRECTORY

	FOOD	DECOR	SERVICE	COST

A&J ⊄ *Chinese* — 25 | 13 | 19 | $19

Rockville | Woodmont Station | 1319 Rockville Pike (Wootton Pkwy.), MD | 301-251-7878

Annandale | 4316 Markham St. (Little River Tpke.), VA | 703-813-8181

"Authentic" Chinese dim sum "shines brightly" at these "well-run machines" in Annandale and Rockville, where "fantastic", "freshly made" noodles and "dishes you rarely see" are delivered with "no-nonsense bustle" in "'80s cafeteria" premises; yes, they're "short on charm", but "who cares" when the lack of ambiance translates into "rock-bottom prices" – just be sure to "bring cash" since they don't take plastic.

Acacia Bistro Ⓜ *American* — 24 | 22 | 24 | $40

Frederick | 129 N. Market St. (bet. Church & 2nd Sts.), MD | 301-694-3015 | www.acacia129.com

This New American "foodie find" in Downtown Frederick puts the focus on "local, fresh and seasonal" ingredients – indeed, you may even see the chef "picking herbs" if you sit in the "wonderful" "secret garden" in back (otherwise, the long, narrow interior has several "tasteful", "cozy" dining rooms); the staff's "cheerful" demeanor goes hand in hand with friendly tabs; P.S. accommodates vegan and gluten-free diners.

Acacia Bistro Ⓢ *Mediterranean* — 20 | 18 | 21 | $40

Upper NW | 4340 Connecticut Ave. NW (Yuma St.) | 202-537-1040 | www.acaciabistro.com

A new chef has brought a bit of the Mediterranean to the small-plates format at this "light, bright" Upper Northwest "shoe box–sized bistro" that's prized for its "thoughtful cooking", "pleasant service" and relatively "reasonable pricing"; add in a "charming patio" and a wine list that offers "a ton of variety" and, in an area with "lackluster" dining options, it "stands far above the crowd."

❷ Acadiana *Contemp. Louisiana* — 24 | 23 | 23 | $45

Mt. Vernon Square/Convention Center | 901 New York Ave. NW (9th St.) | 202-408-8848 | www.acadianarestaurant.com

"Bayou showstoppers" rule at this "classy" Mt. Vernon Square "power spot" with "consistently excellent", "progressive takes" on Cajun-Creole cooking, "genteel" manners and a "beautifully simple" multilevel setting decorated with tasteful nods to New Orleans; it's "a bit pricey", but admirers find "great value" in the Sunday jazz brunch prix fixe.

Acqua al 2 *Italian* — 24 | 21 | 22 | $47

Capitol Hill | 212 Seventh St. SE (North Carolina Ave.) | 202-525-4375 | www.acquaal2dc.com

"This is what pasta is supposed to taste like" say fans of the "dazzling array" on offer at this "charming", "cozy" brick-walled space across from Eastern Market on Capitol Hill (the steaks are also "fabulous", especially with blueberry sauce); the menu is "priced appropriately", i.e. it's "not cheap", but there's always the potential of spotting "a senator wander in."

	FOOD	DECOR	SERVICE	COST

Acre 121 *BBQ/Southern* — 21 | 20 | 20 | $29

Columbia Heights | 1400 Irving St. NW (14th St.) | 202-328-0121 | www.acre121.com

"Surprisingly good" barbecue for a joint that's "smack in the middle" of Columbia Heights is the judgment on the Southern fare (including "some delicious vegetarian options") at this "friendly" spot with a bit of an upscale wine bar look; middling prices, an outdoor patio and a calendar of countrified live music add appeal.

Adam Express 🗷 Ⓜ *Asian/Seafood* — 25 | 18 | 22 | I

Mt. Pleasant | 3211 Mount Pleasant St. NW (Lamont St.) | 202-328-0010

"Good catch" Korean, Chinese and Japanese dishes like "great noo-dles", dumplings and sushi lure Mt. Pleasant urbanites to this tiny yet "appealing" hole-in-the-wall with exposed brick and views of the surrounding neighborhood; fin fans note that the "price isn't too high", either, for the "freshest fish going"; P.S. irregular hours and a small, counter-only room make takeout a good bet.

Addie's *American* — 25 | 19 | 23 | $44

White Flint | 11120 Rockville Pike (Edson Ln.) | Rockville, MD | 301-881-0081 | www.addiesrestaurant.com

"Wonderful", "thoughtfully prepared" New American fare from the Black Restaurant Group (BlackSalt, etc.) is served with "care" at this "little old house" across from the White Flint Mall, with a "quaint", "1930s cottage ambiance"; somewhat "high" prices may be un-avoidable, but diners can escape "close quarters" inside if they "snag a table on the lawn" in front or in the "backyard retreat."

Aditi *Indian* — 23 | 20 | 20 | $25

Greater Alexandria | 5926 Kingstowne Ctr. (Kingstowne Blvd.) | Alexandria, VA | 703-922-6111 | www.myaditi.com

Aditi Indian Kitchen *Indian*

Northeast | Union Station | 50 Massachusetts Ave. NE (Capitol St.) | 202-682-0304

Sense-travel to "Delhi" at this Indian duo via their "well-made and -served" "authentic" specialties, which come cafeteria-style in white-tiled digs at Union Station or in Alexandria's comparatively "cool setting", with its curvy banquettes and room dividers, plus a dramatic crackled wall; staff at both locations is "friendly", and the tabs are "reasonable."

🅉 Adour at the St. Regis *American/French* — 26 | 27 | 25 | $82

Downtown | St. Regis | 923 16th St. NW (K St.) | 202-509-8000 | www.adour-washingtondc.com

Alain Ducasse's "epicurean" French-American showcase near the White House may "ooze sophistication" with "incredibly executed" "drool-worthy" dishes "served in quietly muted splendor" (there's "crystal everywhere"), but there are "no stuck-up waiters" to be found among a staff that "could not be any nicer", its "knowledge-able" sommelier a prime example; in short, one feels "like a million dollars" here – with, of course, "prices to match."

	FOOD	DECOR	SERVICE	COST

Afghan *Afghan*
23 | 14 | 20 | $25

Greater Alexandria | 2700 Jefferson Davis Hwy. (Raymond Ave.) | Alexandria, VA | 703-548-0022 | www.afghanrestaurantva.com
"Overlook" the "less than elegant" setting, and enjoy the "excellent" chow at this Alexandria Afghan where "great kebabs" and other "homestyle" dishes in "ample quantities" keep it "full of Afghani families", some of whom come for music-filled parties in the banquet hall; it's all "inexpensive", but the lunch buffet is the biggest "bargain."

Afghan Kabob House *Afghan*
23 | 14 | 18 | $18

Courthouse | 2045 Wilson Blvd. (N. Courthouse Rd.) | Arlington, VA | 703-294-9999 | www.afghankabobhouse.org
"Honest food" at an "honest price" is the deal at this Arlington Afghani "quick-service" eatery where "wonderful" kebabs, "interesting rice options" and other "excellent" eats trump its "hole-in-the-wall" appearance; night owls note that "it's one of the few late-night spots in the [Courthouse] area" on Friday and Saturday (till 3 AM).

Afghan Kabob Restaurant *Afghan*
25 | 19 | 24 | $20

Springfield | 6357 Rolling Rd. (Old Keene Mill Rd.), VA | 703-913-7008 | www.afghankabobrestaurant.com
Start newbies on Afghan cuisine in this "well-appointed" white-tablecloth Springfielder with "delicious-tasting and -smelling" food and a staff who "willingly explains dishes" and are "kid-friendly" too; don't let the budget prices or "shabby" shopping center surroundings "fool you" – this is a step or two "above typical kebab places."

Againn 🗷 *British*
20 | 21 | 20 | $40

Downtown | 1099 New York Ave. NW (11th St.) | 202-639-9830 | www.againndc.com
Anglophiles summon their "inner duke and duchess" in this Downtown Brit gastropub's clubby-"chic" dining room as they sample "earthy" classics with a "modern twist"; if a full meal's "a little pricey", there's also a "beautiful" zinc bar whose "top-notch" cocktails ("Pimm's cup!") and extensive beer and scotch selection foster "camaraderie."

Agora *Turkish*
23 | 19 | 21 | $37

Dupont Circle | 1527 17th St. NW (bet. Church & Q Sts.) | 202-332-6767 | www.agoradc.net
"Istanbul" in Dupont Circle East offers a "delicious" "tapas-inspired twist" on Turkish and Mediterranean meze delivered by folks who "take real pride" in their work; a meal in the "trendy" low-lit and brick-walled lounge "feels fancy without being overly expensive", or "watch the world go by" on 17th Street from the patio; P.S. there's also an "active bar scene" fueled by "inventive" cocktails and "serious" wines.

Agrodolce *Italian*
23 | 20 | 22 | $30

Germantown | Milestone Shopping Ctr. | 21030 Frederick Ave. (bet. Ridge Rd. & Shakespeare Blvd.), MD | 301-528-6150 | www.agrodolcerestaurant.com
MoCo diners are sweet on the "fresh and flavorful" pastas, "strong" wood-fired pizzas and other "good food for the price" served in

"sunny" Mediterranean digs at this "bit of Italy" in a Germantown strip mall; the vibe is molto "casual", especially at lunch, when you "order at the counter", but the staff is always "friendly", plus there's a "nice" wine selection and a "delightful" patio.

A La Lucia *Italian*
23 | 18 | 22 | $36

Old Town | 315 Madison St. (bet. Fairfax & Royal Sts.) | Alexandria, VA | 703-836-5123 | www.alalucia.com

"Well off the much-traveled" Old Town tourist itinerary is this "much appreciated" "neighborhood favorite", an Italian trattoria that treats its guests like "family" and is prized for "well-prepared" classics and year-round, restaurant-week–like deals (e.g. nightly prix fixe, discount wines Sunday–Tuesday); hence, most shrug off the "garage"-y space's "noisy" echo and "funky" look as adding to the "fun vibe."

Al Crostino *Italian*
23 | 18 | 23 | $38

U Street Corridor | 1324 U St. NW (bet. 13th & 14th Sts.) | 202-797-0523 | www.alcrostino.com

"Custom pastas, delicious sauces" and a varied selection of wines by the glass are the lure at this "cute" lemon-colored Italian "tucked into the hustle and bustle of U Street"; further signs that it's a keeper are the "decent" tabs and "hands-on" mother-daughter management, who treat customers ("cliché, but) like family."

NEW Alegria *Mexican*
- | - | - | M

Vienna | 111 Church St. NW (Dominion Rd.), VA | 703-261-6575 | www.alegriaonchurch.com

Chef-owner Patrick Bazin's new Vienna venture, a small-plates Mexican cantina next door to his eponymous New American, offers a wallet-friendly taste of his creative takes on south-of-the-border staples, plus margaritas and sangria, *por supuesto*; the Spanish-styled setting features wood furniture, patterned walls and deco-style chandeliers, along with a brick-walled seasonal patio.

Al Tiramisu *Italian*
25 | 20 | 24 | $53

Dupont Circle | 2014 P St. NW (bet. Hopkins & 20th Sts.) | 202-467-4466 | www.altiramisu.com

There's "terrific seafood" and "housemade pasta" like you might find at "superb spots in Rome" at "friendly" chef-owner Luigi Diotaiuti's "small" step-down off Dupont Circle, which, though "cramped", retains a "dimly lit, romantic vibe"; the menu's a bit "expensive", but be sure to ask the "very professional waiters" about the "prices for the specials", because those "can be over the top."

American Ice Co. *BBQ*
19 | 23 | 18 | $21

U Street Corridor | 917 V St. NW (bet. 10th St. & Vermont Ave.) | 202-758-3562 | www.amicodc.com

A "Brooklyn dive" on V Street NW, this reclaimed "industrial setting (garage door and chalkboard included)" chills out with a "superb canned beer selection" and "decent" BBQ at "bargain-basement" prices; yes, it's "where the hipsters roam", but staff is "far from pretentious", meaning it's a great place to "grab a beer" and some 'cue "before a show at the 9:30 Club" nearby.

	FOOD	DECOR	SERVICE	COST

Amici Miei *Italian* | 21 | 18 | 20 | $40 |

Potomac | 1093 Seven Locks Rd. (Wootton Pkwy.), MD | 301-545-0966 | www.amicimieiristorante.com

Potomac's "go-to" Italian for "solid" pizza, "fresh pasta" and the like at "midrange prices" can easily "swing from a romantic dinner to a kid-friendly place", offering something for "everyone"; "charming" owners preside over an "attractive" dining room lined with tasteful artwork, but many regulars skip the "hustle and bustle" inside, preferring to sit outdoors.

Amma Vegetarian Kitchen *Indian* | 22 | 11 | 17 | $16 |

Vienna | 344 Maple Ave. E. (Beulah Rd.), VA | 703-938-5328 | www.ammavegkitchen.com

"Dosas are the star" on the "delicious vegetarian" menu at this easy-on-the-wallet South Indian in Vienna; it can be "hard to know what to order" at the counter (no descriptions), and decor is "spartan, with Formica tables", but just sit back, dip your naan into one of the curries and enjoy the "fireworks."

Amsterdam Falafelshop ● *Mideastern* | 25 | 11 | 17 | $11 |

Adams Morgan | 2425 18th St. NW (Columbia Rd.) | 202-234-1969 | www.falafelshop.com

"Eat big and cheap" at this "edgy", always "packed" Adams Morgan late-night "institution" where "amazing, crisp" Belgian-style fries and "gold-standard" falafel in pitas, piled high with "myriad" toppings, "absorb the alcohol in the most wonderful way" for the throngs of club-goers "in line"; for most, the lack of decor, service and utensils is "irrelevant" – they take their nosh in "all its messy glory" to go.

Angeethi *Indian* | 23 | 20 | 21 | $25 |

Herndon | 645 Elden St. (bet. Jackson & Monroe Sts.), VA | 703-796-1527

Leesburg | 1500 E. Market St. (bet. Battlefield & River Creek Pkwys.), VA | 703-777-6785

www.angeethiva.com

"Indian friends" recommend these Herndon and Leesburg subcontinentals for their deft "blend of spices" ("try the vindaloo") and "reasonably priced" lunch buffets stocked with "stuff that Americanized-Indian-food eaters won't recognize"; so maybe the "decor is minimal", but it's "better than many buffets", and besides, these establishments are "calm and quiet" and graced by "good, solid" service.

Ardeo + Bardeo *American/Wine Bar* | 22 | 21 | 21 | $44 |

Cleveland Park | 3311 Connecticut Ave. NW (bet. Macomb & Ordway Sts.) | 202-244-6750 | www.ardeobardeo.com

"Stylish", "sleek and inviting", this Cleveland Park New American offers a dinner menu full of "zest and zing", as well as "breakfastified versions" of dinner menu favorites at its "amazing" weekend brunch; an "attentive" staff easily contends with the "lively setting", which includes a "busy" bar scene, all of which adds up to a "great date place without being insanely expensive" – just don't overdo those "spendy adult beverages."

Argia's *Italian*

| 21 | 18 | 21 | $31 |

Falls Church | 124 N. Washington St. (bet. Broad St. & Park Ave.), VA | 703-534-1033 | www.argias.com

A "solid choice" for an "affordable, family-friendly" night out is this Falls Church Italian dishing up "[more] than just pasta and red sauce" in "hearty and satisfying" portions; the "pleasant" staff keeps an even keel in the "convivial", if "close" and "noisy", main dining area, which brings to life the accompanying murals of "happy Italian townspeople"; P.S. "enjoy a bottle of wine" on the back patio or in the wine bar.

Aroma Indian Cuisine *Indian*

| 23 | 18 | 21 | $26 |

World Bank | 1919 I St. NW (20th St.) | 202-833-4700 🖪
Shirlington | 4052 Campbell Ave. (S. Shirlington Rd.) | Arlington, VA | 703-575-8800
www.aromarestaurant.com

Curry's "seductive scent" sharpens World Bank and Shirlington appetites for the "flavorful" subcontinental fare at these old Indian "gems"; "attentive" service is the rule at both locations, but Shirlington excels with its "well-stocked", "good-value" lunch buffet and "nicely decorated" digs.

Art & Soul *Southern*

| 23 | 22 | 22 | $47 |

Capitol Hill | Liaison Capitol Hill | 415 New Jersey Ave. NW (bet. D & E Sts.) | 202-393-7777 | www.artandsouldc.com

"Artfully crafted" "haute" Southern and New American food is on display at chef-owner Art Smith's hotel venue hard by the Capitol, and though tabs are "pricey", they're not museum quality; lobbyists "feel cool" in the gallerylike dining room hung with contemporary paintings, while its bar/lounge offers "unique cocktails" and the "best mix of Capitol Hill and hipster action."

☑ Artie's *American*

| 25 | 23 | 25 | $31 |

Fairfax | Fairfax Circle Shopping Ctr. | 3260 Old Lee Hwy. (Fairfax Blvd.), VA | 703-273-7600 | www.greatamericanrestaurants.com

All aboard this "comfortable", "classic yacht"–themed Fairfax "treasure" for "always delightful" American fare at "excellent value" prices; repeat visitors "wish all restaurants had servers this good" (if "something doesn't float your boat", "they'll make it right") and recommend using the "call-ahead" service on weekends, when there's often a "long wait."

Arucola *Italian*

| 20 | 17 | 21 | $36 |

Chevy Chase | 5534 Connecticut Ave. NW (bet. McKinley & Morrison Sts.) | 202-244-1555 | www.arucola.com

The "dedicated, long-standing staff" at this "convenient", "reliable" Italian "haunt" in Chevy Chase strives to be "gracious and efficient" in the face of "frantic hordes", some discharged from the nearby cinema; but any concerns about the "limited", faux-rustic space are overcome by the "moderate prices."

	FOOD	DECOR	SERVICE	COST

☒ Ashby Inn Ⓜ *American*   27 | 25 | 26 | $59

Paris | The Ashby Inn | 692 Federal St. (Rte. 50), VA | 540-592-3900 |
www.ashbyinn.com

"Think of heaven" – "rolling hills, green as far as the eye can see" and
"sophisticated" New American cuisine that's "a thrill" for "real
foodies" – and it's "worth the drive" (and expense) to dine at this
"romantic" wine country getaway set in a "charming" inn in Paris,
VA; "gracious" servers and an "accomplished sommelier" enhance
"special occasions", which are even more special if you can "tumble
into bed at the end of the night"; P.S. closed Monday and Tuesday.

Asia Bistro *Asian*   21 | 20 | 21 | $24

Pentagon City | Pentagon Row | 1301 S. Joyce St. (Army Navy Dr.) |
Arlington, VA | 703-413-2002 | www.asia-bistro.com

Zen Bistro & Wine Bar *Asian*

Pentagon City | Pentagon Row | 1301 S. Joyce St. (Army Navy Dr.) |
Arlington, VA | 703-413-8887 | www.zen-bistro.com

The "tasty" Asian fare, including sushi, is "good for the price" at this
"conveniently" located Pentagon Row pair; creative thinkers can chan-
nel a "chic restaurant in the Pacific Rim" by "grabbing a glass of vino"
and some apps in the separate but connected mod-Eastern spaces;
P.S. look for "large crowds" on "speed-dating nights" in the wine bar.

Asian Bistro *Asian*   25 | 20 | 22 | $26

Old Town | 809 King St. (bet. N. Columbus & S. Alfred Sts.) |
Alexandria, VA | 703-836-1515
Fairfax | 3950 University Dr. (North St.), VA | 703-865-4937
www.abistro.com

There's no need to "fight about" whether to have "sushi, Chinese
or Thai", since there are "lots of options" (even Malaysian and
Indonesian) at this Pan-Asian in Old Town and Fairfax; its "prompt
service", "reasonably" priced lunch specials and "classy-enough-
for-the-middle-class" atmosphere especially suit midday meetings,
but it's also favored for "high-quality" delivery/takeout.

Asian Spice *Asian*   23 | 21 | 22 | $30

Chinatown | 717 H St. NW (bet. 7th & 8th Sts.) | 202-589-0900 |
www.asianspice.us

"Multiple Asian cuisines" are prepared with "delicacy and knowledge"
at this Chinatown spot known for its sizable "selection for vegetarians"
and "unfailingly warm" staff; the "lovely, modern" setting in a turreted
19th-century building, along with "sexy cocktails", creates a "romantic" ambiance, and "inexpensive" tabs sweeten the deal.

Assaggi Mozzarella Bar *Italian*   23 | 21 | 20 | $46

Bethesda | 4838 Bethesda Ave. (bet. Arlington Rd. & Woodmont Ave.),
MD | 301-951-1988 | www.assaggirestaurant.com

Assaggi Osteria *Italian*

McLean | 6641 Old Dominion Dr. (Holmes Pl.), VA | 703-918-0080 |
www.assaggiosteria.com

This Italian duo in Bethesda and McLean feature "convivial" bars for
"wine and apps" (e.g. "fabulous mozzarella") along with "somewhat

FOOD DECOR SERVICE COST

costly" but "delicious pastas, meat and fish" in "urbane", "white-tablecloth" surroundings; they're "relaxed" at lunch, with "attentive" service, but if "you can't hear yourself eat" on busy nights in Bethesda, try sitting on its "people-watching" patio.

Athens Grill ⊠ *Greek* 26 | 13 | 21 | $19

Gaithersburg | Goshen Plaza | 9124 Rothbury Dr. (Goshen Rd.), MD | 301-975-0757 | www.athensgrill.com

At this "tiny", "family-owned" storefront Gaithersburg Greek, Hellenic-hunters find "excellent food for the price", including some of the "biggest, best gyros in Greater Washington"; the "nice", "welcoming" staff takes orders at the counter, but "don't expect fast food", as "good food takes time", and given the "cafeteria" ambiance (and no booze), many "do takeaway."

Atlas Room Ⓜ *Eclectic* 25 | 20 | 23 | $41

Atlas District | 1015 H St. NE (bet. 10th & 11th Sts.) | 202-388-4020 | www.theatlasroom.com

On the rapidly "changing" H Street corridor, this "ambitious" Eclectic stands out with its "adventurous" yet "approachable" cooking and "fancy cocktails"; the menu is arranged in an "offbeat" layout (with apps and small and large plates grouped by main ingredient), but the "engaging" staff is there to help diners find their bearings in the dark, "warm" and "cozy" room – decorated, appropriately, with colorful old maps.

Austin Grill *Tex-Mex* 18 | 17 | 19 | $23

Penn Quarter | 750 E St. NW (bet. 7th & 8th Sts.) | 202-393-3776

Silver Spring | 919 Ellsworth Dr. (bet. Fenton St. & Georgia Ave.), MD | 240-247-8969 ◗

Old Town | 801 King St. (Columbus St.) | Alexandria, VA | 703-684-8969

Springfield | 8430 Old Keene Mill Rd. (Rolling Rd.), VA | 703-644-3111

www.austingrill.com

A "home away from home" for "displaced Texans", this "Tex-Mex to the max" chainlet with "huge", "irresistible" margaritas and "laid-back", "colorful" decor is appreciated by "frat boys" and "families" alike (if "you like noise and kids, this is your place"); some say the eats are "pretty commonplace", but "portions are large", "prices are cheap" and the varied menu, with vegetarian and gluten-free options, "satisfies" most.

Azucar *Mexican/Pan-Latin* 24 | 21 | 22 | $28

Silver Spring | Layhill Shopping Ctr. | 14418 Layhill Rd. (Bel Pre Rd.), MD | 301-438-3293 | www.azucarrestaurantmd.com

"Superb" Mexican and Pan-Latin fare – from the complimentary salsa and "deliciously thin" chips, "right down to dessert and drinks" (e.g. "perfect" fresh-fruit daiquiris) – makes this "festively" colored, "candlelit" Silver Spring venue a neighborhood "standout"; add "diligent, unobtrusive" servers to the equation, and it's an all-around "good value."

Bamian *Afghan*

26 | 20 | 22 | $27

Falls Church | 5634 Leesburg Pike (Carlin Springs Rd.), VA | 703-820-7880 | www.bamianrestaurant.com

"The price is right" at this Falls Church "perennial favorite", where "exceptional" Afghani fare is distinguished by "delightful depth of flavor" and "amazing" vegetarian choices ("don't miss the pumpkin!") and is delivered by an "attentive" staff; though set "amid a sea of aging strip malls", the spacious and "surprisingly upscale" space makes a "great place for a party."

Banana Café & Piano Bar *Cuban/Puerto Rican*

19 | 17 | 19 | $27

Capitol Hill | 500 Eighth St. SE (E St.) | 202-543-5906 | www.bananacafedc.com

Peel into this "festive" "Barracks Row hangout", serving "bountiful" heaps of solid, midpriced Puerto Rican and Cuban favorites delivered by an "attentive" staff amid a "predictably yellow"-and-green interior or out on the "popular" patio; the few who find the fare "so-so" or the decor "cheesy" may still enjoy downing "muy bien margaritas" and "singing along" in the upstairs piano bar.

Banana Leaves *Asian*

- | - | - | I

Dupont Circle | 2020 Florida Ave. NW (Connecticut Ave.) | 202-986-1333 | www.mybananaleaves.com

This casual Dupont Circle Pan-Asian favorite got a new leaf on life when it reopened recently, following a devastating fire; the affordable menu spans Asia, running from regional comfort foods to sushi, all served in a spiffy setting of exposed brick, colorful art and wainscoting plus a handful of second-story window tables overlooking a vibrant street scene.

NEW Bandolero *Mexican*

- | - | - | M

Georgetown | 3241 M St. NW (bet. Potomac St. & Wisconsin Ave.) | 202-625-4488 | www.bandolerodc.com

Mike Isabella (Graffiato) goes modern Mexican at this trendy Georgetown spot serving a midpriced menu of small plates and fancified versions of traditional *comida,* all washed down with crafty cocktails and margaritas; just don't bring *abuela* to the loud, rollicking Mexican-Gothic space guarded by reclaimed cemetery gates and decorated with mismatched furniture and Day of the Dead–inspired animal skulls.

Bangkok 54 *Thai*

25 | 21 | 22 | $26

Arlington | 2919 Columbia Pike (Walter Reed Dr.), VA | 703-521-4070 | www.bangkok54restaurant.com

At this "hip Thai" eatery on Columbia Pike, "well-spiced", "affordable" curries and other specialties "shine with rich flavors" and are delivered with "panache" by a "fresh-faced" crew in "modern" Eastern surroundings that are "easy on your eyes", if not always your ears (it's often "noisy" at night); "sit in the lounge for the coolest experience", and sample the "creative" drinks during happy hour.

	FOOD	DECOR	SERVICE	COST

Bangkok Golden *Thai*
24 | **16** | **21** | **$26**

Fort Washington | 9503 Livingston Rd. (Oxon Hill Rd.), MD | 301-248-8810
Fairfax | University Mall | 10621 Braddock Rd. (Ox Rd.), VA | 703-691-0700
Falls Church | Seven Corners Ctr. | 6395 Seven Corners Ctr.
(bet. Arlington Blvd. & Leesburg Pike), VA | 703-533-9480
www.bangkokgoldenrestaurant.com

"Everyone talks about" the "no-longer-secret" Laotian menu at the
Falls Church branch of this "inexpensive" trio (not served at the
other outlets in Fairfax and Fort Washington), but true fans caution
"don't sell the Thai dishes short" – they're "excellent" too; either
way, nobody talks about the basic decor at these strip-mall spots,
though they do speak up for the "earnest" staff that is always ready
with "good advice" for the "adventurous eater."

Bangkok Joe's *Thai*
23 | **22** | **21** | **$29**

Georgetown | Washington Harbour | 3000 K St. NW
(Thomas Jefferson St.) | 202-333-4422 | www.bangkokjoes.com
Dumplings "to die for" with "great cocktails to boot" draw a "lively"
crowd to this "modern" Thai lounge in Georgetown's Washington
Harbour, by the Potomac; its "fast, friendly" service, relative "value"
and location near the AMC cinema make it a natural "dinner-
and-a-movie" spot.

Banh Mi DC *Vietnamese*
21 | **10** | **16** | **$9**

Falls Church | Eden Ctr. | 3103 Graham Rd. (Arlington Blvd.), VA |
703-205-9300
When your "teeth crackle into the sublime baguette" at this "fast",
"cheap" no-frills Falls Church Vietnamese market, you've found a
"classic" Vietnamese sandwich "worth going out of your way for"
enthuse its devotees; there are also other "authentic" prepared snacks
on display, and a handful of tables, but most take things "to go."

Bar Pilar *American*
23 | **19** | **19** | **$20**

U Street Corridor | 1833 14th St. NW (bet. S & T Sts.) | 202-265-1751 |
www.barpilar.com
This "trendy" 14th Street NW gastropub recently expanded upstairs
(possibly outdating the Decor rating), where its "delicious" contemporary American "nose-to-tail cuisine" is served in small and large
formats; hipster foodies hope the expansion lessens the "table-
hovering" waits for seats in the "dark", "arty" bar that's recommended for a "romantic" date and some of the "best bangs for the
buck" on the local scene.

Bastille *French*
24 | **19** | **22** | **$52**

Old Town | 1201 N. Royal St. (Bashford Ln.) | Alexandria, VA |
703-519-3776 | www.bastillerestaurant.com
Those "homesick for France" swear this bistro in North Old Town
takes them back with its "terrific" "modernized takes" on Gallic
classics; "efficient but not intrusive service" helps guests "have a romantic time" in the "intimate" dark-wood dining room or on the
patio that's "fabulous in belle weather"; P.S. prices are "high", so
sou-savers take advantage of the many prix fixe deals.

Batik ☒ *Asian*

22 | 21 | 19 | $21

Gaithersburg | 200 Main St. (Kentlands Blvd.), MD | 301-869-8661 | www.batikasiancuisine.com

"Top-shelf food on a pauper's budget" sums up this Kentlands Pan-Asian street-fare specialist that's a "terrific treat" for families and foodies who dig its "unique" dumpling menu (e.g. American BBQ pork); "friendly smiles" greet visitors to the tiki bar–gone-upscale premises, sealing the deal.

Bayou Ⓜ *Cajun/Creole*

20 | 17 | 21 | $26

West End | 2519 Pennsylvania Ave. NW (bet. 25th & 26th Sts.) | 202-223-6941 | www.bayouonpenn.com

"Finger-lickin'" eats "capture the true flavors of N'Awlins" in an "atmosphere as funky as the bayou" at this "value"-priced West End Cajun-Creole; "cool" (but not "hipper than thou") servers navigate the "lively" scene, which often includes jazz musicians "wailing" upstairs.

Bayou Bakery *Southern*

22 | 18 | 19 | $17

Courthouse | 1515 N. Courthouse Rd. (15th St.) | Arlington, VA | 703-243-2410 | www.bayoubakeryva.com

A "New Orleans sensibility" pervades this "friendly" Courthouse counter-serve bakery/cafe where "terrific" Southern standards, "delicious" beignets, "OMG" desserts and "awesome" coffee keep it humming from breakfast on; in fact, some folks "never want to leave" the "comfy couch" in the corner of the "cute" room, "whimsically decorated" with mason jar lights and salvaged artifacts.

Bazin's on Church Ⓜ *American*

26 | 22 | 23 | $48

Vienna | 111 Church St. NW (bet. Center St. & Lawyers Rd.), VA | 703-255-7212 | www.bazinsonchurch.com

"NoVa foodies" hit this "upscale" "Vienna power spot" for "exciting" New American cooking and "killer" wines; the staff "makes you feel at home" in the "lovely" brick-wall-and-exposed-beam space that's always "happily noisy", thanks in part to the hopping bar, and though it's "pricey", you "get what you pay for: a great dinner"; P.S. the owners recently launched Alegria, a Mexican tapas venture, next door.

Belga Café *Belgian*

25 | 20 | 21 | $39

Capitol Hill | 514 Eighth St. SE (bet. E & G Sts.) | 202-544-0100 | www.belgacafe.com

"Handsome" with "great mussels" sums up why legions "love, love, love" chef-owner Bart Vandaele's "real taste of Belgium" on an "edgy" stretch of Capitol Hill; "outstanding" midpriced eats aside, it's also a "beer destination", which along with the "tight", brick-walled art-"gallery"-like quarters, produces a "notable din", cut through ably by "competent" servers.

Benjarong *Thai*

23 | 20 | 21 | $25

Rockville | Wintergreen Plaza | 885 Rockville Pike (Edmonston Dr.), MD | 301-424-5533 | www.benjarongthairestaurant.com

"Blessedly quiet", with "consistently excellent" Thai fare at "reasonable prices" served by an "attentive" crew – it should come as no surprise that this Rockville stalwart has been "popular" for so many years; longtime loyalists appreciate the "spaciousness" of the Siamese-art-filled digs and remind first-timers that the dishes can "have some serious heat."

Ben's Chili Bowl ●⇎ *Diner*

22 | 14 | 19 | $14

U Street Corridor | 1213 U St. NW (bet. 12th & 13th Sts.) | 202-667-0909 | www.benschilibowl.com

"Junk-food heaven" is a "mouthwatering" 'half-smoke' (spicy hot dog), "drenched chili-cheese fries" and a "creamy" milkshake at this "venerable" DC "icon" with long lines full of blue-collar "workers, college students, U Street partygoers and the tux- and ball-gown–clad" (the POTUS never has to wait); sure, the "'50s diner"-style digs are a bit "dumpy" and "crowded", but the counter staff is "always cheerful", and it's awfully "cheap" for a "piece of history"; P.S. an H Street NE outlet is expected soon.

Bezu ⊠ *American/French*

24 | 21 | 23 | $58

Potomac | Potomac Promenade Shopping Ctr. | 9812 Falls Rd. (River Rd.), MD | 301-299-3000 | www.bezurestaurant.com

The Potomac strip-mall locale "belies the treasure inside" this "small storefront": an "upscale" eatery turning out "surprisingly sophisticated" French–New American cuisine, albeit at "downtown prices"; nonetheless, its "passionate" chef and "helpful" sommelier enhance the "warm and comfortable atmosphere" in the white-and-gold, Eastern-accented space.

BGR, The Burger Joint *Burgers*

22 | 15 | 17 | $15

Dupont Circle | 1514 Connecticut Ave. NW (bet. Dupont Circle & Q St.) | 202-299-1071
Bethesda | 4827 Fairmont Ave. (Woodmont Ave.), MD | 301-358-6137
Old Town | 106 N. Washington St. (bet. Cameron & King Sts.) | Alexandria, VA | 703-299-9791
Arlington | Lyon Vill. | 3129 Lee Hwy. (Custis Memorial Pkwy.), VA | 703-812-4705
Clarendon | 3024 Wilson Blvd. (Highland St.), VA | 703-566-1446
Springfield | 8420 Old Keene Mill Rd. (Rolling Rd.), VA | 703-451-4651
www.bgrtheburgerjoint.com

Chomp a "fancy burger cooked right" and "sweet potato fries to die for" at this inexpensive chain specializing in "juicy goodness on a bun" plus "thick", "yummy" shakes; service veers between "prompt" and "slow" at its varied locations, but the "create-your-own-soda" machines and "'80s flashback" digs (e.g. giant LP covers on the walls) keep most occupied when it gets "crowded."

Bibiana Osteria-Enoteca ⊠ *Italian*

25 | 24 | 24 | $56

Downtown | 1100 New York Ave. NW (entrance on H St. at 12th St.) | 202-216-9550 | www.bibianadc.com

"When Tuscany is too far away", "boldface names" and others head to this Downtown Italian that has "everything going for it": "delightful" cooking that acknowledges the "old country, but for today", a wine list that "would get Bacchus excited" and "impeccable" service; so despite the "expense", it's always a "scene" in the "light, airy" loungelike space.

Biergarten Haus ● *German*   17 | 22 | 18 | $25

Atlas District | 1355 H St. NE (bet. 13th & 14th Sts.) | 202-388-4053 | www.biergartenhaus.com

"Navigate through the sea of hipsters" at this "Germany-meets–H Street" beer hall/garden featuring a 4,000-sq.-ft. outdoor "wonderland" with "rustic wooden tables" and a permanent "Oktoberfest atmosphere" that puts extra oompah into a menu of "great, big beers" and "decent" German grub; *ja,* "service can be slow when it's extremely busy", but staffers "make up for" occasional lapses with "charm and humor."

Big Bear Cafe *American*   - | - | - | M

Bloomingdale | 1700 First St. NW (R St.) | no phone | www.bigbearcafe-dc.com

Chef John Cochran (ex the late Rupperts) has recently elevated this coffeehouse oasis for Bloomingdale neighborhood gentrifiers into a full-fledged restaurant; each night, its college-hangout-esque interior and greenery-swathed patio get dressed up with candles and table service for midpriced New American dinners that put locally sourced ingredients at the center of the plate; P.S. light breakfast and lunch also served.

Birch & Barley Ⓜ *American*   24 | 23 | 24 | $41

Logan Circle | 1337 14th St. NW (bet. P St. & Rhode Island Ave.) | 202-567-2576 | www.birchandbarley.com

Pairing "super-creative" New American food with beer is the mission of this somewhat spendy Logan Circle gastropub, whose "chipper" servers are "great guides" to the "tremendous" brew list (50 on tap, 500 bottles); it's easy to "impress a date" in the "beautiful" "dark" and distressed digs that are "cool" "without being obnoxious about it", and its "indulgent" Sunday brunch is also popular; P.S. sister bar/lounge Churchkey is upstairs.

Bistro Bis *French*   26 | 23 | 24 | $55

Capitol Hill | Hotel George | 15 E St. NW (bet. Capitol St. & New Jersey Ave.) | 202-661-2700 | www.bistrobis.com

The "see-and-be-seen" crowd at this "sophisticated" French rendezvous on Capitol Hill often includes "a senator" or two munching "skillfully served", "modern takes on classic" dishes; "expensive" *oui,* but the "stylish" cherry-wood–paneled room is a "classy" venue for a "power breakfast", "expense-account lunch" or "date night", and what's more, its "bar scene is great."

NEW Bistro Bohem ●Ⓜ *Czech/European*   - | - | - | M

Shaw | 600 Florida Ave. NW (6th St.) | 202-735-5895 | www.bistrobohem.com

Folks are Czech-ing out this trendy, midpriced newcomer that brings Prague to Shaw with Slavic specialties like pierogi and schnitzel updated in a small-plates format, all washed down with absinthe-based cocktails and (of course) beer; the compact space sports a spiffy look, its gray walls brightened with gilded mirrors and eye-popping art, plus there's an outdoor patio; P.S. a next-door bakery/cafe is in the works.

Bistro Cacao *French* | 23 | 22 | 23 | $45 |

Capitol Hill | 320 Massachusetts Ave. NE (bet. 3rd & 4th Sts.) | 202-546-4737 | www.bistrocacao.com

At this Capitol Hill townhouse (by way of the "Right Bank"), "authentic" French bistro dishes and "attentive" service back up the "*completement charmant*" "date-night" setting decorated with antiques and "cozy" curtained booths, while its "lovely" patio is the "place to be spotted" for lunch; it's a bit "expensive" but "worth the coin" say friends (and lovers).

Bistro D'Oc *French* | 23 | 18 | 22 | $40 |

Penn Quarter | 518 10th St. NW (bet. E & F Sts.) | 202-393-5444 | www.bistrodoc.com

Seemingly "plucked right out of Southern France" and transplanted to a "touristy" Penn Quarter location opposite Ford's Theatre, this bistro turns out "well-crafted" classics, like the "amazing cassoulet", at relatively moderate prices; "servers who know each dish" patrol the "homey" bi-level space that's warmed by the bright red and yellow colors of Languedoc's flag.

Bistro Français ● *French* | 21 | 20 | 20 | $41 |

Georgetown | 3124 M St. NW (bet. 31st St. & Wisconsin Ave.) | 202-338-3830 | www.bistrofrancaisdc.com

Francophiles count on this "prototypical bistro" (it's "perfectly named") in Georgetown that "hasn't changed in years" for "well-prepared" Gallic fare that's "reasonably priced" for the area, especially the "excellent-value" prix fixe; a suitably Parisian look and "professional" service are pluses, and it also has the "virtue of staying open later than just about anyone" (till 3 AM weekdays, 4 AM weekends).

Bistro La Bonne ● *French* | 21 | 17 | 19 | $31 |

U Street Corridor | 1340 U St. NW (bet. 13th & 14th Sts.) | 202-758-3413 | www.bistrolabonne.com

"A shot of Paris" in "the middle of the" U Street scene, this "neighborhood spot" specializes in "classic, hearty" French fare that's "*bonne*" if "not *merveilleux*"; the "cute", "simple" decor (vintage posters plus blue, white and red banners) and "friendly" service are nice enough, but the real draw is the "great value", including a "spectacular happy hour."

Bistro LaZeez *Mideastern* | 22 | 16 | 21 | $26 |

Bethesda | 8009 Norfolk Ave. (bet. Auburn & Del Ray Aves.), MD | 301-652-8222 | www.bistrolazeez.com

"Tasty", "authentic" Syrian and Lebanese specialties at "rock-bottom prices" make this "friendly" "family-owned" Mideasterner in Bethesda "worth visiting"; the "tasty" fare can be eaten in the "simple" black, gray and olive "postage stamp" of a dining room, on the patio under bright-yellow umbrellas or taken home.

FOOD | DECOR | SERVICE | COST

☒ Bistro L'Hermitage ☒ *French* | 26 | 26 | 27 | $54

Woodbridge | 12724 Occoquan Rd. (Old Bridge Rd.), VA | 703-499-9550 | www.bistrolhermitage.com

Upon entering this "hidden treasure" in Woodbridge's historic Occoquan area, guests are transported to a "quaint French village" auberge, where one can "dine in decadence" on "wonderful" Gallic cuisine or while away an hour over "pâté and a great wine" at the "warm"-feeling bar; under the eye of owner Youssef Essakl, the "exceptional" staff "never fails to accommodate", so though it's "pricey", "you actually get your money's worth."

Bistro Provence *French* | 26 | 22 | 21 | $66

Bethesda | 4933 Fairmont Ave. (bet. Norfolk Ave. & Old Georgetown Rd.), MD | 301-656-7373 | www.bistroprovence.org

What a "treat" to watch the "artist" (chef Yannick Cam) in the "open kitchen" whipping together "superb", "expertly" crafted contemporary French repasts at his Bethesda bistro; comparatively, "service can leave something to be desired", and being "squeezed" into the "tiny", Provençal-themed dining room tempers an otherwise "exquisite dining" experience that's, all-in-all, "not to be missed if you've got the bucks"; P.S. the stone-walled patio is a "gorgeous" seating alternative.

Bistrot du Coin ◑ *French* | 22 | 20 | 18 | $36

Dupont Circle | 1738 Connecticut Ave. NW (bet. R & S Sts.) | 202-234-6969 | www.bistrotducoin.com

It's "all about the mussels", with "plump" mollusks "available by the bucket" alongside other midpriced "classic bistro" fare at this *très* noisy" "endless party" in Dupont Circle with a *"vieux* Paris" look; "traditionally 'French'" service rubs some the wrong way, but legions of fans ask what's not to "love" about "any place where people drink wine before noon"?

Bistrot Lafayette *French* | 23 | 19 | 21 | $50

Old Town | 1118 King St. (bet. Fayette & Henry Sts.) | Alexandria, VA | 703-548-2525 | www.bistrotlafayette.com

"You can always count on the menu" (it seems like "it never changes") at this "cozy", "unpretentious" peach-colored French bistro in Old Town where "generous portions" of "authentic" Gallic gastronomy (steak tartare, bouillabaisse) are delivered by "attentive" waiters who let you "use your French a bit – what fun!"; it's not cheap, but "reasonable" offerings include a "good prix fixe menu" for lunch and early-birds.

Bistrot Lepic & Wine Bar *French* | 24 | 19 | 22 | $49

Georgetown | 1736 Wisconsin Ave. NW (S St.) | 202-333-0111 | www.bistrotlepic.com

"Worthy of the proximity" to the French embassay is this "authentically" Gallic haven in Upper Georgetown dishing out "expensive" but "high-quality" bistro "classics" "à la the 1950s", including offal; "use your inside voice" when placing orders with the "knowledgeable" servers because it can be "loud" in the "charmingly" "rustic" dining room, though "the upstairs wine bar is a quiet oasis."

NEW Bistro Vivant *French* — | — | — | M

McLean | 1394 Chain Bridge Rd. (Old Dominion Dr.), VA | 703-356-1700 | www.bistrovivant.com

A new venture from industry vets Domenico Cornacchia (Assagi) and Aykan Demiroglu (the erstwhile Locanda), this midpriced French bistro in McLean is where well-heeled locals go to reminisce about their last trip to Paris while sharing regional classics, small plates and vin; natural light filters through lace curtains into the oak-and-burgundy-bedecked dining room, which also boasts a full bar poshly appointed with granite and golden faux-ostrich-covered stools.

Black & Orange ◐ *Burgers* 25 | 18 | 20 | $13

Dupont Circle | 1300 Connecticut Ave. NW (N St.) | 202-296-2242
NEW U Street Corridor | 1931 14th St. NW (bet. U St. & Wallach Pl.) | 202-450-5365
www.blackandorangeburger.com

"Juicy hand-formed patties" helped by "interesting spices", "creative" toppings and "fresh brioche buns" have meatheads piling into these "spare but stylish", industrial-looking fast-casual joints in Dupont and the U Street area; patty partisans also dig the "reasonable" prices and "late-night" hours (till 5 AM Thursday–Saturday).

Blackfinn American Saloon *American* 18 | 17 | 18 | $26

Downtown | 1620 I St. NW (16th St.) | 202-429-4350 | www.blackfinndc.com
Bethesda | 4901 Fairmont Ave. (Norfolk Ave.), MD | 301-951-5681 | www.blackfinnbethesda.com ◐

"Young professionals" congregate at these "sleek and stylized" pubs in Downtown DC and Bethesda, where "affable" crews serve a "diverse" range of American "comfort" eats that are "a step above normal bar food" at everyday prices; however, they're mainly known for their "booming bar scenes", which morph from "great spots to catch a game" to having a "loud" "club feel" geared toward "singles who do not want to engage in conversation."

Black Market Bistro *American* 26 | 23 | 24 | $40

Garrett Park | 4600 Waverly Ave. (Strathmore Ave.), MD | 301-933-3000 | www.blackmarketrestaurant.com

"Like Brigadoon", this "quaint", "old" clapboard house appears to be set in a "place out of time" – Garrett Park, a relic of "small-town beauty" – yet its "incredible" American menu reveals a contemporary, "energetic approach to old favorites" (it's part of the Black restaurant "empire"); also reminiscent of "a quieter day and age" is its "staff that loves to serve", relatively "reasonable prices" and a "dreamy" front porch where you can watch the trains "rattling" by.

Z BlackSalt *American/Seafood* 27 | 21 | 23 | $55

Palisades | 4883 MacArthur Blvd. NW (U St.) | 202-342-9101 | www.blacksaltrestaurant.com

"Inventive, gorgeous and impeccably executed" New American seafood at "not-quite lobbyist prices" is served with "care" at the Black Restaurant Group's "popular" Palisades flagship; if the "decor is not up to the quality of the food", it's not apparent from the "sit-and-be-seen" hordes always packing the "fun bar", "lively" main dining room and somewhat more "intimate" and "elegant" back room; P.S. it's "hard to resist" the "terrific" on-site market for "fresh, fresh, fresh" fish "on your way out."

Black's Bar & Kitchen *American*   24 | 22 | 22 | $49

Bethesda | 7750 Woodmont Ave. (bet. Norfolk Ave. & Old Georgetown Rd.), MD | 301-652-5525 | www.blacksbarandkitchen.com

Happy-hour crowds mob this "wonderful" Bethesda New American seafooder "like salmon swimming upstream" ("single or not") to "oyster up" with "fabulous mojitos" or sit down to "phenomenal mussels" and "fish specials" in the "comfy, fashionable" dining room; insiders note one can "go upscale and spend a lot" or have a "great experience" with lighter fare, and suggest arriving "early" to snag an outdoor table and "watch Bethesda walk by."

BLT Steak ⧄ *Steak*   25 | 23 | 23 | $65

Golden Triangle | 1625 I St. NW (bet. 16th & 17th Sts.) | 202-689-8999 | www.bltsteak.com

At this "classy but not stuffy steak palace", a New York import near the White House, "beautiful", "big slabs of meat" and signature "huge popovers" star in a "power-laden setting" with a "swanky, French bistro kind of feel"; such "great quality and service" "don't come cheap", but for those who "want to dine with politicians" it's worth the "big bucks"; P.S. the recent arrival of chef Jon Mathieson (ex Michel) restored a French accent to some menu selections.

☑ Blue Duck Tavern *American*   27 | 25 | 26 | $64

West End | Park Hyatt | 1201 24th St. NW (bet. M & N Sts.) | 202-419-6755 | www.blueducktavern.com

Birds of a feather are "wowed every time" by the elevated, "beautifully crafted" "comfort food" at this "elegant" West End New American; just as ducky: it's "high on style and low on pretension", with an "extremely gracious" staff that "knows how to show you a good time" in "modern", "Shaker-inspired" environs that are often graced by "famous" faces; P.S. should the bill "make you 'blue'", there are "lower prices" at lunch, and in the bar/lounge.

Blue Ridge Grill *American*   24 | 21 | 23 | $28

Leesburg | 955 Edwards Ferry Rd. NE (Leesburg Bypass), VA | 703-669-5505
Ashburn | Brambleton Towne Ctr. | 22865 Brambleton Plaza (bet. Regal Wood & Soave Drs.), VA | 703-327-1047 www.brgrill.com

It's "hard to choose" among all the "excellent" "culinary comfort food" at these Virginia-based all-Americans, "dependable" "down-home" spots with a "casual" vibe and "friendly" service; families fancying "value for the dollar" keep things "busy" and "a bit noisy", so consider "sitting outside" on the "awesome" patio (Leesburg) or moving quickly on to an after-dinner "movie" (Ashburn).

	FOOD	DECOR	SERVICE	COST

Blue Rock Inn Restaurant 🅼 *American* ▽ 24 | 25 | 25 | $49

Sperryville | Blue Rock Inn | 12567 Lee Hwy. (5 mi. west of Hwy. 522 N.), VA | 540-987-3388 | www.thebluerockinn.com

"Picturesque country dining" that combines "wonderful food and views" of the Blue Ridge Mountains is the thing at this "lovely rural" retreat in a Sperryville inn; the "upmarket", "white-tablecloth" dining room features an "expensive" New American menu, while the casual pub and "comfy" patio offer cheaper eats – either way, service is deft and plenty of "local" wines flow.

Bob & Edith's Diner ◑ *Diner* 20 | 12 | 19 | $14

Arlington | 2310 Columbia Pike (Wayne St.), VA | 703-920-6103 | www.bobandediths.com

"Beloved" by everyone from "disheveled hipsters" to "families", this "friendly", "classic dive diner" in Arlington slings "generous portions" of "kitschy, greasy goodness" at "affordable" tabs; don't let "tough parking", "nothing-fancy" decor or "crazy waits on weekends" deter you – it "scratches the itch", especially for "after-hours partyers" thanks to its 24/7 schedule.

NEW Bobby's Burger Palace *Burgers* 22 | 19 | 19 | $16

West End | George Washington University | 2121 K St. NW (bet. 21st & 22nd Sts.) | 202-974-6260
College Park | Varsity | 8150 Baltimore Ave. (bet. Lakeland Rd. & Navahoe St.), MD | 240-542-4702
www.bobbysburgerpalace.com

Celeb chef Bobby Flay "knows how to cook a burger", as proven by his "funky", "futuristic"-looking College Park and West End chain outposts, where "innovative" "twists on the tried-and-true" include regionally inspired "gourmet" creations washed down by "adult shakes" that are "worth the calories"; perhaps it's "overpriced" for a "joint" where you "order at the counter", but where else can you get "your burger 'crunchified'"?

Bobby Van's Grill *Steak* 23 | 21 | 23 | $57

Downtown | 1201 New York Ave. NW (12th St.) | 202-589-1504

Bobby Van's Steakhouse *Steak*

Downtown | 809 15th St. NW (bet. H & I Sts.) | 202-589-0060
www.bobbyvans.com

"Administration folks having dinner" and "business-lunch" crowds affirm it's "always a quality experience" at these "reliable, friendly" Downtown steakhouses where you'll need "your wallet and your appetite" for the "man-sized beef"; "dark wood" and "traditional" trappings signify an "old boys' club" atmosphere near the White House, while the New York Avenue address is brighter and airier.

Bob's Noodle 66 ☕ *Taiwanese* 22 | 10 | 18 | $17

Rockville | 305 N. Washington St. (bet. Beall Ave. & Martins Ln.), MD | 301-315-6668

Come "as close to Taiwan as you'll get in the States", or at least the DC area, with "cheap", "real-deal" offerings "not for the faint of heart" ("like pig's ear or stomach or stinky tofu") in this "no-frills" Rockville strip-maller; "quick service" may "make you feel rushed", but linger long enough for a heaping of "dreamy" shaved ice; P.S. cash only.

Bodega-Spanish Tapas & Lounge *Spanish*

23 | 23 | 22 | $34

Georgetown | 3116 M St. NW (bet. 31st St. & Wisconsin Ave.) | 202-333-4733 | www.bodegadc.com

You may "want to stick a rose in [your] mouth and tango" after a romantic rendezvous at this Spanish "date spot" in Georgetown with a bullfighting theme to its "dark" black, red and cow-accented interior; the "great ambiance" is backed by "delicious tapas", "stellar sangria" and "original" drinks, all at attractive prices and delivered by a professional crew.

Bombay Bistro *Indian*

24 | 17 | 22 | $26

Rockville | Bell's Corner | 98 W. Montgomery Ave. (Adams St.), MD | 301-762-8798 | www.bombaybistro.com

There's "great bang for your rupee" at the "cheap", "tasty" lunch buffet of this Rockville strip-mall "gem", where "food like your Indian mother would make" satisfies "cravings" for subcontinental "standards"; the "1970s"-style dining room can get "crowded", but the "comfy" "neighborhood atmosphere" offers "a certain warmth" and the staff is a model of "efficiency."

Bombay Club *Indian*

25 | 25 | 25 | $49

Golden Triangle | 815 Connecticut Ave. NW (bet. H & I Sts.) | 202-659-3727 | www.bombayclubdc.com

"Refinement pervades" this "sophisticated Indian" a few "steps from the White House", where "delightful" dishes are served "with style" in "serene", "British raj" environs "tinkling" with live piano – no wonder "Washington-type celebrities abound" at its "luxuriously big tables"; tabs are "upscale but won't break the bank", especially for the "amazing" $28 Sunday brunch, which includes champagne.

Bombay Tandoor *Indian*

26 | 21 | 23 | $30

Tysons Corner | 8603 Westwood Center Dr. (Leesburg Pike) | Vienna, VA | 703-734-2202 | www.bombaytandoor.com

Indian-food devotees are "mesmerized" by the "outstanding quality" cuisine coming out of the kitchen at this subcontinental "hidden" in a Tysons Corner office building; "kudos" extend to its "outstanding service" and "good value", especially at its "amazing" lunch buffet, while the formal-feeling dining room is a "great place for hosting parties."

BonChon Chicken *Korean*

26 | 14 | 15 | $19

Fairfax | 3242 Old Pickett Rd. (Old Lee Hwy.), VA | 703- 865-5688 ◗
Annandale | 6653 Little River Tpke. (Old Columbia Pike), VA | 703-750-1424 ◗
Centreville | 14215 Centreville Sq. (Machen Rd.), VA | 703-825-7711 www.bonchon.co.kr

"How do they get the skin so crispy?" on the "incredible" double-fried chicken cluck fans of these Fairfax County outposts of the

Korean chain where the "addictive" wings compensate for often "scattered service"; some advise skip the "sports-bar atmosphere" and lines that can be "sooo long", and "call in way ahead" to score your birds to go.

Bond 45 *Italian*   22 | 24 | 24 | $61

National Harbor | National Harbor | 149 Waterfront St. (St. George Blvd.), MD | 301-839-1445 | www.bond45.com

It's "all about the view" – an "absolutely incredible" Potomac River panorama – wax couples celebrating "memorable evenings" at this "romantic" Italian steakhouse in National Harbor (an offshoot of the NYC original); "accommodating" servers deliver "great steaks" and "some of the best" housemade burrata to "date night"–worthy dining alcoves in the handsome old-world digs, but it's not for the faint of wallet.

NEW Boqueria *Spanish*   - | - | - | E

Dupont Circle | 1837 M St. NW (19th St.) | 202-558-9545 | www.boqueriarestaurant.com

A hot spot straight out of the gate, Marc Vidal's pricey *bar de tapas* newly arrived in Dupont Circle repeats the successful formula of its NYC siblings, plying a trendy crowd with plenty of vino and a battery of classic tapas, cheese and charcuterie; watching the chefs at work adds more buzz to the energetic, contemporary space, outfitted with blond-wood and sand-colored tiles, and its outdoor patio is a people-watching perch.

Boulevard Woodgrill *American*   20 | 18 | 19 | $26

Clarendon | 2901 Wilson Blvd. (N. Fillmore St.), VA | 703-875-9663 | www.boulevardwoodgrill.com

The "smell of the wood-burning grill" whets the appetite for "fall-off-the-bone ribs" and other "tasty" bites on the "wide-ranging menu" at this "friendly", "value"-priced Clarendon American standby; the simple "upscale"-"casual" setting is bathed in sunlight, though many prefer to "people-watch" at the sidewalk tables, especially during its popular weekend brunch, lubricated by "great Bloody Marys."

NEW Boundary Road ❶ *Eclectic*   - | - | - | M

Atlas District | 414 H St. NE (bet. 4th & 5th Sts.) | 202-450-3265 | www.boundaryrd.com

Edgy Atlas District coordinates haven't kept politicians and foodies from swarming this midpriced Eclectic tavern for fancified eats – like a foie gras torchon PB&J with housemade peanut butter – which can be paired with draft brews, artisanal cocktails or wine; the rustic, exposed-brick-and-wood-beam environs include a roomy bar area for getting together with pals.

NEW Boundary Stone *Pub Food*   ▽ 24 | 26 | 25 | $21

Bloomingdale | 116 Rhode Island Ave. NW (1st St.) | 202-621-6635 | www.boundarystonedc.com

Bloomingdale's young strivers welcome this "awesome neighborhood" watering hole for its "above-par" pub fare served by a pro crew to wooden booths in the "lovely" reclaimed-everything setting;

discerning drinkers note that the "beautiful" bar is stocked with a "well-curated selection of whiskeys and beers", and tame tariffs seal the deal.

Bourbon *Pub Food*

21 | 19 | 19 | $27

Adams Morgan | 2321 18th St. NW (Belmont Rd.) | 202-332-0800
Glover Park | 2348 Wisconsin Ave. NW (Observatory Ln.) | 202-625-7770
www.bourbondc.com

"Bourbon converts" are born at these "friendly" sour-mash specialists in Adams Morgan and Glover Park, where the "extensive collections" of brown spirits are ballasted by "glorified bar food" on the cheap (e.g. "fantastic" tater tots); both locations sport a "classy" and contemporary (i.e. non-tavernlike) look, but the AdMo branch particularly stands out as a "grown-up" spot "in a sea of college bars."

Bourbon Steak *Steak*

25 | 25 | 25 | $70

Georgetown | Four Seasons Hotel Washington DC |
2800 Pennsylvania Ave. NW (28th St.) | 202-944-2026 |
www.bourbonsteakdc.com

"Of course the steaks are superb" at Michael Mina's DC chophouse, but "trust the chefs" to take you on an "amazing adventure" via the rest of the "inventive" New American menu at this "popular" Four Seasons venue – "the place to see, be seen and spend money in Georgetown"; "impeccable service" is de rigueur and "celebrity sightings" are common in the "modern and polished" dining room, as well as the bar that's "rife with power-sippers (and those looking to get attached to them)."

NEW Boxcar Tavern *American*

21 | 21 | 19 | $30

Capitol Hill | 224 Seventh Ave. SE (bet. C & Independence Sts.) |
202-544-0518 | www.boxcardc.com

Despite a Victorian London look, this moderately priced freshman Barracks Row tavern is living in the here and now with its relatively "imaginative" (and mostly American) pub fare and "well-done" beer and wine lists; solid service and a "great vibe" in the "narrow" space mean "seating can be hard to come by on a busy night."

Brabo by Robert Wiedmaier *Belgian/French*

26 | 22 | 24 | $55

Old Town | Lorien Hotel & Spa | 1600 King St. (bet. Diagonal Rd. &
West St.) | Alexandria, VA | 703-894-3440 |
www.braborestaurant.com

An Old Town "favorite", this "upscale", "modern" hotel "respite" offers "fantastic" Belgian-French fare from chef Robert Wiedmaier (Marcel's, Brasserie Beck) with "wine to match"; it's "costly", but you can expect "remarkable" service for a truly "luxe evening"; P.S. next door is Tasting Room, Wiedmaier's "more casual (and affordable)" concept, known for its "can't-be-beat" mussels.

Brasserie Beck *Belgian/French*

25 | 22 | 22 | $49

Downtown | JBG Bldg. | 1101 K St. NW (11th St.) | 202-408-1717 |
www.beckdc.com

"Amazing mussels", a "tremendous beer list" and "relatively moderate" tabs keep Robert Wiedmaier's (of Marcel's) "lusty", "authentic" Belgian brasserie Downtown "crowded" and "boisterous"; since its "power bar" seems to attract "more young lobbyists per square inch" than most, those seeking a quieter "business lunch" or "intimate dinner" should sit in back and enjoy the old-fashioned "European train station" motif.

Brasserie Monte Carlo *French/Mediterranean* | 22 | 18 | 21 | $43 |

Bethesda | 7929 Norfolk Ave. (Cordell Ave.), MD | 301-656-9225 | www.bethesdarestaurant.com

"Far less risky than the casino" is a meal at this French-Med spot with a "solid menu that has stood the test of time" from a chef-owner who "works tirelessly" to deliver "a touch of the Riviera in Downtown Bethesda"; rendering outdoor tables "a big plus" is "close" seating in the "small" saffron-and-orange-hued dining room that's dominated by a mural of Monte Carlo in its heyday.

Bread Line ⊠ *Bakery/Sandwiches* | 23 | 12 | 17 | $15 |

World Bank | 1751 Pennsylvania Ave. NW (bet. 17th & 18th Sts.) | 202-822-8900 | www.breadline.com

"It's the bread, stupid", and the way this gently priced bakery/cafe "down the block" from the White House and World Bank can "pack so many flavors and textures" into one "delicious" sandwich makes for an "unmatched" lunch; at midday, an "efficient" crew moves the "long" queue "fast", though many leave the "stark" industrial premises to sit outside or go "picnicking"; P.S. it's line-free at breakfast, or go for "fine pastry and coffee" in the afternoon.

Brewer's Alley *Pub Food* | 22 | 21 | 22 | $25 |

Frederick | 124 N. Market St. (bet. Church & 2nd Sts.), MD | 301-631-0089 | www.brewers-alley.com

"Upscale pub grub" and "terrific microbrews" from the on-site brewery make this "family-friendly" "fixture" in Downtown Frederick a "go-to" spot whether you "dress up or dress down"; the staff is "passionate about their food and drinks", and the airy, stained-glass-trimmed digs (it's located in an old municipal building/opera house) further the "great value."

NEW The Brixton *Pub Food* | - | - | - | M |

U Street Corridor | 901 U St. NW (Florida Ave.) | 202-560-5045 | www.brixtondc.com

Young, cosmopolitan types hobnob at this midpriced British U Street arrival from the Marvin talents where the action takes place on three levels; a replica English pub on the ground floor serves Brit classics, the upstairs bar/lounge offers a short menu and brews (plus cocktails and wine) in an ornate hunting-lodge setting and the roof deck is fitted out with two more bars and affords DC monument views.

B. Smith's *Southern* | 22 | 24 | 22 | $42 |

Northeast | Union Station | 50 Massachusetts Ave. NE (Capitol St.) | 202-289-6188 | www.bsmith.com

A "beautiful" beaux arts setting from the "heyday of passenger trains" (Union Station's former 'Presidential Suite') provides a "stately" backdrop to enjoy a "stylish" yet "timeless take on Southern food" from the eponymous lifestyle TV personality; critics contend it's a bit "overpriced", but most appreciate the staff's "Southern charm" in this "soothing" "respite from the hectic real world"; P.S. check out the "legendary" Sunday brunch buffet.

Buck's Fishing & Camping Ⓜ *American* | 20 | 19 | 18 | $46 |

Upper NW | 5031 Connecticut Ave. NW (Nebraska Ave.) | 202-364-0777 | www.bucksfishingandcamping.com

A campfirelike "glow" flickers on the "canoes in the rafters" and other rustic trappings at this rustic retreat in the Upper NW backcountry that's known for its "tasty" but "limited" American menu ("perfectly charred" wood-grilled steak, "never-fail" burgers); "inconsistent" service ranges from "helpful" to "rude", but most are willing to make the hike – even though it's "pricier than you might expect given the camping theme."

🆕 Burger, Tap & Shake *Burgers* | 21 | 15 | 19 | $15 |

Foggy Bottom | 2200 Pennsylvania Ave. NW (bet. 22nd & 23rd Sts.) | 202-587-6258 | www.burgertapshake.com

"Not pretentious, just darn good burgers" accessorized with "crisp" Boardwalk-style fries are the hallmark of this upstart counter-serve patty haven and bar near George Washington U. that lets folks eat in "Foggy Bottom for cheap"; its staff "seems to like working" in the spiffy space wrapped with reclaimed wood and floor-to-ceiling windows looking out on Washington Circle; P.S. the "spiked shakes are a dream."

Burma *Burmese* | 22 | 11 | 20 | $23 |

Chinatown | 740 Sixth St. NW (bet. G & H Sts.) | 202-638-1280

"Out of sight" – both literally and figuratively – say fans of this "unassuming gem" with a "slightly obscure" second-story location in Chinatown that serves "well-prepared" "classic Burmese" fare like "hauntingly addictive" tea-leaf salad; decor is at "a minimum", but "kindly" service and "decent" tabs make up for the "plain" digs.

Burma Road *Burmese/Chinese* | 22 | 14 | 21 | $23 |

Gaithersburg | 617 S. Frederick Ave. (bet. Central Ave. & Westland Dr.), MD | 301-963-1429 | www.burmaroad.biz

Adventuresome eaters enjoy the "best of both worlds" at this Burmese-Chinese "match-up" in Gaithersburg, though most "order from the Burmese menu", judging the dishes "unique" and "authentic"; while its Asian-influenced decor and "ambiance could be improved", a "cordial" staff helps make this place one "to return to", especially since the "value is outstanding."

Busara *Thai* | 22 | 19 | 19 | $25 |

Reston | Reston Town Ctr. | 11964 Market St. (bet. Explore & Library Sts.), VA | 703-435-4188
Tysons Corner | 8142 Watson St. (International Dr.) | McLean, VA | 703-356-2288
www.busara.com

"Aromatic and flavorful" plates "presented well" in Tysons Corner and Reston business/shopping hubs make these tandem Thais a "good bet" for "business lunches" or an affordable "night out"; there's nary a straight line in Tysons' "glitzy" bright-blue-orange-and-red space, while Reston's earth tones and right angles are more staid – expect "expeditious" service at both.

☑ Busboys & Poets *American/Eclectic* | 22 | 22 | 21 | $23 |

Mt. Vernon Square/Convention Center | City Vista | 1025 Fifth St. NW (K St.) | 202-789-2227 ●

U Street Corridor | 2021 14th St. NW (V St.) | 202-387-7638 ●

NEW Hyattsville | 5331 Baltimore Ave. (bet. Hamilton & Jefferson Sts.), MD | 301-779-2787

Shirlington | Village at Shirlington | 4251 Campbell Ave. (Arlington Mill Dr.) | Arlington, VA | 703-379-9756 ●

www.busboysandpoets.com

"Is it a bookstore, a coffee shop, a restaurant or a space for activists to gather?" – it's "all of the above", and there's "never a dull moment" in these "friendly" and "happening" "polyglot hangouts" in the DC area; you can "surf the web" while enjoying "affordable" American-Eclectic fare to suit "pretty much any appetite", "grab drinks" at the bar (full range of caffeine and alcohol), "take in some poetry" or sink into one of the "comfy" chairs in the "funky" settings and talk "politics, books or movies."

☑ Buzz *Coffeehouse* | 22 | 20 | 21 | $11 |

Greater Alexandria | 901 Slaters Ln. (Potomac Greens Dr.) | Alexandria, VA | 703-600-2899 | www.buzzonslaters.com

Ballston | 818 N. Quincy St. (Wilson Blvd.) | Arlington, VA | 703-650-9676 | www.buzzbakery.com

"Wonderful" "snack options" – from "real food" like quiche and sammies to "creative" desserts – at everyday prices make these "friendly" Alexandria and Ballston bakery/cafes the DC area's No. 1 value; you can keep your "laptop blazing" while sipping "good coffee", perhaps with one of their signature cupcakes with "lick-your-fingers-good frosting", plus there's wine and beer at night to kindle a "nice 'buzz'" in the "cute", "retro" spaces.

Cacique *Mexican/Spanish* | 24 | 20 | 23 | $28 |

Frederick | 26 N. Market St. (Patrick St.), MD | 301-695-2756 | www.caciquefrederick.com

The "*muy bueno*" "mix of Spanish and Mexican" dishes are "full of flavor" and "reasonably priced", while the "excellent" margaritas and sangrias pack a punch at this "friendly" *posada* "in the heart of Frederick"; there may be more seating in the white-tablecloth interior, but the prime perches are in the "cramped" sidewalk area, "one of the best places to people-watch on Market Street."

Cactus Cantina *Tex-Mex* | 21 | 17 | 19 | $25 |

Cleveland Park | 3300 Wisconsin Ave. NW (Macomb St.) | 202-686-7222 | www.cactuscantina.com

"Never leave hungry and never leave broke" could be the motto of this "reliable" Cleveland Park Tex-Mex known for "enormous" helpings at "starving-artist prices" served by a "genuinely nice" staff; the sidewalk patio is huge, while the interior is "festive"

FOOD DECOR SERVICE COST

but "different than one might expect" (airy and relatively free of kitsch), and though it's "always packed" with "rowdy college kids" and those with "strollers", "somehow you always leave happy – it may be the margaritas."

Cafe Asia *Asian* | 21 | 16 | 18 | $24 |

Golden Triangle | 1720 I St. (bet. 17th & 18th Sts.) | 202-659-2696 | www.cafeasiadc.com ⧉
Rosslyn | 1550 Wilson Blvd. (N. Pierce St.), VA | 703-741-0870 | www.cafeasia.com

The "ultimate happy-hour places" for "twentysomethings", these clublike Pan-Asian purveyors in the Golden Triangle and Rosslyn are "always buzzing" at night, though they're "solid" "lunch spots" too, offering "consistently good" sushi plus a "vast" assortment of Asian staples; service is "so-so" and the "modern" interiors strike some as "sterile" and "cold", but hearts warm to the "affordable" tabs.

Café Bonaparte *French* | 23 | 20 | 18 | $29 |

Georgetown | 1522 Wisconsin Ave. NW (bet. P St. & Volta Pl.) | 202-333-8830 | www.cafebonaparte.com

Georgetown's "cute" "jewel box" of a French cafe "shines" with its "lovely", midpriced menu of "superb" crêpes, "steady" bistro fare plus "great" coffee and wine; while "service can be spotty" and "there's very little 'Elba' room" in this *très* "cozy corner of Paris", at least "they won't rush you", so *"bon appétit!"*

Cafe Deluxe *American* | 20 | 18 | 20 | $29 |

Cleveland Park | 3228 Wisconsin Ave. NW (Macomb St.) | 202-686-2233
Bethesda | 4910 Elm St. (Woodmont Ave.), MD | 301-656-3131
NEW Gaithersburg | Rio Entertainment Ctr. | 9811 Washingtonian Blvd. (Rio Blvd.), MD | 240-403-7082
Tysons Corner | 1800 International Dr. (Chain Bridge Rd.) | McLean, VA | 703-761-0600
www.cafedeluxe.com

"Classic American" "diner" meets "slightly upscale", "European"-feeling cafe at this "friendly" chainlet "popular" with "mixed age groups" for "reasonably priced", "well-prepared" "comfort food" of the kind "you wish your mom used to make"; lest the "decibel count" (beware the "screaming kids") detract, head outside and "linger awhile" on the "lovely" patios; P.S. the chain is a "favorite weekend brunch destination."

Cafe Divan *Turkish* | 24 | 20 | 20 | $32 |

Glover Park | Georgetown Hill Inn | 1834 Wisconsin Ave. NW (34th St.) | 202-338-1747 | www.cafedivan.com

The "refined" Turkish cuisine is "terrific" and "well priced" to boot, at this Ottoman outpost in Glover Park, one of the "few places" serving "Turkish wine" in the area; the "staff greets everyone with a smile", but "the shape of the restaurant's the most fun thing about it", since it's housed in the tip of a flatiron building (ergo you're almost "always near a window" in the "modern", almost sculptural space).

Café du Parc *French*

21 | 20 | 19 | $48

Downtown | Willard InterContinental Hotel |
1401 Pennsylvania Ave. NW (bet. 14th & 15th Sts.) |
202-942-7000 | www.cafeduparc.com

It's "so Parisian" to breakfast *en plein air* on the "pleasant" terrace at
this Downtown French brasserie in the Willard InterContinental or
dig into "inventive takes" on the classics in its blue-and-white dining
room (there's also a separate sidewalk cafe where one can "see the
White House" and "maybe even a politician or two"); sure it's
"crowded", "overpriced" and, being "French, how warm could the servers really be?", but Francophiles insist it's "very much the real thing."

Café Dupont *French*

21 | 21 | 20 | $44

Dupont Circle | Dupont Circle Hotel | 1500 New Hampshire Ave. NW
(19th St.) | 202-483-6000 | www.doylecollection.com

For professional "people-watchers" it's all about "location" – and
this French bistro in the Dupont Circle Hotel delivers with front-row
seats on a "nice" patio, plus a bank of floor-to-ceiling windows lining
the "cool, contemporary" dining room; though "a little pricey", the
Gallic offerings are quite "respectable", the "drinks are generous"
and the staff is "professional."

Cafe Milano ⏺ *Italian*

22 | 21 | 20 | $59

Georgetown | 3251 Prospect St. NW (bet. Potomac St. & Wisconsin Ave.) |
202-333-6183 | www.cafemilano.com

"Get your fabulous on before going" to DC's "'it' place": this
high-end Italian in Georgetown frequented by "pro athletes, politicians" and other "celebrities" who cavort in various "fancy"
dining nooks, some with zany ceiling frescoes (Milan Metro
map, Plácido Domingo); one can certainly "eat well" here (witness "fantastic" risotto, fish "cooked perfectly"), but "people-
watching" is the main event – just "don't expect the best service if
you aren't one of the watched."

Cafe Nola ⏺ *American*

24 | 20 | 22 | $25

Frederick | 4 E. Patrick St. (Market St.), MD | 301-694-6652 |
www.cafe-nola.com

"Expect quality" organic ingredients and "plenty" of "vegetarian
choices" on the New American menu of this all-purpose
coffeehouse/cafe where "local food and music" (and art) "come
together" in Frederick; the "laid-back", "granola" vibe pulses from
the "best" cappuccinos in the morning to "awesome infused" spirits
late at night.

Café Olé *Mediterranean*

20 | 14 | 17 | $27

Upper NW | 4000 Wisconsin Ave. NW (Upton St.) | 202-244-1330 |
www.cafeoledc.com

Tenleytown regulars remark "you can't go wrong" sampling the
"fresh and flavorful" Mediterranean meze at this "simple", peach-
colored Upper NW cafe that's "less pricey and more homey" than
many other DC tapas bars; service is solid, and it has a "pleasant"
patio that's a "relaxing" place to "sit around with friends."

	FOOD	DECOR	SERVICE	COST

Cafe Pizzaiolo *Italian/Pizza*　　24 | 17 | 21 | $20

Greater Alexandria | 1623 Fern St. (Kenwood Ave.) | Alexandria, VA |
703-717-9324
NEW Greater Alexandria | Cameron Station | 4906 Brenman Park Dr.
(Somervelle St.) | Alexandria, VA | 703-894-2250 Ⓜ
Arlington | 507 S. 23rd St. (Eads St.), VA | 703-894-2250
www.cafepizzaiolo.com

"Kids and parents are at ease" at these "friendly" Italian "neighborhood knockouts" where a low-stress, "no-fuss atmosphere" complete
with "board games and puzzles" sets the stage for "off-the-hook"
pies crafted from "simple, fresh ingredients" (the other menu items
are "good too"); decor may be "lacking", but takeout is always an
option and, hey, the "price is right."

❷ Café Renaissance *Continental*　　26 | 26 | 28 | $49

Vienna | 163 Glyndon St. SE (Maple Ave.), VA | 703-938-3311 |
www.caferenaissance.com

"Without a GPS", finding this "elegant, old-world" destination in a
Vienna strip mall takes some doing, but the "consistently outstanding" Continental menu and "fine choice of wines" served by "cordial",
"snappily dressed" waiters make it a "gem" worth hunting for; its intimate, "ornate and gilded" rooms are "romantic", furthering its sta-
tus as a "top choice in Vienna" for a "special", if pricey, meal.

Café Saint-Ex *Eclectic*　　20 | 17 | 18 | $33

Logan Circle | 1847 14th St. NW (T St.) | 202-265-7839 |
www.saint-ex.com

"Space is really tight" at this 14th Street "hangout", but an "interesting crowd" squeezes in for "comforting", midpriced Eclectic eats
and "amazing" brews doled out by a sometimes-"cooler-than-thou"
crew; on the ground floor a "clever aviation theme" flies below a
pretty tin ceiling, downstairs "doubles as a club" with a DJ Tuesday–
Saturday nights and sidewalk seating is "icing on the cake."

Cajun Experience *Cajun/Creole*　　∇ 23 | 16 | 19 | $23

Leesburg | 14 Loudoun St. SE (bet. Church & King Sts.), VA |
703-777-6580 | www.cajunexperience.biz

"Displaced Cajuns" rage about their 'experience' at this affordable
Leesburg Louisianan, musing that the food must be "transported
magically" from a kitchen in "Baton Rouge"; "real nice folks" patrol
the "simple" houselike digs, creating a down-home feel that's like
"being back in NO."

California Tortilla *Tex-Mex*　　22 | 16 | 21 | $11

Chinatown | Gallery Pl. | 728 Seventh St. NW (bet. G & H Sts.) |
202-638-2233
Cleveland Park | 3501 Connecticut Ave. NW (Ordway St.) | 202-244-2447
Bethesda | 4862 Cordell Ave. (bet. Norfolk & Woodmont Aves.),
MD | 301-654-8226
Olney | Olney Village Ctr. | 18101 Village Center Dr.
(Olney Sandy Spring Rd.), MD | 301-570-2522
Potomac | Cabin John Shopping Ctr. | 7727 Tuckerman Ln.
(Seven Locks Rd.), MD | 301-765-3600

(continued)

California Tortilla

Rockville | Rockville Town Sq. | 199 E. Montgomery Ave. (Courthouse Sq.), MD | 301-610-6500
Silver Spring | Burnt Mills Shopping Ctr. | 10721 Columbia Pike/ Colesville Rd. (Hillwood Dr.), MD | 301-593-3955
Greater Alexandria | Hoffman Town Ctr. | 301 Swamp Fox Rd. (Telegraph Rd.) | Alexandria, VA | 703-329-3333
Courthouse | 2057 Wilson Blvd. (bet. Courthouse Rd. & Uhle St.) | Arlington, VA | 703-243-4151
Fairfax | Fair Lakes Promenade Shopping Ctr. | 12239 Fair Lakes Pkwy. (Monument Dr.), VA | 703-278-0007
www.californiatortilla.com
Additional locations throughout the DC area

In "the fast-casual burrito wars" this homegrown chain defends its turf with "some of the best burritos for the money", but its secret weapon is a "sense of humor" extending from "friendly cashiers" to events like Jungle Noise Day to its colorful settings, each sporting a wall filled with "a stunning collection of piquant condiments" (some locations also have mix-your-own-soda stations); even if they're "not places you'd go to propose", they're a "first choice for a dinner with kids."

☑ Capital Grille *Steak*

| 26 | 25 | 26 | $62 |

Penn Quarter | 601 Pennsylvania Ave. NW (6th St.) | 202-737-6200
Chevy Chase | Wisconsin Pl. | 5310 Western Ave. (Wisconsin Ave.), MD | 301-718-7812
Tysons Corner | 1861 International Dr. (Leesburg Pike) | McLean, VA | 703-448-3900
www.thecapitalgrille.com

At these "clubby" steakhouses oozing "sophistication" and "swagger", "toothsome" slabs of beef are matched with "phenomenal" wine by "snazzy" looking servers who "remember who you are"; "you never know who you'll run into" ("members of Congress"?) at Penn Quarter, though all locations are "fine incarnations" of the genre, so expect "prices that reflect the quality."

CapMac *American*

| 23 | 13 | 21 | $10 |

Location varies; see website | 914-489-2897 | www.capmacdc.com

"Ooey-gooey" mac 'n' cheese topped with a "crunchy Cheez-It" crumble has tailgaters "chasing" this orange-and-yellow truck all over DC for what fans claim is a "delicacy more fit to be eaten from a porcelain bowl than a cardboard box"; the el cheapo elbows can be topped with meat and veggies for a small up-charge, while atmosphere is in the form of service "with a smile"; P.S. check website for schedule.

Capri *Italian*

| ▽ 23 | 20 | 25 | $41 |

McLean | Giant Shopping Ctr. | 6825 Redmond Dr. (Chain Bridge Rd.), VA | 703-288-4601 | www.caprimcleanva.com

"Old-school" waiters "work very hard" at this McLean "neighborhood joint" starring seafood "at its finest" and pastas "clearly cooked by someone in the know" (there's a "mama" in the kitchen) and served in a fairly "pleasing", sunny setting; though prices match the area's high-income demographics, it does offer a "true taste of Italy."

	FOOD	DECOR	SERVICE	COST

Caribbean Breeze *Nuevo Latino*

20 | 21 | 19 | $31

Ballston | 4100 N. Fairfax Dr. (Randolph St.) | Arlington, VA |
703-812-7997 | www.caribbeanbreezeva.com

"Everyone seems to be having such a great time" at this Ballston
Nuevo Latino where a "friendly", "laid-back" vibe inspires "great
happy hours" and makes eating "tasty" tapas "fun"; on top of that,
the "cool", colorful dancehall-sized space "turns into a salsa club
on Saturday nights."

Carlyle *American*

25 | 23 | 24 | $36

Shirlington | 4000 Campbell Ave. (Quincy St.) | Arlington, VA |
703-931-0777 | www.greatamericanrestaurants.com

Diners are "greeted with smiles and fed with kindness" – and "unchal-
lenging", "well-executed" New American eats – at this cavernous and
"classy" deco-esque brasserie in Shirlington that's priced for "everyday" but "good enough for special occasions"; hit the "noisy bar scene"
or head upstairs to dine where it's "more conducive to conversation";
P.S. no reservations, so "call ahead" to get on the "wait list."

Carmine's *Italian*

20 | 18 | 20 | $36

Penn Quarter | 425 Seventh St. NW (bet. D & E Sts.) | 202-737-7770 |
www.carminesnyc.com

"Hungry" *paesani* tie on "old-world feedbags" at this "family-
style tomato palace" in the Penn Quarter, feasting on "ginormous
portions" (meatballs like "baseballs") in a woody, 1930s-style
"barracks-sized dining hall" that rings with "loud" "conversation"
and "laughter"; servers are "always there" when needed, and most
leave sighing "money well spent", though a minority call the "assembly-line" experience "a bit stressful"; P.S. the bar menu is a
"best deal" for a twosome.

Carolina Kitchen *Southern*

25 | 23 | 23 | $24

Hyattsville | 6501 America Blvd. (East-West Hwy.), MD | 301-927-2929 |
www.thecarolinakitchen.com

See review in the Baltimore Directory.

Casa Oaxaca Ⓜ *Mexican*

22 | 16 | 17 | $32

Adams Morgan | 2106 18th St. NW (bet. California St. & Wyoming Ave.) |
202-387-2272 | www.oaxacaindc.com

"Holy mole!" it feels like "eating in a restaurant off the Zócalo" at
this "loud", "festive" Adams Morgan townhouse where the midpriced "authentic Mexican regional" menu includes a "variety" of
"incredible" mole and "exotic" treats that make you "forget
cheap Tex-Mex"; service is only "decent" but may seem better after
sampling the mojitos and caipirinhas "muddled to supremacy";
P.S. reservations required.

Cashion's Eat Place Ⓜ *American*

25 | 21 | 24 | $53

Adams Morgan | 1819 Columbia Rd. NW (bet. Biltmore St. &
Mintwood Pl.) | 202-797-1819 | www.cashionseatplace.com

"Expect to find something very special" at chef/co-owner John
Manolatos' Adams Morgan New American "neighborhood destina-

tion" with a "grown-up, slightly glam vibe", whose "informed" staff delivers seasonal, local dishes full of "delicious surprises"; "eclectic in every sense of the word", it's just as "perfect for date night" or "eating alone" at the central bar as for "people-watching" from its sidewalk patio or enjoying an "upscale brunch at not-upscale prices" (it's more costly but still "worth the money" at night).

Cassatt's Café   *New Zealand* | 20 | 17 | 17 | $23 |

Arlington | 4536 Lee Hwy. (Woodstock St.), VA | 703-527-3330 | www.cassattscafe.com

With "the best flat white this side of Wellington", kiwi coffee clutchers also praise Arlington's native New Zealander for its "awesome brunch", "great" desserts and other-hemisphere "noshes" at budget prices; the staff is "efficient" and the "pleasant, "arty" decor – featuring rotating works by local artists, "some of whom train in the basement" here – would make the cafe's namesake Impressionist proud.

Caucus Room ⊠ *American* | 23 | 25 | 24 | $63 |

Penn Quarter | 401 Ninth St. NW (D St.) | 202-393-1300 | www.thecaucusroom.com

"Lobbyists cutting deals" "wow" clients and "power brokers" with "truly old-school", "expense-account eating" (featuring "succulent steaks", natch) in a "traditional clubby atmosphere" with service to match at this Penn Quarter New American; "you get what you pay for, however, you pay quite a bit" – though Social Reform, the casual bar/lounge up front, offers a more democratically priced menu.

Cava Mezze   *Greek* | 25 | 20 | 21 | $34 |

Capitol Hill | 527 Eighth St. SE (Pennsylvania Ave.) | 202-543-9090
Rockville | 9713 Traville Gateway Dr. (Shady Grove Rd.), MD | 301-309-9090
NEW Clarendon | 2940 Clarendon Blvd. (Fillmore St.), VA | 703-276-9090
www.cavamezze.com

The "flaming cheese" will "light up your palate" as well as the "dark" "caverns" that house this moderately priced Greek chainlet that also wows with "diptastic" spreads and "bold" small plates; "generous" staffers ferry "potent" cocktails that help fuel the "high decibel levels."

Cava Mezze Grill   *Greek* | 22 | 15 | 18 | $15 |

NEW Columbia Heights | 3105 14th St. NW (bet. Irving & Kenyon Sts.) | 202-695-8100
Bethesda | 4832 Bethesda Ave. (bet. Arlington Rd. & Woodmont Ave.), MD | 301-656-1772
NEW Tysons Corner | Tysons Corner Ctr. | 8048 Tysons Corner Ctr. (bet. Chain Bridge Rd. & Westpark Dr.) | McLean, VA | 703-288-0005
www.cavagrill.com

At these "in-and-out" Greek spots (a spin-off concept from sit-down parent Cava Mezze), "delicious" pitas, bowls or salads are assembled "Chipotle-style" in a "pick-what-you-like"-for-toppings line by "fast", "friendly" crews; "fast-food prices" and raw-industrial settings that are "nicer than similar" spots draw a cava-lcade of fans.

FOOD | DECOR | SERVICE | COST

Cedar Restaurant *American*

23 | 19 | 22 | $46

Penn Quarter | 822 E St. NW (bet. 8th & 9th Sts.) | 202-637-0012 | www.cedardc.com

This "chic basement hideout" with "fine", if pricey, New American fare is an "appealing stop on the Penn Quarter circuit" for "first dates", "pre-theater dinners" and "post-work drinks"; a "tall wall of mirrors" and "tree murals well disguise" the fact that it's "below ground", and the "engaging" staff lends a *Cheers* quality to it."

Ceiba *Nuevo Latino*

24 | 22 | 23 | $45

Downtown | 701 14th St. NW (G St.) | 202-393-3983 | www.ceibarestaurant.com

"Different and delightful" Nuevo Latino fare awakens the "passion in your palate" in an "exuberant" and "elegant" Downtown setting where "singles" often meet over "creative cocktails" at the bar or in the low-lit, modern lounge area; it's a Goldilocks kind of place, with "not too much, not too little" service, and though not cheap (except for the "competitively priced" happy hour), you can go "with confidence."

☷ Central Michel

26 | 21 | 23 | $54

Richard ☒ *American/French*

Penn Quarter | 1001 Pennsylvania Ave. NW (11th St.) | 202-626-0015 | www.centralmichelrichard.com

"Proving Michel Richard doesn't need beaucoup bucks to be brilliant", his "high-energy brasserie" in Penn Quarter dazzles with its "outstanding" riffs on tradition that run from New American (fried chicken that "slaps the Colonel in the face") to French ("I'm going to marry their faux gras"); a "welcoming" staff and a "casual" vibe let ordinary folk feel like the "movers and shakers" that line the "striking" "modern" dining room and "hopping" bar – in short, a "winner."

NEW Cesco Osteria *Italian*

19 | 21 | 18 | $46

Bethesda | Bethesda Metro | 7401 Woodmont Ave. (bet. Edgemoor & Montgomery Lns.), MD | 301-654-8333 | www.cesco-osteria.com

Longtime followers of "real Tuscan chef" Francesco Ricchi praise a "good move" to fresh, comparatively "cavernous" digs in Bethesda, where he's added a dash of "fun" (happy hour at the huge bar, live music) while maintaining an Italian menu that "does not disappoint"; prices remain high, and mixed service marks suggest there are still a few kinks, but the "beautiful" wood-lined interior and huge patio with "flaming torches" are "enjoyable."

C.F. Folks ☒ *Eclectic*

24 | 10 | 20 | $19

Dupont Circle | 1225 19th St. NW (bet. M & N Sts.) | 202-293-0162 | www.cffolksrestaurant.com

"It's time someone declared" this Eclectic luncheonette below Dupont Circle "a national treasure" say longtime loyalists who depend daily on its "gourmet" "homestyle" eats like "can't-go-wrong" sandwiches, some of DC's "best" crab cakes and "delicious" specials; its "counter is packed with Washington power" and regulars who swear the staff's "friendly/edgy attitude grows on you"; P.S. if it's too "cramped", "eat outside", or take it to go.

	FOOD	DECOR	SERVICE	COST

Charlie Palmer Steak ☒ *Steak*   26 | 26 | 25 | $69

Capitol Hill | 101 Constitution Ave. NW (bet. 1st St. & Louisiana Ave.) | 202-547-8100 | www.charliepalmer.com

You might "find your congressman" at this "top-end" Capitol Hill chophouse, where lobbyists get "whiplash" scanning the "sleek, so-phisticated" room, and tourists are awed by "wonderful views of the Capitol" from the window tables; it's "pricey", of course, but the steaks are "cooked to perfection" (there's "excellent" fish too) and complemented by "fabulous" American wines, and "even if you're not a VIP", you'll be treated like one.

Chart House *Seafood*   23 | 25 | 23 | $45

Old Town | 1 Cameron St. (N. Union St.) | Alexandria, VA | 703-684-5080 | www.chart-house.com

A "wonderful view" of the Potomac and an "especially nice" outdoor patio are the main reasons to chart course to this "classic"-looking dockside seafooder in Old Town, but bolstering the case are the "fantastic" fin fare and prime rib, plus a "fabulous" salad bar; aye, cap'n, it's priced for "once-in-a-while" dining, but "attentive" ser-vice and the "incredible" location make it a popular "place to take visitors" or mark a "special occasion."

NEW Chasin' Tails *Cajun/Creole*   - | - | - | I

Arlington | 2200 N. Westmoreland St. (Washington St.), VA | 703-538-2565 | www.chasintailscrawfish.com

The main event at this sporty, new brick-walled watering hole in Greater Arlington (near Falls Church) takes place when robustly seasoned crawfish, boiled in a bag, are dumped on the table, and folks roll up their sleeves and dig in; for those diners not up for messy, hands-on eating, the menu offers other easy-on-the wallet Cajun-Creole specialties.

☑ Cheesecake Factory *American*   24 | 22 | 22 | $30

Upper NW | Chevy Chase Pavilion | 5345 Wisconsin Ave. NW (Western Ave.) | 202-364-0500
White Flint | White Flint Mall | 11301 Rockville Pike (Nicholson Ln.) | Rockville, MD | 301-770-0999
Clarendon | Market Common Clarendon | 2900 N. Wilson Blvd. (Fillmore St.), VA | 703-294-9966
Fairfax | Fair Oaks Shopping Ctr. | 11778 Fair Oaks Mall (Lee Jackson Memorial Hwy.), VA | 703-273-6600
Tysons Corner | Tysons Galleria | 1796 International Dr. (Chain Bridge Rd.) | McLean, VA | 703-506-9311
Sterling | Dulles Town Ctr. | 21076 Dulles Town Circle (Nokes Blvd.), VA | 703-444-9002
www.thecheesecakefactory.com
See review in the Baltimore Directory.

Chef Geoff's *American*   21 | 19 | 20 | $36

Downtown | 1301 Pennsylvania Ave. NW (E St.) | 202-464-4461
Upper NW | 3201 New Mexico Ave. NW (Lowell St.) | 202-237-7800

(continued)

(continued)

Chef Geoff's

Tysons Corner | Fairfax Sq. | 8045 Leesburg Pike (Gallows Rd.) | Vienna, VA | 571-282-6003
www.chefgeoff.com

"Solid American food with some tasty twists" that's "fairly priced", and dished up in "vibrant" environs is the format at Geoff Tracy's bistros in the DC area; they all have "active" bar scenes, with "two-fisted" happy hours, yet they're "surprisingly kid-friendly", which can make them "cacophonous" – still, adept service and "great gluten-free offerings" help keep them "busy."

Chesapeake Room   *American/Seafood* | 20 | 21 | 19 | $38 |

Capitol Hill | 501 Eighth St. SE (E St.) | 202-543-1445 | www.thechesapeakeroom.com

Arguably DC's "coolest" 300-plus–gallon fish tank hovers over the bar in this Barracks Row bistro, handsomely decorated with maple trim, leather seats and oil paintings, and serving "reliably good" American fare that sources local surf 'n' turf; service is solid, and the prices are right, giving it "lots of potential", though it may be "best enjoyed in warm weather, when you can sit on the large", luxe patio.

NEW Chez Billy Ⓜ *French* | - | - | - | M |

Petworth | 3815 Georgia Ave. NW (bet. Quincy & Randolph Sts.) | 202-506-2080 | www.chezbilly.com

At this French bistro in Petworth's landmarked Billy Simpson's building, flickering candles and ornate chandeliers cast a glow over its bi-level bar, while the separate dining room sparkles with verve and class with its wood-backed booths, vintage lighting and tiled floor; in both settings, moderately priced favorites like mussels, steak frites and duck confit are enjoyed with classic cocktails, French wines and international beers by its cosmopolitan clientele.

Chicken on the Run   *Chicken/Peruvian* | 24 | 11 | 19 | $14 |

Bethesda | 4933 St. Elmo Ave. (Old Georgetown Rd.), MD | 301-652-9004 | www.chickenbethesda.com

"Fabulous Peruvian spit-roasted chicken" and deep-fried yuca have Bethesdans racing to this counter-serve joint where "cheap" prices and "huge portions" add up to a big "bang for your buck"; there's "no decor" and minimal seating, so "takeout" may be the way to go – just be warned that your car may "smell so good you can hardly wait to get your order home."

Chima   *Brazilian* | 26 | 24 | 25 | $58 |

Tysons Corner | 8010 Towers Crescent Dr. (Leesburg Pike) | Vienna, VA | 703-639-3080 | www.chimasteakhouse.com

"You'll never want to eat again, but in a good way" after a trip to this "high-class rodizio" in Tysons Corner, with its "never-ending" parade of meat backed by a "salad bar the length of a bus" ("get your money's worth"); the waiters running around with "swords" are "a hoot", yet the "chic", "contemporary", Brazilian wood-accented environs make for a "classy night" out.

	FOOD	DECOR	SERVICE	COST

China Bistro *Chinese*

| 24 | 9 | 17 | $15 |

Rockville | 755 Hungerford Dr. (Martins Ln.), MD | 301-294-0808
"Dumplings, dumplings, dumplings" are the draw at this "casual" Rockville Asian counter-serve, where a Chinese 'mama' with a "golden touch turns out luscious" packets of "homemade goodness" (along with other "authentic" eats) at "attractive" prices; prime-time "lines" and sometimes "not friendly" service don't deter fans, and while a post-Survey remodel spruced it up a bit, it's still not ritzy.

China Garden *Chinese*

| 22 | 16 | 18 | $29 |

Rosslyn | Twin Towers | 1100 Wilson Blvd., 2nd fl. (bet. Kent & Lynn Sts.), VA | 703-525-5317 | www.chinagardenva.com
"Chinese tour buses disgorge" loads of tourists for the "yum yum" dim sum (weekends only) at this "reliable", "reasonably priced" Rosslynite that's "efficient at moving large crowds through"; the "huge" office tower venue has uninspiring "standard Chinese restaurant" decor, but locals say it works for a "super-fast lunch" during the week, when it offers a "varied menu" of Cantonese cuisine.

China Jade *Chinese*

| 25 | 18 | 22 | $21 |

Rockville | 16805 Crabbs Branch Way (Shady Grove Rd.), MD | 301-963-1570 | www.chinajaderockville.com
This "authentic" Chinese in a Rockville shopping center may feel "halfway to China" for some, but is "worth" a drive on account of its "complex yet well-balanced" Sichuan and Cantonese specialties; the typical digs are pleasant enough, and patrons appreciate the cheap tabs and "friendly", "helpful" staffers.

China Star *Chinese*

| 24 | 14 | 16 | $19 |

Fairfax | Fair City Mall | 9600 Main St. (Pickett Rd.), VA | 703-323-8822
"There is no need to ask for extra-spicy" at this Fairfax strip-mall spot: the "authentic" Sichuan cuisine "tortures" the tongues of the biggest heat-seekers (for those who cower at the low end of the Scoville heat scale, there's also a roster of Americanized Chinese fare); service is "not the greatest", and there's "zero atmosphere", but it's still a "wonderful buy."

Chinatown Express *Chinese*

| 23 | 8 | 15 | $17 |

Chinatown | 746 Sixth St. NW (H St.) | 202-638-0424
"C'mon, you didn't come here for the decor" say those who stand "transfixed at the entrance ogling" the "guy making noodles and dumplings in the window" before descending into Chinatown's "dirt-cheap" den for noodles "tasty and chewy" enough to ensure you "steer clear of the rest" of the standard eats; service is so "quick" here, "they practically throw the food at you."

Ching Ching Cha *Tearoom*

| ▽ 20 | 25 | 25 | $21 |

Georgetown | 1063 Wisconsin Ave. NW (M St.) | 202-333-8288 | www.chingchingcha.com
"Cheaper than a massage but almost as effective" coo visitors to this "tranquil" Chinese tearoom in Georgetown, where lounging on plush pillows and being treated by serene servers provides "a cool, quiet get-

FOOD | DECOR | SERVICE | COST

away" from busy lives; more than 70 freshly brewed teas dominate a menu with a modest selection of "snacks" like dumplings and cookies that perhaps work "better for relaxing than [as] a full meal."

Chop't Creative Salad *American* 21 | 14 | 19 | $12

Chinatown | 730 Seventh St. NW (bet. G & H Sts.) | 202-347-3225
Downtown | Metro Ctr. | 618 12th St. NW (G St.) | 202-783-0007
Dupont Circle | 1300 Connecticut Ave. NW (N St.) | 202-327-2255
Farragut | 1629 K St. NW (17th St.) | 202-688-0333 ⑤
Golden Triangle | 1105 19th St. NW (L St.) | 202-955-0665 ⑤
Northeast | Union Station | 50 Massachusetts Ave. NE (Capitol St.) | 202-688-0330
Rosslyn | 1735 N. Lynn St. (Wilson Blvd.), VA | 703-875-2888
www.choptsalad.com

The mixmasters behind the counters "keep things moving at a fast clip" – er, chop – at these "high-volume", "assembly-line" lunch spots that offer a "bewildering variety of salad" fixin's for "customizable" bowls (they also have wraps); wilted wallets worry they're paying "too much green for the greens", but most health-seekers find the "gigantic" "end products" "worth" the mild "splurge."

Chutzpah *Deli* 23 | 12 | 18 | $18

Fairfax | Fairfax Towne Ctr. | 12214 Fairfax Towne Ctr. (Monument Dr.), VA | 703-385-8883 | www.chutzpahdeli.com

"Sandwiches too big to finish in one sitting" plus "delicious" breakfast items and other "authentic" deli favorites answer the "craving" for "Jewish soul food" at this Fairfax shopping-center noshery; some say oy vey about the authentically "surly" service and "NYC-style" check, but even if "you'll never confuse this with a real NY deli", it's "not a bad start for Northern Virginia."

Circa *American* 20 | 21 | 20 | $32

Dupont Circle | 1601 Connecticut Ave. NW (Q St.) | 202-667-1601 | www.circaatdupont.com ●
NEW Foggy Bottom | 2221 I St. NW (22nd St.) | 202-506-5589 | www.circaatfoggybottom.com ●
Clarendon | 3010 Clarendon Blvd. (Garfield St.), VA | 703-522-3010 | www.circaatclarendon.com

These "sleek, trendy" New American bistros in Dupont Circle, Foggy Bottom and Clarendon are "hopping" meet-up spots, where "consistently solid" food with the "right level of creative flair" anchors "vibrant bar" scenes chock-full of "twentysomethings"; staff members are generally "helpful" and the prices "fair", but you have to be "lucky to snag" a table in one of the "lovely" outdoor areas.

Circle Bistro *American* 20 | 17 | 19 | $46

West End | One Washington Circle Hotel | 1 Washington Circle NW (L St.) | 202-293-5390 | www.thecirclehotel.com

At this West Ender "hidden" in a hotel, a "small but well-balanced menu" of "fine" New American dishes is ferried to tables by "attentive" help; its "quiet, simply decorated" earth-toned dining room, bar/lounge with fireplace and "sweet", secret-feeling patio are so "convenient to the Kennedy Center" that "more people should know about" it – and its "bargain" pre-theater menu.

Citronelle *French*
(aka Michel Richard Citronelle)

– | – | – | VE

Georgetown | Latham Hotel | 3000 M St. NW (30th St.) | 202-625-2150 | www.citronelledc.com

Michel Richard's modern French flagship in Georgetown is temporarily closed at press time due to water damage to the hotel housing it; it is expected to reopen in early 2013.

City Lights of China *Chinese*

19 | 13 | 18 | $26

Dupont Circle | 1731 Connecticut Ave. NW (bet. R & S Sts.) | 202-265-6688 | www.citylightsofchina.com
Bethesda | 4820 Bethesda Ave. (Woodmont Ave.), MD | 301-913-9501 | www.bethesdacitylightsofchina.com

"Large portions" of "cheap", "classic" Chinese "standards" ("crispy beef" is the "standout") have kept these "friendly" and "reliable" Dupont Circle and Bethesda joints going for years; given their "hole-in-the-wall" looks, happily they're known for "fast delivery."

☒ CityZen 🅂🅼 *American*

27 | 27 | 27 | $115

SW | Mandarin Oriental | 1330 Maryland Ave. SW (12th St.) | 202-787-6006 | www.mandarinoriental.com

Chef Eric Ziebold "delivers taste, imagination and fun" via a multi-course menu that adds up to a "fabulous meal full of pleasant surprises" at this "stunningly beautiful" "Nouvelle American" "destination" in the Mandarin Oriental; a "personal touch from the minute you walk in the door" enhances the experience, which leads flush foodies to exult "fine dining is still alive and worth every cent"; P.S. the "very hip" bar offers a "real-bargain" tasting menu.

☒ Clyde's ● *American*

22 | 23 | 22 | $33

Chinatown | Gallery Pl. | 707 Seventh St. NW (bet. G & H Sts.) | 202-349-3700
Georgetown | Georgetown Park Mall | 3236 M St. NW (bet. Potomac St. & Wisconsin Ave.) | 202-333-9180
Chevy Chase | 5441 Wisconsin Ave. (bet. Montgomery St. & Wisconsin Circle), MD | 301-951-9600
Rockville | 2 Preserve Pkwy. (bet. Tower Oaks Blvd. & Wootton Pkwy.), MD | 301-294-0200
Greater Alexandria | Mark Ctr. | 1700 N. Beauregard St. (bet. Rayburn Ave. & Seminary Rd.) | Alexandria, VA | 703-820-8300
Reston | Reston Town Ctr. | 11905 Market St. (bet. Reston & Town Ctr. Pkwys.), VA | 703-787-6601
Tysons Corner | 8332 Leesburg Pike (Rte. 123) | Vienna, VA | 703-734-1901
Broadlands | Willow Creek Farm | 42920 Broadlands Blvd. (bet. Belmont Ridge Rd. & Claiborne Pkwy.), VA | 571-209-1200
www.clydes.com

"Nostalgic" themes (old farmhouse, Adirondack lodge, the Golden Age of Travel) make each location of this homegrown American saloon feel like a "unique" "adventure", so it's no wonder they're "popular" stops for everyone from "kids" to "grandma" – indeed, they're Greater

DC's Most Popular places to dine; "upbeat" service also plays a role, along with the fact that diners are sure to "get their money's worth" via a "value"-packed menu of "solidly appealing", "honest" eats.

Coal Fire *Pizza*   22 | 18 | 20 | $21

NEW **Frederick** | 7820 Wormans Mill Rd. (Rte. 15), MD | 301-631-2625
Gaithersburg | 116 Main St. (Kentlands Blvd.), MD |
301-519-2625
www.coalfireonline.com
See review in the Baltimore Directory.

Z Coastal Flats *Seafood*   24 | 22 | 23 | $30

Fairfax | Fairfax Corner | 11901 Grand Commons Ave. (Monument Dr.),
VA | 571-522-6300
Tysons Corner | Tysons Corner Ctr. | 7860 Tysons Corner Ctr.
(International Dr.) | McLean, VA | 703-356-1440
www.greatamericanrestaurants.com
"To-die-for" crab cakes, "overflowing" lobster rolls and loads of other "plate-licking" piscatorial preparations reel in Tysons Corner and Fairfax mall shoppers to these midpriced "islandy" "theme parks" (colorful decor, sculptures of underwater critters hanging overhead) sporting "lively bar scenes"; the resulting "madhouse" crowds are "well managed" by "Johnny-on-the-spot" serving teams – still, to avoid waits, "go early or call ahead."

Co Co. Sala ● *Eclectic*   24 | 24 | 21 | $41

Penn Quarter | 929 F St. NW (bet. 9th & 10th Sts.) | 202-347-4265 |
www.cocosala.com
"Chocoholics'" "dreams are answered" at this "sexy" Penn Quarter Eclectic lounge, where "snazzy" decor (curvy ceilings, shimmering walls) and staffers who "enjoy" themselves set the stage for "clever sweet and savory takes" on the cocoa bean – "decadent" desserts, sure, but "even the salad" is chocolaty; "small plates meant for savoring, not devouring" may leave big eaters "hungry" and with an "emptier wallet", but "sweet tooths" swear it's "worth the investment."

Columbia Firehouse *American*   23 | 23 | 22 | $35

Old Town | 109 S. Asaph St. (King St.) | Alexandria, VA | 703-683-1776 |
www.columbiafirehouse.com
Old Town's "cool remake of an old firehouse" offers a "moderately" priced American menu alight with "interesting twists", served by an "attentive" crew amid "lots of seating options": an "airy" exposed-brick atrium, a "classy" upstairs salon and a "charming" patio; but it's at its best, perhaps, when one is sipping "tasty, old-fashioned drinks" with the "power brokers" in the "beautiful" barroom.

Comet Ping Pong *Pizza*   20 | 15 | 16 | $25

Upper NW | 5037 Connecticut Ave. NW (Nebraska Ave.) | 202-364-0404 |
www.cometpingpong.com
When this Upper Northwest "pizza, Ping-Pong and live music" venue is on its game, it's a "fun place" for "cheap" "family outings" or an "unusual date", with "crunchy" New Haven–style pies and "addictive" wings; it loses points for its warehouse decor, "uncomfortable"

bench seating and a half-hearted serve from the "so-so" staff, but paddle partisans call it a winner, citing, duh, free "Ping-Pong!"

Commissary *American* 19 | 17 | 18 | $24

Logan Circle | 1443 P St. NW (bet. 14th & 15th Sts.) | 202-299-0018 | www.commissarydc.com

All-in-one bar/coffeehouse/restaurant, Logan Circle's "refreshingly inexpensive", "cozy" "neighborhood dive" does it all with a "solid" American menu "broad enough to suit just about anyone", "comfortable" armchairs and "free WiFi"; locals "doing some work" or "meeting up" for happy hour appreciate a "welcoming" vibe from the staff.

Comus Inn Ⓜ *American* 20 | 24 | 22 | $46

Dickerson | 23900 Old Hundred Rd. (Comus Rd.), MD | 301-349-5100 | www.thecomusinn.com

Dining "out in the middle of nowhere" has its charms when "magnificent" views of Sugarloaf Mountain set the stage for "romantic" dinners, "lovely" receptions, a scenic brunch or "happy hour on the patio" at this historic Montgomery County farmhouse; its "perfectly good" New American fare strikes some as "overpriced" – still, the staff makes everyone "feel like a celebrity"; P.S. reservations are "a must"; closed Monday and Tuesday.

Coppi's Organic *Italian* 23 | 20 | 20 | $34

U Street Corridor | 1414 U St. NW (bet. 14th & 15th Sts.) | 202-319-7773 | www.coppisorganic.com

Spinning "flavorful" wood-fired pizzas plus "tasty" entrees amid "bicycling memorabilia" honoring its namesake racing cyclist, this "cozy" Ligurian is a "great value for the money", even if it's a "bit steep" for U Street; fans also dig the "dimly lit" date-night setting, "attentive" service and "sustainable", "organic shtick."

🄩 Corduroy 🄢 *American* 28 | 25 | 26 | $68

Mt. Vernon Square/Convention Center | 1122 Ninth St. NW (bet. L & M Sts.) | 202-589-0699 | www.corduroydc.com

"Every morsel from the kitchen is a thing of beauty", and matched by "excellent" wines, at Tom Power's "civilized" New American in a townhouse opposite the Convention Center; service that's "polished yet the antithesis of stuffy" and "clean-lined", "modern" decor both strike a balance between "elegant" and "casual", adding up to an "expensive but worth it" experience; P.S. the "hideaway upstairs bar" offers what may be the "best" three-course "bar bargain" in town.

Cork Ⓜ *American* 25 | 22 | 23 | $44

Logan Circle | 1720 14th St. NW (bet. R & S Sts.) | 202-265-2675 | www.corkdc.com

At this über-trendy Logan Circle wine bar, "a huge array of wines by the glass without an outrageous mark-up" is paired with "delightful" New American small plates with an "extra edge of creativity" courtesy of chef Robert Weland (ex Poste); the "well-informed" staff doubles as "eye candy" in the "stylish", brick-walled, "dimly-lit" space that gets "loud" and "crowded" late, so best come "early."

	FOOD	DECOR	SERVICE	COST

Cosmopolitan Grill ⓜ *E European*   ▽ 27 | 17 | 24 | $31

Greater Alexandria | 7770 Richmond Hwy. (Belford Dr.) | Alexandria, VA | 703-360-3660 | www.restaurant-cosmopolitan.com

"Great goulash", "Wiener schnitzel like your mother used to make" and other "wonderful" Balkan specialties at "reasonable prices" make this "hidden gem" a nice alternative in Alexandria; "high standards of hospitality" are upheld, and the "no-frills" decor leaves guests to focus on "food not found everywhere."

The Counter *Burgers*   21 | 15 | 18 | $17

Reston | Reston Town Ctr. | 11922 Democracy Dr. (Bluemont Way), VA | 703-796-1008 | www.thecounterburger.com

"Bring your appetite and creative spirit" to this "friendly" Reston branch of a West Coast chain for the "drool-worthy" burgers "made to your liking" with near-"endless" options for customization; supporters cite a "stylish" industrial setting and low cost, and wonder "who can resist" the 'adult' milkshakes that make good use of the full bar.

Crème *Southern*   21 | 16 | 19 | $31

U Street Corridor | 1322 U St. NW (13th St.) | 202-234-1884

"Brunch!" is the word on this "cool" Southern belle on U Street, where folks "stand in line" on weekends for "delicious every-which-way Benedicts" and hearty fare like chicken and waffles; the "tiny", industrial digs serve as a reliable "date" or "meeting spot" for dinner too, bolstered by solid service and everyday tabs.

Crisp & Juicy *Chicken/Peruvian*   24 | 10 | 17 | $13

Upper NW | 4533 Wisconsin Ave. (River Rd.) | 202-966-1222
Gaithersburg | 18312 Contour Rd. (Lost Knife Rd.), MD | 301-355-7377
Rockville | Sunshine Sq. | 1331 Rockville Pike (Templeton Pl.), MD | 301-251-8833
Silver Spring | 1314 E. West Hwy. (Colesville Rd.), MD | 301-563-6666
Silver Spring | Leisure World Plaza | 3800 International Dr. (Georgia Ave.), MD | 301-598-3333
Wheaton | Westfield Wheaton | 11160 Veirs Mill Rd. (University Blvd. W.), MD | 301-962-6666
Arlington | 4540 Lee Hwy. (Woodstock St.), VA | 703-243-4222
Falls Church | 913 W. Broad St. (bet. Spring & West Sts.), VA | 703-241-9091
www.crispjuicy.com

"Lip-smacking" rotisserie chicken "falls off the bone" at these Peruvian counter joints where fried yuca and other "tasty" sides "complete the feast" – still, their real "secret" is a dipping sauce so addictive some wonder if they "mix crack in"; bar cooking at home, it may be one of the "cheapest ways to feed a family", but "nonexistent" service and decor leave some squawking "takeout preferred."

Crystal Thai *Thai*   23 | 18 | 20 | $25

Arlington | Arlington Forest Shopping Ctr. | 4819 Arlington Blvd. (Park Dr.), VA | 703-522-1311 | www.crystalthai.com

"An early standout" on the Thai restaurant scene is this aging Arlingtonian, whose "loyal patrons" keep coming back to its "pleasant" Eastern-accented dining room, dressed up by "friendly" servers in traditional attire; classic dishes, like its "dream-come-true" crispy fish, and "reasonable" prices, especially at lunch, seal the deal.

Cuba de Ayer ⓜ *Cuban*　　　25 | 17 | 23 | $24

Burtonsville | 15446 Old Columbia Pike (Spencerville Rd.), MD | 301-476-9622 | www.cubadeayerrestaurant.com

A real "asset to Burtonsville" is this "unassuming" Cuban "gem" where "authentic", "*muy rico*" benchmarks of its native cuisine come to the table at prices reflecting its "down-home sensibility"; despite "unremarkable" dinerlike decor, the "lively" salsa soundtrack and "gracious" staff "welcome" make a visit feel like a "vacation"; P.S. reservations recommended.

Cuba Libre Restaurant & Rum Bar　*Cuban*　　20 | 24 | 20 | $38

Penn Quarter | 801 Ninth St. NW (H St.) | 202-408-1600 | www.cubalibrerestaurant.com

Leave Penn Quarter behind via this "over-the-top", "Disney"-esque nuevo Cubano where an "Old Havana" town "plaza" – complete with wrought-iron balconies, lush plants and street lamps – offers "plenty of room to rumba" when not partaking of the comparatively "toned-down" fare; still, the "reasonably priced" plates "come quickly", and "inspiring" rum drinks ("grilled pineapple" mojito, anyone?) complete the "transporting" affair.

Cubano's　*Cuban*　　　　　23 | 19 | 21 | $32

Silver Spring | 1201 Fidler Ln. (Georgia Ave.), MD | 301-563-4020 | www.cubanosrestaurant.com

No "government license to travel" is needed to partake of "authentic" ropa vieja or lechón asado at this "relaxed" Cuban joint "hidden away" in Silver Spring; its mojitos "will light up your experience" and, along with "friendly" servers, lend an "upbeat" vibe to the already "colorful" space, making the "pricey"-for-the-genre ticket price "worth it."

NEW Curious Grape Wine, Dine & Shop ⓜ *Eclectic*　　- | - | - | M

Shirlington | Shirlington Vill. | 2900 S. Quincy St. (bet. Campbell Ave. & Randolph St.) | Arlington, VA | 703-671-8700 | www.curiousgrape.com

The name says it all at Shirlington's all-in-one bastion of Bacchus: part wine shop and part spiffy wine bar/restaurant serving a full Eclectic dinner menu (with budget-friendly half-size options), as well as cheese and charcuterie, to pair with vino at a circular bar or at tables in the urbane dining room; as if that weren't enough, there's also an all-day cafe and specialty market.

Curry Mantra　*Indian*　　▽ 23 | 20 | 22 | $27

Fairfax | 9984 Main St. (bet. Fairfax Sq. & Tedrich Blvd.) | Fairfax City, VA | 703-218-8128 | www.dccurrymantra.com

Indian-food lovers praise this Fairfax standard bearer's "fresh and pungent and very authentic" regional specialties, featuring many vegetarian dishes, served with aplomb in a dining room that recently doubled in size, warmed by "memorable" curry-colored decor; its lunch buffet is a "great-value" way to try lots of "different foods" at once.

Da Domenico ⓩ *Italian*   23 | 19 | 24 | $40

Tysons Corner | 1992 Chain Bridge Rd. (Leesburg Pike) | McLean, VA | 703-790-9000

There's a "campy", "old-school feel" (nonna and nonno "would have loved this place in 1950") to this fancy, candlelit Tysons Corner "staple" where "roaming" singers occasionally break into "arias" as "attentive" servers deliver "tasty" Southern Italian fare; regulars insist it has the "world's best veal chop", while the opera-adverse note the live performances are Friday and Saturday nights only.

Dangerously   21 | 13 | 18 | $15
Delicious Pies *American/Bakery*

Atlas District | 1339 H St. NE (bet. 13th & 14th Sts.) | 202-398-7437 ●

www.dangerouspiesdc.com

"Tempting treats" lure ardent calorie-counters to these "hip" but "tiny" bakeries in DC and Baltimore selling "scratch"-made "slices of heaven" in the form of sweet and savory pies; skeptics scoff it's best known for "being on the Food Network" (maybe that explains "premium" prices), but crust-cravers parry it "ain't pretty, but it sure is good"; P.S. DC denizens should keep an eye out for the food truck.

Daniel O'Connell's ● *Pub Food*   20 | 23 | 20 | $29

Old Town | 112 King St. (bet. Lee & Union Sts.) | Alexandria, VA | 703-739-1124 | www.danieloconnells.com

This "rambling" tavern (it's "like four pubs in one") may be the "classiest" spot in Old Town to savor "a good pint" while "sitting by the fireplace" thanks to "quaint" Emerald Isle decor with plenty o' "old-world style"; the "slightly upscale" pub grub may be "an afterthought", but it's perfectly "fine", moderately priced and served by an amenable staff.

DC Coast *American*   23 | 22 | 23 | $52

Downtown | Tower Bldg. | 1401 K St. NW (14th St.) | 202-216-5988 | www.dccoast.com

"K Street types" gravitate to this "steady" seafood-strong New American spot on account of its "consistently performing" kitchen and "professional" staff that delivers a "value-oriented" "power lunch" in a "very DC" atmosphere; the art deco, former bank space is "stylish and architecturally distinct", so "sit upstairs and enjoy the view", though some prefer "hanging at the bar" downstairs with the "lobbyists."

DC Noodles *Thai*   23 | 18 | 20 | $23

U Street Corridor | 1410 U St. NW (bet. 14th & 15th Sts.) | 202-232-8424 | www.dcnoodles.com

Some patrons swear by the "perfect" pad Thai, while others cure "colds" with "giant bowls" of "spicy broth" at this "cheap" Asian "noodle joint" on U Street; both factions scarf down their fill in its compact "bright red and silver" quarters tended by "quick" servers, or opt for its "takeaway."

	FOOD	DECOR	SERVICE	COST

DC-3 *Hot Dogs* | 18 | 18 | 19 | $12

Capitol Hill | 423 Eighth St. SE (bet. E St. & Pennsylvania Ave.) | 202-546-1935 | www.eatdc3.com

Buckle up for a trip around the US wiener scene via this airplane-themed "hot dog heaven" on Capitol Hill, where an "interesting" range of "regionally" themed franks – e.g. Philly (Whiz wit), California (veggie dog, avocado) – arrive "fast" at the gate; a "friendly" crew runs the counter-serve setup, and you fly at "non-DC prices (i.e. affordable)."

Dean & DeLuca *Eclectic* | 23 | 16 | 18 | $27

Georgetown | 3276 M St. NW (33rd St.) | 202-342-2500 | www.deandeluca.com

"Terrific" sandwiches and "tasty" Eclectic "snacks" from DC's outpost of the "fancy" NYC gourmet grocer come with people-watching perks at Georgetown's "foodie Mecca"; decor is "n/a", but the shelves themselves offer a "feast for the eyes", so cruise the "mile-long display case" of prepared foods before heading to the outdoor cafe area – all in all, it's "a splurge that's worth it."

Degrees *French* | ∇ 22 | 19 | 24 | $47

Georgetown | Ritz-Carlton Georgetown | 3100 South St. NW (bet. 31st St. & Wisconsin Ave.) | 202-912-4100 | www.ritzcarlton.com

Paris in Georgetown describes this recently re-branded Ritz-Carlton venue that serves expensive Gallic fare from breakfast through the late evening; the contemporary space sports exposed brick and plush red curtains, and its inviting bar pours cocktails, craft beers and wine (*bien sûr*) to pair with internationally inspired bar bites.

NEW Del Frisco's Grille ● *Steak* | - | - | - | VE

Downtown | 1201 Pennsylvania Ave. NW (12th St.) | 202-450-4686 | www.delfriscosgrille.com

Power players, desk jockeys and tourists can tuck into the signature steaks and seafood, along with comfort classics and lighter fare, at this national chainlet steakhouse that recently debuted in the Penn Quarter; bills can be high, in keeping with the handsome, modern setting that features a wall of wine at the entrance and a classy island bar with windows opening to a spacious, canopied terrace.

Delhi Club *Indian* | 24 | 13 | 21 | $23

Clarendon | 1135 N. Highland St. (Clarendon Blvd.), VA | 703-527-5666 | www.delhiclub.com

"Look no further" than this "friendly" subcontinental "holding down the fort for Indian food in Clarendon" say locals who love its "authentic", "correctly prepared" cuisine; true, it's a tiny bastion with "just a few tables" near its big windows, but if decor is not an "issue", go for "consistently good food" at a "reasonable price."

Delhi Dhaba *Indian* | 20 | 11 | 17 | $19

Courthouse | 2424 Wilson Blvd. (Barton St.) | Arlington, VA | 703-524-0008 | www.delhidhaba.com

This "down-market but downright tasty" Punjabi stands as "one of the few remaining bits of old Arlington", and locals have long counted on its "good, basic curries" and "mix-and-match platters" at "almost giveaway prices"; the red and yellow no-frills setting and "cafeteria-style" service suggest "takeout" may be "best", though the recently expanded patio is also a good bet.

Dickson Wine Bar *Eclectic*   ∇ 21 | 22 | 18 | $33

U Street Corridor | 903 U St. NW (bet. 9th & 10th Sts.) | 202-332-1779 | www.dicksonwinebar.com

A "smart", "sexy" design makes this midpriced Eclectic wine bar on U Street seem "more NYC than DC", with its "extensive" wine collection displayed on three open floors, and young folks catching views of the action around them; "enjoyable" small plates (foodies "recommend" the pork belly banh mi) are designed to match the vino and fancy cocktails ferried by the "caring" staff.

The Diner ● *Diner*   21 | 16 | 20 | $20

Adams Morgan | 2453 18th St. NW (bet. Belmont & Columbia Rds.) | 202-232-8800 | www.dinerdc.com

"When everywhere else is closed", this 24/7 Adams Morgan diner just keeps on slinging its "consistently tasty", "reasonably priced" grub served "with a smile" in deco-esque premises that are "a bit classy" for the genre; still, it feels like home – whether you're digging into an "early-morning" breakfast when "strollers take over", waiting in line for an "amazing brunch" or satisfying post-"wild-night-on-the-town" "munchies."

Dino *Italian*   24 | 19 | 22 | $42

Cleveland Park | 3435 Connecticut Ave. NW (bet. Macomb & Ordway Sts.) | 202-686-2966 | www.dino-dc.com

Cleveland Park's "great little restaurant with the big heart" is a real "keeper" for its "off-the-beaten-track Italian" fare, an "encyclopedic yet reasonably priced wine list" and "best of all, Dino himself", aka Dean Gold, the "charming" chef-owner; the contempo-Euro furnishings are "comfortable", and the staff treats diners with "genuine warmth", so "take advantage" – "if this place was situated Downtown", "prices would be double."

Dish + Drinks *American*   ∇ 21 | 18 | 21 | $44

Foggy Bottom | The River Inn | 924 25th St. NW (bet. I & K Sts.) | 202-338-8707 | www.dishanddrinks.com

At this Foggy Bottom New American, dishes with "familiar foundations" are given fresh appeal with "interesting" flavor combinations in a "little" "modern" dining room that puts on the dog with large William Wegman prints; although it's near Kennedy Center and "suitable for pre-theater dining", an "obscure" address keeps it more a spot for neighborhood "regulars" and "hotel guests" who get "attentive" treatment.

District ChopHouse & Brewery *Steak*   21 | 20 | 20 | $39

Penn Quarter | 509 Seventh St. NW (bet. E & F Sts.) | 202-347-3434 | www.chophouse.com

This "wonderful cross between upscale steakhouse and comfortable sports bar" in Penn Quarter serves "good-value" chops

FOOD | DECOR | SERVICE | COST

along with "tasty" sides and a "nice selection" of its own "artisan beers" in "casual, crowded and noisy" environs; though some say the fare "rarely knocks your socks off", it also "rarely disappoints", and "efficient" servers get guests to nearby Verizon Center events on time.

NEW District Commons *American*   22 | 22 | 22 | $43

Foggy Bottom | 2200 Pennsylvania Ave. NW (bet. 22nd & 23rd Sts.) | 202-587-8277 | www.districtcommonsdc.com

This "posh, sassy addition to the Foggy Bottom dining scene" (from the Passion Food group) updates the tavern concept with a "cool", "modern" look featuring huge windows, plus a "cheeky" menu that "reimagines" American comfort food; service "hits the mark", and though some find the tabs "pricey for what it is", the real issue is that when it gets "busy" it can really "put the 'din' in dinner."

NEW District Kitchen *American*   ∇ 24 | 20 | 26 | $48

Woodley Park | 2606 Connecticut Ave. NW (Calvert St.) | 202-238-9408 | www.districtkitchen.com

Chef-owner Drew Trautmann's "clever use of interesting", locally sourced ingredients distinguishes the "outstanding" New American plates that emerge from his rookie Woodley Park kitchen, to be served in a rustic dining room with brick walls and engaging artifacts; it's a bit expensive, but imbued with a warm "neighborhood feel" that "encourages folks to return."

NEW District of Pi *Pizza*   23 | 20 | 20 | $22

Penn Quarter | 910 F St. NW (bet. 9th & 10th Sts.) | 202-681-3141 | www.pi-dc.com

"Carb up before a Caps game" with "fabulous" deep-dish Chicago pizza and St. Louis–style pies (featuring super-thin crust) at this new chain outpost close to Verizon Center, where "delicious" gluten-free and vegan options make it a "game-changer when it comes to team outings"; its "deft" staffers sling the dough in a "huge", "fancier"-than-expected space full of reclaimed wood and exposed brick.

☑ Dogfish Head Alehouse *Pub Food*   21 | 20 | 22 | $24

Gaithersburg | 800 W. Diamond Ave. (Quince Orchard Rd.), MD | 301-963-4847
Fairfax | 13041 Lee Jackson Memorial Hwy. (bet. Majestic Ln. & Springfellow Rd.), VA | 703-961-1140
Falls Church | Seven Corners Ctr. | 6363 Leesburg Pike (Rte. 7), VA | 703-534-3342
www.dogfishalehouse.com

"Knock-you-on-your-backside" craft beers on a "seasonally changing" slate take "center stage" at these "popular" suburban showcases for the famed Delaware brewer; the "reasonably priced" bar food may be "secondary" but it's "solid" and staffers are "cheerfully attentive", so if some say the "simple" "pub-style" environs are "too loud, even for bars", most toast the "warm, inviting atmosphere."

	FOOD	DECOR	SERVICE	COST

NEW Dolce Veloce Cicchetti
Wine Bar ⊠ *Italian*

- | - | - | M

Fairfax | 10826 Fairfax Blvd. (Fairchester Dr.), VA | 703-385-1226 | www.dolceveloce.com

At chef-owner Giuseppe 'Joe' Ricciardi's latest Fairfax venture, an intimate osteria next to his Dolce Vita restaurant, Italian-style tapas (cicchetti) are paired with vino by the glass or bottle in a relaxed, informal setting wrapped with shelves of wine; pizza cones (filled wraps shaped for handheld eating) are among the many inexpensive small dishes that can serve as a snack or add up to a full meal.

Dolce Vita *Italian*

25 | 20 | 23 | $33

Fairfax | 10824 Lee Hwy. (Main St.), VA | 703-385-1530 | www.dolcevitafairfax.com

They're "eager to please" at this Fairfax trattoria whose "amazing" Italian fare, graced with "homemade touches", has *paesani* clamoring for seats in its "small" "old-world" room; it's "well priced" to boot, has a "nice wine list" and "you won't be rushed out the door"; P.S. its new wine bar next door, Dolce Veloce Cicchetti, should ease waits.

Domku Bar &
Café Ⓜ *E European/Scandinavian*

∇ 22 | 19 | 16 | $23

Petworth | 821 Upshur St. NW (bet. 8th St. & Georgia Ave.) | 202-722-7475 | www.domkucafe.com

Where else in DC can one "order pickled herring without getting weird looks" than at this Petworth purveyor with a menu of "rib-sticking" Scandinavian and Eastern European fare that notably includes "varied vegetarian offerings", plus "refreshing" aquavits; "hipsters" say the "thrift-store" finds give it a "homey feel", but many sniff that "slow" service leaves them "colder than a night in Warsaw."

Don Pollo *Chicken/Peruvian*

23 | 12 | 19 | $18

Chevy Chase | 7007 Wisconsin Ave. (bet. Bradley Blvd. & Leland St.), MD | 301-652-0001
Rockville | Twinbrooke Shopping Ctr. | 2206 Veirs Mill Rd. (bet. Atlantic Ave. & Meadow Hall Dr.), MD | 301-309-1608
www.donpollorestaurant.com

Feathered friends "looove" the "fabulous", "well-seasoned" Peruvian spit-roasted chicken served with "spicy, flavorful traditional sauces" and "excellent" sides at "rock-bottom" prices at this Maryland mini-chain; there is "no decor" to speak of, so some surveyors opt for "fast" takeout, but most don't mind the "casual" feel.

Ⓩ Double T Diner *Diner*

20 | 16 | 21 | $18

Frederick | Francis Scott Key Mall | 5617 Spectrum Dr. (Genstar Dr.), MD | 301-620-8797 | www.doubletdiner.com

See review in the Baltimore Directory.

Duangrat's *Thai*

26 | 20 | 22 | $30

Falls Church | 5878 Leesburg Pike (Glen Forest Dr.), VA | 703-820-5775 | www.duangrats.com

"Dishes not normally seen in standard Thai restaurants" can make ordering at this "white-linen-tablecloth" Falls Church venue "seem overwhelming"; but not to worry since its "attentive" staff in traditional dress can help diners choose a specialty from an "extensive" menu that offers "excellent quality and value"; P.S. there's a popular Thai-style dim sum menu on weekends.

Dukem ❶ *Ethiopian*   24 | 15 | 19 | $25

U Street Corridor | 1114-1118 U St. NW (12th St.) | 202-667-8735 | www.dukemrestaurant.com

"Look Ma, no utensils!", just "perfect spongy, tangy injera bread" to scoop up "tasty" Ethiopian kitfo, tibs (the lamb's "amazing") and the like, including many veggie options, at these "traditional" outposts in DC and Baltimore; "ho-hum" decor afflicts both locales, but "attentive" service and "reasonable" tabs make them handsome choices for most; P.S. there's an "elaborate" coffee ceremony on Sunday at both branches, and live music in DC Wednesday–Sunday.

Dutch's Daughter *American*   25 | 24 | 25 | $41

Frederick | 581 Himes Ave. (Rte. 40), MD | 301-668-9500 | www.dutchs.info

This "class act" in Frederick is a "special-occasion" magnet thanks to a "beautiful" facility that feels like a "hunter's mansion", plus a "consistently excellent" upmarket American menu ("crab cakes reign supreme") and "impeccable" service; though some say it's a place your "grandmother" would love, it's also a hit with the prom squad and brunchers, as well as locals who gather downstairs in the comparatively "cool" bar.

Eamonn's – A Dublin Chipper/PX *Irish*   23 | 16 | 18 | $18

Old Town | 728 King St. (Columbus St.) | Alexandria, VA | 703-299-8384 | www.eamonnsdublinchipper.com

"Grease stains on the brown paper bags" signify that "something good lies within" – namely "perfectly crisp, piping hot" fish and spuds - at Old Town's "easy"-on-the-wallet fish 'n' chips counter from Eve's Cathal Armstrong (other "fried goodness" includes candy bars); the publike space is often "crowded" with "nowhere to linger" at the few communal tables, so just "grab and go"; P.S. the "speakeasy"-style lounge upstairs, PX, mixes "unique" cocktails.

🆕 East Pearl *Chinese*   – | – | – | M

Rockville | 838 Rockville Pike (bet. Edmonston Dr. & Wootton Pkwy.), MD | 301-838-8663

Joining the Rockville Chinese fray is this moderately priced arrival featuring two separate kitchens that each handle a different side of the menu - the small kitchen up front preps noodle dishes, while the main one in back handles all the other Hong Kong–style fare; also setting it apart is the bright, contemporary space that displays upscale touches.

Eat First ❶ *Chinese*   22 | 8 | 20 | $21

Chinatown | 609 H St. NW (bet. 6th & 7th Sts.) | 202-289-1703
Check out "what Chinatown used to be" like at this subterranean "treasure" that "rewards" intrepid eaters with "incredible"

FOOD | DECOR | SERVICE | COST

Cantonese "specials marked on the mirrored walls", plus "extremely well-prepared" standards on "the American menu"; should the "joint" look "tired", focus on "hospitable and quick" service and "good food for the price."

Eatonville *Southern*
23 | 24 | 22 | $35

U Street Corridor | 2121 14th St. NW (bet. V & W Sts.) | 202-332-9672 | www.eatonvillerestaurant.com

At this culinary tribute to Zora Neale Hurston, one of the "greats of the Harlem Renaissance", "down-home" touches like "drinks served in mason jars" and an "indoor porch with rocking chairs" set a twangy scene for "terrific" Southern cuisine "with a modern twist" just off U Street; everyday prices and "energetic, knowledgeable servers" complete the picture-perfect "Southern charm."

Eggspectation *American*
21 | 20 | 21 | $22

Silver Spring | 923 Ellsworth Dr. (bet. Fenton St. & Georgia Ave.), MD | 301-585-1700
Chantilly | Westone Plaza | 5009 Westone Plaza Dr. (Westfields Blvd.), VA | 703-263-7444
Leesburg | Wegmans Shopping Ctr. | 1609 Village Market Blvd. SE (Market St.), VA | 703-777-4127
www.eggspectations.com

"Eggs any way you like them" star at these "upscale diners" that also offer a "quirky menu" of "to-swoon-for" pancakes, "freshly squeezed" juices and "anything you can imagine doing to a bagel", and even some lunch and dinner options; some say it's "expensive for breakfast food" and the "brightly lit" venues are "too loud", but most eggheads leave feeling "well cared for" and "satiated."

8407 Kitchen Bar *American*
24 | 23 | 23 | $42

Silver Spring | 8407 Ramsey Ave. (bet. Bonifant St. & Wayne Ave.), MD | 301-587-8407 | www.8407kb.com

"Silver Spring has sprung" onto the food scene via this "innovative" New American "destination" ("shockingly hip" for the area) with an "industrial" dining room full of "exposed beams and rafters", and a similarly neo-rustic bar/lounge downstairs serving the likes of "creative" charcuterie and martinis with a "kick"; if some find it "a little pricey for a regular night", it's still a "go-to spot for dates", complete with a "welcoming" crew.

El Centro D.F. *Mexican*
21 | 20 | 20 | $32

Logan Circle | 1819 14th St. NW (bet. S & T Sts.) | 202-328-3131 | www.elcentrodf.com

A "super-sexy vibe" permeates Richard Sandoval's "always crowded" 14th Street Mexican triplex (near his Masa 14) serving moderately priced, "innovative" takes on Mexican "street eats" backed by a "beyond-amazing selection of tequila" poured by folks who "know about the stuff"; "trendy" types "get the night started" at the rooftop bar before descending to the "dungeon-esque" basement tequileria that pulses like an "underground club in Mexico City."

El Chalan ⊠ *Peruvian*

22 | 14 | 19 | $33

Foggy Bottom | 1924 I St. NW (20th St.) | 202-293-2765 | www.elchalandc.com

"Step down and arrive in South America" at this Foggy Bottom Peruvian serving "zesty ceviche" and "ever-reliable lomo saltado" to "World Bank, IMF and embassy crowds"; the "small" subterranean digs, decorated simply with regional paintings, may "need the help they get from the bar's pisco sours", but the food is the reason why it's "still a favorite" after so many years.

NEW El Chucho Cocina Superior ● *Mexican*

- | - | - | I

Columbia Heights | 3313 11th St. NW (bet. Lamont St. & Park Rd.) | 202-290-3313

Named for a legendary 19th-century bandit, this sun-washed Columbia Heights Mexican (from the Jackie's team in Silver Spring) slings inexpensive, upgraded takes on classic taqueria fare, plus margaritas on tap and 60-plus types of tequila; the downstairs bar boasts a colorful industrial-mod look, while the roof deck has picnic tables and vintage wrought-iron decorations.

Elephant Jumps *Thai*

26 | 18 | 23 | $25

Falls Church | 8110 Arlington Blvd. (Gallows Rd.), VA | 703-942-6600 | www.elephantjumps.com

"Worth the trip from DC", this "bargain" Falls Church favorite offers "imaginative" Thai cuisine via a "creative" menu with "elements of fusion" – check out the 'East Meets West' section for items "unseen elsewhere" (e.g. drunken spaghetti chicken); with a "friendly" owner who will "offer a detailed tour" of the options, and the whimsical if bare-bones decor, regulars "can't recommend it enough."

Elevation Burger *Burgers*

21 | 13 | 18 | $12

National Harbor | National Harbor | 108 Waterfront St. (National Harbor Blvd.), MD | 301-749-4014
Hyattsville | 5501 Baltimore Ave. (Jefferson St.), MD | 301-985-6869
Rockville | 12525 Park Potomac Ave. (Montrose Rd.), MD | 301-838-4010
Arlington | Lee Harrison Shopping Ctr. | 2447 N. Harrison St. (bet. Lee Hwy. & 26th St.), VA | 703-300-9467
Falls Church | 442 S. Washington St. (Annandale Rd.), VA | 703-237-4343
www.elevationburger.com

Burgers get the "organic" treatment at these bright and airy "natural fast food" counter-serves slinging "high-quality" grass-fed, free-range beef along with vegetarian options and "crispy" fries cooked in olive oil; some judge it "a little pricey" for its milieu, and the "friendly" service can seem "a bit slow", but remember, "they cook your food to order."

El Golfo *Pan-Latin*

∇ 23 | 15 | 24 | $23

Silver Spring | 8739 Flower Ave. (Piney Branch Rd.), MD | 301-608-2121 | www.elgolforestaurant.com

"Family-friendly" describes this "welcoming" Silver Springer with its "cheerful" crew ferrying "full" plates of "delicious" Pan-Latin fare to all ages; while it's "not big on decor" (a few South American textiles on pink walls) fans rely on this "trusty" performer for "excellent-value", "low-maintenance" meals.

NEW Elisir ⑤ *Italian* ▽ 26 | 24 | 23 | $67

Penn Quarter | 427 11th St. NW (bet. E St. & Pennsylvania Ave.) | 202-546-0088 | www.elisirrestaurant.com

Chef Enzo Fargione (ex Teatro Goldoni) "gets it right" at his "delight-ful" new Penn Quarter "gastro-Italian", where his "signature" "out-of-this-world" showman touches (witness the "amazing" branzino served in a smoking cigar box) are unveiled in "blissfully quiet", ultra-suave surroundings while the "staff waits on you hand and foot"; if it seems too "high priced", try the $19 two-course bar lunch.

Ella's Wood-Fired Pizza *Pizza* 21 | 17 | 19 | $24

Penn Quarter | 901 F St. NW (entrance on 9th St.) | 202-638-3434 | www.ellaspizza.com

"Tasty" wood-fired pizza with "crisp yet slightly chewy" crust and "fantastic" craft beers come at a "bargain in a high-cost neighbor-hood", ensuring this Penn Quarter pie shop is always "super-busy"; the "casual" stone-wall-accented setting turns into a "madhouse" during sporting events at nearby Verizon Center, but the "prompt and efficient" crew keeps its cool.

El Manantial *Mediterranean* 24 | 23 | 24 | $41

Reston | Toll Oaks Village Ctr. | 12050 North Shore Dr. (Wiehle Ave.), VA | 703-742-6466 | www.elmanantialrestaurant.com

"They will make any occasion a special one" at this "out-of-the-way" Reston "gem" whose "outstanding" seafood-centric Mediterranean menu sparkles like the storied inland sea pictured on the trompe l'oeil murals; best of all, it comes without the "hassle" of "more crowded Reston Town Center" venues, so very few quibble about the tab.

El Mariachi *S American/Tex-Mex* 25 | 18 | 24 | $23

Rockville | Ritchie Ctr. | 765 Rockville Pike (Wootton Pkwy.), MD | 301-738-7177 | www.elmariachirockville.com

"You can't go wrong" with this "popular neighborhood" Tex-Mex (and South American) cantina in a Rockville strip mall say longtime loyalists who laud its "tasty homemade salsa" and "authentically flavored" entrees served by an "outstanding" staff; the space is "plain but pleasant", with white tablecloths, and prices are "quite reasonable", so it "stays busy."

El Pollo Rico *Chicken/Peruvian* 26 | 10 | 19 | $12

Wheaton | 2517 University Blvd. (bet. Georgia & Grandview Aves.), MD | 301-942-4419
Arlington | 932 N. Kenmore St. (bet. Fairfax Dr. & Wilson Blvd.), VA | 703-522-3220
Woodbridge | 13470 Minnieville Rd. (Smoketown Rd.), VA | 703-590-3160
www.welovethischicken.com

The Peruvian chicken is so "finger-lickin' good" that folks are eating it "before they're done paying" at these "bare-bones" counter-serve

	FOOD	DECOR	SERVICE	COST

roasters; indeed, everyone from "Anthony Bourdain" to "three-piece suits to day laborers" raves about the "delicious greasiness" that can be had for just a "few bucks", and since service is "quick", nobody clucks too much about occasional "lines out the door."

El Tamarindo ● *Mexican* | 21 | 14 | 20 | $24 |

Adams Morgan | 1785 Florida Ave. NW (18th St.) | 202-328-3660 | www.eltamarindodc.com

One can "satisfy a Mexican-food craving", a yen for *"auténtico"* Salvadoran specialties like "hot and melty" pupusas, or a thirst for "knee-knocking margaritas" at this long-running, late-night Adams Morgan standby; "affordable" tabs, "easy seating" and a "nice" staff compensate for festive "hole-in-the-wall" decor that leaves something "to be desired" – and really, "after a night of drinking", who cares?

Eola 🅂Ⓜ *American*   ∇ | 25 | 18 | 20 | $85 |

Dupont Circle | 2020 P St. NW (Hopkins St.) | 202-466-4441 | www.eoladc.com

"Expect to spend the evening" dining "on the cutting-edge" at this "innovative" Dupont Circle New American, where a $65 five-course prix fixe menu (no à la carte) is served at a "leisurely pace" in a "quiet" townhouse "sparsely" decorated with exposed bricks and ochre walls; its "smart" wine list is parsed by "knowledgeable" servers, though the staff "isn't as polished" as "such an ambitious menu" would suggest.

Equinox *American* | 25 | 22 | 24 | $68 |

Golden Triangle | 818 Connecticut Ave. NW (bet. H & I Sts.) | 202-331-8118 | www.equinoxrestaurant.com

Chef/co-owner Todd Gray (and executive chef Karen Nicholas) "can just plain cook", using "locally sourced" ingredients in "creative" ways in the "outstanding" New American dishes that grace the tables at this "pricey" fine-dining spot steps from the White House; "polished" service is "worthy of that special night" out but "also establishment enough for business lunches", when one spots famous faces in the "sleek", contemporary rooms.

Estadio *Spanish* | 25 | 23 | 21 | $44 |

Logan Circle | 1520 14th St. NW (Church St.) | 202-319-1404 | www.estadio-dc.com

"Bustling with energy", this "spirited" Logan Circle Spanish tapas destination is "big on creative flavors", with an "ever-changing" menu of "earthy", "sometimes daring" delights (take care: the bill "can add up"); however, it's "small on space", so come early to avoid "painful waits" for a table in the "playful" "Moorish-meets-Almodóvar" space – or if you must wait, the "knowledgeable" bartenders can mix you a "fancy drink", like the "famous slushito."

Etete ● *Ethiopian* | 24 | 14 | 18 | $26 |

U Street Corridor | 1942 Ninth St. NW (U St.) | 202-232-7600 | www.eteterestaurant.com

This "sparse" but "modern" nook in DC's 'Little Ethiopia' (in the U Street Corridor) is like being in "Addis Ababa", where diners scoop up "spicy" and "filling" stews with spongy injera bread; service is "friendly if not super-quick", but for those looking for "something different" (e.g. eating with your hands), it's a "great alternative" in "a sea of sameness", and cheap too.

Ethiopic Ⓜ *Ethiopian*   24 | 21 | 21 | $31

Atlas District | 401 H St. NE (4th St.) | 202-675-2066 | www.ethiopicrestaurant.com

Ethiopian food is staged for "cosmopolitans" at this "upscale" West African in the burgeoning Atlas District, where basketweave tables, rich colors and homeland art provide a "lovely" backdrop for "very flavorful" cuisine, served "graciously"; while it lacks the "raw feel of similar joints on Ninth Street", this slightly "pricier" version is "very popular", ergo reservations are "a must."

Et Voila *Belgian/French*   25 | 17 | 21 | $45

Palisades | 5120 MacArthur Blvd. NW (bet. Arizona Ave. & Dana Pl.) | 202-237-2300 | www.etvoiladc.com

"Cramped but delicious" describes this "charming European-style bistro tucked away" in the Palisades, where "hearty" French-Belgian fare "elevated with just enough elegance and finesse" is delivered by waiters from "central casting", who adroitly navigate the "runway" of its long, narrow room; "outstanding moules frites" matched with "very good" wine and "even better" Belgian beer – it's all "well worth the price."

☒ Eve, Restaurant Ⓢ *American*   27 | 25 | 26 | $86

Old Town | 110 S. Pitt St. (bet. King & Prince Sts.) | Alexandria, VA | 703-706-0450 | www.restauranteve.com

"You don't just dine" at Cathal Armstrong's "pitch-perfect" Old Town New American, you get a taste of "perfection" as you are "cosseted" in "plush" banquettes in the "romantic" tasting room, where "personalized" multicourse menus evince the chef's "passion" and "attention to detail"; or head to the connecting bistro and bar to "savor the delicious food" on the cheap – it offers à la carte choices and, at lunch, there's a two-course "bargain" prix fixe for around $15.

Evening Star Cafe *Southern*   23 | 20 | 21 | $38

Del Ray | 2000 Mt. Vernon Ave. (Howell Ave.) | Alexandria, VA | 703-549-5051 | www.eveningstarcafe.net

Del Rey's "upscale Southern" lodestar boasts a new chef, Jim Jeffords (ex CityZen), who puts "updated twists" on Dixie favorites in a diner-esque dining room sporting "clever fixtures" and artwork repurposed from vintage finds (there's also a back bar and upstairs lounge with live music); further points of light include solid service, "reasonable" tabs and "amazing" wines from its next-door shop, Planet Wine.

Eventide ⓈⓂ *American*   23 | 26 | 23 | $45

Clarendon | 3165 Wilson Blvd. (Hudson St.), VA | 703-276-3165 | www.eventiderestaurant.com

"Guests dressed to the nines" live up to the "soaring", "sumptuous" surroundings ("love those velvet curtains"), lingering over "well-executed" New American dishes and "indulgent" treatment at Clarendon's "date-night destination"; "inventive" cocktails (and tamer tariffs for food) can be had at the "sophisticated" yet casual street-level bar or "divine" rooftop patio.

Evo Bistro *Mediterranean*

| 22 | 18 | 20 | $44 |

McLean | Salona Shopping Ctr. | 1313 Old Chain Bridge Rd. (Dolley Madison Blvd.), VA | 703-288-4422 | www.evobistro.com

"Meet friends and share small plates" at McLean's restaurant for "wine lovers" that offers a "well-done" variety of Mediterranean bites and entrees to pair with "terrific" vino from self-serve vending machines (the bartenders are "helpful" too) in a "low-key", earth-toned space flooded with "natural light"; just be wary since "it's easy to rack up quite a bill", or stick to the $5 pours and plates during happy hour.

Extra Virgin *Italian*

| 21 | 20 | 21 | $40 |

Shirlington | 4053 Campbell Ave. (Randolph St.) | Arlington, VA | 703-998-8474 | www.extravirginva.com

For "pre-theater dinner and post-show drinks", guests "can't say enough" about this midpriced Italian near Arlington's Signature Theatre, where "bright", "fresh" dishes are delivered by "accommodating" servers; the space is curvy and contemporary with a "relaxing bar" area, and it also hosts occasional themed wine dinners and live music, bringing diners "back for more."

Ezmè *Turkish*

| 22 | 21 | 24 | $34 |

Dupont Circle | 2016 P St. NW (bet. Hopkins & 21st Sts.) | 202-223-4304 | www.ezmedc.com

Fans say this Dupont Circle spot "competes with Istanbul" when it comes to Turkish meze, offering "authentic" dishes served on "the prettiest plates" paired with flights of vino; "responsive" servers tend to the "relaxing", loungelike room that's lined with wine racks, a solid venue for a "romantic" date that won't empty the wallet.

Faccia Luna Trattoria *Pizza*

| 23 | 17 | 21 | $24 |

Old Town | 823 S. Washington St. (bet. Green & Jefferson Sts.) | Alexandria, VA | 703-838-5998

Clarendon | 2909 Wilson Blvd. (Fillmore St.), VA | 703-276-3099 www.faccialuna.com

"Craveable" "gourmet pizzas" and pastas at "reasonable" prices, including "awesome lunch deals", make these Clarendon and Old Town trattorias "longtime favorites" of local folks, some of whom have "been there a couple hundred times"; "helpful" staffers and "casual", "comfortable" settings with booth seating make them especially "friendly to families."

NEW Family Meal *American/Diner*

| - | - | - | M |

Frederick | 880 N. East St. (8th St.), MD | 301-378-2895 | www.voltfamilymeal.com

Bryan Voltaggio's (Volt) modern American diner offers easy-on-the-wallet all-day meals in a former Frederick car dealership transformed by clever design and raw, natural materials into an open, airy space, with a long counter fronting an open kitchen; its menu elevates the comfort-food canon, while adult beverages include boozy milkshakes as well as wine, beer and cocktails.

Farrah Olivia M *American* ▽ 23 | 15 | 20 | $65

Crystal City | 2250 Crystal Dr. (23rd St.) | Arlington, VA | 703-445-6571 | www.farraholiviarestaurant.com

One "must do a little searching" for this "restaurant within a restaurant" hidden in the small purple-hued back room of Kora in Crystal City, but seekers are rewarded by "clever", "inventive" New American repasts; prices are high, and a few say it "doesn't always work", but when it does, it's "amazing"; P.S. open Wednesday–Sunday for dinner only.

Faryab M *Afghan* 24 | 16 | 22 | $33

Bethesda | 4917 Cordell Ave. (bet. Norfolk Ave. & Old Georgetown Rd.), MD | 301-951-3484

Diners are invariably "impressed" by this "moderate" Bethesda Afghan option serving "excellent" Middle Eastern fare, including "delicious" kebabs, "savory" aushak and "distractingly good" pumpkin dishes; service is "prompt", and the "simple" environs hung with native tapestries are "pleasant", so bring guests and "harvest the compliments."

Fast Gourmet *Pan-Latin* ▽ 27 | 10 | 18 | $13

U Street Corridor | 1400 W St. NW (14th St.) | 202-448-9217 | www.fast-gourmet.com

"Fill up both tanks" at this U Street Corridor "gourmet gas station" (seriously, the pumps work) where a "friendly" counter crew slaps together Latin sandwiches that are "meaty masterpieces", like the "monumental" Uruguayan *chivito* stuffed with various meats, mozzarella, egg and olives; the decor is upscale Mobil Mart (a few tables and chairs next to a rack of Slim Jims), but "don't let it put you off" – it's cheap, and open way-late on weekends.

15 Ria *American* 22 | 20 | 21 | $39

Scott Circle | DoubleTree by Hilton Hotel Washington DC | 1515 Rhode Island Ave. NW (15th St.) | 202-742-0015 | www.15ria.com

"Cozy" club chairs and "attractive place settings" contribute to an "inviting", "upscale" ambiance that belies this New American spot's setting "off the lobby of a chain hotel" – a DoubleTree near Scott Circle; chef Janis McLean, whose work is reflected in the Food rating, departed in early 2012, but the "good values" and "well-trained staff" remain, making it "great for a date" or a "post-work happy hour, especially if you can nab a patio seat."

Filomena Ristorante *Italian* 24 | 21 | 23 | $44

Georgetown | 1063 Wisconsin Ave. NW (M St.) | 202-338-8800 | www.filomena.com

With "pasta mamas" making noodles in the front window, one might think this "bustling" Georgetown trattoria would be like "your Italian grandmother's kitchen" – but it's "cavernous" inside, and even nonna never had so much "kitsch" or "gaudy" ("yet somehow fabulous")

holiday decor; still, the "thoughtful" staff makes it feel like "home" to legions of locals, "tourists" and "celebrities" who've stuffed themselves for years on the "rich", "massive" red-sauce plates; P.S. the weekend buffet is a way around "high prices."

Finemondo ⓔ *Italian*   20 | 19 | 20 | $44

Downtown | 1319 F St. NW (bet. 13th & 14th Sts.) | 202-737-3100

"Simple" "Italian country meals" are served under a vaulted ceiling in the "romantic", "relaxed" old-word dining room of this expensive Downtown spot; while thespians count it as a "nice pre-theater option", citing "efficient" service, tipplers get comfortable in "overstuffed chairs" amid the warm, woody surroundings of its "humming" bar.

ⓩ Fiola ⓔ *Italian*   27 | 25 | 26 | $68

Penn Quarter | 601 Pennsylvania Ave. NW (entrance on Indiana Ave. bet. 6th & 7th Sts.) | 202-628-2888 | www.fioladc.com

"Wow", Fabio Trabocchi's "sensational" Penn Quarter venue offers the "complete package" – "his elegant magic touch" with rustic Italian cuisine, a "fabulous" and "unstuffy" villalike ambiance plus "extremely engaging" help; aim for a table in the rear to "ogle" the objets d'art and the (sometimes famous and) "lively crowd", and though it's not cheap, tabs are an "unbelievable" value given the "truly wonderful dining experience."

Firefly *American*   23 | 23 | 21 | $42

Dupont Circle | 1310 New Hampshire Ave. NW (N St.) | 202-861-1310 | www.firefly-dc.com

At this Dupont Circle "hideaway", chef Daniel Bortnick's New American "funked-up comfort food" is displayed in an "engaging" setting that's built around an "enormous indoor tree", managing to be both "romantic" and "kid-friendly"; the staff is "great", and if the bill is big, at least it's cute – it "comes in a mason jar" flickering with light.

Firestone's Ⓜ *American*   26 | 24 | 25 | $34

Frederick | 105 N. Market St. (Church St.), MD | 301-663-0330 | www.firestonesrestaurant.com

There's a "fantastic, lively energy" humming at this Downtown Frederick brick-and-wood tavern where the "phenomenal" New American fare may come as a "happy shock" given the "casual" environment and moderate prices; the mezzanine is quieter and affords stellar "people-watching" of the "active" bar scene below, but up or down, the service is "exceptional"; P.S. its adjacent shop offers prepared foods and gourmet gadgetry.

Fire Works Pizza *Pizza*   24 | 20 | 21 | $23

Courthouse | 2350 Clarendon Blvd. (Adams St.) | Arlington, VA | 703-527-8700
Leesburg | 201 Harrison St. SE (Royal St.), VA | 703-779-8400
www.fireworkspizza.com

"Rock-star" pizza sporting "flavorful" crusts and "locally sourced ingredients", plus "really freaking good" garlic knots, whet the appetite for the "fantastic" beer selections at these "casual" Courthouse and Leesburg "wood-fired" siblings with "reasonable" checks and "snappy" service; inside they're "industrial" and "noisy", while outside large patios provide "primo" seating in nice weather.

NEW Fishnet M *Seafood* ▽ 24 | 16 | 20 | $17

College Park | 5010 Berwyn Rd. (Baltimore Ave.), MD | 301-220-1070 | www.eatfishnet.com

Inspired by the grilled fish sandwiches sold as street food in his native Istanbul, Ferhat Yalcin (ex Corduroy) sources "fresh fish daily" to replicate them at this new "bare-bones" College Park counter-serve; the "carefully prepared" catch, topped with a "special Turkish sauce" and accompanied by fries you "can't pass up" and "intriguing" Turkish soft drinks, makes for a "a blessed relief from fast-food chains."

Z Five Guys *Burgers* 24 | 14 | 21 | $12

Chinatown | 808 H St. NW (bet. 8th & 9th Sts.) | 202-393-2900

Georgetown | 1335 Wisconsin Ave. NW (Dumbarton St.) | 202-337-0400

Bethesda | 4829 Bethesda Ave. (bet. Arlington & Clarendon Rds.), MD | 301-657-0007

Frederick | Shops at Monocacy | 1700 Kingfisher Dr. (Rte. 26), MD | 301-668-1500

Greater Alexandria | 4626 King St. (Beauregard St.) | Alexandria, VA | 703-671-1606

Greater Alexandria | 7622 Richmond Hwy. (Boswell Ave.) | Alexandria, VA | 703-717-0090

Old Town | 107 N. Fayette St. (King St.) | Alexandria, VA | 703-549-7991

Herndon | Fox Mill Ctr. | 2521 John Milton Dr. (Fox Mill Rd.), VA | 703-860-9100

Springfield | 6541 Backlick Rd. (Old Keene Mill Rd.), VA | 703-913-1337

Manassas | Manassas Corner | 9221 Sudley Rd. (Centerville Rd.), VA | 703-368-8080

www.fiveguys.com

Additional locations throughout the DC area

"Hot, juicy and smothered in whatever your heart desires", this is "the way a burger should be" say fans of these über-"popular" counters, voted the DC area's Most Popular chain; while the "sparse" white-and-red-tiled settings earn few raves, "who cares" when "the prices are right" and there are free peanuts to shell while you wait – which won't be long since the "hard-working" crews fill orders "fast."

Fleming's Prime Steakhouse & Wine Bar *Steak* 25 | 24 | 25 | $61

Tysons Corner | 1960 Chain Bridge Rd. (International Dr.) | McLean, VA | 703-442-8384 | www.flemingssteakhouse.com

"Quality" cuts of "properly prepared" steak bring beef-eaters to the Tysons Corner and Harbor East links of this "expense-account" chophouse chain; adding to the "excellent" experience are the "top-notch" servers who ably tend the "crowded" dining rooms and "busy" bar with "dark and woody", "man's club" decor.

Floriana Restaurant *Italian* 24 | 22 | 23 | $40

Dupont Circle | 1602 17th St. NW (Q St.) | 202-667-5937 | www.florianarestaurant.com

In the diadem of "reasonably priced Italians", this Dupont row-house "gem" shines, with a "brilliant" staff dishing up "lasagna just as good

as it was 30 years ago" (at a prior location) along with more recent in-
novations; its "intimate" "Victorian" charm works for a "celebration
meal" or for casual drinks with friends on "half-price wine nights."

Florida Ave. Grill Ⓜ *Diner* | 22 | 12 | 20 | $17 |

Shaw | 1100 Florida Ave. NW (11th St.) | 202-265-1586 |
www.floridaavenuegrill.com

A "true DC vibe" flavors the "down-home" Southern food "cooked with
experience and served up hot" and "greasy" at this old-time Shaw
diner lined with "pictures of famous diners" and not much else; the
staff is "friendly", and its customers get "plenty of food for the price",
especially if they come Tuesday–Friday for the early-bird deal.

☑ Fogo de Chão *Brazilian/Steak* | 27 | 24 | 27 | $61 |

Penn Quarter | 1101 Pennsylvania Ave. NW (11th St.) | 202-347-4668 |
www.fogodechao.com

"It's all about the meat" at this "well-appointed" Brazilian steakhouse chain (with outposts in DC's Penn Quarter and Baltimore's
Inner Harbor), "a carnivore's version of paradise" thanks to "gaucho"-
attired servers who "cruise the floor" doling out "familiar" and "unusual" cuts of skewered beef, pork and poultry "until you beg them
to stop"; it may be "spendy", but with the "all-you-can-eat" policy,
guests leave "stuffed"; P.S. there's a "well-stocked salad bar" too.

Fontaine Caffe & Creperie *French* | ▽ 25 | 20 | 22 | $31 |

Old Town | 119 S. Royal St. (bet. King & Prince Sts.) | Alexandria, VA |
703-535-8151 | www.fontainecaffe.com

This "adorably cute" French cafe "in the heart of" Old Town's historic
district fills affordable sweet and savory crêpes "for every taste" and
pairs them with "surprisingly good wines" and European ciders; its
blue-walled dining room or a table outside makes a "darling" rendezvous for a "fantastic brunch", "spur-of-the-moment" nosh or "not-too-
formal date"; P.S. the buckwheat crêpes are naturally gluten-free.

Fontina Grille *Italian* | 20 | 18 | 18 | $28 |

Rockville | King Farm Village Ctr. | 801 Pleasant Dr. (Redland Blvd.),
MD | 301-947-5400 | www.fontinagrille.com

"There's always a crowd" at this "reliable" Rockville ristorante
where the "tasty" Italian entrees and wood-fired pizza earn fans;
"reasonable" tabs, a "smiling" staff and "cozy", wood-trimmed digs
make it a "decent neighborhood joint to take the family."

Food Corner Kabob House *Afghan* | 25 | 15 | 21 | $16 |

Dupont Circle | 2029 P St. NW (21st St.) | 202-331-3777
Annandale | 7031 Little River Tpke. (bet. Carrico & John Marr Drs.),
VA | 703-750-2185
Springfield | 7031 Brookfield Plaza (Backlick Rd.), VA | 703-866-7834
Tysons Corner | 8315 Leesburg Pike (bet. Chain Bridge & Gosnell Rd.) |
Vienna, VA | 703-893-2333
Centreville | 14220 Centreville Sq. (Lee Hwy.), VA | 703-543-7166
www.foodcornerkabob.com

For "a lot of healthy food for very little money", frugal foodies recommend these Afghan "grab"-and-eat joints serving "superb" ke-

FOOD DECOR SERVICE COST

bab platters, "freshly baked" breads and "melt-in-your-mouth" meats; "average" decor is overlooked thanks to "flexible", "friendly" counter staffers who can "make combinations upon request."

Food Wine & Co. *American* | 22 | 20 | 20 | $40 |

Bethesda | 7272 Wisconsin Ave. (bet. Bethesda Ave. & Elm St.), MD | 301-652-8008 | www.foodwineandco.com

A "versatile venue", this midpriced Bethesda New American appeals to "all generations" as a place to "grab a drink" with friends in the dark-wood bar or partake of a "nice sit-down dinner" of "reliably good" food in its high-ceilinged, tall-windowed dining area; service is "relaxed" but "professional", and "wine prices are sane", so locals say it's a "perfect way to end a long day at the office."

Ford's Fish Shack *New England/Seafood* | 26 | 21 | 23 | $30 |

Ashburn | Ice Rink Plaza | 44260 Ice Rink Plaza (Farmwell Rd.), VA | 571-918-4092 | www.fordsfishshack.com

Folks from "Maine" feel like they're back home when chowing down on the "authentic" specialties (lobster rolls, whoopie pies) at this casual, maritime-themed fishouse in Ashburn's Ice Rink Plaza; it's "always busy", but the staff makes everyone "feel special" and doesn't charge much for the pleasure.

Fortune *Chinese* | 22 | 14 | 18 | $22 |

Falls Church | Seven Corners Ctr. | 6249 Arlington Blvd. (Wilson Blvd.), VA | 703-538-3333

Dim sum devotees praise the "amazing" offerings at this massive Seven Corners banquet hall; of course, it's "always chaotic" and "rushed", and "the only ambiance is provided by the clientele (so many people)", but folks who "come hungry leave sated – with leftovers!"; P.S. there's also a Cantonese seafood menu at dinner.

❷ Foti's Ⓜ *American* | 27 | 23 | 25 | $52 |

Culpeper | 219 E. Davis St. (East St.), VA | 540-829-8400 | www.fotisrestaurant.com

It's "worth the drive" to Frank and Sue Maragos' "charming" Downtown Culpeper foodie "haven", where the former Inn at Little Washington talents serve "sophisticated", "imaginative" New American fare that "holds its own when compared with more expensive places"; what's more, you "never feel rushed" by the "earnest" staff while savoring "perfect wine pairings" in the glowing, brick-and-dark-wood storefront; P.S. closed Monday and Tuesday.

❷ Founding Farmers *American* | 24 | 22 | 20 | $35 |

World Bank | IMF Bldg. | 1924 Pennsylvania Ave. NW (20th St.) | 202-822-8783

NEW **Potomac** | 12505 Park Potomac Ave. (Seven Locks Rd.), MD | 301-340-8783 ◑

www.wearefoundingfarmers.com

These "buzzing", cooperative-grower-owned all-Americans have planted their "farm-to-table"-themed comfort cuisine in "rustic-chic" digs in DC's IMF Building and Potomac, MD, where "homey" vittles like "awesome cornbread" and "bacon lollies" are ferried by "youthful" farmhands, while "artisanal" drinks are swilled at the "packed bars"; service is "solid but nothing stellar", and though many complain about the "unbearable" noise, most are "impressed with how affordable" it is.

Four Sisters *Vietnamese*   25 | 20 | 21 | $28

Merrifield | Merrifield Town Ctr. | 8190 Strawberry Ln. (bet. Gallows Rd. & Lee Hwy.), VA | 703-539-8566 | www.foursistersrestaurant.com

A "huge selection" of "authentic", "consistently excellent" dishes brings diners to this "bargain-priced" Vietnamese spot, a "subdued" space decorated with "beautiful flower displays" in Merrifield Town Center; "gracious", "helpful" servers further explain why this "family-friendly" place is a "popular" pick.

Franklin's *Pub Food*   21 | 22 | 23 | $24

Hyattsville | 5123 Baltimore Ave. (Gallatin St.), MD | 301-927-2740 | www.franklinsbrewery.com

For "affordable" "good old American standards" like burgers and ribs and "distinctive" "proprietary brews", Hyattsville residents visit this "airy", industrial bi-level brew pub with an adjacent general store selling "quirky" and "nostalgic" gifts; "pleasant" staffers lend to the "casual", "irreverent" vibe, though a few shout it can be "so loud it's hard to talk."

Freddy's Lobster & Clams *Seafood*   19 | 14 | 18 | $26

Bethesda | 4867 Cordell Ave. (bet. Old Georgetown Rd. & Woodmont Ave.), MD | 240-743-4257 | www.freddyslobster.com

It feels "very summer-at-the-shore" at this "casual" Bethesda seafood shack where New England specialties like fried whole-belly clams, peel-and-eat shrimp and "fab" lobster rolls are eaten at "wood picnic tables", with vintage boating gear adding to the "nostalgic" vibe; still, critics carp that it's "a bit underwhelming for the price", though the service is "fast" and "friendly", and the beer list is "phenomenal."

NEW Fuel Pizza & Wings *American/Pizza*   – | – | – | I

Penn Quarter | 600 F St. NW (bet. 6th & 7th Sts.) | 202-547-3835
Downtown | 1606 K St. NW (bet. 16th & 17th Sts.) | 202-659-3835
www.fuelpizza.com

NY-style pizza pulls up at these new gas station–themed refueling spots where pies and slices with every conceivable topping are doled out at the counter, and spicy wings and subs fly out the door too; cheap tabs, delivery service and late weekend hours are powerful attractions for the young and hungry, while grease monkeys get revved scoping out the automotive memorabilia.

NEW Fujimar ●Ⓩ *Asian/Pan-Latin*   – | – | – | E
(fka Lima)

Downtown | 1401 K St. NW (14th St.) | 202-789-2800 | www.fujimarrestaurant.com

At this dazzling second-floor Downtown venue, high-end sushi, ceviche and other seafood dishes – all given Asian-Latin twists – glisten against an ultra-mod backdrop comprising two loungey dining areas, several bars and a futuristic sushi counter; diners dressed to kill knock back fancy cocktails and terroir-driven wines at commensurate prices.

Full Kee ❶ *Chinese* — 23 | 8 | 16 | $20

Chinatown | 509 H St. NW (bet. 5th & 6th Sts.) | 202-371-2233 | www.fullkeedc.com

The "dead ducks" in the window and "Formica-filled" interior ID this Chinese eatery as a "hard-core, real-deal" Chinatown spot where the "amazingly long menu" (much of it posted on the wall) ranges from Hong Kong's "traditional soups" to "rare and interesting delicacies" that come at "rock-bottom" prices; the "ornery" service just "makes the experience more genuine"; P.S. the same-named Falls Church operation is separately owned.

Full Kee ❶ *Chinese* — 22 | 13 | 16 | $21

Falls Church | 5830 Columbia Pike (Leesburg Pike), VA | 703-575-8232

The kee to this "no-frills" (but late-night) Falls Church Chinese is to "go with a group" so you can order lots of bargain-priced, "not-Americanized" Cantonese food to share (don't miss the "heavenly" shrimp dumplings or "must-have" oyster casserole); while its "menu looks similar" to some other local Chinese eateries, fans swear that the "taste is a cut above."

Full Key ❶ *Chinese* — 25 | 12 | 19 | $20

Wheaton | Wheaton Manor Shopping Ctr. | 2227 University Blvd. W. (bet. Amherst & Georgia Aves.), MD | 301-933-8388

"Authentic Hong Kong–style" specialties, like "outstanding noodle soups" and "rich roast meats", are the key to ordering at this "unassuming" Wheaton Chinese where there's "not much decor" but there is "great congee" (it also serves "American-Chinese" standards); the staff is "nice", and it's "one of the cheapest places in town", which means it's often full.

Fu Shing Cafe *Chinese* — 22 | 14 | 20 | $19

Bethesda | 10315 Westlake Dr. (Lakeview Dr.), MD | 301-469-8878 | www.fushingcafebethesda.com

An "oldie but goodie", this strip-mall "hole-in-the-wall" in Bethesda is the "neighborhood Chinese go-to" spot for a "cheap", "flavorful" fill-up; service is "fast" and "friendly", and if the "tight quarters" are "no place to 'dine'" (you "order at the counter", and food's "brought to the table"), there's always "carryout and delivery."

Fyve *American* — ▽ 24 | 22 | 23 | $54

Pentagon City | Ritz-Carlton Pentagon City | 1250 S. Hayes St. (bet. Army-Navy Dr. & 15th St.) | Arlington, VA | 703-412-2762 | www.ritzcarlton.com

"Super service", always expected from the Ritz-Carlton brand, highlights this Pentagon City resto-lounge where "delicious" albeit "pricey" American bistro fare and "martinis served in your own personal shaker" are found in "quiet", elegant surroundings that work well for "sitting by the fireplace with friends"; bonus: formal tea is served on weekends.

Gadsby's *American*   21 | 25 | 21 | $34

Old Town | 138 N. Royal St. (Cameron St.) | Alexandria, VA |
703-548-1288 | www.gadsbystavernrestaurant.com

"A true Revolutionary experience" awaits at this "historical"
Alexandria tavern space that once hosted our first president, and
where "Colonial characters" and "period" musicians now provide
"excellent entertainment" while you sup on midpriced Traditional
American fare that's "nicely done"; while some say it's "not for those
looking for a culinary experience", the historically minded argue you
do have the opportunity to try George Washington's "favorite duck
recipe" – and hey, "maybe James Madison" will talk to you!

Georgia Brown's *Southern*   22 | 22 | 22 | $42

Downtown | 950 15th St. NW (bet. I & K Sts.) | 202-393-4499 |
www.georgiabrowns.com

At this "Low Country" "magnet for high-powered regulars" just
"blocks from the White House", you never know who you'll see "digging into the fried tomatoes" and other "high-end comfort food"
ferried by "down-home, Southern-friendly" folk in its "packed-
beyond-reason" room; even if the "classy", "Clinton-era decor"
could stand an "update", it's got "staying power", and there "ain't
nothin' like" its "amazing" Sunday jazz brunch.

Geranio *Italian*   25 | 22 | 23 | $46

Old Town | 722 King St. (bet. Columbus & Washington Sts.) |
Alexandria, VA | 703-548-0088 | www.geranio.net

A "perennial favorite" since 1976, this pretty, rustic Old Town
Italophiles' haunt is home to "pleasant" servers who present
"not-to-be-missed" lobster risotto and seasonal specials that are
"relatively pricey" but "delicious"; flush wallets favor it for "special-
occasion dinners" or a "romantic evening", while thinner wads find
cheaper prices at lunch.

Good Fortune *Chinese*   ▽ 22 | 13 | 16 | $24

Wheaton | 2646 University Blvd. W. (bet. Georgia Ave. &
Veirs Mill Rd.), MD | 301-929-9818

Perhaps "best for weekend dim sum", when the rolling carts make it
"fun", this affordable Chinese eatery near the Westfield Wheaton
shopping complex also serves the "terrific" bites off its regular
menu all week long; the "large" dining area may be low on frills, but
first-timers especially count themselves fortunate that the staff is
so "patient and helpful."

Good Stuff Eatery ⊠ *Burgers*   23 | 15 | 17 | $15

Capitol Hill | 303 Pennsylvania Ave. SE (bet. 3rd & 4th Sts.) |
202-543-8222

NEW **Crystal City** | 2110 Crystal Dr. (23rd St.) | Arlington, VA |
703-415-4663

www.goodstuffeatery.com

Former *Top Chef* contender Spike Mendelsohn is behind this "popular" Capitol Hill counter serve (and newer Crystal City sibling) woo-
ing "celebrities", "pols" and "policy wonks" with "creative", "juicy"

burgers, "perfectly seasoned" fries and "unbelievably decadent" milkshakes ("heaven in a plastic cup"), all doled out "fast" in upscale-industrial "fast-food" digs; despite "limited" seating, occasional "long" waits and tabs some consider "pricey" for the genre, it's still usually "jam packed."

Grace's Mandarin *Asian*   25 | 28 | 25 | $41

National Harbor | 188 Waterfront St. (Fleet St.), MD | 301-839-3788 | www.gracesrestaurants.com

"Delightful" Asian fusion and "so good" sushi are backed by "superior" service at Grace Tang's waterfront spot, and though it's "pricey, that's National Harbor for ya"; making it further worth the while is an "awesome" view of the Potomac, though the exuberant Eastern decor is also "intriguing" ("love the huge Buddha").

🆕 Graffiato ● *Italian/Pizza*   24 | 18 | 21 | $43

Chinatown | 707 6th St. NW (bet. G & H Sts.) | 202-289-3600 | www.graffiatodc.com

Top Chef's Mike Isabella delivers "Italian comfort food like none other" at this somewhat "pricey" Chinatown addition where the pizzas are "creative", the "tapas-style" plates "pack a punch" and, yes, the famous pepperoni sauce is indeed "worth bathing in"; service is "efficient" and the bi-level "industrial-chic" setting has a "high-energy", "rock 'n' roll" vibe (read: "loud") that provides a "fun way to dine on a date" or "with friends."

Granville Moore's *American/Belgian*   24 | 19 | 21 | $30

Atlas District | 1238 H St. NE (bet. 12th & 13th Sts.) | 202-399-2546 | www.granvillemoores.com

"Even Popeye would be jealous" of the "phenomenal" mussels at this affordable Belgian-American gastropub in the Atlas District, which "packs a lot" of "hipsters" scarfing "gourmet bar food" into its rough-hewn, "pocket-sized" space; you may "have to wait for a seat", but glass-half-full types see it as a perfect time to flag down one of the amenable staffers and dive into the "deep, rich and wide beer list."

Grapeseed ⊠ *American*   23 | 19 | 21 | $49

Bethesda | 4865 Cordell Ave. (bet. Norfolk & Woodmont Aves.), MD | 301-986-9592 | www.grapeseedbistro.com

The staff will "steer you right" for "imaginative food with tasteful wine pairings" at this vine-centric Bethesda New American whose contemporary space includes "romantic" two-person booths for "date night", private "wine cellar" rooms for small groups and a chef's table overlooking the kitchen that keeps kids "occupied"; a few sour grapes say it's "noisy" and "pricey" but they're crushed by great bunches of folks who "love this place."

🆕 Green Pig *American*   - | - | - | M

Clarendon | 1025 N. Fillmore St. (11th St.), VA | 703-888-1920 | www.greenpigbistro.com

This mod-rustic, moderately priced Clarendon American arrival reflects chef Scot Harlan's passion for nose-to-tail cooking – watch

	FOOD	DECOR	SERVICE	COST

him craft 'redneck' charcuterie in the open kitchen – and for giving French classics a decidedly American push; the bar and dining rooms, decorated with vintage kitchen collectibles, offer both intimate and communal seating arrangements.

The Grille   *American/French*

▽ 25 | 23 | 27 | $63

Old Town | Morrison Hse. | 116 S. Alfred St. (bet. King & Prince Sts.) | Alexandria, VA | 703-838-8000 | www.thegrillealexandria.com

"Feeling far from the madding crowd" in an Old Town hotel, this "understated yet elegant" American-French place treats diners like "honored guests", pampering them with "wonderful" service and "very carefully" prepared food; it's "expensive", but also a "perfect spot for a celebration" given its "charm and sophistication."

Grillfish   *Seafood*

20 | 18 | 20 | $37

West End | 1200 New Hampshire Ave. NW (M St.) | 202-331-7310 | www.grillfishdc.com

"Simply prepared seafood" "lets the fish do the talking" at this West End eatery serving "fresh" aquatica at prices "you don't have to take out a second mortgage to afford"; "friendly" servers put diners at ease in the "comfy", "unpretentious" dining room with columns and faux-stone walls and out on the "pleasant" sidewalk.

Grill from Ipanema   *Brazilian*

24 | 20 | 23 | $41

Adams Morgan | 1858 Columbia Rd. NW (Belmont Rd.) | 202-986-0757 | www.thegrillfromipanema.com

This "little piece of Brazil in Adams Morgan" proffers "classic" Carioca cooking like moqueca (fish stew) that "makes the mouth mambo" served by an "attentive" staff in tropical-themed environs; it's not cheap, but its "hearty" weekend brunch is a "deal" for under $20, and evokes a "relaxing day in Rio" – especially after one or two caipirinhas.

NEW Grillmarx Steakhouse & Raw Bar   *Steak*

22 | 22 | 20 | $41

Olney | Fairhill Shopping Ctr. | 18149 Town Center Dr. (Olney Sandy Spring Rd.), MD | 301-570-1111 | www.grillmarxsteakhouse.com

A "great" "upmarket" addition to Olney say locals who welcome this steakhouse and raw bar serving "smoky" ribs, tasty chowders and "well-prepared" entrees in a "noisy" bar area or a "more spacious, quieter" dining room trimmed with exposed brick, wood beams and leather banquettes; if some say it's "a bit pricey", others point to a "fairly priced" wine list.

Guajillo   *Mexican*

21 | 16 | 19 | $25

Courthouse | 1727 Wilson Blvd. (bet. Quinn & Rhodes Sts.) | Arlington, VA | 703-807-0840 | www.guajillogrill.com

"Savor the smoky flavors of Mexico" at this "authentic", affordable Arlington Courthouse–area cantina known for its "no-competition" moles, "clever" tacos and "complex" margaritas; it's "crowded but fun" in the brightly painted nook stuffed with traditional leather chairs handcrafted in Mexico, and "quick" service gives it a boost.

Guapo's *Tex-Mex* ⟶ 22 | 18 | 21 | $25

Upper NW | 4515 Wisconsin Ave. NW (Albemarle St.) | 202-686-3588
Bethesda | 8130 Wisconsin Ave. (River Rd. NW), MD | 301-656-0888
Gaithersburg | Rio | 9811 Washingtonian Blvd. (Rio Blvd.), MD |
301-977-5655
Shirlington | 4028 Campbell Ave. (S. Shirlington Rd.) | Arlington, VA |
703-671-1701
Fairfax | Fairlakes Shopping Ctr. | 13050 Fairlakes Shopping Ctr.
(Lakes Blvd.), VA | 703-818-0022
www.guaposrestaurant.com

Guests "never leave hungry" at this "good, basic" multilocation "Tex-Mex machine", a "kids' favorite" on account of "tasty" tacos and fajitas – while many adults may gravitate to the "feel-good margarita pitchers"; festive, "informal surroundings" are further "brightened by a happy, helpful staff", adding up to a "great value" that "holds its own" against similar chains.

Guardado's 🅼 *Pan-Latin/Spanish* 23 | 14 | 21 | $32

Bethesda | 4918 Del Ray Ave. (bet. Norfolk Ave. & Old Georgetown Rd.),
MD | 301-986-4920 | www.guardadosnico.com

"Tantalizing tapas minus all the glam and glitz" of other area tapas joints is the attraction at this "homey", "good-value" Bethesda Spanish-Latin "mom-and-pop" co-owned by chef Nicolas José Guardado and his wife, Reyna; together, they oversee a "cheerful" staff that sets a "comfortable, pleasurable" mood for an "informal meal."

Haad Thai *Thai* ▽ 21 | 15 | 20 | $28

Downtown | 1100 New York Ave. NW (bet. 11th & 12th Sts.) |
202-682-1111 | www.haadthairestaurant.com

"For a quick Thai fix", Downtown denizens duck into this "dependable" "neighborhood standby" for midpriced Southeast Asian "comfort food"; a large mural depicting the silhouette of a Thai long-tail boat sets a "soothing" tone in the casual space, one that's furthered by the "accommodating", "warm" service.

Haandi *Indian* 24 | 17 | 21 | $29

Bethesda | 4904 Fairmont Ave. (Norfolk Ave.), MD | 301-718-0121
Falls Church | Falls Plaza Shopping Ctr. | 1222 W. Broad St. (Gordon Rd.),
VA | 703-533-3501
www.haandi.com

"Standard-setting Indian food" has long been the draw at these "unwaveringly steady" subcontinentals in Bethesda and Falls Church with waiters who are "helpful, approachable" and "ready to share their culture"; they're "reasonably" priced too, especially the "impressive" lunch buffets that "attract a crowd" daily to the "pleasant" (and "pink") settings; P.S. the Bethesda location is planning a move nearby.

Hama Sushi *Japanese* ▽ 25 | 18 | 22 | $32

Herndon | Village Center at Dulles | 2415 Centreville Rd.
(Sunrise Valley Dr.), VA | 703-713-0088 | www.hama-sushi.com

"You would never know it from the outside", but this traditional-looking strip-mall Japanese in Herndon is a winner among local "sushi lovers" thanks to "very creative" rolls and "interesting" specials;

	FOOD	DECOR	SERVICE	COST

solid service, a midsized sake selection and moderate prices further its appeal.

NEW The Hamilton ◑ *American* | 20 | 25 | 18 | $36 |

Downtown | 600 14th St. NW (F St.) | 202-787-1000 |
www.thehamiltondc.com

This "massive", new late-night eatery/performance venue (from the Clyde's folks), in a "prime" spot near the White House, will "blow you away" with its "high-ceilinged hunting lodge" look featuring stately, "active" bars and private booths, plus its downstairs live-music area; the "something-for-everyone" American menu leaves diners "with enough money to pay the mortgage" – and though some call the service "indifferent", glass-half-full fans see it as "still getting the hang of it."

Hank's Oyster Bar *American/Seafood* | 24 | 17 | 21 | $38 |

NEW Capitol Hill | 633 Pennsylvania Ave. SE (7th St.) | 202-733-1971
Dupont Circle | 1624 Q St. NW (bet. 16th & 17th Sts.) | 202-462-4265
Old Town | 1026 King St. (bet. Henry & Patrick Sts.) | Alexandria, VA | 703-739-4265 Ⓜ
www.hanksrestaurants.com

"Oysters and clams and lobster rolls, oh my" trill fans of these "classic" raw bars in Dupont Circle, Old Town and Capitol Hill; "congeniality" and "fair value" inspires some happy shuckers to say they "could slurp oysters all day" in the "comfortable" New England (by way of *Martha Stewart Living*) digs.

Hard Times Cafe *American* | 22 | 17 | 21 | $18 |

Bethesda | 4920 Del Ray Ave. (bet. Norfolk Ave. & Old Georgetown Rd.), MD | 301-951-3300
Germantown | 13032 Middlebrook Rd. (Century Blvd.), MD | 240-686-0150 ◑
College Park | 4738 Cherry Hill Rd. (Baltimore Ave.), MD | 301-474-8880
Rockville | Woodley Gdns. | 1117 Nelson St. (Montgomery Ave.), MD | 301-294-9720
Old Town | 1404 King St. (West St.) | Alexandria, VA | 703-837-0050
Clarendon | 3028 Wilson Blvd. (Highland St.), VA | 703-528-2233 ◑
Fairfax | 4069 Chain Bridge Rd. (Sager Ave.), VA | 703-267-9590 ◑
Springfield | Springfield Plaza | 6362 Springfield Plaza (Commerce St.), VA | 703-913-5600 ◑
Manassas | 7753 Sudley Rd. (bet. Broken Branch Ln. & Sudley Manor Dr.), VA | 703-365-8400 ◑
Woodbridge | Potomac Festival Plaza | 14389 Potomac Mills Rd. (bet. Opitz Blvd. & Potomac Mills Rd.), VA | 703-492-2950 ◑
www.hardtimes.com
Additional locations throughout the DC area

"God said 'let there be chili'" before creating this regional chain "staple" say fans of the "superb" variations (Texas, Cincinnati, spicy, vegetarian) available by the bowl or in many of its less-lauded pubby menu items – though some say those are "surprisingly good" too; "prompt" service, "value" and a "honky-tonk" atmosphere with "sports bar leanings" that includes a "decent" beer selection make them great places to "catch a game."

	FOOD	DECOR	SERVICE	COST

Harry's Smokehouse *BBQ/Burgers*
▽ 21 | 22 | 22 | $23

Pentagon City | The Fashion Centre at Pentagon City | 1100 S. Hayes St. (Army Navy Dr.) | Arlington, VA | 703-416-7070 | www.harryssmokehouse.com

Inside Pentagon City's Fashion Centre mall, this "good ol' American barbecue" spot serves "melt-in-your-mouth" brisket and other down-home eats at "great prices"; plasma TVs, craft beers and a large open kitchen anchoring the raw-wood-and-stone space provide "a good escape" from shopping.

Härth *American*
▽ 23 | 27 | 23 | $58

Tysons Corner | Hilton McLean Tysons Corner | 7920 Jones Branch Dr. (Westpark Dr.) | McLean, VA | 703-847-5000 | www.harthrestaurant.com

"Fabulously chic and sexy decor" meshing woodsy elements with fiery accents (including the wood-burning oven it's named for) imparts a "cool atmosphere" to this high-priced Tysons Corner New American at the Hilton; the "not-your-average-hotel-restaurant" feel extends to the "delicious" comfort food, including "outstanding" pastas and flatbreads, an "amusing" iPad drinks list and "courteous" service that make it "worth fighting traffic" to dine here.

NEW Haven *Pizza*
- | - | - | I

Bethesda | 7137 Wisconsin Ave. (bet. Leland St. & Willow Ln.), MD | 301-664-9412 | www.havenpizzeria.com

New Haven–style pizzas fired in two 2,200-degree coal ovens – most notably the tribute to Connecticut's famed 'white-clam tomato pie' – have been drawing crowds to this new Bethesda pie shop since day one; its handsome, brick-trimmed setting is family-friendly and casual with roomy booths and a granite bar dispensing wine and beer, and it's priced friendly too; P.S. leave room for homemade gelato for dessert.

Hee Been *Korean*
23 | 18 | 19 | $29

Greater Alexandria | 6231 Little River Tpke. (Beauregard St.) | Alexandria, VA | 703-941-3737
NEW Arlington | 3600 S. Glebe Rd. (Jefferson Davis Hwy.), VA | 703-567-4036
www.heebeen.com

Those who "can't decide between Korean barbecue and Japanese" find an affordable fix at this Asian "feast" with outlets in Alexandria and Arlington, where "fun tabletop grilling" rubs shoulders with "enormous" "all-you-can-eat" buffet spreads that leave guests full for "days"; "industrial" decor suits the largely self-serve model, with diners focused on chowing "to their heart's delight."

Heritage India *Indian*
22 | 20 | 20 | $34

Glover Park | 2400 Wisconsin Ave. NW (Calvert St.) | 202-333-3120 | www.heritageindiausa.com

Go "upscale Indian" "without losing authenticity" at this Glover Park subcontinental serving "rich" and "spicy" classics plus Indian street food–inspired tapas; considering the "pleasant" ambiance that flows from the "friendly" staff and "beautiful" heritage on display (brocaded fabrics, British colonial paintings), it's reasonably priced.

	FOOD	DECOR	SERVICE	COST

Hill Country *BBQ* | 21 | 19 | 16 | $28 |

Penn Quarter | 410 Seventh St. NW (bet. D & E Sts.) | 202-556-2050 | www.hillcountrywdc.com

This "li'l bit of Texas" (via NYC, and with "Manhattan" prices) brings "finger-lickin'" ribs and "moist" brisket to this "barn"-sized "Disney-did-Lockhart" BBQ spot in Penn Quarter; its "meal-ticket"-based, "cafeterialike service" is "fun", "kitschy", "confusing" or perhaps all three – but most agree that "cold beer" and "great live music" in the downstairs club add to an "awesome concept."

Himalayan Heritage *Indian/Nepalese* | 21 | 19 | 20 | $27 |

Adams Morgan | 2305 18th St. NW (Kalorama Rd.) | 202-483-9300 | www.himalayanheritagedc.com

"Spicy", "complex" Nepalese-Indian fare is "served with pride and love" via "warm", "friendly" sherpas who guide diners through the "adventurous menu" at this purveyor "right in the thick of things" in Adams Morgan; the "cozy" space has a Himalayan lodge feel, which, along with "reasonable" prices, brings folks back "over and over."

Hinode *Japanese* | 20 | 16 | 19 | $28 |

Bethesda | 4914 Hampden Ln. (bet. Arlington Rd. & Woodmont Ave.), MD | 301-654-0908

Frederick | 50 Carroll Creek Way (Market St.), MD | 301-620-2943 | www.hinode-frederick.com

Rockville | 134 Congressional Ln. (bet. Jefferson St. & Rockville Pike), MD | 301-816-2190

Locals depend on these "friendly" suburban Maryland Japanese joints for a "terrifically wide variety" of "competently done" sushi; at the sparsely decorated Bethesda and Rockville links it's all about the "bargain" lunch buffets, and though Frederick lacks the buffet, it boasts a "charming" creekside setting.

Hollywood East Cafe *Chinese* | 24 | 15 | 18 | $24 |
(aka Hollywood East on the Boulevard)

Wheaton | Westfield Wheaton | 11160 Veirs Mill Rd. (University Blvd. W.), MD | 240-290-9988 | www.hollywoodeastcafe.com

Its "worth getting up early" and heading to this Wheaton Chinese on weekends, to dig your chopsticks into its "fantastic" Cantonese dim sum the "friendly" staff brings around on carts (weekdays, it's available à la carte); there's also a large "authentic" menu "ranging from the common to the extraordinary" served in a modern-industrial setting that some say is "hard to find" inside a shopping mall.

Honey Pig Gooldaegee | 23 | 13 | 17 | $24 |
Korean Grill ● *Korean*
(aka Seoul Gool Dae Gee)

Annandale | 7220 Columbia Pike (Maple Pl.), VA | 703-256-5229
Centreville | 13818 Braddock Rd. (Old Centreville Rd.), VA | 703-830-5959
www.eathoneypig.com

"Prepare to smell like" the "wonderful" barbecue meats grilling "right in front" of you at the table at these "hip", "lively" Seoul sisters in Annandale, Centreville and Ellicott City, which are popular "after-clubbing" destinations since they're open 24/7 (except Monday, when it's closed from 2–11 AM) and blare "upbeat K-pop music" "as loud as a club" with the "industrial" "decor to match"; most non-Korean speakers can work around the staff's "minimal English" to seek out the strong "price-to-flavor ratio."

Hong Kong Palace *Chinese* | 27 | 11 | 16 | $21 |

Falls Church | 6387 Seven Corners Ctr. (Leesburg Pike), VA | 703-532-0940 | www.hkpalace.webs.com

"Long lines" don't lie at this "friendly", "real Sichuan" "hole-in-the-wall", a "favorite" of the "local Asian" community and others in the know for "amazing, authentic Chinese" so "well done" it leaves folks wondering "what did Falls Church do to deserve this place?"; you don't need to bring much money, but "be prepared for spicy."

Hooked *Seafood* | 20 | 21 | 16 | $42 |

Sterling | Potomac Run Ctr. | 46240 Potomac Run Plaza (bet. Cascades Pkwy. & Rte. 7), VA | 703-421-0404 | www.hookedonseafood.com

A "swanky, cool vibe" filled with glitz provides an "upscale" "change of pace" for Sterling say fans of this Potomac Run venue that proffers "well-prepared" seafood and sushi; some detractors note "unreliable" service and "steep" tabs, though most locals are reeled in by the "reliably tasty" eats and attractive bait like a "nice", huge "outdoor patio."

Horace & Dickie's Seafood | 22 | 6 | 20 | $12 |
Carryout *Seafood*

Atlas District | 809 12th St. NE (H St.) | 202-397-6040

NEW **Horace & Dickie's Seafood** 🅢🅜 *Seafood*

Takoma | 6912 Fourth St. (bet. Blair Rd. & Butternut St.) | 202-248-4265 | www.horaceanddickies.com

It's a little late to "not tell anyone" about this Atlas District "landmark" carryout (and new, more polished Takoma sibling) and its "dynamite", "good-eating" seafood and soulful sides that have been giving folks their "money's worth" for years; occasional "lines out the door" prove that "lack of decor and ambiance" is no deterrent to business when they "give you plenty of fish" in your sandwich.

Hot 'N Juicy Crawfish *Cajun/Creole* | ∇ 20 | 17 | 20 | $24 |

Woodley Park | 2651 Connecticut Ave. NW (bet. Calvert St. & Woodley Rd.) | 202-299-9448 | www.hotandjuicycrawfish.com

Pick a "spice level", grab "plenty of napkins" and indulge in "crawfish-sucking, shrimp-peeling, crab-cracking madness" at this Cajun-Creole chain outpost in Woodley Park where "friendly and prompt" servers keep the cold beer coming; yes, it's a "very casual" atmosphere (plastic-covered tables, bibs) but the good times roll "in the summer when you can sit outside."

NEW Howard Theatre *Southern* | - | - | - | M |

Shaw | Howard Theatre | 620 T St. NW (7th St.) | 202-803-2899 | www.thehowardtheatre.com

Reopened after an eye-popping renovation, this storied African-American theater in Shaw, where the likes of Duke Ellington came to fame, now serves a sophisticated, moderately priced Southern-accented American supper-club menu designed by consulting chef Marcus Samuelsson (Harlem's Red Rooster) on performance nights; the weekly Sunday gospel buffet brunch is also worthy of the limelight.

Hudson ● *American* ▽ 18 | 20 | 20 | $42

West End | 2030 M St. NW (21st St.) | 202-872-8700 | www.hudson-dc.com

There's a "cosmopolitan" feel to this pricey West End New American gathering spot sporting a "modern", "open" setting "smartly de-signed" to separate the nibblers and cocktail sippers from the serious diners digging into its "well-crafted, seasonal" fare; most are "pleased with the service", and regulars recommend "snagging an outside table" to people-watch.

Hunan Dynasty *Chinese* ▽ 20 | 16 | 21 | $36

Capitol Hill | 215 Pennsylvania Ave. SE, 2nd fl. (bet. C St. & Independence Ave.) | 202-546-6161

"Longtime staff members are friendly and warmly welcome" regulars, like "members of Congress", who bipartisanly approve the "solid", "flavorful" Chinese fare at this Capitol Hill "mainstay" that does sushi and Thai too; typical restaurant chinoiserie is par for the course, as are "reasonable" tabs.

Hunter's Head Tavern Ⓜ *British* ▽ 23 | 23 | 20 | $30

Upperville | 9048 John Mosby Hwy./Rte. 50 (Parker St.), VA | 540-592-9020 | www.huntersheadtavern.com

It's "well worth the drive" to scenic Upperville to visit this "ersatz British pub" housed in a historic 18th-century home, where guests dine inside the "cozy" "country tavern" or on the "beautiful outdoor patio"; after placing initial orders at the bar, the "efficient" staff de-livers the "very good", midpriced pub grub (bangers 'n' mash, Welsh rarebit), much of it made from organic local meats and produce from neighboring Ayrshire Farm.

Huong Viet ⊄ *Vietnamese* 25 | 14 | 20 | $23

Falls Church | Eden Ctr. | 6785 Wilson Blvd. (bet. Arlington & Roosevelt Blvds.), VA | 703-538-7110 | www.huong-viet.com

This "no-contest" pick in Falls Church's Eden Center epitomizes "true Vietnamese cuisine" swear fans, citing its "great noodle dishes", "excellent" bun, indeed, pretty much everything on its looong menu; with "willing, friendly service", most "don't care about" the "no-frills" decor or that one must "bring cash" to pay the "cheap" bill.

Il Canale *Italian/Pizza* 22 | 18 | 20 | $33

Georgetown | 1063 31st St. NW (M St.) | 202-337-4444 | www.ilcanaledc.com

Taste buds are "transported to Italy" via "genuine, wood-fired" Neapolitan pizza (plus "delicate" pasta and other "authentic" fare) at this "friendly" Georgetowner "romantically" "tucked away" near the C&O Canal; the good value is bolstered by a "peerless wine list" with a "fair corkage policy" and a plethora of distinctive seating op-

	FOOD	DECOR	SERVICE	COST

tions: "lovely" sidewalk, "modern" "industrial" ground floor, "quaint rooftop" or by a "magical" window upstairs.

Il Fornaio *Italian* | 25 | 23 | 23 | $43 |

Reston | Reston Town Ctr. | 11990 Market St. (bet. Reston & St. Francis Pkwys.), VA | 703-437-5544 | www.ilfornaio.com
"Remarkable" house-baked breads presage a "sumptuous" Italian meal at Reston's "terrific, classy trattoria" chain place, where a "really nice staff" ferries plates through a Tuscan "movie set"; a few penne-pinchers say it's "pricey", but everyone loves happy hour when there's $5 pizza at the bar.

Il Pizzico 🗷 *Italian* | 27 | 20 | 24 | $41 |

Rockville | Suburban Park | 15209 Frederick Rd. (Gude Dr.), MD | 301-309-0610 | www.ilpizzico.com
You'd think that "more than two decades" of dishing up "beautiful homemade pastas" and other simply "amazing food for the price" would have put this Rockville Italian on the foodie radar screen, but its "unassuming strip-mall" location has kept it something of a local "find"; that doesn't mean you won't "wait" for a prime-time table in the Tuscanesque setting – so go "early", "inhale the atmosphere", "salute the wines" and banter with the "helpful", "talkative" waiters.

Il Porto Ristorante *Italian* | 24 | 22 | 23 | $36 |

Greater Alexandria | 121 King St. (S. Lee St.) | Alexandria, VA | 703-836-8833 | www.ilportoristorante.com
Yes, it's "been there forever", and this midpriced Alexandria Italian remains "an all-time favorite" of supporters who swear by its sauces, both "light and complex" and so "rich" and "meaty" they taste as if they'd "been cooking for hours", proffered by "polite" servers; "retro in a good way", the plaster-beam-and-stone construction lends it an "old-world charm."

India Palace Bar & Tandoor *Indian* | ∇ 26 | 23 | 26 | $23 |

Germantown | Fox Chapel Shopping Ctr. | 19743 Frederick Rd. (Gunners Branch Rd.), MD | 301-540-3000 | www.indiapalacegermantown.com
"Run and frequented by Indians", this Germantown shopping-center subcontinental offers "appealing", affordable fare (including a "great buffet selection" at lunch) in a simple, traditionally decorated setting that works for "date night" or a meal with "the whole family"; the service is as "exceptional" as the food, with "inviting" staffers tending to every need.

Indique *Indian* | 23 | 21 | 21 | $37 |

Cleveland Park | 3512-14 Connecticut Ave. NW (bet. Ordway & Porter Sts.) | 202-244-6600 | www.indique.com

Indique Heights *Indian*

Chevy Chase | 2 Wisconsin Circle (Western Ave.), MD | 301-656-4822 | www.indiqueheights.com
"Exciting, high-end" riffs on Indian "street food" at these "upper-end" Cleveland Park and Chevy Chase subcontinentals raise them to "Himalayan heights" say supporters who also give high marks to

"pleasant" service; "mezzanine seating" at DC's "beautiful" bi-level space strikes a "romantic" note, while "casbahlike" dining on "cushions" lends a "relaxing" vibe just over the district line in Maryland.

☑ Inn at Little Washington
Restaurant *American*

`29` `29` `29` `$205`

Washington | Inn at Little Washington | 309 Middle St. (Main St.), VA | 540-675-3800 | www.theinnatlittlewashington.com

"Simply the best", Patrick O'Connell's hunt-country New American "citadel" earns the No. 1 rating for Food, Decor and Service in the Greater DC area for what amounts to "a life-altering experience"; guests get "pampered in all directions" in an "intimate", richly embroidered setting, where "revelatory" multicourse repasts are "prepared with extraordinary skill" and seasoned with a "touch of whimsy" – in short, it's "worth every penny . . . and that's a lot of pennies!"; P.S. "spend the night for the ultimate indulgence."

I Ricchi ☑ *Italian*

`24` `23` `24` `$65`

Dupont Circle | 1220 19th St. NW (bet. M & N Sts.) | 202-835-0459 | www.iricchi.net

"Power brokers unite" at this "old-world" Dupont Circle Italian, whose "divine" classics and "professional" service have "stood the test of time"; regulars who "feel pampered" in its "lovely", villa-esque room counter protests that "you have to be one of the ricchi indeed to afford to eat here", by conceding that, yes, prices are "high" but so is the "quality."

Irish Inn at Glen Echo *Irish*

`20` `19` `22` `$36`

Glen Echo | 6119 Tulane Ave. (MacArthur Blvd.), MD | 301-229-6600 | www.irishinnglenecho.com

"Genuine Irish hospitality" powers this "charming" Glen Echo eatery where "familiar" Irish (and American) "comfort food" is "well represented" on the midpriced menu, but is bolstered by fancier items from further afield; choose from several "adorable", "conversation"-friendly rooms or "skip the food" to down a "pint" in the bar or on the outdoor deck; P.S. there's occasional live music.

NEW Irish Whiskey Public
House ❶ *Pub Food*

`-` `-` `-` `M`

Dupont Circle | 1207 19th St. NW (bet. M & N Sts.) | 202-463-3010 | www.irishwhiskeydc.com

Serious tipplers drink to this newly inaugurated Irish pub near Dupont Circle, where bars on three floors pour an impressive roster of whiskeys and noteworthy beers, and are backed by a midpriced menu of spirited Auld Sod classics (e.g. beer-battered fish 'n' chips, shepherd's pie with Guinness gravy); the modern-Dublin-in-DC setting features gleaming dark wood, barrel-and-brick-lined walls, fireplace seating and an outdoor patio.

Iron Bridge Wine Company *American*

`25` `23` `23` `$41`

Warrenton | 29 Main St. (1st St.), VA | 540-349-9339 | www.ironbridgewines.com

See review in the Baltimore Directory.

	FOOD	DECOR	SERVICE	COST

Isabella's *Spanish*

26 | 22 | 23 | $32

Frederick | 44 N. Market St. (Rte. 144), MD | 301-698-8922 |
www.isabellas-tavern.com

At this "popular" midpriced Spanish in Frederick, "helpful" staffers
"guide diners through the amazing array" of tapas that are designed to
"share" but which are so "fantastic" you "may not want to"; a "super"
happy hour enlivens the "casual" setting with exposed-brick walls.

It's About Thyme 🏷Ⓜ *Eclectic*

25 | 21 | 23 | $38

Culpeper | Thyme In Culpeper | 128 E. Davis St. (Main St.), VA |
540-825-4264 | www.thymeinfo.com

"Outstanding", reasonably priced Eclectic food is "beautifully prepared and happily served" by a "knowledgeable" staff at this
Culpeper "destination" with a "small town feel"; the "distinctive" interior, with its tin ceiling and European landscape murals, can get "a
bit crowded", but it's definitely "worth the squeeze."

Jackie's *American*

23 | 20 | 20 | $38

Silver Spring | 8081 Georgia Ave. (entrance on Sligo Ave.), MD |
301-565-9700 | www.jackiesrestaurant.com

What used to be an "old muffler shop" hides Silver Spring's "nifty",
"funky '60s"-looking resto-lounge with "inventive" American "cuisine that doesn't take itself too seriously" and "won't break the
bank" that's "delivered in style" by an "unfailingly friendly" crew;
"crafty cocktails" are poured at its next-door sibling, Sidebar.

Jack Rose Dining Saloon *American*

▽ 20 | 24 | 18 | $45

Adams Morgan | 2007 18th St. NW (Florida Ave.) | 202-588-7388 |
www.jackrosediningsaloon.com

"There are few cooler spaces" than this spirits-centric saloon in
Adams Morgan with its "wall of bourbon and whiskey", "a glorious
sight to behold" while partaking of the non-liquid accompaniments,
i.e. the "decent" if "slightly expensive" American food; it's also "worth
a trip to sip" and nosh on tasty "bar nibbles" on the upstairs terrace.

Jackson's Mighty Fine Food & Lucky Lounge *American/Seafood*

23 | 21 | 23 | $31

Reston | Reston Town Ctr. | 11927 Democracy Dr. (Library St.), VA |
703-437-0800 | www.greatamericanrestaurants.com

Folks flock to Reston Town Center's "never-miss" American pub for its
"broad menu" of "great-tasting" "familiar" favorites served in "hearty"
portions at "moderate" prices; the "thoughtful" staff caters to the "lit-
tlest needs" in an "expansive" sea of "comfortable", "roomy booths"
surrounded by 1940s-inspired decor, and though a few complain it's
"hard to have a conversation", most enjoy the "energetic" atmosphere,
especially the "hopping bar scene" with its many "upscale singles."

Jackson 20 *American*

21 | 21 | 21 | $39

Old Town | Hotel Monaco | 480 King St. (Pitt St.) | Alexandria, VA |
703-842-2790 | www.jackson20.com

The kitchen takes "old Southern dishes you remember and gives
them" a New American "kick" at this Old Town Alexandria hotel

spot with a look that's both "chic" (dark and modern with an open kitchen) and "quirky" ("an unusual amount of pigs"); "crazy-busy" brunches are handled with an "efficient approach" – at other times it's a nice place to "relax and unwind" with one of the 20 bottles of wine under $20.

Jaipur *Indian*
25 | 22 | 25 | $27

Fairfax | 9401 Lee Hwy. (Circle Woods Dr.), VA | 703-766-1111 | www.jaipurcuisine.com

"Intoxicating", "exotic aromas" hint at the "amazing" traditional food found at this "colorfully" decorated Fairfax Indian, where the curries "dance in your mouth"; a "popular" and affordable lunch buffet and staffers who "go out of their way" put it "heads and tails above" many other nearby options.

ⓩ Jaleo *Spanish*
24 | 20 | 21 | $39

Penn Quarter | 480 Seventh St. NW (E St.) | 202-628-7949
Bethesda | 7271 Woodmont Ave. (Elm St.), MD | 301-913-0003
Crystal City | 2250 Crystal Dr. (23rd St.) | Arlington, VA | 703-413-8181
www.jaleo.com

A "pitcher of sangria" and a "steady stream" of "delicious", "witty" tapas at this trio overseen by "rock-star" Spanish chef José Andrés are the answer to a "bruising work week", "out-of-town guests" or a "date-night" dilemma; "terrific" crews deftly handle the "racket and bustle" in "festively" decorated settings that feel as "fresh and exciting as ever", though costs can "add up quickly" – especially if you "have to try everything"; P.S. Penn Quarter recently had a bold, designer redo not reflected in its Decor rating.

J&G Steakhouse *American/Steak*
24 | 24 | 23 | $68

Downtown | W Hotel | 515 15th St. NW (bet. F St. & Pennsylvania Ave.) | 202-661-2440 | www.jgsteakhousewashingtondc.com

Jean-Georges Vongerichten's "modern take" on the steakhouse genre brings some of the "best" "juicy" cuts to Downtown, though often the "stars of the meal" are his "transcendent" New American dishes; just off the W Hotel's "disco-feeling lobby", the dining room, with its high ceilings and suave appointments, exudes an "understated" "chic" matched by its "polite" servers; P.S. the less pricey "hidden wine bar" downstairs is "perfect for an illicit tryst."

Java Green ⓩ *Vegan/Vegetarian*
22 | 16 | 20 | $18

Golden Triangle | 1020 19th St. NW (K St.) | 202-775-8899 | www.javagreen.net

Even a "meat-eater" could "love the vegan offerings" at this "eco-friendly" self-serve cafe in Golden Triangle, with its "varied selection" of "interesting" eats: salads, soups, wraps and sandwiches, plus "great smoothies too"; finding a seat at this "simple" vegetarian's "lunch heaven" can be iffy at prime times, so check the outdoor tables or do "takeout."

	FOOD	DECOR	SERVICE	COST

Joe's Noodle House *Chinese* `23` `9` `14` `$18`

Rockville | 1488 Rockville Pike (Congressional Ln.), MD | 301-881-5518 | www.joesnoodlehouse.com

"Chinese families in search of a taste of home" pack this "crowded", "divey" Rockville spot where "adventurous palates" find "authentic" Sichuan "kick and flavor" ("experience the burn") and "amazing value for money"; the "vast" menu with "hundreds of dishes" can seem "overwhelming", but the counter staff is "willing to help" before you sit down and "wait" for your picks to arrive.

Johnny's Half Shell 🖹 *American/Seafood* `21` `20` `20` `$47`

Capitol Hill | 400 N. Capitol St. NW (Louisiana Ave.) | 202-737-0400 | www.johnnyshalfshell.net

Super-"fresh" seafood, seasoned with the "Congressional or Supreme Court gossip" that can be overheard during this Capitol Hill New American's "active bar" or in its "more reserved" dark-wood dining area, powers Ann Cashion and John Fulchino's "tightly run ship"; time-honored Gulf and Chesapeake recipes are "prepared with skill and served with speed", and live jazz enlivens the weekends.

Juice Joint Cafe 🖹 *Health Food* ▽ `23` `13` `21` `$11`

Downtown | 1025 Vermont Ave. NW (K St.) | 202-347-6783 | www.juicejointcafe.com

The "rare" combo of "healthy and delicious" keeps a "daily lunch crowd coming back" to this Downtown canteen with a "huge" list of "inventive" salads, stir-fries, sandwiches and other casual fare; despite the "long line" at lunch, the "friendly" team takes "great care of their customers"; P.S. a recent renovation nearly doubled seating indoors and out (not reflected in the Decor rating).

Juniper *American* ▽ `24` `24` `26` `$55`

West End | Fairmont Hotel | 2401 M St. NW (24th St.) | 202-457-5020 | www.fairmont.com

A true sleeper, this "quiet" West Ender in the Fairmont is "not your typical hotel restaurant", providing "exquisite", "imaginative" New American meals; expect to pay a premium for the "elegant" service and "luxurious" setting overlooking a "beautiful courtyard" that qualify it "for a romantic dinner."

Kabob Bazaar *Persian* `25` `17` `21` `$20`

Bethesda | 7710 Wisconsin Ave. (Old Georgetown Rd.), MD | 301-652-5814
Clarendon | 3133 Wilson Blvd. (N. Herndon St.), VA | 703-522-8999
www.kabobbazaar.com

"Authentic" Persian dishes make for "balanced", "virtuous" and "reasonably priced" meals at these Bethesda and Clarendon "neighborhood gems" serving "delightful" kebabs, stews and "exotic specials"; "simple" brick-lined surrounds are tended by "helpful servers", though some folks just grab a seat at the bar for a quick spot of "Persian tea."

	FOOD	DECOR	SERVICE	COST

Kabob N Karahi ● *Nepalese/Pakistani* ▽ 26 | 8 | 23 | $15

Silver Spring | 15521 New Hampshire Ave. (Briggs Chaney Rd.), MD | 301-879-0044 | www.kabobnkarahi.com

It may be "just a [disposable] plate and fluorescent light kind of place" but this Silver Spring strip-mall "hole-in-the-wall" serves "expertly done" kebabs and other Pakistani-Nepalese treats at prices "you won't even blink at"; what's more, "courteous" servers make patrons feel "like visitors in someone's home."

Kabob Palace Family Restaurant *Mideastern* 26 | 12 | 20 | $18

Crystal City | 2333 S. Eads St. (bet. 23rd & 24th Sts.) | Arlington, VA | 703-979-3000 | www.kabobpalaceusa.com

"People in the know" come to this Arlington Mideasterner for "authentic" kebabs of "unfailing" quality plus an "excellent" lunch buffet at affordable prices; it's "always busy" despite "no decor" and "informal" service, bringing "all ages, races and creeds together in pursuit of awesome food."

NEW Kangaroo Boxing Club ● *BBQ* – | – | – | I

Columbia Heights | 3410 11th St. NW (Park Rd.) | 202-505-4522 | www.kangaroodc.com

PORC *BBQ*

Location varies; see website | no phone | www.porcmobile.com

The PORC food-truck talents have put down roots in Columbia Heights with this new brick-and-mortar venue, allowing expanded menu offerings of their inexpensive, house-smoked BBQ; the space has a rustic, been-there-forever quality with a cozy window nook, bar topped with an ornate fireplace mantel, classic jukebox and vintage photos of DC; P.S. the food truck is still rolling, so check its website for locations and times.

Kazan ☒ *Turkish* 25 | 20 | 25 | $40

McLean | Chain Bridge Corner Shopping Ctr. | 6813 Redmond Dr. (Chain Bridge Rd.), VA | 703-734-1960 | www.kazanrestaurant.com

After more than three decades, this McLean Turk sure "knows how to serve flavorful food", most notably its "out-of-this-world" doner kebab – and at "reasonable prices for the quality"; what's more, chef-owner Zeynel Uzun is almost "always on-site" overseeing a "most accommodating" staff, and while "sophisticated Turkish decor" doesn't quite transcend the "strip-mall" locale, it at least feels like a strip mall in Istanbul.

Kaz Sushi Bistro ☒ *Japanese* 25 | 17 | 21 | $47

World Bank | 1915 I St. NW (bet. 19th & 20th Sts.) | 202-530-5500 | www.kazsushi.com

Japanophiles give props to the "classical and innovative, new-age sushi" and "amazingly creative" small plates at Kaz Okochi's World Bank bistro; "yes, it is pricey" – except at lunchtime, when "hearty" bento boxes offer "terrific value" – and sure, the "sterile" decor could use an "upgrade", but most feel that the "pristine" sushi and "great" service more than "compensate."

	FOOD	DECOR	SERVICE	COST

Kellari Taverna *Greek*

23 | **21** | **21** | **$62**

Golden Triangle | 1700 K St. NW (Connecticut Ave.) | 202-535-5274 |
www.kellaridc.com

"Swim" to this "elegant Greek" seafooder in the Golden Triangle
"that can rival any in Athens" with its "beautifully done" fish and
tasty meze in a "bright", airy room that will "impress a business as-
sociate"; although choosing from the "mouthwatering" display of
"fish on ice" "can get expensive", there's a "steal" of a three-course
lunch, a pre-theater prix fixe and "free cheese and olives at the bar"
that expresses its Hellenic hospitality.

☑ Kinkead's *Seafood*

25 | **21** | **23** | **$62**

Foggy Bottom | 2000 Pennsylvania Ave. NW (I St.) | 202-296-7700 |
www.kinkead.com

At Bob Kinkead's Foggy Bottom "legend", folks who "know fish"
"consistently" prepare "exceptional", "camera"-worthy seafood
dishes while servers make guests feel "pampered" in the "quiet",
white-linen "corporate atmosphere"; "maybe it's not trendy", but
the "power lunches" show no sign of slowing down; P.S. hit the
downstairs bar/cafe for a cheaper, less "formal" meal.

☑ Kobe Japanese Steak &
Seafood House *Japanese*

27 | **24** | **25** | **$41**

Leesburg | Leesburg Plaza | 514 E. Market St. (Plaza St.), VA |
703-443-8300 | www.kobejs.com

See review in the Baltimore Directory.

☑ Komi ☒Ⓜ *American/Mediterranean*

28 | **22** | **28** | **$176**

Dupont Circle | 1509 17th St. NW (P St.) | 202-332-9200 |
www.komirestaurant.com

Johnny Monis leads diners on a "gastro-adventure" at his Dupont
Circle American-Med "temple" offering a "dazzling variety of dishes
beautifully prepared and executed" in a "subdued", "understated"
setting, made more "relaxing" by a staff that's "detailed oriented
without being uptight"; "expect to spend the evening" as they "serve
and serve and serve" a fixed-price "parade" of plates along with
"witty wine pairings" – and while the "high price" and "hard-to-get
reservations" give "mere eaters" pause, food fanatics chant "just go."

Konami *Japanese*

▽ **23** | **18** | **19** | **$36**

Tysons Corner | 8221 Leesburg Pike (Chain Bridge Rd.) | Vienna, VA |
703-821-3400 | www.konamirestaurant.com

"Even the pickiest of palates" will enjoy the "delicious" sushi and
other midpriced à la carte items at this Tysons Corner Japanese with
solid service; it "doesn't look like much from the outside" but it's
spacious and attractively lit inside, and hey, there's "free parking."

Kora ☒ *Italian*

17 | **20** | **17** | **$34**

Crystal City | 2250 Crystal Dr. (23rd St.) | Arlington, VA |
571-431-7090 | www.korarestaurant.com

A "soaring", "modern" dining room lined with floor-to-ceiling windows
and eggplant hues is the backdrop for "casual" Italian meals, including

	FOOD	DECOR	SERVICE	COST

pizza, at this Crystal City eatery catering to "office" workers and "families"; a few say it's "unmemorable"' but most find it "solid" with decent service and middling tabs; P.S. the owners' American restaurant within a restaurant, Farrah Olivia, is located in the back room.

Kotobuki *Japanese* | 25 | 10 | 18 | $27 |

Palisades | 4822 MacArthur Blvd. NW (U St.) | 202-625-9080 | www.kotobukiusa.com

"Good things come in small packages" at this "quirky" Palisades Japanese where a "focused selection" of "high-quality" sushi plus *kamameshi*, a rice-based hot pot, come at "very reasonable prices"; the "tiny", "square box" of a space (above Makoto, on the second story) is made more fab by a "Beatles-heavy play list" and "prompt and courteous" service; P.S. it's also a "favorite" take-out spot.

Kramerbooks & Afterwords Cafe ❶ *American* | 19 | 18 | 18 | $27 |

Dupont Circle | 1517 Connecticut Ave. NW (bet. Dupont Circle & Q St.) | 202-387-1462 | www.kramers.com

"Eating surrounded by books is such a treat" at this bookstore cafe "institution" in Dupont Circle with an American menu of "casual" fare served up in a "lively", "cosmopolitan" setting that "makes you feel smarter" just being there; prices are "fair", service is "friendly" and the "always-packed" weekend brunch is "one of the best" around ("browse the fantastic" reading selection while you wait); P.S. open 24 hours on the weekend.

Kushi *Japanese* | 25 | 21 | 21 | $44 |

Mt. Vernon Square/Convention Center | City Vista | 465 K St. NW (bet. 4th & 5th Sts.) | 202-682-3123 | www.eatkushi.com

"The best seats are at the bar" watching the "fascinating" chefs in action at this "hip" Mount Vernon Square Japanese izakaya that goes "beyond the usual sushi" (though that's "beautifully" prepared) with "tasty" kushiyaki, robata and raw-bar selections, plus small-batch sake and microbrews; its lofty, "minimalist" quarters exude a "contemporary Tokyo vibe" as do the "accompanying prices", but you pay for the "privilege of authenticity."

La Bergerie *French* | 26 | 24 | 24 | $58 |

Old Town | Crilley Warehse. | 218 N. Lee St. (bet. Cameron & Queen Sts.) | Alexandria, VA | 703-683-1007 | www.labergerie.com

"Fantastic" French "classics" – like "superb" sole meunière and "heavenly" soufflés – continue to "exceed the highest expectations" at this "old-style" Old Towner; "sublime" service and a "quiet", "elegant" dining room with brick walls, crystal chandeliers and "well-spaced" booths make it excellent for "special occasions", leading most to deem it "worth the cost."

La Canela *Peruvian* | 23 | 22 | 21 | $37 |

Rockville | Rockville Town Sq. | 141 Gibbs St. (bet. Beall Ave. & Middle Ln.), MD | 301-251-1550 | www.lacanelaperu.com

"Want to visit Peru? start here" say fans of this Rockville "charmer" that "elevates" the country's cuisine with "superb" takes on regional specialties, like "divine" ceviche and "heavenly" chicharrón, all washed down with "so-good" pisco sours; considering the "not particularly expensive" prices, "attentive" service and "nicely appointed" interior (wrought-iron accents, "larger-than-life mirrors"), it's a "real gem."

La Caraqueña *S American*   ▽ 25 | 15 | 22 | $25

Falls Church | 300 W. Broad St. (Little Falls St.), VA | 703-533-0076 | www.lacaraquena.com

"Holy cow" – "the arepas are incredible" at this "charmer" that dishes up "some of the best South American food this side of the equator" according to fans; connected to a "nothing" motor lodge in Falls Church, it's got a "motel-chic" vibe that's definitely "not fancy", but "friendly service" and prices that please the crowds "jammed" into the "teeny-tiny" space make reservations "essential."

La Chaumière ✗ *French*   26 | 24 | 24 | $58

Georgetown | 2813 M St. NW (bet. 28th & 29th Sts.) | 202-338-1784 | www.lachaumieredc.com

One can "almost imagine Julia [Child] and Jacques [Pepin] sharing a cozy meal" of "excellent" classics at this "long-lived, much-loved" Georgetown "country French" *auberge,* with its "rustic stone fireplace", proper tablecloths and a sound level that would have allowed them "to converse"; "been-there-forever" pros ensure that there are "not many empty chairs at peak times", especially since it's a "wonderful value" (if "not cheap").

NEW **LacoMelza Ethio Cafe & Gallery** *Ethiopian*   - | - | - | I

Silver Spring | 7912 Georgia Ave. (Eastern Ave.), MD | 301-326-2435

Ethiopian culture pervades this affordable Silver Spring newcomer, from the colorful art for sale on the walls to the brilliantly hued food on the plates; that's right, the stews and such are piled on plates, not spongy bread as at many other Ethiopian venues, which may make for an easy introduction to this cuisine for newbies.

La Côte d'Or Café *French*   24 | 22 | 23 | $45

Arlington | 6876 Lee Hwy. (Westmoreland St.), VA | 703-538-3033 | www.lacotedorcafe.com

Francophiles find a "little bit of France in the Arlington suburbs" thanks to the "consistently excellent" classics served up in "unpretentious" country-cafe digs at this long-running "neighborhood" bistro with "welcoming owners"; locals judge the considerable prices "fair" for a "romantic rendezvous" or "special occasion."

Lafayette Room *American*   ▽ 27 | 28 | 26 | $80

Golden Triangle | The Hay-Adams | 800 16th St. NW (bet. H & I Sts.) | 202-638-2570 | www.hayadams.com

You might be too busy rubbernecking the "familiar faces at breakfast and lunch" to notice the "superb execution of the classics" and "professional" service at this "beautiful, formal" American hotel dining room with a view across to the White House; you'll pay a pretty penny, but as "one of the last" of its kind, it's an "experience not to be missed"; P.S. no dinner Saturday or Sunday.

La Ferme *French*   24 | 25 | 23 | $51

Chevy Chase | 7101 Brookville Rd. (bet. Taylor & Thornapple Sts.), MD | 301-986-5255 | www.lafermerestaurant.com

This "long-standing" Chevy Chase French bastion's "elegant" farmhouse ambiance (lightened and brightened in spring 2012, possibly outdating its Decor rating) along with its "expensive" repertoire of "classic" dishes "prepared to perfection" unite for a "visual and culinary escape" for its largely "older, established" clientele who appreciate the "professional" level of service; regulars' advice to young 'uns: don't dismiss it as "a little passé" because "this old chestnut seems [even] tastier today."

NEW La Forchetta *Italian/Pizza*   - | - | - | M

Upper NW | 3201 New Mexico Ave. NW (Lowell St.) | 202-244-2223 | www.laforchettadc.com

Roberto Donna is back in town and cooking up a storm at restaurateur Hakan Ilhan's sleek, contemporary modern Italian in Wesley Heights, offering a broad, midpriced menu that features trattoria-style small bites, pastas and entrees, as well as Donna's popular Neapolitan-style pizza; there's a molded concrete bar for nibbling and sipping and lots of table-seating for families and duos beneath elaborate chandeliers.

La Fourchette *French*   23 | 20 | 23 | $41

Adams Morgan | 2429 18th St. NW (bet. Columbia & Kalorama Rds.) | 202-332-3077 | www.lafourchettedc.com

"Providing a calm center" in the "heart of Adams Morgan", this "sweet, little" French old-timer is "just what a bistro should be", proffering "simple" takes on the "classics" in an "unpretentious" atmosphere; decorated with an oversized mural, the "cozy" space is "charming" and the service is "fantastic", all adding up to a "terrific value."

La Limeña *Cuban/Peruvian*   23 | 14 | 20 | $22

Rockville | Ritchie Ctr. | 765 Rockville Pike (Wootton Pkwy.), MD | 301-424-8066

"Packed" at lunch and weekends, this "unpretentious" Rockville strip-maller is "deservedly popular" for "amazing" Peruvian (and some Cuban) dishes like "outstanding" anticuchos, "exceptional" tamales and "dream"-worthy ceviche; a "family-friendly" atmosphere pervades the simple space decorated with paintings and roof tiles that evoke old Lima, and with "courteous" service and "excellent prices", regulars reckon it's "a grand bargain."

Landini Brothers *Italian*   25 | 22 | 23 | $48

Old Town | 115 King St. (bet. Lee & Union Sts.) | Alexandria, VA | 703-836-8404 | www.landinibrothers.com

Old Town's "brassy Italian with an established clientele" that includes local notables delivers the kind of "mouthwatering" and "hearty" "old-fashioned" food that leaves you with a "stuffed feeling", even if it costs

FOOD | DECOR | SERVICE | COST

"much money"; it's "see and be seen" in the "dimly lit", "clubby" interior while its *bellíssimo* patio delights romantics.

Las Canteras ⓜ *Peruvian* ▽ 24 | 22 | 24 | $40

Adams Morgan | 2307 18th St. NW (Kalorama Rd.) | 202-265-1780 | www.lascanterasdc.com

Decked with handcrafted artwork and a "cozy" red color palette, this two-story Adams Morgan Andean reataurant/bar offers a "chic" environment for enjoying "flavorful" Peruvian standards – lomo saltado, ceviche, "not-to-be-missed" *parihuela* (seafood soup) – alongside some "interesting" nuevo notions; service is "proficient", and though it's not cheap, there are weekday early-bird specials and half-priced wine on Tuesdays.

Las Tapas *Spanish* 24 | 23 | 23 | $39

Old Town | 710 King St. (N. Washington St.) | Alexandria, VA | 703-836-4000 | www.lastapas.us

It pays to "be adventurous" at this brick-walled Spaniard that "transposes you right into Seville" from Old Town with a "wonderful selection" of "scrumptious", midpriced small plates; "very good" sangria and "quick and friendly" service add to the vibrant atmosphere – and to really get "immersed in the culture", come on Tuesday, Wednesday or Thursday evenings for live flamenco performances.

La Strada *Italian* ▽ 23 | 20 | 24 | $41

Del Ray | 1905 Mt. Vernon Ave. (bet. Bellefonte & Howell Aves.) | Alexandria, VA | 703-548-2592 | www.lastrada-ontheave.com

"To-die-for" housemade pasta is an "art form" with "great wines to match" at this "tasty", family-style Northern Italian osteria/enoteca that "impresses" Del Ray locals; it's not always cheap, but there's a lot of "love" for the "pleasant" staff and the "cute" wine-cellar decor and sunny patio.

La Taberna del Alabardero *Spanish* 26 | 24 | 25 | $62

World Bank | 1776 I St. NW (18th St.) | 202-429-2200 | www.alabardero.com

The "Rolls-Royce of Spanish" restaurants, this venerable World Banker takes diners on an "atmospheric mini-trip to Spain" via "opulent" decoration (elaborate chandeliers, lace, gilt accents), "exquisite", "refined" food and a "magnificent" Iberian wine collection, all of it made "memorable" by a "professional and friendly" staff; yet it's "open to informality" too: happy-hour "tapas at the bar are a wonderful bargain", and "sangria on the patio" is a summer delight.

La Tasca *Spanish* 21 | 22 | 20 | $32

Chinatown | 722 Seventh St. NW (bet. G & H Sts.) | 202-347-9190
Rockville | Rockville Town Sq. | 141 Gibbs St. (bet. Beall Ave. & Middle Ln.), MD | 301-279-7011
Old Town | 607 King St. (St. Asaph St.) | Alexandria, VA | 703-299-9810
Clarendon | 2900 Wilson Blvd. (Fillmore St.), VA | 703-812-9120
www.latascausa.com

"Over-the-top" Iberian decor – stucco walls, mosaics, plenty of wrought iron – plus "deadly" sangria and "fantastic" happy-hour deals make this "spicy" Spanish chainlet "best enjoyed with groups" who don't mind it "loud" and "crowded"; a "vast" menu of "reasonably" priced small plates "offers something for everyone", though some say "sampling is an adventure" with eats ranging from just "ok" to "excellent."

La Tomate *Italian*
19 | 17 | 19 | $41

Dupont Circle | 1701 Connecticut Ave. NW (R St.) | 202-667-5505 | www.latomatebistro.com

Early birds at this "wedge-shaped", light-filled Dupont Circle eatery "get a window corner seat" and "watch the throngs" stroll by or, if those are taken, snag a table on the "pleasant patio" of this neighborhood Italian "standby"; cheap? no, but its "old favorites" and "interesting new dishes" are "reliably" "well prepared" and served by an "attentive" crew.

☑ L'Auberge Chez François Ⓜ *French*
28 | 27 | 28 | $81

Great Falls | 332 Springvale Rd. (Beach Mill Rd.), VA | 703-759-3800

Jacques' Brasserie Ⓜ *French*
Great Falls | 332 Springvale Rd. (Beach Mill Rd.), VA | 703-759-3800
www.laubergechezfrancois.com

This "fairy-tale destination" in Great Falls, VA, is "like a fine wine that ages beautifully", eternally providing visitors with "wonderful", "gemütlich" Alsatian cuisine that's in perfect harmony with its "charming", "rustic" farmhouse setting; the "unstuffy" staff "pampers" diners during "long and leisurely" multicourse repasts, and though the air is "rarefied", the prix fixe menu means there's "no wincing" over surprises on the bill; P.S. thrifty types may prefer the more "casual ambiance" of the cellar brasserie, whose à la carte menu has "less impact on your wallet."

L'Auberge Provençale Restaurant *French*
▽ 26 | 25 | 26 | $86

Boyce | L'Auberge Provençale | 13630 Lord Fairfax Hwy. (Rte. 50), VA | 540-837-1375 | www.laubergeprovencale.com

After touring Virginia's wine country, oenophiles can "come 'home'" to this "beautiful" Boyce retreat for a "magnificent" meal amid "authentic French country style" – there's even a fireplace to warm "chilly nights"; expect a "sophisticated" (and "pricey") prix fixe menu accompanied by "world-class" service in a "comfortable", antiques-filled setting, and, if you "spend the night" (and you should), the "breakfasts are superb."

Lauriol Plaza *Mexican*
21 | 19 | 20 | $28

Dupont Circle | 1835 18th St. NW (T St.) | 202-387-0035 | www.lauriolplaza.com

"Sip a margarita and socialize" because it often "takes awhile to get a table" at this "sprawling", light-filled multilevel Dupont Circle East Mexican – after all, you're competing with "an army of twenty-somethings" who down "overflowing pitchers" and some of the "best bang-for-the-peso" chow of its class, all "served with smiles";

purists call it a "factory", but with its "gorgeous roof deck" and ample "people-watching", "no wonder it's mobbed constantly."

Lavandou *French*

| 23 | 20 | 22 | $45 |

Cleveland Park | 3321 Connecticut Ave. NW (bet. Macomb & Ordway Sts.) | 202-966-3002 | www.lavandoudc.com

"Year after year", this "wonderful neighborhood bistro" brings "joie de vivre" to a "devoted" Cleveland Park clientele with "tasty" French fare (including "tremendous" mussels) bolstered by "charming" service and "excellent" nightly deals like corkage-free Mondays; the "rustic" setting feels like "spending an evening in the countryside in Provence", and if it's "perhaps too cozy" for some – "hope for friendly neighbors."

Layalina ● *Lebanese/Syrian*

| 24 | 22 | 22 | $33 |

Arlington | 5216 Wilson Blvd. (bet. Emerson & Greenbrier Sts.), VA | 703-525-1170 | www.layalinarestaurant.com

"Stupendous" Syrian and Lebanese specialties – like "the freshest meze" and a signature lamb shank dish – are served up in this "atmospheric" Arlington eatery crowded with "celebrating families" and crammed with rugs and artwork that "transport you to Beirut"; it's a warm", "friendly" place, and fans note you'd "pay twice as much elsewhere" for food this good.

Lebanese Taverna *Lebanese*

| 23 | 20 | 21 | $29 |

Bethesda | 7141 Arlington Rd. (bet. Bethesda Ave. & Elm St.), MD | 301-951-8681

Rockville | Rockville Town Sq. | 115 Gibbs St. (bet. Beall Ave. & Middle Ln.), MD | 301-309-8681

Rockville | Congressional Plaza | 1605 Rockville Pike (bet. Congressional Ln. & Halpine Rd.), MD | 301-468-9086

Silver Spring | 933 Ellsworth Dr. (Rte. 29), MD | 301-588-1192

Arlington | 4400 Old Dominion Dr. (bet. Lorcom Ln. & Upton St.), VA | 703-276-8681

Arlington | 5900 Washington Blvd. (McKinley Rd.), VA | 703-241-8681

Pentagon City | Pentagon Row | 1101 S. Joyce St. (Army Navy Dr.) | Arlington, VA | 703-415-8681

Tysons Corner | Tysons Galleria | 1840 International Dr. (Chain Bridge Rd.) | McLean, VA | 703-847-5244

www.lebanesetaverna.com

"The hummus will ruin you for all other hummus" at this "small, casual" chain ("that never feels like one") where "the multiple joys of Lebanese cuisine" include "excellent" vegetarian options and "wonderful" meze platters perfect for groups; the "family-friendly" settings are "modern" with "traditional" touches that "don't overdo it", and there's the added attraction of a "great price-to-quality ratio."

Le Chat Noir *French*

| 20 | 18 | 20 | $42 |

Upper NW | 4907 Wisconsin Ave. NW (41st St.) | 202-244-2044 | www.lechatnoirrestaurant.com

"If you have a hankering for crêpes" and other "reliable" bistro fare, this "touch of France" in Upper NW is "a must try", catering to a "mostly neighborhood" crowd with its simple, "comfortable and low-key" setting and "cordial" service; there's also a "very good" selection of wines, some of which thrifty types point out are offered at half-price on Tuesday and Wednesday (as well as on weekends in the upstairs lounge).

Ⓩ Ledo Pizza *Pizza*   **23**   **15**   **20**   **$17**

Georgetown | 1721 Wisconsin Ave. NW (S St.) | 202-342-0091
Northeast | 7435 Georgia Ave. NW (bet. Geranium & Hemlock Sts.) | 202-726-5336
Bethesda | 10301 Westlake Dr. (Arizina Circle), MD | 301-469-6700
Bethesda | 5245 River Rd. (Brookside Dr.), MD | 301-656-5336
Wheaton | 2638 W. University Blvd. (Grandview Ave.), MD | 301-929-6111
Arlington | 1035 S. Edgewood St. (Columbia Pike), VA | 703-521-5336
Courthouse | 1501 Arlington Blvd. (N. Fairfax Dr.) | Arlington, VA | 703-528-3570
Falls Church | 7510 Leesburg Pike (Pimmit Dr.), VA | 703-847-5336
Reston | 2254 Hunters Woods Plaza (Colts Neck Rd.), VA | 703-758-9800
www.ledopizza.com
Additional locations throughout the DC area
This "cheap-and-cheerful", "tried-and-true" local pizza chain eschews the circular standard in favor of cheesy "squares of pure delight" with "flaky", "buttery", "French pastry dough–quality" crusts, a "tart but sweet" sauce and toppings "piled high"; aside from "nonexistent decor" ("who needs it anyway?"), each location "maintains a single-store atmosphere fairly well" with a "nice family" feel and "quick" service.

Ledo Restaurant, Original *Italian/Pizza*   **24**   **15**   **20**   **$18**

College Park | 4509 Knox Rd. (Yale Ave.), MD | 301-422-8122 | www.ledorestaurant.com
A "local favorite" since 1955, this pizza joint in College Park maintains a devoted following thanks to pies that are "unique from the cheese to the crust", which is rich, flaky and "rectangular"; it's still priced like yesteryear and family-owned, and though in a newer, "nondescript" location, that doesn't stop "loyalists" from returning for "slices you don't have to fold" and "Italian-American food too."

Legal Sea Foods *Seafood*   **23**   **20**   **22**   **$39**

Chinatown | 704 Seventh St. NW (bet. G & H Sts.) | 202-347-0007
Bethesda | Montgomery Mall | 7101 Democracy Blvd., 2nd fl. (I-270), MD | 301-469-5900
Crystal City | 2301 Jefferson Davis Hwy. (23rd St.) | Arlington, VA | 703-415-1200
Tysons Corner | Tysons Galleria | 2001 International Dr. (Chain Bridge Rd.) | McLean, VA | 703-827-8900
www.legalseafoods.com
"Always a safe choice for a fine meal", this Boston-based piscine purveyor "looks like a chain" but "tastes much better" with "swimmingly delicious" standards, like its "famous" New England clam chowder; "attractive", contemporary settings and "upbeat", "well-trained" staffs make the tabs "reasonable" for the overall "quality."

FOOD | DECOR | SERVICE | COST

Leopold's Kafe & Konditorei *Austrian* 23 | 21 | 18 | $29

Georgetown | 3315 M St. NW (bet. 33rd & 34th Sts.) | 202-965-6005 |
www.kafeleopolds.com

"You'd think you were in Vienna" when sipping Austrian wines by
the "fountain" at this Georgetown cafe/bistro's back alley patio – or
ensconced at a window table in its "sleek", "stylish" Euro interior;
further "transporting" is the "hearty" fare like bratwurst for lunch
and a pastry case for "sophisticated adults" to "salivate over", not to
mention the Germanic "efficiency" of the service.

Le Pain Quotidien *Bakery/Belgian* 21 | 18 | 17 | $22

Capitol Hill | 660 Pennsylvania Ave. SE (bet. 6th & 7th Sts.) |
202-459-9148

Dupont Circle | Blaine Mansion | 2000 P St. NW (bet. Hopkins &
20th Sts.) | 202-459-9176

Georgetown | 2815 M St. NW (bet. 28th & 29th Sts.) |
202-315-5420

Upper NW | 4874 Massachusetts Ave. NW (49th St.) |
202-459-9141

Bethesda | Bethesda Row | 7140 Bethesda Ln. (bet. Bethesda Ave. &
Elm St.), MD | 301-913-2902

Old Town | 701 King St. (N. Washington St.) | Alexandria, VA |
703-683-2273

Clarendon | 2900 Clarendon Blvd. (Filmore St.), VA | 703-465-0970
www.lepainquotidien.com

"Phenomenal" bread with a "crunchy crust" and "delicate crumb",
"fabulous" pastries, "heavenly" chocolate spreads and other "imaginative" bites "perfect for a quick lunch" make these Belgian bakery/
cafes "hard not to like"; communal tables and "rustic" decor are
"very Euro" – likewise what some call "touch-and-go" service and
somewhat "steep" tabs, though many say the "yummy carbs just lift
you up and away."

Le Refuge 🗷 *French* 26 | 21 | 25 | $47

Old Town | 127 N. Washington St. (bet. Cameron & King Sts.) |
Alexandria, VA | 703-548-4661 | www.lerefugealexandria.com

It's "the restaurant that time forgot (and that's not so bad)" say supporters of this family-run Old Towner that's been cooking up "superb" French standards that "warm the soul" for roughly three
decades; the "country French"–style dining room may be a "little
cramped", but the "cozy atmosphere" is enhanced by "wonderful"
service, leading admirers to deem it "worth the splurge."

Levante's *Mideastern* 21 | 19 | 20 | $33

Dupont Circle | 1320 19th St. NW (Dupont Circle) | 202-293-3244 |
www.levantes.com

"Large portions" and "quality ingredients" make the "reliable" "traditional dishes" like baba ghanoush, dolma and falafel a "good
value" at this Middle Eastern oasis near Dupont Circle; service is
"cordial", and the sleek, Mediterranean-looking dining room is
"vivifying" – throw in a "nice" outdoor terrace and most say it's a
"great lunch spot."

	FOOD	DECOR	SERVICE	COST

NEW Le Zinc M French   ∇ 22 | 21 | 21 | $51

Cleveland Park | 3714 Macomb St. NW (Wisconsin Ave.) | 202-686-2015 |
www.lezincdc.com

At this "friendly" Cleveland Park rookie, a French menu "with a
modern touch" (now under the direction of a new chef, possibly
outdating the Food rating) goes hand in hand with the "lively", tin-
ceilinged "bistro" setting lined with "wonderful" photos that reflect
the proprietor's music-industry roots (as does the "great" playlist);
it's "expensive for the neighborhood", but even so most call it a
"great new addition."

Lia's American/Italian   21 | 20 | 20 | $39

Chevy Chase | 4435 Willard Ave. (Wisconsin Ave.), MD |
240-223-5427 | www.liasrestaurant.com

Hitting the sweet spot between "neighborhood hang" and "fine dining", Geoff Tracy's Chevy Chase restaurant satisfies all comers with
a "great variety" of "consistently tasty" contemporary American-
Italian fare served by a "personable" staff in a "sleek", almost
"Scandinavian"-looking space; its generally "good price point" is
further improved by a "screaming deal" early-bird dinner and some
of the "best" happy-hour specials around.

Liberty Tavern American   24 | 20 | 21 | $36

Clarendon | 3195 Wilson Blvd. (Washington Blvd.), VA | 703-465-9360 |
www.thelibertytavern.com

At this split-level Clarendon New American, an "interesting", "ever-
changing" menu and a "wonderful" brunch please folks dining in the
"quiet but never dull" Arts and Crafts–style dining room upstairs,
while downstairs there's a "happening bar scene of twenty- and thirty-
somethings" drinking their way through an "awesome" beer collection and noshing "very serious" pub grub; a "well-trained staff" and
"good prices" keep both floors "packed."

Liberty Tree American/Pizza   ∇ 23 | 17 | 22 | $27

Atlas District | 1016 H St. NE (bet. 10th & 11th Sts.) | 202-396-8733 |
www.libertytreedc.com

"Keep this place a secret" smile supporters of this "small" Atlas
District room with a "cozy" "New England vibe" that may "not [get]
a lot of buzz" but does "do nicely with fish", "cracker-thin"-crusted
pizza and other American eats; add "above-average" beers and
"personal service" to its recommendations for a "quiet" meal "on a
street more known for its rowdy bar scene."

Z Lightfoot American   26 | 27 | 23 | $42

Leesburg | 11 N. King St. (Market St.), VA | 703-771-2233 |
www.lightfootrestaurant.com

There's an "enduring" "sense of history" at this New American in
Downtown Leesburg housed in a "beautiful" Romanesque Revival
former bank building "gloriously appointed" with cozy fireplaces
and Venetian chandeliers – and yet for all its "elegance", there's a
"relaxed" atmosphere; satisfied surveyors say the "creative", "delicious" dishes (e.g. "dream"-inducing fried green tomatoes) and

FOOD DECOR SERVICE COST

"strong service" make it an "excellent place to celebrate", concluding it's "not cheap" but "you get what you pay for."

Lighthouse Tofu *Korean*
∇ 24 | 14 | 18 | $19

Rockville | 12710 Twinbrook Pkwy. (bet. Rockville Pike & Veirs Mill Rd.), MD | 301-881-1178

"Talk about your great finds", this Korean "comfort-food" kitchen in Rockville pumps out "top-notch" "cheap eats" including "amazing" seafood, meat and veggie tofu stews (they "can't be beat in chilly weather"), "delish" BBQ ribs and other traditional favorites; it "isn't a fancy place", but service is "kind and attentive enough" and the "price is right."

Lincoln *American*
20 | 23 | 20 | $40

Downtown | 1110 Vermont Ave. NW (L St.) | 202-386-9200 | www.lincolnrestaurant-dc.com

The "young, trendy and loud" hit this Downtown New American's bar for "creative and perfectly made" cocktails, then head to the dining room for "conversation" and a "wide variety of decent-tasting" small plates at "great-for-the-waistline" prices that "inhibit" ordering too many; service is "professional", and the decor's "homage" to Honest Abe ("pennied floor", "big white chair") is "fun" if "a bit odd."

Little Fountain Cafe Ⓜ *Eclectic*
∇ 23 | 22 | 22 | $42

Adams Morgan | 2339 18th St. NW (Belmont Rd.) | 202-462-8100 | www.littlefountaincafe.com

A "refuge from the glitz and squalor of 18th Street NW" is this "quaint and romantic" subterranean spot where "love and care" go into each "imaginative" Eclectic dish served by the "nice people" who work here; a "decent" wine list (half-price Wednesday nights) and a prix fixe deal seals its "date-night" appeal; P.S. the menu is also available at its upstairs bar, Angles.

🅉 NEW Little Serow *Thai*
28 | 19 | 27 | $60

Dupont Circle | 1511 17th St. NW (bet. P & Q Sts.) | no phone | www.littleserow.com

"Small in size but packed with flavor and flair", chef-owner Johnny Monis' new Issan-style Thai in Dupont Circle (DC's top-rated newcomer) "transports" taste buds with "intense and unusual", "kick-your-ass spicy" fare; it's "easier on the pocket" than his celebrated Komi (upstairs next door), and you should "check your control freak at the door" of this "super-dark" cave and let the "incredibly knowledgeable" staff guide you through the "delicious" set-menu journey.

Local 16 *American/Pizza*
∇ 17 | 19 | 19 | $27

U Street Corridor | 1602 U St. NW (16th St.) | 202-265-2828 | www.localsixteen.com

An "awesome rooftop bar" and "good music" make this "night-clubby" U Street "hot spot" a meeting ground for "attractive singles"; but food fans say it "deserves a visit before 11 PM too" thanks to "surprisingly good pizza" (improved thanks to input from consulting chef Edan MacQuaid) and its "mission to use fresh, local ingredients" in its midpriced American fare, backed by dependable service.

	FOOD	DECOR	SERVICE	COST

Logan Tavern *American*   20 | 17 | 18 | $31

Logan Circle | 1423 P St. NW (bet. 14th & 15th Sts.) | 202-332-3710 |
www.logantavern.com

There's "nothing too exotic" about this Logan Circle "neighborhood
favorite", but the airy, industrial space is "always full of locals" enjoying "hearty" American comfort food in a "friendly, relaxed" atmosphere; it's a "first choice" for pre–Studio Theatre dining and Sunday
brunch ("you can't beat the Bloody Marys") – throw in "pretty people-
watching" and reasonable prices and "what's not to love?"

Lost Dog Cafe *Pub Food*   23 | 18 | 21 | $18

Arlington | 2920 Columbia Pike (Walter Reed Dr.), VA | 703-553-7770
Arlington | 5876 Washington Blvd. (McKinley Rd.), VA | 703-237-1552
McLean | 1690 Anderson Rd. (Magarity Rd.), VA | 703-356-5678
www.lostdogcafe.com

"Every taste" is accounted for at these "funky" area eateries with a
huge menu of "darned good" pizza, a "refreshing diversity of sandwiches" and an "enormous" craft beer selection; pet-lovers "applaud"
its "soft spot for our four-legged friends" (a portion of profits go to dog
and cat rescue), "kids" are "entertained" by the "colorful", "adorable"
animal murals – and everyone else digs the "affordable" tabs and "nicest staff on earth"; P.S. Washington Boulevard is separately owned.

NEW **Lost Society** ☒Ⓜ *American/Steak*   ▽ 18 | 21 | 17 | $41

U Street Corridor | 2001 14th St. NW (U St.) | 202-618-8868 |
www.lostsociety-dc.com

"Urban and sexy", this New American steakhouse arrival on U
Street is a "place to see and be seen" – whether imbibing "handcrafted" cocktails at the rooftop or second-story bars, or ensconced
in its "romantic-yet-funky" dining room, which is dressed with curtained booths, velvet sofas and chandeliers; "interesting" entrees
skew comforting, though expensive.

Ⓩ Lucky Corner Vietnamese   28 | 19 | 23 | $21
Cuisine *Vietnamese*

Frederick | 700 N. Market St. (7th St.), MD | 301-624-1005 |
www.luckycornerrestaurant.com

"Pho-get about getting Vietnamese anywhere else in Frederick" declare devotees of this under-the-wire place serving "mouthwatering"
hot pots, noodle dishes and seafood specialties at a "great value";
an "attentive" staff tends to the "cute", simply decorated dining
room that nonetheless is "very small" (it's "great for takeout").

Luke's Lobster *Seafood*   23 | 14 | 17 | $23

Penn Quarter | 624 E St. NW (bet. 6th & 7th Sts.) |
202-347-3355
NEW **Bethesda** | Bethesda Row | 7129 Bethesda Ln. (Arlington Rd.),
MD | 301-718-1005
www.lukeslobster.com

"No need to go to Maine" (or to the NYC original) say claw-noisseurs
of the "fresh", "meaty" rolls with "subtle seasoning" at these "mock
lobster shacks" in Penn Quarter and Bethesda; "lobster costs what

FOOD | DECOR | SERVICE | COST

"lobster costs", which makes it "pricey" for a counter-serve with "basic" amenities, but New England rusticators sigh "the only thing missing is the ocean."

Luna Grill & Diner *Diner/Vegetarian*   19 | 16 | 19 | $22

Dupont Circle | 1301 Connecticut Ave. NW (N St.) | 202-835-2280
Shirlington | 4024 Campbell Ave. (Quincy St.) | Arlington, VA | 703-379-7173
www.lunagrillanddiner.com

Folks "know what to expect" at this "reliable" Dupont and Shirlington diner duo: "cheap", "tasty" "comfort food" from a "varied" menu that offers "something for everyone", vegetarians and "picky eaters" included; "low-pressure" service and "homey", "comfortable" surroundings make them "good for relaxing and talking."

NEW Lunchbox *American*   24 | 19 | 23 | $12

Frederick | 50 Carroll Creek Way (Market St.), MD | 301-360-0580 | www.voltlunchbox.com

Bryan Voltaggio has "struck gold again" with this counter-service place sporting a posh-"high-school-cafeteria" look near Frederick's "picturesque" Carroll Creek, a few blocks from his flagship Volt; a "nostalgic"-leaning menu of "yummy", "high-quality" sandwiches, salads and soups, plus cookies for dessert, incorporates the owner's considerable "culinary talents", hence your "lunch money is well spent"; P.S. open lunch to early evening.

Lyon Hall ⚫ *French/German*   24 | 19 | 22 | $38

Clarendon | 3100 N. Washington Blvd. (Highland Ave.), VA | 703-741-7636 | www.lyonhallarlington.com

"Meat-heavy" Alsatian "treasures" chased by "unique" beers, all at "reasonable prices", have Clarendon's "trendy who's who" thronging this French-German brasserie, causing its *"Midnight in Paris*-like space" to get "crowded and loud" on weekends; "divine" homemade donuts at brunch and "thoughtful" servers are among the touches that attract a "late-thirties set who have enough pride to avoid chain dining."

Mad Fox Brewing Company *American*   20 | 20 | 20 | $25

Falls Church | Shops at Spectrum | 444 W. Broad St. (bet. Pennsylvania & Virginia Aves.), VA | 703-942-6840 | www.madfoxbrewing.com

"Foxy for sure", this affordable Falls Church brew-'n'-eatery "lives up to the 'gastropub' moniker" with "made-from-scratch" nosh like "wonderful" pizza and fried pickles that "are a taste of foodie heaven" – still, "beer is obviously the name of the game", with "fantastic" seasonal selections; the "contemporary" space with a 60-ft. bar is "casual", "fun" and ably served by a "personable" staff.

Madhatter *American/Pub Food*   18 | 20 | 18 | $24

Dupont Circle | 1319 Connecticut Ave. NW (bet. Dupont Circle & N St.) | 202-833-1495 | www.madhatterdc.com

"More of a mad keg party than tea party", this "popular" Dupont Circle American tavern approximates "Alice's Wonderland" with themed decor like white-rabbit prints and a giant floating top hat; "young, hip individuals flock here" for "solid chow" that's just "a step above pub fare" at "reasonable prices" and "great beer", so "go early or get trampled by the post-collegiate meet-market crowd."

Z Maggiano's Little Italy *Italian*   23 | 22 | 23 | $34

Upper NW | 5333 Wisconsin Ave. NW (bet. Jenifer St. & Western Ave.) | 202-966-5500
Tysons Corner | Tysons Galleria | 2001 International Dr. (Chain Bridge Rd.) | McLean, VA | 703-356-9000
www.maggianos.com

"Always good for celebrating", especially with "large groups", these Upper NW and Tysons chain links "never waiver" in providing "full-flavored" "red-sauce" "classics" in portions suitable for "King Kong" at a "fair price"; if the "checkered-tablecloth", wood-paneled rooms seem "noisy" to some, most say they're a "wonderful environment" for a "family-style" meal on account of "smooth" service that makes everyone "feel special."

Z Magnolias at the Mill *American*   25 | 27 | 25 | $35

Purcellville | 198 N. 21st St. (Main St.), VA | 540-338-9800 | www.magnoliasmill.com

In a "beautiful", "rustic mill" that "reflects its heritage" with "quilts", farming implements and "worn wood", this midpriced New American enclave in Purcellville is an "attractive" stop "after a day in wine country" (or "go cycling first" since it's just off the W&OD Trail); with "excellent" choices that run the gamut "from burgers to steaks and some traditional Southern dishes", all ferried by "friendly" help, most "leave with a smile."

Mai Thai *Thai*   23 | 20 | 20 | $26

Dupont Circle | 1200 19th St. NW (M St.) | 202-452-6870
Georgetown | 3251 Prospect St. NW (bet. Potomac St. & Wisconsin Ave.) | 202-337-2424
Old Town | 6 King St. (Union St.) | Alexandria, VA | 703-548-0600
www.maithai.us

There are "no real surprises" on the menu at these "bit-more-upscale"-than-the-norm Thai places that turn out "consistently tasty" "standards" delivered "fast" by "accommodating" servers at prices that "won't break the bank" – though there is an "interesting and affordable wine list"; all boast colorful, modern interiors, while the Old Town original has "beautiful views" of the Potomac.

The Majestic *American*   24 | 19 | 23 | $44

Old Town | 911 King St. (bet. Alfred & Patrick Sts.) | Alexandria, VA | 703-837-9117 | www.majesticcafe.com

"Home cookin' like your mama wished" she made (including a kids' menu with a healthy bent) star at this "casual" Old Town American from the Restaurant Eve team – and for "much less money" than a meal at its fancier "big brother"; while this venue looks more like a "diner", the "same quality and attention to detail" that marks the brand means that "meatloaf can rise to a gourmet experience", service is "as it should be" and "reservations can be hard to come by" (try the bar).

	FOOD	DECOR	SERVICE	COST

NEW Majestic Bar & Grille ◑ *American/Eclectic*

| - | - | - | I |

Bethesda | 7141 Wisconsin Ave. (bet. Willow Ln. & Woodmont Ave.), MD | 301-312-6043 | www.themajesticbethesda.com
This urbane Bethesda gastropub arrival offers an Eclectic, affordably priced menu featuring family Greek recipes along with upgraded pub fare, Southern comfort food and more; its spiffy setting, replete with an impressive tin ceiling, includes a long bar and hightops set against sunny windows, plus a large backyard patio.

Z Makoto M *Japanese*

| 27 | 19 | 23 | $78 |

Palisades | 4822 MacArthur Blvd. NW (U St.) | 202-298-6866
"Leave your shoes – and your ego – at the door" of this tiny Palisades Japanese temple where the "exquisite jewel-box plates" on its multi-course *omakase* menu come to the table the "chef's way"; the setting is simple and traditional, with "hard" bench seating, but it's "unparalleled in DC" say those who "know the difference", so a little patience and a thick wallet will transport you "half a world away."

Mala Tang *Chinese*

| 22 | 18 | 19 | $30 |

Arlington | 3434 Washington Blvd. (Kirkwood Rd.), VA | 703-243-2381 | www.mala-tang.com
Named for the hot and "numbing" sensation that distinguishes Sichuan food, this "fun" Arlington eatery is outfitted with special tables for individual hot pots that allows everyone to cook "in their own style and level of spiciness" (don't worry: the staff is "helpful" if needed); there are also other dishes that would be found in the Chengdu street stalls depicted in the back wall mural, all of them offering a "good value for the money."

Malaysia Kopitiam *Malaysian*

| 23 | 11 | 18 | $24 |

Dupont Circle | 1827 M St. NW (bet. 18th & 19th Sts.) | 202-833-6232 | www.malaysiakopitiam.com
A "giant" picture menu makes it easy to envision the "tasty", "no-compromise" Malaysian dishes at this Dupont Circle "jewel" that connoisseurs claim is the "only place in town that comes close to the real thing"; there is "no pretense" and "nothing to look at" in the subterranean digs, but it's still a "bargain" – and "you can't eat the atmosphere anyway."

Mamma Lucia *Italian*

| 22 | 16 | 21 | $23 |

Bethesda | 4916 Elm St. (bet. Arlington Rd. & Woodmont Ave.), MD | 301-907-3399
Frederick | Shops of Monocacy | 1700 Kingfisher Dr. (Rte. 26), MD | 301-694-2600
Olney | Olney Village Ctr. | 18224 Village Center Dr. (Olney Sandy Spring Rd.), MD | 301-570-9500
College Park | College Park Plaza | 4734 Cherry Hill Rd. (bet. Autovill Dr. & 47th Ave.), MD | 301-513-0605
Rockville | Federal Plaza | 12274 Rockville Pike (Twinbrook Pkwy.), MD | 301-770-4894
Rockville | Fallsgrove Village Shopping Ctr. | 14921 Shady Grove Rd. (bet. Blackwell Rd. & Fallsgrove Blvd.), MD | 301-762-8805

(continued)

Mamma Lucia

Silver Spring | Blair Shops | 1302 E. West Hwy. (Colesville Rd.), MD | 301-562-0693

Reston | North Point Vill. | 1428 North Point Village Ctr. (Reston Pkwy.), VA | 703-689-4894

www.mammaluciarestaurants.com

Neighborhood folks visit these "reliable" eateries for "generous portions" of "solid standby Italian" and "mmm" "NY-style" pizza served in "very casual" environs or via "quick" take-out; service "varies by location", but the staff generally "makes you feel at home", so if some dissenters deem the food merely "decent", most ask "at these prices, who cares?"

Mandalay *Burmese*
23 | 13 | 19 | $25

Silver Spring | 930 Bonifant St. (bet. Fenton St. & Georgia Ave.), MD | 301-585-0500 | www.mandalayrestaurantcafe.com

This "friendly", "family-run" Burmese in Downtown Silver Spring "artfully combines" "simple ingredients" and "tantalizing spices" for "complex flavors" – and "when they say spicy, they really mean it" (though "wimps" note they can "turn down the heat"); "un-fancy" decor doesn't deter those who dub it "a value eatery"; P.S. there are "tons" of vegetarian and vegan options.

M&S Grill *Seafood/Steak*
22 | 21 | 21 | $38

Downtown | 600 13th St. NW (F St.) | 202-347-1500

Reston | Reston Town Ctr. | 11901 Democracy Dr. (Discovery St.), VA | 703-787-7766

www.mandsgrill.com

"Less stuffy" little brothers of McCormick & Schmick's, these "reliable" American grills offer "something for everyone" with "consistently" "tasty" if "not inventive" seafood and steaks that "don't cost an arm or leg"; if a few call them "typical businessman's lunch" places, a passel of partisans praise the "comfortable" clubby decor, "effective" service and happy hours with "wonderful selections."

Mandu *Korean*
23 | 16 | 20 | $28

Dupont Circle | 1805 18th St. NW (bet. S & Swann Sts.) | 202-588-1540

Mt. Vernon Square/Convention Center | City Vista | 453 K St. NW (bet. 4th & 5th Sts.) | 202-289-6899 ◖

www.mandudc.com

Seoul searchers satisfy Korean "cravings" with "wonderful" dumplings, "sizzling" bibimbop and "dangerous" sojutinis, "all priced right" in a "21st-century hip-hop setting" (Mt. Vernon Square) or in "warmth and intimacy" (Dupont Circle); "efficient yet relaxed" service and happy-hour deals make most want to "man-do it again"; P.S. Mt. Vernon serves a late-night bar menu that includes Asian tacos.

Mannequin Pis *Belgian*
23 | 17 | 19 | $45

Olney | Olney Ctr. | 18064 Georgia Ave. (Olney Laytonsville Rd.), MD | 301-570-4800 | www.mannequinpis.com

It's "worth a visit" to this "out-of-the-way" Olney "mussel paradise" to sample over a dozen "divine" bivalve preparations (an "art form"

FOOD | DECOR | SERVICE | COST

they have "perfected") along with other Belgian standbys and, *naturellement,* a "great" selection of imported brews; a few call the service "erratic", but the mellow, wood-paneled dining room is "cozy" and a Monday night prix fixe helps deflate the bill.

🆕 Maple ●Ⓜ *Italian*

- | - | - | M

Columbia Heights | 3418 11th S. NW (bet. Monore St. & Park Rd.) | 202-588-7442 | www.dc-maple.com

Light, midpriced Italian fare – bruschetta, panini, pasta and such – soaks up the drinks at this new cool 'n' casual Columbia Heights watering hole; as for the liquid refreshment, expect a focus on well-chosen Italian vino (some on tap), craft beers and digestives poured at a gleaming tiger-maple-wood bar.

Maple Ave Restaurant Ⓜ *Eclectic*

- | - | - | M

Vienna | 147 Maple Ave. W. (bet. Center St. & Courthouse Rd.), VA | 703-319-2177 | www.mapleaverestaurant.com

This midpriced Eclectic on Vienna's main drag turns out farm-fresh small and large plates (and exciting cocktails) that reflect chef-owner Tim Ma's Asian-Latin sensibility and time at NYC's Momofuku; though it flew under the foodie radar for the first years of its life, now the few tables in its simple, earth-toned room often require reservations; P.S. don't miss the funnel cakes for dessert.

🇿 Marcel's *Belgian/French*

28 | 26 | 28 | $95

West End | 2401 Pennsylvania Ave. NW (24th St.) | 202-296-1166 | www.marcelsdc.com

"Build your own feast" at this "refined" West End modern French-Belgian by choosing from its "expansive" prix fixe menu selections, all of which showcase the "intricacy" and "subtlety" of Robert Wiedmaier's "brilliant" cuisine; factor in "pampering" service and an "elegant", "special-occasion" atmosphere and you get "full value" for the "expensive" tab; P.S. for a real deal, there's a pre-theater option that includes shuttle service to the Kennedy Center.

Mark's Duck House *Chinese*

25 | 11 | 18 | $24

Falls Church | Willston Ctr. | 6184 Arlington Blvd. (Patrick Henry Dr.), VA | 703-532-2125 | www.marksduckhouse.com

"Succulent Peking duck" hits a "home run" at this Falls Church Cantonese joint, but it's hardly the only star in a lineup that includes Hong Kong–style dim sum that'll "rock-your-socks off"; the simple, "bustling" storefront "can get cramped" at times, but just consider the "looong" lines "confirmation that the food is very good"; P.S. duck and pork roasts are sold by the pound for takeout.

Mark's Kitchen *Eclectic*

21 | 9 | 18 | $18

Takoma Park | 7006 Carroll Ave. (Laurel St.), MD | 301-270-1884 | www.markskitchen.com

It may "look ordinary", but "there's a reason" this Takoma Park storefront is "packed day and night": it has "a little bit of everything" from "reliable hipster diner food" to Korean fare to "interesting" vegetarian choices and "great" desserts – all at "good value"; the "hip, friendly" staff will keep things "laid-back" amid the "hustle and bustle."

⊠ Marrakesh ⇗ *Moroccan* 24 | 26 | 23 | $49

Shaw | 617 New York Ave. NW (bet. 6th & 7th Sts.) | 202-393-9393 | www.marrakesh.us

"This isn't just a dinner, it's an experience" say those who've been transported to "another world" (Morocco) via the "gorgeous" traditional decor, "seating on pillows" and "fun" belly-dancing performances at this venerable Shaw extravaganza; the food-focused claim the "absolutely delectable dishes" on the seven-course, prix fixe menu "melt in your mouth" and arrive at "perfectly paced" intervals, adding up to a cultural trip that's "worth the money."

Marrakesh P Street *Moroccan* ▽ 23 | 24 | 21 | $35

Dupont Circle | 2147 P St. NW (bet. 21st & 22nd Sts.) | 202-775-1882 | www.marrakeshpstreet.com

"Fantastic" traditional decor of intricate mosaic tiles, fountains and a souk-like scattering of rugs and pillows at this Dupont Circle Moroccan creates a "welcoming" backdrop for "excellent" standards like tagines, couscous and kebabs at "great prices"; it can get "busy", but service is "good", and the nightly belly-dancing performances are "cool."

Martin's Tavern *American* 20 | 21 | 21 | $37

Georgetown | 1264 Wisconsin Ave. NW (N St.) | 202-333-7370 | www.martins-tavern.com

"Ghosts of administrations past" haunt this "historic" Georgetown tavern that's been hosting locals, pols and presidents in the "narrow" wooden booths in its "cozy" confines since the New Deal; the "reliably good" American menu, which includes items not found elsewhere (e.g. the signature "hot brown" sandwich), has "endured the test of time", and prices remain "reasonable."

Marvin *American/Belgian* 23 | 22 | 20 | $36

U Street Corridor | 2007 14th St. NW (U St.) | 202-797-7171 | www.marvindc.com

What's going on at this "friendly", midpriced U Street bistro (and homage to Marvin Gaye) is a "delicious" mix of flavors from Belgium and the American South, like "must"-have moules frites and "fantastic" chicken and waffles washed down by a "nice choice of beers"; dine downstairs in a "dark", "cool" setting featuring a mural of its namesake crooner, or "head upstairs" to the "awesome" rooftop for a drink.

Masa 14 ● *Asian/Pan-Latin* 23 | 22 | 20 | $40

Logan Circle | 1825 14th St. NW (bet. S & T Sts.) | 202-328-1414 | www.masa14.com

"Creative Latin-Asian fusion" and tapas collide in the little dishes "bursting with flavor" served by a "knowledgeable" crew at this "trendy" late-night Logan Circle "hot spot" from Richard Sandoval (Zengo) and Kaz Okochi (Kaz Sushi); the airy industrial space features a "long concrete bar stocked with plenty of eye candy" in the form of a "spirited, young" crowd; P.S. prices are moderate, but the $35 all-you-can-eat-and-drink brunch is such a "deal", it's almost a "community service."

Masala Art *Indian*
25 | 17 | 19 | $34

Upper NW | 4441 Wisconsin Ave. NW (Albemarle St.) | 202-362-4441 | www.masalaartdc.com

The "superb", "authentic" Indian menu at this Upper NW subcontinental includes some regional specialties "not commonly found", piquing purists' interest; its compact storefront space, decorated with native art, is a "modest" backdrop for such "exciting" fare, and while a few say service is "slow" at times, the staff is "pleasant", and there's "great value" to be had, especially at the "bargain" lunch buffet.

☑ Matchbox *American*
23 | 22 | 21 | $29

Capitol Hill | 521 Eighth St. SE (bet. E & G Sts.) | 202-548-0369
Chinatown | 713 H St. NW (bet. 7th & 8th Sts.) | 202-289-4441
Rockville | Congressional Plaza | 1699 Rockville Pike (Halpine Dr.), MD | 301-816-0369
www.matchboxchinatown.com

"Awesome" wood-fired pizzas with "high-quality" toppings, and "nasty-good" sliders "piled high" with onion straws kindle a blaze of praise for these "go-to" New American "hangouts" – and a "very nice" selection of beer and wine fans the flames; add in "kind" service, chic "industrial"-designer digs and "great prices", and it's no surprise there's often a "wait."

Matisse *French/Mediterranean*
23 | 21 | 22 | $54

Upper NW | 4934 Wisconsin Ave. NW (Fessenden St.) | 202-244-5222 | www.matisserestaurantdc.com

"Delightful" French-Med fare is "prepared in a contemporary manner" (i.e. "without a lot of sauces") at this "higher-end" Upper NW retreat, whose "open", "airy" dining room, managed by a "nice" staff, is graced with "soft lighting, copious mirrors and muted decor"; hence, it draws a clientele that skews "a little old", and who enjoy a "quiet dinner" and can afford the "expensive" tabs.

Matuba *Japanese*
23 | 15 | 21 | $32

Bethesda | 4918 Cordell Ave. (bet. Norfolk Ave. & Old Georgetown Rd.), MD | 301-652-7449 | www.matuba-sushi.com

At this Bethesda Japanese "institution" it's easy for regulars to "embarrass themselves" by gobbling so much of the "reliable, classic" fin fare – especially at the "fun" conveyor-belt lunch buffet (the price is "awesome for all-you-can-eat"); the dining area is "plain", but service is "friendly" and "kids" are welcome.

NEW Mayfair & Pine *British*
- | - | - | M

Glover Park | 2218 Wisconsin Ave. NW (Calvert St.) | 202-333-2090 | www.mayfairandpine.com

'Family friendly' could be the motto of the moderately priced menu featuring childhood favorites reimagined for adults (yes, there's a kids' menu too) at this new gastropub from a former *Top Chef* con-

FOOD | DECOR | SERVICE | COST

testant that recently debuted in Glover Park; craft beer and wine are perfectly at home in the pubby bi-level setting.

McCormick & Schmick's *Seafood*　　23 | 22 | 23 | $45

Penn Quarter | 901 F St. NW (9th St.) | 202-639-9330
Golden Triangle | 1652 K St. NW (bet. 16th & 17th Sts.) | 202-861-2233
Crystal City | 2010 Crystal Dr. (20th St.) | Arlington, VA | 703-413-6400
Reston | Reston Town Ctr. | 11920 Democracy Dr. (bet. Discovery & Library Sts.), VA | 703-481-6600
Tysons Corner | Ernst & Young Bldg. | 8484 Westpark Dr. (Leesburg Pike) | McLean, VA | 703-848-8000
www.mccormickandschmicks.com

"Trusted" by legions for its "wide selection" of "fresh" and "delicious" seafood dishes, this "quasi–fine-dining" chain wins over fin fans with a "refined-without-being-snooty" atmosphere and a "hopping happy hour with good specials"; "very attentive" service and "clubby" dining rooms create a "relaxing" vibe, leading most patrons to declare the sizable bills "money well spent."

Medium Rare *Steak*　　22 | 18 | 21 | $32

Cleveland Park | 3500 Connecticut Ave. NW (Ordway St.) | 202-237-1432 | www.mediumrarerestaurant.com

This Cleveland Parker "keeps it simple and does it well" with a single "no-choices" set menu for $19.50, consisting of bread, salad, "crispy fries" and a dry-aged sirloin cap "done perfectly", plus a "big surprise: second helpings"; the "friendly" staff herds dishes through the "noisy" modern bistro or to a patio with "terrific people-watching", and while add-ons like "smartly selected wines and beers" and "huge" desserts drive up costs, it's still an "excellent value."

Meiwah *Chinese*　　21 | 17 | 19 | $28

West End | 1200 New Hampshire Ave. NW (M St.) | 202-833-2888
Chevy Chase | Chase Tower | 4457 Willard Ave. (Wisconsin Ave.), MD | 301-652-9882
www.meiwahrestaurant.com

"Reliable, repeatable results" that "always please" make these "Americanized Chinese" twins in the West End and Chevy Chase "hugely popular" – and it doesn't hurt that they're "fairly priced"; floor-to-ceiling windows lend a bright feel to the simple, contemporary spaces, and "speedy" service, whether dine-in or delivery, "will give you whiplash."

Me Jana *Lebanese*　　24 | 21 | 24 | $36

Courthouse | Navy League Bldg. | 2300 Wilson Blvd. (Adams St.) | Arlington, VA | 703-465-4440 | www.me-jana.com

"Warm", "attentive" staffers go "out of their way to make you feel at home" at this affordable Arlington Courthouse purveyor of "authentic" Lebanese specialties and "excellent meze" ("order anything and everything") that make it a perfect "destination for a group"; the contemporary interior, with large windows, is "inviting", and the "nice atmosphere" continues outside on the umbrella-shaded sidewalk patio.

NEW Mellow Mushroom *Pizza* | 25 | 20 | 22 | $20 |

Adams Morgan | 2436 18th St. NW (Columbia Rd.) | 202-290-2778 | www.mellowmushroom.com

"Finally" sigh fans of this fresh Adams Morgan link in the ever-expanding, psychedelic-themed pizzeria chain – though "you'd never know it" was a chain given the location-specific "funky decor" and calendar of events; servers aiming to "please without being fawning" sling "excellent" pizzas with "unique, chewy crusts" and "satisfying" piled-high toppings, as well as calzones, salads and an "admirable" draft beer selection.

NEW Menomale *Pizza* | - | - | - | I |

Northeast | 2711 12th St. NE (Evarts St.) | 202-248-3946 | www.menomale.us

Real-deal Neapolitan pizza, calzones and panuozzos come to restaurant-starved Brookland courtesy of Ettore Rusciano, a Naples-certified maestro pizzaiolo who crafts gourmet pies and more using a wood-fired oven imported from Italy; pair the cheap bites with a smart list of craft brews in the tidy, white-walled bistro with tomato-red accents brightened by a charming picture window.

Meridian Pint ● *Pub Food* | 20 | 19 | 21 | $24 |

Columbia Heights | 3400 11th St. NW (Park Row) | 202-588-1075 | www.meridianpint.com

The "friendly" "bartenders know their brews" at this inexpensive tavern in Columbia Heights, where "rotating" drafts "quench your thirst" in a modern-rustic dining room or a basement den equipped with "draw-your-own-pint" machines; while "mostly known for its beer", it cooks up a full slate of "better-than-average" pub grub.

Merzi *Indian* | ▽ 20 | 14 | 16 | $12 |

Penn Quarter | 415 Seventh St. NW (bet. D & E Sts.) | 202-656-3794 | www.merzi.com

A "choose-your-own-adventure" approach that's "good, cheap and fast" governs this counter-serve concept in the Penn Quarter, where guests choose naan, chaat, rice or salad as a base for "yum" "mix 'n' match" meats, vegetables and sauces; its simple modern storefront, dressed up with intriguing red designs, is a "convenient" stop after visiting nearby museums and the Mall.

Meskerem *Ethiopian* | 22 | 18 | 20 | $26 |

Adams Morgan | 2434 18th St. NW (bet. Belmont & Columbia Rds.) | 202-462-4100 | www.meskeremonline.com

This "granddaddy of Ethiopian cuisine in Adams Morgan" remains "a good intro" to the "classics" of this affordable genre – sopping up "delicious" meat or vegetarian samplers with "tasty" injera bread is "a fun break to the monotony" of fork-and-knife dining; likewise the traditional hassock seating in the spice-colored triplex, so even if a few sigh that the service seems occasionally "overwhelmed", most are happy to return "again and again."

	FOOD	DECOR	SERVICE	COST

Mezè ● *Mideastern* — 24 | 20 | 22 | $39

Adams Morgan | 2437 18th St. NW (bet. Belmont & Columbia Rds.) |
202-797-0017 | www.mezedc.com

Adams Morgan's "exotic getaway" is this stylish bi-level Middle
Eastern offering a "wide selection" of "delicious" small plates (and
a few entrees) washed down by "extraordinary" mojitos that taste
even better when they're half-price during the weekday happy hour;
a "great late-night menu" plus "open-air" seating and smooth service make for a "reasonably priced", "romantic night out."

Mia's Pizzas *Pizza* — 25 | 17 | 20 | $25

Bethesda | 4926 Cordell Ave. (bet. Norfolk Ave. & Old Georgetown Rd.),
MD | 301-718-6427 | www.miaspizzasbethesda.com

"Love the 'za!" say fans of the "wonderful" wood-fired pies with
"beautifully charred" thin crusts and "tangy-sweet tomato sauce" at
this Bethesda "favorite" with solid service; if some say the "small",
airy interior can get "hectic" with "noisy kids", most note that it's
"easy on the wallet", and there's always the patio (and takeout).

Michael's Noodles *Chinese* — 22 | 11 | 18 | $19

Rockville | 10038 Darnestown Rd. (Travilah Rd.), MD | 301-738-0370 |
www.michaelsnoodles.com

There are many Taiwanese "dishes you can't find anywhere else" on
the broad-ranging Chinese menu of this simple Rockville storefront,
so foodies skip the General Tso's and "order something unusual" off
the 250-item list; seating is "limited" at this "genuinely delicious
place" with "decent prices", so "come early" or opt for takeout.

Mike's "American" *American* — 26 | 24 | 26 | $31

Springfield | 6210 Backlick Rd. (Commerce St.), VA | 703-644-7100 |
www.greatamericanrestaurants.com

Credit this "classy" Springfield mainstay's "attraction" to its "super-
solid" American fare – be it a "fresh, colorful salad, a tender grilled fish
or a large, juicy steak" – and moderate tabs (you can "eat a lot for a little"); "eager", young servers make it work as well for "family" outings
as for "meeting business associates or just an after-work get-together"
in the "happening" bar, but given its near-universal appeal, there's
nearly "always a wait", so call ahead" to be placed on the list.

Minerva *Indian* — 23 | 14 | 18 | $20

Gaithersburg | 16240 Frederick Rd. (Shady Grove Rd.), MD |
301-948-9898 | www.minervacuisine.com
Fairfax | 10364 Lee Hwy. (University Dr.), VA | 703-383-9200 |
www.minervafairfax.com
Herndon | Village Center at Dulles | 2443 Centreville Rd.
(Sunrise Valley Dr.), VA | 703-793-3223 | www.minervacuisine.com
Chantilly | Chantilly Park | 14513 Lee Jackson Memorial Hwy.
(Airline Pkwy.), VA | 703-378-7778 | www.minervacuisine.com

Especially if you like it "spicy", it's "hard to beat" this South Asian
chainlet for "authentic" Indian dishes, some of which you "can't find
elsewhere", plus a weekday buffet with a "wide variety" of "affordable" options; service reviews are mixed ("indifferent" to "great"),

FOOD | DECOR | SERVICE | COST

and interior decoration is "lacking", but large flat-screen TVs make it easy "to catch up on Bollywood movies."

Minh's Restaurant Ⓜ *Vietnamese* | 24 | 16 | 18 | $27 |

Courthouse | 2500 Wilson Blvd. (Cleveland St.) | Arlington, VA | 703-525-2828

Its location in an Arlington Courthouse office building "isn't special, but the food is" assert fans of this Vietnamese venue offering a "tremendous variety" of "outstanding" dishes, representing "both Northern and Southern styles"; it "usually isn't too crowded" in the "relaxing", white-tablecloth dining room, and though a few say service is like "rolling dice", most find it "friendly" and "reasonably" priced.

Ⓩ Minibar by José Andrés *Eclectic* | 28 | 21 | 27 | VE |

Penn Quarter | 855 E St. NW (bet. 8th & 9th Sts.) | 202-393-0812 | www.minibarbyjoseandres.com

José Andrés' "rock-my-world" Eclectic "culinary adventure" (closed at press time) is slated to reopen in fall 2012 in new Penn Quarter digs with more than double the capacity of its old six-seat location, thus outdating the Decor rating; the "mind-bending" multicourse meals, prepared by "engaging" chefs, should remain the same – an "expensive" "treat of a lifetime" – though the expanded space may lessen the "hassle" of snagging what was a "nearly impossible" reservation.

NEW Mintwood Place Ⓜ *American* | – | – | – | M |

Adams Morgan | 1813 Columbia Rd. NW (Biltmore St.) | 202-234-6732 | www.mintwoodplace.com

There's a been-here-forever feel about this convivial, midpriced addition to Adams Morgan, showcasing Cedric Maupillier's (ex Central Michel Richard) French-accented American cooking, much of it done in a wood-burning oven; the farmhouse-moderne look (pale wainscoting, antique implements) instills an easygoing ambiance, and there's a sidewalk patio for watching the neighborhood pass by.

Mio Ⓩ *Nuevo Latino* | 26 | 24 | 24 | $41 |

Downtown | 1110 Vermont Ave. NW (L St.) | 202-955-0075 | www.miorestaurant.com

"New energy, creativity and addictive flavors permeate" this high-end Downtown Nuevo Latino thanks to its latest chef, Giovanna Huyke, who puts an "emphasis on Puerto Rican food"; a "friendly atmosphere" pervades the "stylish" interior accessorized with modern art plus an "active bar scene" fueled by some of "the best mojitos in town."

Mi Rancho *Tex-Mex* | 22 | 18 | 21 | $25 |

Germantown | 19725 Germantown Rd. (Middlebrook Rd.), MD | 301-515-7480
Rockville | Congressional Plaza | 1488 Rockville Pike (Congressional Ln.), MD | 240-221-2636
Silver Spring | 8701 Ramsey Ave. (bet. Cameron St. & Colesville Rd.), MD | 301-588-4872
www.miranchotexmexrestaurant.com

The "simple and great-tasting" Tex-Mex at this "comfortable", "unassuming" chainlet may not blow away anyone who "comes from west of the Mississippi", but portions are "plentiful", margaritas are "fabulous" and "homemade" tortillas are a nice touch; "vibrant colors", "festive" lighting and servers with "constant smiles" are "good for families" – and you "won't go broke" or "go away hungry."

Mitsitam Café *American*   ▽ 23 13 13 $24

SW | National Museum of the American Indian | 950 Independence Ave. SW (4th St.) | 202-633-7039 | www.mitsitamcafe.com

This "honest-to-goodness gourmet" oasis in the National Museum of the American Indian offers "delicious" seasonal specialties of indigenous peoples (think cedar-planked salmon from the Pacific Northwest and "fantastic" soft tacos from Mesoamerica); it's a "typical cafeteria" ("crowded", you "buss your own trays"), but pros profess it's "the best place to eat on the Mall", only "wishing it stayed open" after museum hours.

Moby Dick *Persian*   23 11 17 $15

Dupont Circle | 1300 Connecticut Ave. NW (N St.) | 202-833-9788 🖂
Georgetown | 1070 31st St. NW (bet. K & M Sts.) | 202-333-4400
Bethesda | 7027 Wisconsin Ave. (Leland St.), MD | 301-654-1838
Gaithersburg | Market Sq. | 105 Market St. (Kentlands Blvd.), MD | 301-987-7770
Germantown | 12844 Pinnacle Dr. (Century Blvd.), MD | 301-916-1555
Rockville | Fallsgrove Village Shopping Ctr. | 14929 Shady Grove Rd. (bet. Blackwell Rd. & Fallsgrove Blvd.), MD | 301-738-0005
Silver Spring | 909 Ellsworth Dr. (Fenton St.), MD | 301-578-8777
Arlington | 3000 Washington Blvd. (Highland St.), VA | 703-465-1600
Fairfax | Fairfax Towne Ctr. | 12154 Fairfax Towne Ctr. (Ox Rd.), VA | 703-352-6226
McLean | 6854 Old Dominion Dr. (Chain Bridge Rd.), VA | 703-448-8448
www.mobysonline.com
Additional locations throughout the DC area

"Go straight for" the "juicy, flavorful" kebabs (the lamb is "to die for") at this local Persian-style street-eats chain that "never fails" in its quest to produce "off-the-charts-good" faves like "tangy" grape leaves, "delicious" hummus and "melt-in-your-mouth" baklava, all served up in portions "big enough for Ahab and his men"; "no-frills" surroundings may call for carryout, but with this much "bang for the buck", you will "forget about the decor."

Mon Ami Gabi *French*   22 21 21 $40

Bethesda | 7239 Woodmont Ave. (Elm St.), MD | 301-654-1234
Reston | Reston Town Ctr. | 11950 Democracy Dr. (Library St.), VA | 703-707-0233
www.monamigabi.com

You "may not be in Paris" – just Bethesda or Reston – "but you can pretend for a few hours" at this "lively" and "cute" art deco–esque Gallic chain where the French onion soup is "mouthwatering" and you "can't beat" the steak frites and "excellent wines by the glass"; it's "not inexpensive" – and a few say *non* to a "cacophonous", "Disney-like" atmosphere – but service is "American" (read: "friendly"), and a "loyal following" means "reservations are a must."

	FOOD	DECOR	SERVICE	COST

☒ Monocacy Crossing Ⓜ American
28 | 21 | 26 | $43

Frederick | 4424 Urbana Pike (bet. Araby Church & Ball Rds.), MD | 301-846-4204 | www.monocacycrossing.com

"Don't let the outside appearance fool you" say Frederick denizens who laud the "fabulous", "innovative" American cuisine (whiskey duck nachos are "out of this world") "elegantly" served at this "unassuming"-looking "farmhouse" on a "country road"; "strong" drinks and somewhat "expensive" tabs make this "simply" decorated "rustic gem" worthy of an "adult-only date night."

The Monocle ☒ American
21 | 22 | 24 | $49

Capitol Hill | 107 D St. NE (1st St.) | 202-546-4488 | www.themonocle.com

Peek "behind the curtain" of government at this "old-school" American establishment in the "shadow of the Capitol", where politicians and other powerful faces are "greeted by name", and tourists in its clubby booths feel that they're "sitting in the heartbeat of the USA"; the traditional fare is "darn good" too, but it's the "power" and the "history" that keep this "landmark" humming, especially at lunch; P.S. closed weekends.

Montmartre Ⓜ French
25 | 20 | 23 | $45

Capitol Hill | 327 Seventh St. SE (Pennsylvania Ave.) | 202-544-1244 | www.montmartredc.com

"Which arrondissement are we in?" ask *amis* of this "charmingly French" "sanctuary" on Capitol Hill, where "remarkable", "real-deal" bistro eats like "braised rabbit and escargot" are well "worth" the "not-cheap" price; the "attentive" staff treats guests "like family", albeit in a "small and crowded" room, so in *bonne* weather, many prefer to sit on the patio and "watch passersby."

Morrison-Clark Restaurant American
▽ 24 | 25 | 24 | $51

Downtown | Morrison-Clark Inn | 1015 L St. NW (bet. 10th & 11th Sts.) | 202-898-1200 | www.morrisonclark.com

Set in a "stately" "historic" inn, this Downtown vet remains a "well-kept secret" with "wonderful architecture" – including marble fireplaces and crystal chandeliers – that creates a "grand old atmosphere" for enjoying "memorable" New American cuisine served by a solicitous staff; prix fixe dinner and brunch options prevent wallet shock.

Morton's The Steakhouse Steak
26 | 24 | 26 | $71

Georgetown | 3251 Prospect St. NW (bet. Potomac St. & Wisconsin Ave.) | 202-342-6258

Golden Triangle | Washington Sq. | 1050 Connecticut Ave. NW (bet. K & L Sts.) | 202-955-5997

Bethesda | Hyatt Regency | 7400 Wisconsin Ave. (Old Georgetown Rd.), MD | 301-657-2650

Crystal City | Crystal City Shops | 1750 Crystal Dr. (bet. 15th & 18th Sts.) | Arlington, VA | 703-418-1444

Reston | Reston Town Ctr. | 11956 Market St. (Freedom Sq.), VA | 703-796-0128

www.mortons.com

Sure it's a chain, but this "quintessential" steakhouse has "distinguished itself" time and again with "power steaks" that "melt in your mouth" and "superb" seafood in "comfortable" "dark, clubby" digs; with always "impeccable" service and even a bit of a "meat show" (when waiters bring out the uncooked goods for inspection), it's perfect for "cutting a deal" – just put it on the "expense account."

Mosaic Cuisine & Café *Eclectic* | 23 | 18 | 22 | $25 |

White Flint | Congressional Shopping Ctr. | 186 Halpine Rd. (Rockville Pike) | Rockville, MD | 301-468-0682 | www.mosaiccuisine.com

There's no waffling about the focus of this "refreshing" Rockville "concept place" – what with multiple breakfast variations, "sandwiches on waffles", dessert waffles, etc. – but the affordable menu also includes "divine" soups, salads and "creative" entrees, many with a French accent; "incredibly friendly" servers work a "crowded" dining room of "soothing hues" and "tasteful wall art"; P.S. Wicked Waffle, its counter-serve spinoff Downtown, offers breakfast and lunch items to go.

Mourayo *Greek* | 25 | 18 | 23 | $45 |

Dupont Circle | 1732 Connecticut Ave. NW (bet. R & S Sts.) | 202-667-2100 | www.mourayous.com

"Inventive modern Greek fare" makes this pricey Dupont Circle "culinary find" not "your regular gyro place" – rather, it excels with "fresh fish" dishes and "refined" renditions of classics plus interesting Hellenic wines; "available but unobtrusive" servers keep an even keel in the "unpretentious", "nautically themed" space, resulting in a "simply delightful dining experience."

Mrs. K's Toll House Ⓜ *American* | 23 | 24 | 24 | $42 |

Silver Spring | 9201 Colesville Rd. (Dale Dr.), MD | 301-589-3500 | www.mrsks.com

"One of a kind", this sprawling Silver Spring "institution" has a Tudor "inn"-like setting that's "quaintly elegant" and just right for "highly civilized" (though "pricey") repasts of "interesting" contemporary American cuisine; it's been a "family favorite" with "fabulous" service since the '30s, but these days the winepress room attracts a "younger crowd" that prefers not to "dine with their grandmothers' friends."

Murasaki *Japanese* | ∇ 23 | 15 | 20 | $30 |

Upper NW | 4620 Wisconsin Ave. NW (bet. Brandywine & Chesapeake Sts.) | 202-966-0023 | www.murasakidc.com

"Appearance matters to the chefs" behind the sushi counter at this "well-priced" Upper NW Japanese "neighborhood" spot, which is why the "creative" rolls are not only "tasty" but "good looking"; solid service contributes to its "reliable" reputation, and a "comfortable" patio is an alternative to the typical blond-wood interior.

Mussel Bar ❶ *Belgian* | 20 | 17 | 18 | $34 |

Bethesda | 7262 Woodmont Ave. (Elm St.), MD | 301-215-7817 | www.musselbar.com

"The name says it all" at Robert Wiedmaier's tribute to his Belgian heritage in Bethesda, where "great" mussels flex their stuff alongside a "huge, well-thought-out beer selection" that lubricates a "hopping" bar scene; a few critics contend it's "the one dud in the

Wiedmaier collection" and plead "they've got to do something about the acoustics" (it's "all hard wood and metal"), but service is solid, and if you dig mussels, "this is the place to go in the 'burbs."

Myanmar ⓜ *Burmese* ▽ 24 | 11 | 14 | $22

Falls Church | Merrifalls Plaza | 7810 Lee Hwy. (Hyson Ln.), VA | 703-289-0013

It's "where Burmese expats go", so you know the "curries" et al. are "authentic" and "reliably terrific" at this "tiny, out-of-the-way" joint in Falls Church; "modest trappings" and service snags that bother some don't deter "adventurous eaters", who assert it's well worth the modest tabs for this "unique" ethnic food.

Mykonos Grill ⓜ *Greek* 23 | 22 | 23 | $35

Rockville | 121 Congressional Ln. (Rockville Pike), MD | 301-770-5999 | www.mykonosgrill.com

"The warm breeze of the Mediterranean wafts through" this "always reliable" and "moderately priced" veteran Greek in Rockville, where "wonderful seafood" and "flavorful" specialties are served by "polite", "professional" waiters; dining in the "bright" white-and-blue room is "always a pleasure", though it can get "busy", so "make reservations or come early."

Nage *American/Seafood* 21 | 16 | 18 | $37

Scott Circle | Marriott Courtyard Embassy Row | 1600 Rhode Island Ave. NW (bet. 16th & 17th Sts.) | 202-448-8005 | www.nagerestaurant.com

Net "creative seafood dishes" at dinner and "great snacks and drinks for happy hour" (or a "terrific" "bottomless brunch") at this "lively" Scott Circle New American that provides "service with a smile"; the contemporary corporate decor "reminds you that it's a hotel restaurant", but supporters say it offers "better fare than most" such venues.

Nam-Viet *Vietnamese* 21 | 12 | 20 | $24

Cleveland Park | 3419 Connecticut Ave. NW (bet. Macomb & Ordway Sts.) | 202-237-1015

Clarendon | 1127 N. Hudson St. (bet. 13th St. & Wilson Blvd.), VA | 703-522-7110

www.namviet1.com

Standouts like "fabulous" lemongrass chicken and "fantastic" pho that really "hits the spot" star on an otherwise "reliable", "well-done" Vietnamese menu at these long-running "neighborhood gems" in Clarendon and Cleveland Park; a "sincere" staff adds warmth to the "simple", "unassuming" settings, and prices are "more than fair."

Nando's Peri-Peri *Chicken* 22 | 19 | 19 | $17

Chinatown | 819 Seventh St. NW (bet. H & I Sts.) | 202-898-1225

Dupont Circle | 1210 18th St. NW (Connecticut Ave.) | 202-621-8603

NEW **Bethesda** | 4839 Bethesda Ave. (bet. Arlington Rd. & Hager Ln.), MD | 301-500-2182

NEW **Gaithersburg** | Washingtonian/Rio Ctr. | 224 Boardwalk Pl. (Sam Eig Hwy.), MD | 240-408-7146

National Harbor | 191 American Way (Fleet St.), MD | 301-686-8388

Silver Spring | 924 Ellsworth Dr. (bet. Fenton St. & Georgia Ave.), MD | 301-588-7280

(continued)

Nando's Peri-Peri
Pentagon City | 1301 S. Joyce St. (Army Navy Dr.) | Arlington, VA | 571-858-9953
www.nandosperiperi.com

"Addictive" rotisserie chicken "spiced to perfection" brings "repeat" customers to this Portuguese/South African chain where "unique" sauces (including "fiery" ones "from the depths of hell") and "amazing" sides play able wingmen to the big bird; you "wait in line to order", then the "food is brought to your table" in "pleasant", woody digs – it's an "ingenious fast-food concept" that's "quick, cheap and fun."

Napoleon Bistro *French*   ▽ 24 | 24 | 19 | $36
Adams Morgan | 1847 Columbia Rd. NW (bet. Biltmore St. & Mintwood Pl.) | 202-299-9630 | www.napoleondc.com

This "very French" Adams Morgan spot serving "delicious" mid-priced bistro fare, most notably "excellent" crêpes, recently got a redo (possibly outdating its Decor rating), and now features dark walls, black velvet and glowing candles, which should enhance it as a perfect place "for hand-holding and eye-gazing"; if a few are less enamored of the service ("not so great"), most say it's "friendly", and the popular brunch "never disappoints."

Nava Thai *Thai*   26 | 16 | 20 | $25
Wheaton | 11301 Fern St. (Price Ave.), MD | 240-430-0495

"Sublime", "big and bold" curries exemplify the "interestingly un-routine" dining possibilities at this Thai eatery that, along with "real value", make it "well worth the trek to Wheaton"; so worth it, indeed, that there's often a "wait" for a table in its basic, yellow-hued dining rooms where "friendly" servers create a "warm and inviting" feel.

Negril 🖾 *Jamaican*   24 | 13 | 20 | $15
Anacostia | 2863 Alabama Ave. SE (30th St.) | 202-575-7555
U Street Corridor | 2301 Georgia Ave. NW (Bryant St.) | 202-332-3737
Silver Spring | 965 Thayer Ave. (Georgia Ave.), MD | 301-585-3000
www.negrileats.com

"Yeah mon", the "awesome" "homestyle" meals at this Jamaican chainlet bring island flavor to Greater DC and Baltimore via "delicious" beef patties, roti and more; some locations are counter service only, and overall a few suggest the "colorful" decor "could use some help", but staffers are "helpful and friendly", and the price "cannot be beat."

Neisha Thai *Thai*   20 | 19 | 20 | $27
Upper NW | 4445 Wisconsin Ave. NW (Albemarle St.) | 202-966-7088
Tysons Corner | Tysons Corner Ctr. | 7924 Tysons Corner Ctr. (Chain Bridge Rd.) | McLean, VA | 703-883-3588
www.neisha.net

Tysons Corner and Upper NW denizens rely on this family-owned Thai duo for "always dependable" fare from a large menu ("get the passion beef"); the "modern Asian decor" strikes some as a "bit dark", but bright spots include the fact that it's "reasonably priced" and that "everyone is so friendly."

	FOOD	DECOR	SERVICE	COST

New Fortune ● *Chinese*

| 23 | 13 | 19 | $21 |

Gaithersburg | 16515 S. Frederick Ave. (Westland Dr.), MD | 301-548-8886 | www.newfortunedimsum.com

"Never-ending carts" of "wonderful" dim sum rush by at a "frenetic pace" at this "huge" Gaithersburg Cantonese during lunchtime hours; the authenticity of its "traditional" dishes is "confirmed" by "lots of Asian diners" at its family-style round tables, and "reasonable" prices won't dent your personal fortune.

New Heights ⊠ *American*

| 22 | 20 | 20 | $59 |

Woodley Park | 2317 Calvert St. NW (Connecticut Ave.) | 202-234-4110 | www.newheightsrestaurant.com

Longtime loyalists joke "every time you turn around, there's a new chef" at this "high-end" Woodley Park New American, most recently, the well-regarded Ron Tanaka (ex Cork); service is solid upstairs in the "contemporary Arts and Crafts" dining room, while at the downstairs bar "knowledgeable" mixologists make full use of the "unsurpassed array of gin."

New Kam Fong ● *Chinese*

| ∇ 25 | 11 | 18 | $28 |

Wheaton | 2400 University Blvd. (Elkin St.), MD | 301-933-6388

For "excellent" Cantonese fare, including BBQ and some "very exotic dishes", head to this "friendly" Wheaton storefront that's considered "one of the best" and as "authentic" as the "ducks and pigs hanging" in the display case would suggest; the simple setup is "brightly" lit, illuminating budget-worthy bills.

Newton's Table *American*

| 22 | 18 | 21 | $54 |

Bethesda | 4917 Elm St. (bet. Arlington Rd. & Woodmont Ave.), MD | 301-718-0550 | www.newtonstable.com

The "attractively plated, inventive" New American food "tastes as good as it looks" at chef-owner Dennis Friedman's place in Bethesda; maybe it's "pricey for the 'burbs", and a few find the contemporary ambiance "bland", but with "polished" service and "delicious" food, it's considered by most a "nice addition" to the local scene.

Neyla *Lebanese*

| 24 | 21 | 21 | $46 |

Georgetown | 3206 N St. NW (Wisconsin Ave.) | 202-333-6353 | www.neyla.com

"Sense-tingling, lively dishes" are "designed to be shared" at this "high-end" Lebanese resto-lounge that some consider the "best-kept secret in Georgetown"; though a few say it's "overpriced", most are happy to place themselves in the hands of the "accommodating" staff and relax with a drink in the "exotic" environs, which include a room "draped like an Arab tent"; P.S. there's a "nightclubbish" vibe on weekends.

Nick's Chophouse *Steak*

| 21 | 22 | 21 | $44 |

Rockville | 700 King Farm Blvd. (bet. Gaither & Shady Grove Rds.), MD | 301-926-8869 | www.nickschophouserockville.com

Rockville's carnivores gather at this "dependable", "suburban" steakhouse to relish "simple", if expensive, meaty fare served profession-

	FOOD	DECOR	SERVICE	COST

ally; the light, airy dining room is formal but not fussy, the lounge bar is spacious and, as both are "never very crowded", locals relish it as a "quiet" place for "happy-hour eats" or dinner "at the last minute."

901 Restaurant & Bar *American/Asian*   22 | 23 | 21 | $41

Mt. Vernon Square/Convention Center | 901 Ninth St. NW (I St.) | 202-524-4433 | www.901dc.com

"Dim lighting" casts a "cool", "Miami-esque" glow over this "friendly", "upscale" Convention Center watering hole whose "big" bar works well for large groups soaking up the "plethora of beer on tap" (it's a showcase for big papa Capitol City Brewing) during its "loud" and "fun" happy hour; LED menus describe "interesting" American-Asian small plates and entrees, though a minority are less impressed by the "discolike" atmosphere and "portion sizes that don't reflect the prices."

1905 🗷 M *French*   21 | 22 | 19 | $35

Mt. Vernon Square/Convention Center | 1905 Ninth St. NW (bet. T & U Sts.) | 202-332-1905 | www.1905dc.com

"Get your green fairy on" with the "hot crowd" sipping absinthe at this "hip", "friendly" Mt. Vernon Square "speakeasy" (it's "upstairs and hidden") where you can also sup on "fairly inexpensive" "feel-good" French fare; the "dark, cozy" space, furnished with an "eclectic" mix of fittings and curios (and the rooftop space) is "great for a date that you hope will last way past dinner."

Niwano Hana *Japanese*   26 | 16 | 23 | $26

Rockville | Wintergreen Plaza | 887 Rockville Pike (Edmonston Dr.), MD | 301-294-0553 | www.niwanohana.com

No wonder this Rockville Japanese has been a local "favorite" for decades – its "incredible" sushi (both "classic" and "edgy" rolls) always includes "generous, well-proportioned pieces" of "so-fresh" fish; there's "not much maneuvering room" in the "crowded" traditional-looking digs, but that just makes it "feel more like Japan" – besides, the "polite" staff always keeps your teacup "full", and best of all is the "very reasonable price."

Nooshi *Asian*   21 | 15 | 17 | $21

Golden Triangle | 1120 19th St. NW (bet. L & M Sts.) | 202-293-3138 | www.nooshidc.com

"All things noodles and sushi" ferried by "rushed but efficient" servers makes this cheap, "consistently good" Golden Triangle Pan-Asian a "crowded" "work-lunch" spot; during the "super-affordable happy hour", however, the "tight" quarters are ceded to a "young, loud" GW crowd bent on "having a good time."

Nora 🗷 *American*   26 | 23 | 24 | $65

Dupont Circle | 2132 Florida Ave. NW (R St.) | 202-462-5143 | www.noras.com

"Farm-to-table before it was fashionable" (more than 30 years ago), Nora Pouillon's Dupont Circle New American standard-bearer remains "eternally new" by always treating the "freshest" "local" ingredients with "sophistication" yet "without fuss"; the "adorable" and "intimate" environs, complete with "eavesdropping opportunities", are tended by a staff that "makes you feel like a millionaire", which makes sense given the tab.

Northside Social *Coffeehouse*   22 | 18 | 18 | $16

Clarendon | 3211 Wilson Blvd. (Fairfax Dr.), VA | 703-465-0145 | www.northsidesocialarlington.com

It's "like my own living room" say folks who sink into "comfy old sofas" or "camp out on laptops" while sipping "froufrou" java and noshing "great" baked goods and sandwiches at this "hip" "hangout" in Clarendon; those who find it "overpopulated" can ascend to the more "intimate" second-floor wine bar for small plates and vino, but up or down, the vibe is "friendly" and the tabs low.

Nostos 🅱 *Greek*   26 | 24 | 25 | $47

Tysons Corner | 8100 Boone Blvd. (bet. Aline Ave. & Gallows Rd.) | Vienna, VA | 703-760-0690 | www.nostosrestaurant.com

This "sparkling" gem in Tysons Corner (a sibling of Mykonos Grill) offers "too many" "tempting" choices for just one meal – from "incredible" lollipop lamb chops to "delightful" fish – claim fans who "go back again and again"; sure, the prices are high, but "even the restrooms are posh" in this "beautifully" designed "modern" setting (light-gray stone walls, interesting art) that's warmed by skilled waiters who can help "navigate the extensive Greek wine list."

Notti Bianche *Italian*   22 | 17 | 22 | $43

Foggy Bottom | George Washington University Inn | 824 New Hampshire Ave. NW (bet. H & I Sts.) | 202-298-8085 | www.nottibianche.com

"What's not to like" about this "intimate" Italian in Foggy Bottom, with a "small" but "pricey" menu that's "well chosen", "well prepared" and well served by a "hospitable" staff in the "quiet", film-poster-bedecked room; the pre-theater prix fixe makes it a "wonderful" go-to "before a Kennedy Center performance."

Oakville Grille & Wine Bar *American*   21 | 19 | 21 | $44

Bethesda | Wildwood Shopping Ctr. | 10257 Old Georgetown Rd. (Democracy Blvd.), MD | 301-897-9100 | www.oakvillewinebar.com

A "quiet, classy neighborhood spot", this Bethesda bistro has a "varied" American menu that strikes some as "old-fashioned" but appeals to the "mix of suits and plaid shirts" and "ladies who lunch", who don't blink at the "premium prices" and appreciate the "lovely" California-heavy wine list; staffers are "unobtrusive" and want to "please diners", making this a "dependable" destination "for stopping after shopping."

🅉 Obelisk 🅱🅜 *Italian*   28 | 20 | 26 | $98

Dupont Circle | 2029 P St. NW (bet. 20th & 21st Sts.) | 202-872-1180

From the antipasto "spectrum of delights" to sweet endings like "candied fennel ice cream", a "stellar" prix fixe dinner (no à la carte) at Peter Pastan's Dupont Circle Italian soars to "heights taller than the Washington Monument", DC's other obelisk; the "intimate", "informal" townhouse setting allows diners to focus on "what Italian cooking is really about": "simple but expertly prepared food served by pros", which along with "superb" wines, is "worth every euro."

Occidental Grill & Seafood *Seafood/Steak* 23 | 24 | 24 | $65

Downtown | Willard Plaza | 1475 Pennsylvania Ave. NW (bet. 14th & 15th Sts.) | 202-783-1475 | www.occidentaldc.com

"Washington powers" have been tucking into the "reliably" "terrific" surf 'n' turf for years at this "touch of old-time DC" just steps from the White House, and lined with "portraits of statesmen" peering down from on high; sure, it's "expensive" (as is the small-plates menu in the attached wine room), but "good service will never go out of style", and "establishment" types affirm it's important "to dine here at least once a year."

Oceanaire Seafood Room *Seafood* 24 | 23 | 24 | $58

Downtown | 1201 F St. NW (bet. 12th & 13th Sts.) | 202-347-2277 | www.theoceanaire.com

Essentially a "steakhouse for fish", this "upper-end" chain sea-fooder, with links in DC and Baltimore, attracts a "power" crowd with its "invariably delicious and fresh" fish "prepared to perfection" and suited to "business dinners" and "special occasions"; you'll need to "bring your gold card", but it's "money well spent", especially given the "sleek", "elegant" setting (think 1930s steamliner) and "fabulous" happy hour.

Olazzo *Italian* 24 | 19 | 22 | $29

Bethesda | 7921 Norfolk Ave. (Cordell Ave.), MD | 301-654-9496
Silver Spring | 8235 Georgia Ave. (Thayer Ave.), MD | 301-588-2540
www.olazzo.com

"Terrific lasagna" is the highlight of the menu at this Bethesda–Silver Spring duo owned by a pair of brothers who serve up "delicious" Italian fare and "jump in" to help out with the "delightful" service; they don't take reservations, but with such "cozy", rustic, flatteringly lit digs, plus "spectacular" martinis, it's perfect for "date night" and "reasonably priced" to boot.

Old Angler's Inn *American* 20 | 24 | 20 | $58

Potomac | 10801 MacArthur Blvd. (Clara Barton Pkwy.), MD | 301-365-2425 | www.oldanglersinn.com

An "incomparable" setting near the C&O Canal in Potomac sets a "romantic" mood throughout this old favorite – out on the "divine" terrace or informal beer garden, inside for drinks by the "roaring fire" or up narrow stairs in the dining rooms; the "quality" New American fare is "well served", though "expensive" tabs keep it a "special-occasion place."

☑ Old Ebbitt Grill ☻ *American* 23 | 24 | 23 | $42

Downtown | 675 15th St. NW (bet. F & G Sts.) | 202-347-4800 | www.ebbitt.com

Imagine if the "walls could talk" at this "iconic" DC tavern "convenient" to the White House, since day and night its vast space "bustles" with an "interesting" mix of "tourists" and "politicos" seated in the "rich, paneled" "Victorian"-style rooms or perched at the "long, stately bars"; happily, the "tasty" American menu "fits all budgets" – on the low end, check out the "excellent" burgers and "one of the best happy-hour deals for oyster-lovers" around.

Old Glory All-American BBQ *BBQ*   19 | 15 | 18 | $28

Georgetown | 3139 M St. NW (Wisconsin Ave.) | 202-337-3406 | www.oldglorybbq.com

"At the crossroads of crowded and delicious" lies this Georgetown BBQ joint beloved by "coeds and tourists", where the "old-fashioned" ribs and such, "multiple" sauces and standard sides sometimes take a backseat to the "college scene" and "watching a game"; while the ephemera-filled space is "nothing fancy", it's been around for over two decades – and the rooftop seating is mighty appealing.

Old Hickory Steakhouse *Steak*   ∇ 26 | 26 | 24 | $111

National Harbor | Gaylord National Hotel | 201 Waterfront St. (St. George Blvd.), MD | 301-965-4000 | www.gaylordhotels.com

"Superb steaks and wonderful, imaginative sides", together with "excellent cheeses" cared for and served by a dedicated "cheese sommelier", make this lesser-known steakhouse in the Gaylord National Hotel something of a destination dinner spot; the light and elegant environs evoke a Georgetown mansion, so the "expensive" bill should not come as a surprise (it's "worth it"); P.S. "get a window seat" to enjoy views of the Potomac.

NEW 100° C Chinese Cuisine *Chinese*   24 | 21 | 22 | $30

Fairfax | Fair Ridge Ctr. | 3903 Fair Ridge Dr. (bet. Fairfax County Pkwy. & Ox Rd.), VA | 703-537-0788 | www.100degreehot.com

"As the name implies, the spicy specialties are the best" at this Hunan standard-bearer in Fairfax, where a roomful of people enjoying family-style meals is a testament to the menu's "authenticity"; "reasonable" prices, a staff that "really cares" and a "modern" "minimalist Asian" setting featuring multicolored lanterns and a wall sculpture add up to a real "neighborhood find."

Oohhs & Aahhs Ⓜ⇄ *Southern*   ∇ 23 | 7 | 17 | $21

U Street Corridor | 1005 U St. NW (10th St.) | 202-667-7142 | www.oohhsnaahhs.com

At this U Street soul food "pit stop", "down-home" Southern fare in helpings that would "easily serve two" "make up" for its "nothing-to-write-home-about" decor; some moan that it's "overpriced", but BYO helps compensate, and the staff is "nice and friendly."

Open City ⏺ *Diner*   21 | 17 | 20 | $21

Woodley Park | 2331 Calvert St. NW (24th St.) | 202-332-2331 | www.opencitydc.com

"Quality" diner fare at a "decent price" – from "pizza to all-day breakfast" seasoned with "just the right amount of funk" – has a mix of "zoo tourists", "locals" and "conventioneers" "crowding" into this eatery in Woodley Park; despite its "bustling" nature, the service is generally "attentive" in the airy, tin-ceilinged interior and out on the "lovely" patio.

	FOOD	DECOR	SERVICE	COST

The Orchard ⊠Ⓜ *Eclectic* | 25 | 22 | 25 | $24 |

Frederick | 45 N. Market St. (Church St.), MD | 301-663-4912 | www.theorchardrestaurant.com

An "oasis" in Downtown Frederick for its "lighter-than-most" menu of "organic and local" eats (stir-fries, salads, veggie/vegan choices), this Eclectic eatery works for a casual "first date" or a "girls' night out"; the "homey" storefront has a "charming" atmosphere, "always great" service and budget prices that speak to a "real find."

Oriental East *Chinese* | 23 | 14 | 16 | $23 |

Silver Spring | 1312 East-West Hwy. (Colesville Rd.), MD | 301-608-0030 | www.orientaleast.com

"Crowds stretch out the door and down the sidewalk on weekends" for the "delicious" "value"-priced dim sum at this Silver Spring Chinese, which fans claim is worth braving the "zoo" for; there's "not much decor", and the staff "isn't there to exchange pleasantries", but the food arrives "rapidly" and "piping hot", so really the "hardest part is deciding when to stop"; P.S. pros show up well before opening time on weekends.

Oro Pomodoro *Italian/Pizza* | 21 | 18 | 20 | $29 |

Rockville | Rockville Town Sq. | 33 Maryland Ave. (bet. Beall Ave. & Middle Ln.), MD | 301-251-1111 | www.oropomodoro.com

"Delicious" pizza, certified by the Verace Pizza Napoletana Association, "is the star", though the other Italian "selections are worth considering" too at this Rockville Town Square spot that reminds guests of a "sophisticated city pizzeria in Roma", especially on the "pleasant" patio in the venue's central piazza; inside, an "impressive" bar dominates a glitzy gold-toned room where "timely" service and "reasonable" tabs please most.

Oval Room ⊠ *American* | 26 | 23 | 25 | $69 |

Golden Triangle | 800 Connecticut Ave. NW (bet. H & I Sts.) | 202-463-8700 | www.ovalroom.com

Deep "in lobbyist territory" close to the White House, this "sophisticated" New American trades in "inventive" dishes served with "panache and style", at prices that may "not be for the 99%"; still, it's a "great experience" dining among "power" in the "quiet and understated" green-and-red (but not oval) room, with tables spread "far enough apart for good conversation."

❷ Oya *Asian* | 24 | 27 | 22 | $45 |

Penn Quarter | 777 Ninth St. NW (H St.) | 202-393-1400 | www.oyadc.com

"Fireplaces, mirrors, glass and white leather" give a "Vegas" vibe to this "gorgeous" resto-lounge in Penn Quarter pairing "creative sushi" and Asian fusion fare "done right" with an "off-the-wall" wine list; such a combo of "hip and chic" means it's *"très cher"*, but it's also a "great first-date" location, with service that provides "attention without hovering"; P.S. the lunch and dinner prix fixe deals "can't be beat."

	FOOD	DECOR	SERVICE	COST

Oyamel ❶ *Mexican*
25 | 22 | 21 | $42

Penn Quarter | 401 Seventh St. NW (D St.) | 202-628-1005 | www.oyamel.com

"No burritos or chimichangas here!" cheer fans of the "delightful, creative" tapas and street food given "a typical José Andrés twist" (e.g. grasshopper tacos "you'll jump for") at this high-end Penn Quarter Mexican with a "funky", "loud" atmosphere; some say that service, while "friendly", "doesn't match the quality of the food", but for most, niceties like "super-strong" margaritas and the "edible entertainment" of guacamole made tableside extend the fiesta feeling.

Ozzie's Corner Italian *Italian*
24 | 24 | 24 | $31

Fairfax | Fairfax Corner | 11880 Grand Commons Ave. (Monument Dr.), VA | 571-321-8000 | www.greatamericanrestaurants.com

"Fresh housemade pasta" is a favorite of the "delicious" fare that comes in "plentiful" portions at this Fairfax Corner "Italian with a twist", where the "price is right"; the "big" space feels "cozy" on account of comfy red-leather booths and "welcoming" staff that "makes you feel at home"; P.S. there are no reservations at busy times, but "phone ahead to get on the seating list."

Pacci's Neapolitan Pizzeria *Pizza*
23 | 19 | 21 | $24

Silver Spring | 8113 Georgia Ave. (Sligo Ave.), MD | 301-588-1011 | www.paccispizzeria.com

In the "wasteland" of Maryland pizza, the "soupy, yummy tomato-and-cheese goodness" atop a "delicious thin crust" produced by this Silver Spring pie-maker counts as a "major addition" to the scene, and is supported by a "very passable" wine selection; add in "friendly" service and a "warm", "cozy" brick-lined setting, and one can make an "inexpensive date happen" here.

NEW Pacci's Trattoria & Pasticceria Ⓜ *Italian*
▽ 23 | 17 | 19 | $24

Silver Spring | 6 Post Office Rd. (Seminary Rd.), MD | 301-588-0867

Recently setting up shop in Forest Glen's historic old Post Office & General Store building, this "neighborhood Italian" (a sibling of Pacci's Neapolitan Pizzeria) remains somewhat "undiscovered"; but locals report a "limited" menu featuring "very nice pastas" plus "beautiful, inexpensive treats to quench your wine palate", all for an affordable price in rustic, wood-beamed digs.

❷ Palena *American*
27 | 22 | 24 | $98

Cleveland Park | 3529 Connecticut Ave. NW (bet. Ordway & Porter Sts.) | 202-537-9250 | www.palenarestaurant.com

"Ambrosia fit for the gods" is on the menus at Frank Ruta's Cleveland Park New American, and fans swear the "quiet", "dimly lit" back room's prix fixe (no à la carte) is "worth" the "expense", while noting the "casual" front cafe is "one of the best bargains in town", with its "succulent" burgers, entrees and a bread basket "worth paying for" – and, indeed, they do charge for it; service throughout matches the kitchen's "high competency", and a market annex sells "superb" desserts and savories.

The Palm *Steak*
25 | 21 | 25 | $69

Dupont Circle | 1225 19th St. NW (bet. M & N Sts.) | 202-293-9091
Tysons Corner | 1750 Tysons Blvd. (Rte. 123) | McLean, VA | 703-917-0200
www.thepalm.com

The "famous, rich and powerful" crowd these "classic", "clubby" steakhouse chain spots near Dupont Circle and in Tysons Corner, famed for their "superb" chops, "excellent" wine and "outstanding" service; "you never know who you might see" at the next table (or gazing down from the wall in "caricature" form), just "don't expect to hear your own thoughts" above the "noise", and bring a "full" wallet.

Panache Restaurant 🗷 *Mediterranean*
21 | 20 | 19 | $45

Golden Triangle | 1725 Desales St. NW (bet. Connecticut Ave. & 17th St.) | 202-293-7760
Tysons Corner | Pinnacle Towers S. | 1753 Pinnacle Dr. (Chain Bridge Rd.) | McLean, VA | 703-748-1919
www.panacherestaurant.com

Glamorous and grown-up, these stylish Mediterranean spots in the Golden Triangle and Tysons Corner boast "generous", "varied" tapas selections, well suited to "share with friends" at the "chic", "hopping" bars backed by "awesome" staff – or there's a full menu for a "cozy dinner for two"; "nice" servers, upscale prices and an "interesting" red-and-white color scheme rule at both locations, though Tysons Corner is much larger and more sleek.

Panjshir *Afghan*
▽ 25 | 19 | 25 | $28

Falls Church | 924 W. Broad St. (West St.), VA | 703-536-4566 | www.panjshirrestaurant.com

Far-flung fans "schlep to Falls Church just to eat" at this "outstanding" Afghan stalwart, many of them praising "the most amazing *kadu* (pumpkin) you will ever eat"; a "lovely and welcoming" staff brightens the simple, traditionally decorated storefront, and "nice prices" seal the deal.

Paolo's *Californian/Italian*
21 | 19 | 21 | $36

Georgetown | 1303 Wisconsin Ave. NW (N St.) | 202-333-7353 ◗
Reston | Reston Town Ctr. | 11898 Market St. (Reston Pkwy.), VA | 703-318-8920
www.paolosristorante.com

A "reliably good" range of "well-prepared" pizza, pasta and mains make these "sleek" Cal-Ital spots in Georgetown and Reston Town Center solid "standbys", but it's the standout "perfect" salads and "addicting" free "breadsticks and olive tapenade" that keep many "coming back"; "friendly personnel", moderate prices and "awesome" happy hours are added draws.

Parkway Deli *Deli*
22 | 11 | 19 | $19

Silver Spring | Rock Creek Shopping Ctr. | 8317 Grubb Rd. (E. West Hwy.), MD | 301-587-1427 | www.theparkwaydeli.com

"Where else can you find a tongue sandwich" inside the Beltway? ask lovers of this "low-priced" Jewish deli in Silver Spring, with "huge" "classic" sandwiches and other "traditional" noshes delivered by an

FOOD | DECOR | SERVICE | COST

"efficient" staff; a few kvetch it "comes up short" "if you're from NYC", and critique the "tacky" purple decor, but most say it's still "good after all these years" – and, hey, you "can't beat the [free] pickle bar!"

Pasha Cafe *Mediterranean*

∇ 23 | 17 | 24 | $29

Cherrydale | 3911 N. Lee Hwy. (Pollard St.) | Arlington, VA | 703-528-1111 | www.pashacafe.com

Boosters applaud "excellent food in an unlikely location" at this Mediterranean in a Cherrydale strip mall, which gets props for its Greek salads and pita sandwiches; the "casual", wood-accented digs are served by "friendly" staffers who "don't rush" customers, and "prices are just right" for a "neighborhood cafe."

Passage to India *Indian*

24 | 22 | 23 | $38

Bethesda | 4931 Cordell Ave. (bet. Norfolk Ave. & Old Georgetown Rd.), MD | 301-656-3373 | www.passagetoindia.info

"Entering the mosiac tile door" of this "upscale" Bethesda Indian, one senses its "authenticity", and indeed, its "divided-by-region" menu presents "perfectly spiced" dishes "rarely seen" elsewhere; for most who have booked passage, "gracious" treatment in a set-ting appointed with "Colonial elegance" further "justifies the price."

PassionFish *American/Seafood*

26 | 24 | 24 | $52

Reston | Reston Town Ctr. | 11960 Democracy Dr. (Explorer St.), VA | 703-230-3474 | www.passionfishreston.com

"Downtown flair and finesse" pervade this seafood-focused American "showplace" in Reston, where "fresh, delicious, well-seasoned" choices "aren't just a rehash of classic fish dishes" (look for "Asian influences" and "amazing" sushi); even if "it ain't cheap", service is "top-notch", and its "Miami-like" bi-level space is "open, airy and al-ways inviting", and consequently favored as a "date location" or "high-end after-work dinner"

Pasta Mia 🖂Ⓜ🚫 *Italian*

26 | 14 | 16 | $27

Adams Morgan | 1790 Columbia Rd. NW (18th St.) | 202-328-9114

"Beautiful Bolognese and ravishing ravioli" in "portions that will last you all week" is the rich reward for the "pain" of waiting in the "club-style line" outside this dinner-only Adams Morgan Italian "institution" and abiding by its rigid rules (e.g. "cash only", "no substitutions"); with its "impersonal" service and humble "red-and-white checker-board tablecloths", it's maybe "not for first dates", but "terrific" prices keep the hordes "coming back."

Paul *Bakery*

22 | 19 | 18 | $19

Penn Quarter | 801 Pennsylvania Ave. (bet. 8th & 9th Sts.) | 202-524-4500
NEW **Farragut** | 1000 Connecticut Ave. NW (K St.) | 202-524-4860
NEW **Georgetown** | 1078 Wisconsin Ave. NW (bet. M & Potomac Sts.) | 202-524-4630
www.paul-usa.com

"Ooh-la-la", it's "like being in a Parisian cafe" – "even the cashiers say '*merci*'" – aver fans of this "authentic" French bakery import that fills "baguette sandwich cravings" and leaves "no time to diet" with its "buttery", "rich" pastries; if some say it's "not cheap" for what it is and complain of "disorganized" service, dedicated Francophiles "bliss" out with the "beautiful bread" on the "comfy" sofas and chairs.

Peacock Cafe *American*

22 | 20 | 22 | $36

Georgetown | 3251 Prospect St. NW (bet. Potomac St. & Wisconsin Ave.) | 202-625-2740 | www.peacockcafe.com

A "Georgetown institution" for "girls' night outings" or "ladies' lunch", this "consistent" performer satisfies with its midpriced, "tasty" American dishes and solid wine selection, with over a dozen by the glass, served by a "fine" crew; there's good "people-watching" too, in the "trendy", industrial-lite digs (and outside, weather permitting).

NEW Pearl Dive Oyster Palace *Seafood*

26 | 23 | 23 | $42

Logan Circle | 1612 14th St. NW (bet. Corcoran & Q Sts.) | 202-319-1612 | www.pearldivedc.com

This "skyrocketing" new "superstar" from the Black Restaurant Group, near Logan Circle, is crewed by an "outstanding" staff that serves up "superb" oysters and other "fabulous" seafood-centric fare with a "distinctly Gulf Coast focus", like "rich and satisfying" gumbos; with its crumbling "New England"–boardwalk look, it's a "very cool place to hang your hat", and though pricey, "if they took reservations", some "would probably spend all their money here"; P.S. the upstairs bar is a "fun" place to wait and play bocce.

☑ Peking Duck Restaurant Ⓜ *Chinese*

28 | 18 | 23 | $35

Greater Alexandria | 7531 Richmond Hwy. (Woodlawn Trail) | Alexandria, VA | 703-768-2774 | www.pekingduck.com

No canard, "authentic barely begins to describe" this venerable but unassuming-looking Peking duck specialist "all the way out" near Fort Belvoir in Greater Alexandria, where the roasted fowl is sliced "in front of you" just "like in Peking" (er, Beijing); if that doesn't sound ducky, ask the "superb" staff for "suggestions" (hint: "delicious" soups), and have no fear of the bill – it won't bite.

Peking Gourmet Inn *Chinese*

25 | 17 | 22 | $35

Falls Church | Culmore Shopping Ctr. | 6029 Leesburg Pike (Glen Carlyn Rd.), VA | 703-671-8088 | www.pekinggourmet.com

"Duck in early to avoid huge crowds" clamoring for this "premier" Pekingese purveyor's signature bird, "crisp and delicate and beautifully served tableside" by real "pros" in a sprawling, "old-fashioned" space in Falls Church; if a few feel it's "overpriced", most say it's "worth it" – heck, even Democrats agree that "there's more to this restaurant than the pictures of ex-presidents" ("Bush I and Bush II") on the wall.

Perrys *American/Eclectic*

22 | 22 | 22 | $45

Adams Morgan | 1811 Columbia Rd. NW (Biltmore St.) | 202-234-6218 | www.perrysadamsmorgan.com

"A delightful trip" away from Adams Morgan beckons diners up the stairs at this pricey Eclectic-New American stronghold where "prompt" servers dish out "interesting" fare in a "warmly decorated" room; there's a "totally different feel" on the "fabulous" roof deck, with its "little lights" and cityscape views, while "Sunday brunch will literally pull you" up out of your seat (there's a boisterous drag show).

Persimmon *American*

25 | 17 | 21 | $51

Bethesda | 7003 Wisconsin Ave. (bet. Leland & Walsh Sts.), MD | 301-654-9860 | www.persimmonrestaurant.com

In Bethesda, this blue-chip bistro "stands out" for its "consistently" "excellent" New American fare and "strong" wine list served by some of the "nicest people" around, though it's temporarily closed at press time for a renovation that will result in a more casual feel to the space, as well as a slightly retooled, lower-priced menu (which puts the Food and Decor ratings in question).

Pesce ⊠Ⓜ *Seafood*

26 | 17 | 23 | $50

Dupont Circle | 2002 P St. NW (bet. Hopkins & 20th Sts.) | 202-466-3474 | www.pescedc.com

Regine Palladin's "firm hand on the tiller" keeps her Dupont Circle seafooder on its "excellent, creative", "fin-tastic" course; the simple, airy sliver of a space is a "delightful retreat from Washington's bustle", in which servers provide "reliable advice" about the "best available" "fish you've never heard of" on the chalkboard menu – in short, for the "quality", it's a relative "bargain."

Pete's New Haven Style Apizza *Pizza*

22 | 14 | 17 | $20

Columbia Heights | 1400 Irving St. NW (14th St.) | 202-332-7383
Upper NW | 4940 Wisconsin Ave. NW (Fessenden St.) | 202-237-7383
Clarendon | 3017 Clarendon Blvd. (Garfield St.), VA | 703-527-7383
www.petesapizza.com

New Haven–style 'za – "the way God intended", with "thin crusts" and "slightly scorched" bottoms – keeps this inexpensive, "gourmet" pizzeria mini-chain "swarming with kids", though more grown-up palates also report "fantastic" salads, market-driven antipasti, pastas and brews; folks order at the counter and are served at tables by staff who "move things along" in the "light and airy" spaces.

Petits Plats *French*

▽ 22 | 18 | 21 | $48

Woodley Park | 2653 Connecticut Ave. NW (bet. Calvert St. & Woodley Rd.) | 202-518-0018 | www.petitsplats.com

This "adorable" bistro in a converted Woodley Park house takes diners "back to France" with its "cravable" mussels, steak frites and the like (there's also sandwiches on "fresh" baguettes for a take-out lunch); relax by one of the fireplaces, bask in attention from a "wonderful" owner who "takes good care of his clientele" and appreciate prices that are "decent" given the sizable quality of the *plats*.

⊉ P.F. Chang's China Bistro *Chinese*

23 | 23 | 22 | $30

Chevy Chase | Shops at Wisconsin Pl. | 5046 Wisconsin Ave. (Williard Ave.), MD | 301-654-4350
White Flint | White Flint Mall | 11301 Rockville Pike (Nicholson Ln.) | Rockville, MD | 301-230-6933
Ballston | Arlington Gateway | 901 N. Glebe Rd. (Fairfax Dr.) | Arlington, VA | 703-527-0955
Fairfax | Fairfax Corner | 4250 Fairfax Corner Ave. (Monument Dr.), VA | 703-266-2414
Tysons Corner | Tysons Galleria | 1716 International Dr. (Chain Bridge Rd.) | McLean, VA | 703-734-8996

(continued)

P.F. Chang's China Bistro

Sterling | Dulles Town Ctr. | 21078 Dulles Town Circle (Nokes Blvd.), VA | 703-421-5540
www.pfchangs.com

"Tantalizing" "twists" on Chinese food (including the "famous", "addictive" lettuce wrap) in a "classy", "cool" Asian-inspired setting, plus "agreeable" service and "affordable" tabs add up to an "unbeatable combination" at this "upscale" Chinese chain; while maybe "not for the purist", it's a "regular favorite" for many, including families, groups and those who appreciate the "awesome" gluten-free items, though few relish the sometimes "horrendous" waits.

Phillips *Seafood* | 20 | 19 | 20 | $39 |

SW | 900 Water St. SW (7th St.) | 202-488-8515 | www.phillipsseafood.com
See review in the Baltimore Directory.

Pho DC *Vietnamese* | ▽ 24 | 21 | 21 | $22 |

Chinatown | 608 H St. NW (bet. 6th & 7th Sts.) | 202-506-2888 | www.phodc.com

This slim spot in Chinatown serves a variety of "tasty", "inexpensive" Vietnamese specialties, but regulars say that a "large" bowl of "fabulous, steaming pho is the way to go"; "attentive" staff gets to "know" regulars who frequent the "stylish, little" brick-walled space, complete with a mod wall of color-changing LED lights.

Pho 14 *Vietnamese* | 25 | 17 | 22 | $15 |

Columbia Heights | 1436 Park Rd. NW (bet. 14th & 15th Sts.) | 202-986-2326 | www.dcpho14.com

Whether it's the "best pho in Columbia Heights" or "in the District" (or "this side of the Pacific"), many agree there's an "extra little bit of something" that sets apart this "neighborhood place" – even the veggie pho "has really complex flavors"; "quick and polite" servers deliver "super-value" namesake soups plus "out-of-this-world" banh mi and other traditional eats in a simple storefront nook.

Pho 75 ⊅ *Vietnamese* | 24 | 8 | 16 | $13 |

Langley Park | 1510 University Blvd. E. (bet. New Hampshire Ave. & Riggs Rd.), MD | 301-434-7844
Rockville | 771 Hungerford Dr. (Mannakee St.), MD | 301-309-8873
Clarendon | 1721 Wilson Blvd. (Quinn St.), VA | 703-525-7355
Falls Church | Eden Ctr. | 3103 Graham Rd. (Arlington Blvd.), VA | 703-204-1490
Herndon | 382 Elden St. (Herndon Pkwy.), VA | 703-471-4145
www.pho75.tumblr.com

"A big bowl of steaming-hot love", with broth that "lives up to the hype" and "many options for extras", stars on the menu at these local Vietnamese "standard-bearers"; despite decor that makes "elementary school cafeterias look like the Four Seasons", service is "fast" and it's "cheap, cheap, cheap"; P.S. cash only and most locations close at 8 PM nightly.

| | FOOD | DECOR | SERVICE | COST |

Pie-Tanza *Pizza*

23 | 16 | 20 | $21

Arlington | Lee Harrison Shopping Ctr. | 2503 N. Harrison St. (bet. Lee Hwy. & 26th St.), VA | 703-237-0200
Falls Church | Falls Plaza Shopping Ctr. | 1216 W. Broad St. (Gordon Rd.), VA | 703-237-0977
www.pie-tanza.com

"Put on Sinatra" to get in the mood for these "cozy", "family-friendly" pizzerias in Falls Church and Arlington that wow "all ages" with thin-crust, wood-fired wonders (they also serve "other Italian favorites"); add in low prices, "extremely nice" servers and open kitchens that allow patrons to see all the pie-throwing action, and regulars say they "couldn't ask for more out of a small neighborhood" joint.

NEW The Pig *American/Eclectic*

- | - | - | M

Logan Circle | 1320 14th St. NW (bet North St. & Rhode Island Ave.) | 202-290-2821 | www.thepigdc.com

Pork, unsurprisingly, is the focus at this Logan Circle American-Eclectic entry with a snout-to-corkscrew-tail bent, where the kitchen turns out midpriced fodder ranging from boar spoonbread to pig ramen to an ice cream sundae topped with bacon-peanut brittle; the lofty industrial space feels rustic-modern thanks to repurposed barn lumber and white tiles on the walls.

Ping by Charlie Chiang's *Asian*

23 | 22 | 22 | $28

Shirlington | Village at Shirlington | 4060 Campbell Ave. (Randolph St.) | Arlington, VA | 703-671-4900 | www.charliechiangs.com

This "sleek", "sexy" Asian restaurant/lounge with a "hip clientele" in Shirlington gets buzzy at its "awesome happy hour" on account of its "great drinks list" ("the craft-beer menu puts most bars to shame") and impresses with its "creative" Chinese-leaning fare, plus sushi; "accommodating" staffers love "what they do and it shows", plus the bill "won't chokeslam your wallet."

Ping Pong Dim Sum *Asian*

21 | 22 | 19 | $34

Chinatown | 900 Seventh St. NW (I St.) | 202-506-3740
NEW Dupont Circle | 1 Dupont Circle NW (bet. New Hampshire Ave. & P St.) | 202-293-1268
www.pingpongdimsum.us

"Ultra-modern" settings filled with moody dark lacquer are the first clue that these Dupont Circle and Chinatown Asian venues are "not your normal" dim sum houses, offering instead "creative", "tapas-style" takes on traditional nibbles alongside "gigantic" cocktails ("if you can move past the wonderful teas"); a few call it "kinda pricey" and complain of "uncomfortable" backless seats and "inconsistent" service, but the "urban-chic" vibe keeps most happy, especially "groups."

Piola *Italian/Pizza*

∇ 21 | 19 | 18 | $24

Rosslyn | 1550 Wilson Blvd. (N. Pierce St.), VA | 703-528-1502 | www.piola.it

Rosslyn regulars "recommend that you stick with what they do best" and opt for the "fantastic" "thin, crusty" pizza baked in a brick oven with "quality" ingredients at this Italian chain direct from The Boot;

service is solid, and a "lively" atmosphere plays well for either "commuter's happy hour" or dine-in, when regulars recommend taking a gander at the month's art installation; P.S. there's a patio too.

Pizzeria Da Marco *Pizza* ▽ 23 | 20 | 22 | $25

Bethesda | 8008 Woodmont Ave. (bet. Cordell & St. Elmo Aves.), MD | 301-654-6083 | www.pizzeriadamarco.net

"No, pizzas are not sliced", and yes, crusts are "charred" and centers a bit "soggy" when they're "authentic" Neapolitans like the "delicious" rounds baked in this Bethesda Italian's imported brick oven; servers who "really like" their patrons make both the "open, airy" brick-walled room and the "lovely" terrace feel "inviting", and moderate prices, especially the "great-deal" happy hour, make folks positively pie-eyed.

Pizzeria Orso *Pizza* 22 | 17 | 18 | $27

Falls Church | 400 S. Maple Ave. (Tinners Hill St.), VA | 703-226-3460 | www.pizzeriaorso.com

You'll want to "check out the small plates" whipped up by chef Will Artley (ex Evening Star), who also turns out authentic "cracker-thin" Neapolitan "brick-oven" pizzas at this "casual", sunny Falls Church Italian-influenced kitchen; though a few find service "wanting", this place is "kid-friendly" and "popular" with "parents who like to drink" (Italian margarita, anybody?).

Pizzeria Paradiso *Pizza* 23 | 17 | 19 | $26

Dupont Circle | 2003 P St. NW (bet. Hopkins & 20th Sts.) | 202-223-1245
Georgetown | 3282 M St. NW (bet. Potomac & 33rd Sts.) | 202-337-1245
Old Town | 124 King St. (bet. Lee & Union Sts.) | Alexandria, VA | 703-837-1245
www.eatyourpizza.com

These midpriced "pizza nirvanas" in Dupont Circle, Georgetown and Old Town Alexandria are "delicious enough for serious foodies but still casual enough for an outing with family and friends"; service is generally "ok" in the "pleasant", "cosmopolitan" brick-walled settings, and if they tend to get "crowded" and "loud" at times, "beer geeks" recommend the "ameliorating" powers of the "impressive" brew list.

P.J. Clarke's ☛ *Pub Food* 18 | 19 | 19 | $38

Downtown | 1600 K St. NW (16th St.) | 202-463-6610 | www.pjclarkes.com

"Knowledgeable bartenders and enthusiastic young wait staff" are on the team of this "road version" of an NYC-based "burgers-and-beer" joint, strategically located near the White House; some sniff the "solid but not great" food means there are "better places to drop your bar-food dollars", but the clubby, dark-walled environs offer a "chill atmosphere" in which to "meet for drinks"; P.S. there's a more limited version of the menu upstairs at Sidebar.

Plaka Grill *Greek* 24 | 13 | 19 | $18

Vienna | 110 Lawyers Rd. NW (Maple Ave.), VA | 703-319-3131 | www.plakagrill.com

It's "worth a trip to the suburbs" of Vienna for "soulful", "value"-priced Hellenic cooking, including some of "the best gyros around" ("stuffed with fries!") and hummus that "must be whipped by the goddess Hestia herself"; a picturesque mural of a Greek street scene provides a bit of color to the "tiny", "not-fancy" cafe setting that's serviced by "fast and friendly" help.

☑ Plume ⓈⓂ American   26 | 28 | 29 | $109

Downtown | The Jefferson | 1200 16th St. NW (M St.) | 202-448-3227 | www.jeffersondc.com

"Not just a feather in the [Hotel] Jefferson's cap but a full plume" enthuse guests who exalt this "impeccably dressed restaurant with a gracious and elegant personality" crafting "superb", classically grounded New American food inspired by Thomas Jefferson's gustatory interests; there's also an "unbelievable" cellar that would have impressed the oenophilic founding father himself, but as so much "marble and gilt" signify, "expect to open up the wallet."

Policy Ⓜ American   22 | 19 | 19 | $35

U Street Corridor | 1904 14th St. NW (T St.) | 202-387-7654 | www.policydc.com

"Interesting and tasty" midpriced New American small plates plus "innovative" cocktails and craft beer draw the "hipster U Street" crowd to this "urban destination" with a "fab interior" sporting diner-esque red booths on the lower level and a "graffiti-glam" lounge upstairs; a few report being "underwhelmed" by the service, but most find the staff "friendly" and agree that it's a "great place to go with friends."

Pollo Campero Central American   19 | 12 | 17 | $11

Columbia Heights | 3229 14th St. NW (Park Rd.) | 202-745-0078
Gaithersburg | Lakeforest Mall | 701 Russell Ave. (Lakeforest Blvd.), MD | 240-403-0135
Takoma Park | 1355 University Blvd. E. (New Hampshire Ave.), MD | 301-408-0555
Wheaton | 11420 Georgia Ave. (Hickerson Dr.), MD | 301-942-6868
Falls Church | 5852 Columbia Pike (Moncure Ave.), VA | 703-820-8400
Herndon | 496 Elden St. (Grant St.), VA | 703-904-7500
Manassas | 7913 Sudley Rd. (Lomond Dr.), VA | 703-368-1824
www.global.campero.com

"Fill up on a budget" at this Latin American "fast-food" franchise specializing in "crisp", "juicy" poultry dispensed with efficiency along with "a large selection" of sides; ok, so maybe the bright-yellow-and-orange interiors are a bit "sterile", and it may "not win any gastronomical awards", but legions of "locals looking for a chicken fix" attest that "once you start eating", it's "tough to stop."

🆕 Pork Barrel BBQ Restaurant BBQ   ▽ 19 | 17 | 16 | $19

Del Ray | 2312 Mount Vernon Ave. (bet. Del Rey & Oxford Aves.) | Alexandria, VA | 703-822-5699 | www.porkbarrelbbq.com

Two former Senate staffers–turned–national BBQ champs recently debuted this Del Ray smoker dispensing "good Southern BBQ with some very tasty sides", though service and kitchen bumps lead some to bark it needs to "get its act together"; still, the price is right, even if the setup is "quirky" - the bar is full-service, but for food you "order at the counter and then find a table" in the "retro" room.

	FOOD	DECOR	SERVICE	COST

Poste Moderne Brasserie *American*   `20` `22` `20` `$50`

Penn Quarter | Hotel Monaco | 555 Eighth St. NW (bet. E & F Sts.) | 202-783-6060 | www.postebrasserie.com

Hotel Monaco's New American "hidden enclave" reveals a "gorgeous" courtyard patio "perfect for summer canoodling" and a "trendy" yet "quiet" dining room; its latest chef, Dennis Marron (ex The Grille), puts a "thoughtful", "sustainable" spin on seasonal menus and, yes, it's "pretty pricey", but "good" service and "subtle mixology" help ease the sting, and there are "values" at lunch.

Posto *Italian*   `23` `20` `22` `$46`

Logan Circle | 1515 14th St. NW (bet. Church & P Sts.) | 202-332-8613 | www.postodc.com

Before saying 'bravo' next door at Studio Theatre, practice saying "*buono*" at this "delicious" but "pricey" Italian near Logan Circle, a spin-off of Penn Quarter's Tosca; the "open, bright" "contemporary" digs "can get noisy", but "quality" service helps keep it a pre-theater "favorite", despite having no set-menu deal.

Praline *Bakery/French*   `23` `16` `20` `$38`

Bethesda | Sumner Pl. | 4611 Sangamore Rd. (MacArthur Blvd.), MD | 301-229-8180 | www.praline-bakery.com

Its "suburban shopping-center" setting "might mislead", but "just try to stop the flakes from flying" when you bite into what are arguably the "best croissants in Greater DC" say fans of this "little slice of Paris" in Bethesda that, while not cheap, will "save you airfare" overseas; upstairs from the bakery/cafe, "bistro classics" are well served in a sunny setting, but better yet is a rendezvous in the "lovely", "easy-going" rooftop patio.

Present Restaurant *Vietnamese*   `26` `23` `25` `$32`

Falls Church | 6678 Arlington Blvd. (Annandale Rd.), VA | 703-531-1881 | www.presentcuisine.com

"Sleeping Duck on the Golden Pond" and other "poetic names" "lyrically" describe the "creative" dishes at this "surprising" Vietnamese "oasis" that brings "upscale" dining at a "reasonable cost" to an "unlikely" location in a Falls Church strip mall; step inside and walk past the "fountain" to an "elegant" dining room where "attentive" waiters are always happy to "explain" the menu.

Pret A Manger *Sandwiches*   `19` `13` `18` `$14`

Chinatown | 1155 F St. NW (11th St.) | 202-464-2791
NEW **Downtown** | 1432 K St. NW (Vermont Ave.) | 202-559-8000 🖪
Farragut | 1828 L St. NW (19th St.) | 202-689-1982 🖪
Golden Triangle | 1825 I St. NW (bet. 18th & 19th Sts.) | 202-403-2992 🖪
NEW **Northeast** | Union Station | 50 Massachusetts Ave. (F St.) | 202-289-0186
www.pret.com

"Why can't American fast food be this tasty?" ask fanciers of this British import making waves for its "always fresh" "grab-and-go" sandwiches, salads and soups (plus "delish" cookies); though "somewhat expensive for a sandwich", most agree it's "worth it", citing "convenience", "friendly" counter service and "nice" metal-trimmed interiors.

❷ Prime Rib ⊠ *Steak*   28 | 26 | 28 | $71
Golden Triangle | 2020 K St. NW (bet. 20th & 21st Sts.) | 202-466-8811 | www.theprimerib.com
See review in the Baltimore Directory.

Primi Piatti ⊠ *Italian*   19 | 16 | 20 | $52
Foggy Bottom | 2013 I St. NW (bet. 20th & 21st Sts.) | 202-223-3600 | www.primipiatti.com

This Foggy Bottom Italian trattoria's owner occasionally performs "remarkable table-to-table magic tricks", but some in the audience feel there's a bit of "pizzazz missing" from the "solid", "genuinely good" fare that nonetheless "never disappoints"; it's "inviting" inside among mirrors and marble, and "pleasant" on the patio, even if it's on the "pricey" side.

Proof *American*   24 | 23 | 23 | $56
Penn Quarter | 775 G St. NW (bet. 7th & 8th Sts.) | 202-737-7663 | www.proofdc.com

"Find your own 'proof'" of this Penn Quarter New American's virtues via its "wonderfully original" food paired with "amazing" wines in "noisy", "sexy" and "dark" modern rusticity ("good for a date on which you want to lean in to 'hear better'", not so good to "read the menu"), where "power brokers and tourists collide"; "knowledgeable" servers and "savvy wine" pros "impress the 1%", while its $12 lunch special (entree plus a glass of wine) pleases the proletariat.

PS 7's ⊠ *American*   23 | 22 | 22 | $55
Penn Quarter | 777 I St. NW (bet. 7th & 8th Sts.) | 202-742-8550 | www.ps7restaurant.com

Peter Smith imparts a "deft and creative touch" to the "splendid" New American fare at his pricey Penn Quarterite with a contemporary, light-filled dining room that's "well run" and recommended for a "top-notch business lunch", a "group of 20" or an "intimate dinner"; at happy hour, "beautiful young people hang at the bar" where "killer" housemade hot dogs pair with "outstanding" cocktails.

🆕 Pulpo *Spanish*   - | - | - | M
Cleveland Park | 3407 Connecticut Ave. NW (bet. McComb & Ordway Sts.) | 202-450-6875 | www.pulpodc.com

Cleveland Park recently saw the debut of this ambitious Spanish taperia serving a midpriced menu that runs the gamut from Iberian wine-bar classics to bites of newfangled molecular gastronomy; the interior aesthetic is loftlike and dimly lit, with exposed brick and an open kitchen overlooking four communal tables.

Pupatella Pizzeria ⊠ Ⓜ *Pizza*   26 | 15 | 19 | $19
Arlington | 5104 Wilson Blvd. (Edison St.), VA | 571-312-7230 | www.pupatella.com

"Incredibly authentic", "mighty good" pizza with a "perfectly charred and textured crust" and "just the right balance of toppings" earns this "friendly" Arlington Neapolitan pie-and-fry (it also serves rice balls and croquettes) the top pizza rating in Greater DC; the "arty", graffitied space recently doubled in size and added table service (possibly outdating its Decor and Service ratings), and the prices are easy to stomach; P.S. the original Ballston food truck operates at special events.

Queen Vic ⓂBritish
▽ 23 | 21 | 21 | $23

Atlas District | 1206 H St. NE (bet. 12th & 13th Sts.) | 202-396-2001 | www.thequeenvicdc.com

"Quick-witted" publicans pull "superb" drafts and dish up "melt-in-your-mouth" Sunday roast, fish 'n' chips and other inexpensive forms of "traditional" British "comfort" at this Atlas District tavern; an "Old English" vibe pervades the dark-wood digs, and there's an attached tuck shop selling imported staples like McVitie's and Ribena.

🆕 Quench American
- | - | - | M

Rockville | Traville Village Ctr. | 9712 Traville Gateway Dr. (Shady Grove Rd.), MD | 301-424-8650 | www.quenchnation.com

This sleek entry in Rockville's Traville Village Center slakes MoCo thirsts with craft cocktails and muddles in moderately priced, contemporary American bar bites, plus small and large plates; the loungey digs are decidedly more urbane, with faux–animal skin rugs and cut-off logs serving as rustic tables.

Rabieng Thai
25 | 17 | 22 | $30

Falls Church | Glen Forest Shopping Ctr. | 5892 Leesburg Pike (Glen Forest Dr.), VA | 703-671-4222 | www.rabieng.com

Duangrat's "baby brother", this midpriced Falls Church Siamese is around the corner in humbler yet "cozy" digs and does its elder proud with "delicious" Northern Thai specialties and weekend Thai dim sum; "thoughtful waiters who warn" patrons about spicing levels establish a "relaxed" environment for sampling unusual dishes, so the only "problem is trying something new – because you want to get what you had the last time."

Rail Stop Ⓜ American
▽ 23 | 19 | 20 | $48

The Plains | 6478 Main St. (Fauquier Ave.), VA | 540-253-5644 | www.railstoprestaurant.com

For "great food in horse country", this "tiny", "country-casual" American in The Plains fits the bill with a "homespun" menu that does the chef "proud", complemented by a "short" but apropos wine list; it's "pricey", but that doesn't stop enthusiasts from declaring it a "real treat" with "friendly" service; P.S. don't miss the patio or the toy train that circles above diners' heads.

Raku Asian
23 | 18 | 20 | $34

Dupont Circle | 1900 Q St. NW (19th St.) | 202-265-7258
Bethesda | 7240 Woodmont Ave. (bet. Bethesda Ave. & Elm St.), MD | 301-718-8681
www.rakuasiandining.com

With "sushi down to a science" and a "great variety" of other Japanese, Chinese and Thai bites "done with aplomb", these

FOOD | DECOR | SERVICE | COST

"friendly", "go-to" Asian spots in Bethesda and Dupont Circle make for a "quick, solidly good, inexpensive meal"; sensitive ears cite "deafening" noise in the consistently "crowded" contemporary environs that are hung with brightly colored paper umbrellas, so outside seating is a "nice plus."

Rangoli *Indian* ▽ 24 | 23 | 24 | $27

South Riding | South Riding Market Sq. | 24995 Riding Plaza (Riding Center Dr.), VA | 703-957-4900 | www.rangolirestaurant.us

The "superb" Indian specialties at this sunny-yellow South Riding venue come at a "great price", especially at its "wonderful" lunch buffet; service gets a thumbs-up too, and the overall positive experience has frequenters saying it "should be at the top of everyone's list."

❑ Rasika 🅂 *Indian* 28 | 25 | 26 | $51

Penn Quarter | 633 D St. NW (bet. 6th & 7th Sts.) | 202-637-1222

NEW **West End** | 1190 New Hampshire Ave. NW (M St.) | 202-466-2500
www.rasikarestaurant.com

"Only superlatives" describe the "mind-blowing" "modern Indian" food that gives diners a "mouthgasm" at this "wildly popular", "classy" Penn Quarter destination (and its new, cosmopolitan West End sister) that has diners "salivating" for dishes like its crispy spinach; "luxurious" appointments, a "knowledgeable" wait staff and a sommelier "savant" create a "sophisticated" environment that further makes it a "bargain for the quality" – translation: "plan early" for a reservation, or "eat at the bar."

Ravi Kabob House ⊘ *Pakistani* 25 | 8 | 14 | $18

Arlington | 250 N. Glebe Rd. (Pershing Dr.), VA | 703-816-0222 Ⓜ

Arlington | 305 N. Glebe Rd. (Pershing Dr.), VA | 703-522-6666 ◗

www.ravikabobusa.com

"Mouthwatering", "wonderfully tasty" kebabs with "all the fixin's" rave devotees of these Greater Arlington Pakistani joints practically across the street from one another; "decor and ambiance are nonexistent", and service is only fair, but no one argues as it's so "cheap", with "quality" that's "much higher than the cost"; P.S. cash only.

Ray's Hell Burger ⊘ *Burgers* 26 | 10 | 16 | $16
(aka Ray's Butcher Burgers)

Courthouse | Colonial Vill. | 1725 Wilson Blvd. (bet. Quinn & Rhodes Sts.) | Arlington, VA | 703-841-0001 | www.rayshellburger.com

"In the world of burgers", there's simply "no comparison" to this "incredibly well-priced" Courthouse paragon, its "epic" patties made from "quality" "steak cuttings", with "juices dripping down your forearm"; "fanatics" will stand on line with "everyone from union members to heads of state" for the "hectic" ordering experience in this "no-frills" counter-serve "hole-in-the-wall", and remember to "bring cash", since it doesn't take cards.

	FOOD	DECOR	SERVICE	COST

Ray's The Classics *Steak* | 25 | 19 | 22 | $43 |

Silver Spring | 8606 Colesville Rd. (Georgia Ave.), MD | 301-588-7297 | www.raystheclassics.com

"Any cut will satisfy" at Michael 'Ray' Landrum's Silver Spring chophouse where "steaks of the highest quality" put the "big boys to shame on price" and are accompanied by "delicious" sides and "bargain" wines (there's also "excellent" seafood); service is generally "attentive", and though the "fancy" white tablecloths are steakhouse-esque, the decor feels "more gender-neutral than most"; P.S. "burgers in the bar area" are even more of a "deal."

❷ Ray's The Steaks *Steak* | 27 | 18 | 22 | $46 |

Courthouse | Navy League Bldg. | 2300 Wilson Blvd. (Adams St.) | Arlington, VA | 703-841-7297 | www.raysthesteaks.com

"No-frills deliciousness" sums up Mike 'Ray' Landrum's Courthouse beefeteria that "rays-es the bar on great steaks" at "bargain-basement prices" – the "breathtaking" hunks are served with two sides along with "affordable" wines in "sparse" white surroundings by "knowledgeable", "efficient" servers; "why pay for decor and snootiness at 'fine' steakhouses?" ask acolytes who appreciate "not being nickeled, dimed and dollared", saying this may be the "best restaurant idea in history."

Ray's The Steaks at East River 🅂🅼 *Burgers/Steak* | ▽ 25 | 18 | 21 | $32 |

Northeast | 3905 Dix St. NE (bet. 40th St. & Minnesota Ave.) | 202-396-7297 | www.rayseastriver.com

"Juicy" steaks take up "most of the plate" at Michael 'Ray' Landrum's "good-value" outpost in a Northeast DC neighborhood with few sit-down dining options; neighborhood denizens also "chow down" on "super" burgers, smoked/fried chicken and a few other hearty options served by a "genuinely friendly and efficient" staff in simple bistro surroundings.

🆕 Ray's to the Third *American/Steak* | 25 | 14 | 22 | $31 |

Courthouse | 1650 Wilson Blvd. (bet. Pierce & Quinn Sts.) | Arlington, VA | 703-974-7171 | www.raystothethird.com

"Ray's a toast" – with a glass from the "superior-for-a-neighborhood-place" wine selection – to Michael 'Ray' Landrum's new "bistro version" in Courthouse that features steak frites "done very well" at prices that "can't be beat"; its unassuming premises are also home to his signature burger as well as "excellent" shrimp and chicken, and decadent shakes.

Red Curry *Asian* | ▽ 22 | 20 | 18 | $29 |

Old Town | 100 King St. (Union St.) | Alexandria, VA | 703-739-9600 | www.redcurry.us

Diners on a budget in Old Town Alexandria head to this "fairly" priced Pan-Asian purveyor for everything from "great" pad Thai to "outstanding" orange chicken and "worth-a-visit" sushi; service is average, but the airy contemporary space has a touch of Zen about it.

FOOD | DECOR | SERVICE | COST

Red Hook Lobster
Pound *New England/Seafood*

25 | 12 | 20 | $20

Location varies; see website | 202-341-6263 | www.redhooklobsterdc.com

"People actually chase these food trucks" to "cure the urge" for a "succulent", "chunky" lobster roll offered "Maine-style with mayo or Connecticut-style with butter" ("the toughest call of the day"), with a whoopie pie to follow; "lines can be very long", making it hard for some folks to "justify the cost", while "longtime fans" advise: check its whereabouts online and "go early."

Red Hot & Blue *BBQ*

22 | 18 | 20 | $21

Gaithersburg | Grove Shopping Ctr. | 16811 Crabbs Branch Way (Shady Grove Rd.), MD | 301-948-7333
Greater Alexandria | 6482 Lansdowne Ctr. (Beulah St.) | Alexandria, VA | 703-550-6465
Rosslyn | 1600 Wilson Blvd. (N. Pierce St.), VA | 703-276-7427
Fairfax | 4150 Chain Bridge Rd. (Rte. 236), VA | 703-218-6989
Falls Church | Tower Sq. | 169 Hillwood Ave. (Douglass Ave.), VA | 703-538-6466
Herndon | 2403 Centreville Rd. (Sunrise Valley Dr.), VA | 703-870-7345
Manassas | 8366 Sudley Rd. (Irongate Way), VA | 703-367-7100
Leesburg | Bellwood Commons Shopping Ctr. | 541 E. Market St. (Plaza St.), VA | 703-669-4242
www.redhotandblue.com

If you're "hard up for Memphis-style barbecue", this "trustworthy" chain will "scratch" the "itch" say bolsters who praise "finger-licking" mains like "must-try" pulled pork and "catfish that makes a Delta-lover happy", accompanied by "traditional" sides; interiors are "nothing fancy", but service is "timely" and tabs are "inexpensive", so it's a "super place to hang your hat and get messy."

RedRocks ☻ *Pizza*

21 | 18 | 20 | $22

Columbia Heights | 1036 Park Rd. NW (11th St.) | 202-506-1402
Old Town | 904 King St. (bet. Alfred & Patrick Sts.) | Alexandria, VA | 703-717-9873
www.redrocksdc.com

"Tasty artisanal pizzas in the Neapolitan style" (some topped with house-cured meats) and an "excellent" beer and cocktail menu draw admirers to this inexpensive duo with "welcoming" service; the "rustic-with-a-dash-of-hipster" Columbia Heights branch sports a "pleasure" of a patio and a "go-to" brunch, while the more spacious Old Town location features an open kitchen.

Redwood *American*

19 | 22 | 18 | $42

Bethesda | Bethesda Row | 7121 Bethesda Ln. (bet. Bethesda Ave. & Elm St.), MD | 301-656-5515 | www.redwoodbethesda.com

"Wonderful for alfresco dining" on the "shaded" patio, this New American "respite" attracts a ladies lunch crowd who also "sits by the big open windows" in the "contemporary" redwood-accented dining room, and sips vino and nibbles "solid" "California-inspired" fare; some find it "a bit pricey" and service "slow at times", but most "can't stay away" because it's just so darn "pleasant."

	FOOD	DECOR	SERVICE	COST

The Regent *Thai*
▽ 24 | 20 | 21 | $29

Dupont Circle | 1910 18th St. NW (bet. Florida Ave. & T St.) | 202-232-1781 | www.regentthai.com

This "flavorful" midpriced Thai in Dupont Circle with "terrific presentation" is favored for its "dark", "chic" atmosphere and "interesting" mixed drinks; those who like to linger also note that with "warm", "friendly" service, there's "no rush" to get you out.

Renato at River Falls *Italian*
22 | 17 | 20 | $47

Potomac | 10120 River Rd. (Falls Rd.), MD | 301-365-1900 | www.riverfallsseafood.com

Something of a "local club" for its tony Potomac neighbors, this "intimate" suburban ristorante "consistently" does Italian fare "well and with the best ingredients", including seafood from the co-owned fish market next door; its "friendly" staff facilitates the mealtime gatherings that make this place a "highlight" of the area's social scene, to whom it's "pricey" but "worth it."

Ren's Ramen ⊘ *Japanese/Noodle Shop*
▽ 24 | 11 | 14 | $15

Wheaton | 11403 Amherst Ave. (University Blvd.), MD | 301-693-0806 | www.rens-ramen.com

Forget about the much-maligned dorm-room staple – the "soul-satisfying", "authentic" Japanese ramen of this "one-dish Wheaton powerhouse" may be "the best soup you have ever had" with its "amazing pork-based broth" (or veggie broth option); but "be prepared to wait" at peak times, since "crowding tends to slow things down" in this "small", minimally decorated spot; P.S. cash only.

Ricciuti's *Italian*
24 | 21 | 22 | $32

Olney | 3308 Olney Sandy Spring Rd. (Georgia Ave.), MD | 301-570-3388 | www.ricciutis.com

A "gem of a place" in a "warm, cozy old house", this Italian spot charms Olneyites with "foodie" sensibilities with its "wonderful", seasonal small and large plates plus brick-oven pizzas; a staff that's "willing to please" ensures that diners "never feel rushed", setting a "peaceful" tone for many a "date night."

Rice *Thai*
22 | 19 | 20 | $33

Logan Circle | 1608 14th St. NW (bet. Q & R Sts.) | 202-234-2400 | www.ricerestaurant.com

"Terrific Thai classics" meet with "a twist of art and experimentation" at this moderately priced Logan Circle "date spot" where every dish "impresses"; low lighting and an exposed-brick and earth-toned interior lend a "cool NYC vibe", though "friendly" service "with a big smile" runs warm.

NEW Rice Paper *Vietnamese*
- | - | - | I

Falls Church | Eden Ctr. | 6775 Wilson Blvd. (bet. Arlington & RooseveltBlvds.), VA | 703-538-3888 | www.ricepaper-tasteofvietnam.com

A stylish, glitzy setting belies the serious, traditional cookery at this new arrival to Falls Church's Vietnamese enclave, Eden Center; its inexpensive menu of multiregional classics intrigues experts as well as beginners, and features hard-to-find broken-rice dishes.

Ripple *American*   23 | 20 | 23 | $49

Cleveland Park | 3417 Connecticut Ave. NW (Ordway St.) | 202-244-7995 | www.rippledc.com

"Relax with a wonderful glass of wine" and "serious" cheese and charcuterie plus "innovative" small and large plates at this colorful, vibrant Cleveland Park New American wine bar, where the "farm-to-table concept is truly experienced" at a "fairly reasonable price (by Washington standards)"; staffers are "extremely knowledgeable" about "the origins of every item of food", causing one wag to tag it "*Portlandia* ensconced in Washington."

Ris *American*   25 | 22 | 24 | $57

West End | 2275 L St. NW (23rd St.) | 202-730-2500 | www.risdc.com

If only the "government was run as well as" Ris Lacoste's West End New American bistro sigh surveyors, citing "gold-star" service and a "polished kitchen" turning out "exciting" "market-fresh" dishes in a "sophisticated", "modern" setting; various deals offer a way around high prices, so whether headed for Kennedy Center, meeting "friends and family" or hanging at the bar, it suits the whole neighborhood.

NEW River Falls Tavern *American*   - | - | - | E

Potomac | 10128 River Rd. (Falls Rd.), MD | 301-299-0481 | www.thetavernatriverfalls.com

Tony Potomac locals have taken to this American tavern newcomer from the talents behind nearby Renato, serving crab cakes along with burgers and other comfort fare in a trim, rustic-modern dining room decorated with area photographs and kaleidoscopic wall treatments; meanwhile, its granite-topped bar offers a low-key backdrop for meet-ups with friends.

Rocklands *BBQ*   22 | 14 | 18 | $19

Glover Park | 2418 Wisconsin Ave. NW (Calvert St.) | 202-333-2558
Rockville | Wintergreen Plaza | 891 Rockville Pike (Edmonston Dr.), MD | 240-268-1120
Greater Alexandria | 25 S. Quaker Ln. (Duke St.) | Alexandria, VA | 703-778-9663
Arlington | 3471 Washington Blvd. (Lincoln St.), VA | 703-528-9663
www.rocklands.com

Though proponents can't agree if "finger-licking BBQ is the order of the day" or the "flavorful" "side dishes are the real stars", they do swear "no one walks away hungry" from this "smoky and delicious" area chain; service is "just fine" in the "low-key" settings with "road-house decor" ("a roll of paper towels on each table"), and with "right-on" prices they also do a "tremendous take-out business."

NEW Rogue 24 🗷 🅜 *American*   23 | 25 | 25 | $145

Mt. Vernon Square/Convention Center | 922 N St. NW (bet. 9th & 10th Sts.) | 202-408-9724

RJ Cooper "swings for the fences" at his Mt. Vernon New American where everything is a "real adventure" – from the hidden "back-alley entrance", to the showpiece "open kitchen smack in the middle" of the "wonderfully industrial" room, to the "imaginative" multicourse tasting marathons coordinated by a "knowledgeable" staff and paired with a "variety of drinks" (16- or 24-course options only), "not just wine"; accordingly, the "entertaining" experience is priced like "dinner and a show", though wallet-watchers note the lounge is à la carte.

Rolls 'N Rice *Japanese*   ▽ 22 | 20 | 19 | $16

Rockville | 1701 Rockville Pike (Halpine Rd.), MD | 301-770-4030 | www.rollsnrice.com

"Cheap and cheerful" sushi, Japanese mains (and even some "reimagined Chinese" and Korean dishes) strike Rockville regulars as ideal for a "quick bite" in a "bright", "family-friendly" environment; most find the counter staff "friendly" and the overall experience "convenient."

Roof Terrace at the Kennedy Center *American*   16 | 20 | 17 | $51

Foggy Bottom | Kennedy Ctr. | 2700 F St. NW (bet. New Hampshire & Virginia Aves.) | 202-416-8555 | www.roofterracerestaurant.com

"It's all about the view" and "super-convenient" pre-event dining at this "elegant", white-tablecloth New American atop the Kennedy Center; besides an "inspired" brunch, the food is merely "acceptable" (and "expensive" to boot), but don't worry about missing your show since "fast" service is "geared for meeting curtain deadlines."

Room 11 *Eclectic*   ▽ 26 | 23 | 25 | $36

Columbia Heights | 3234 11th St. NW (Lamont St.) | 202-332-3234 | www.room11dc.com

Columbia Heights has the number on what "may be the perfect restaurant" concept: take a "cozy" zinc-topped wine bar, add a large patio and serve "excellent, inventive" Eclectic small plates paired with "fabulous" wines; with its "Brooklyn"-"hipster" vibe and "tremendous bang for the buck", no wonder its neighbors say it's "worth the wait" (though waits may subside after an upcoming expansion).

Rosa Mexicano *Mexican*   23 | 23 | 21 | $39

NEW **Chevy Chase** | 5225 Wisconsin Ave. NW (Western Ave.) | 202-777-9959
Penn Quarter | Terrell Pl. | 575 Seventh St. NW (bet. E & F Sts.) | 202-783-5522
National Harbor | 153 Waterfront St. (St. George Blvd.), MD | 301-567-1005
www.rosamexicano.com

"Traditional dishes with a modern twist" are the hallmark of this "upscale Mexican" chain, though at press time a revamped menu (by chef-lebrity Jonathan Waxman) is about to debut, shifting to a local, market-driven focus and adding new dishes, including ceviche, possibly outdating the Food rating (don't worry – the favorites will remain, like its "killer" tableside guacamole and "outstanding" pomegranate margaritas); "fast" service keeps things rosy in the colorful, contemporary settings, so even if some feel the midpriced fare is "steep", the majority "loves" it.

	FOOD	DECOR	SERVICE	COST

Roti Mediterranean Grill *Mediterranean*   22 | 15 | 19 | $13

Downtown | 1311 F St. NW (13th St.) | 202-499-4145 🛒
Farragut | 1629 K St. (16th St. NW) | 202-499-2091 🛒
NEW **Foggy Bottom** | 2221 I St. (22nd St. NW) | 202-499-2095
World Bank | 1747 Pennsylvania Ave. NW (bet. 17th & 18th Sts.) | 202-466-7684 🛒
NoMa | 1275 First St. NE (N St.) | 202-618-6969 🛒
SW | L'Enfant Plaza Metro Station | 480 L'Enfant Plaza SW (10th St.) | 202-618-6965
Courthouse | 1501 Wilson Blvd. (N. Oak St.) | Arlington, VA | 571-257-3295
www.roti.com

Dubbed the "Mediterranean version of Chipotle" by admirers, this expanding chain fills a niche with "healthy, cheap and filling" pita-centered sandwiches, salads and platters that customers design themselves in industrial Aegean (orange-and-blue-tiled) settings; its "fast service despite the long lines" attracts office workers and others "in a rush", who rely on it for a "quick lunch."

Royal Mile Pub *Scottish*   23 | 20 | 22 | $25

Wheaton | 2407 Price Ave. (bet. Elkin St. & Georgia Ave.), MD | 301-946-4511 | www.royalmilepub.net

"Hours can go by" easily at this "cozy" Scottish pub, a "well-kept Wheaton secret" known for "step-beyond pub fare" at a reasonable price; aye, it's a "great place to drink" too, thanks to the "international" ale selection, one of the "best scotch lists" in the area and a "friendly" owner; P.S. there's occasional live music.

RT's *Cajun/Creole*   26 | 16 | 24 | $39

Greater Alexandria | 3804 Mt. Vernon Ave. (Glebe Rd.) | Alexandria, VA | 703-684-6010 | www.rtsrestaurant.net

Long a "favorite" for those "craving New Orleans" flavors in Greater Alexandria, this Cajun-Creole classic has a "deft touch" in the kitchen, whipping up "outstanding" dishes such as its "famous" Jack Daniel's shrimp; yes, perhaps the old-time-saloon look "needs a shake-up", but the bayou brigade wouldn't change anything about the "excellent" food, "fine" service or reasonable tabs.

☑ Ruan Thai *Thai*   27 | 15 | 21 | $22

Wheaton | 11407 Amherst Ave. (University Blvd.), MD | 301-942-0075 | www.ruanthaiwheaton.com

"Everything is just so good" on the menu – notably "not-to-be-missed" deep-fried watercress – at this Wheatonite known for its "real" Thai cuisine "priced well"; "fast", "friendly service keeps the "bustling" scene and "very busy carry-out" operation under control, so who cares if the digs are "sparse", since you "don't go for the ambiance."

Russia House *Russian*   21 | 20 | 20 | $45

Dupont Circle | 1800 Connecticut Ave. NW (Florida Ave.) | 202-234-9433 | www.russiahouselounge.com

"*Na zdorovie!*" toasts the "beautiful crowd" reveling in the "decadency of the czars" at this Russian retreat occupying an "opulent" yet "cozy" four-story townhouse in Dupont Circle; the food is "well prepared" if "expensive", but comrades claim it's really all about the "stunning" vodka collection and "choice" caviar dropped off by "knowledgeable" staff to backdrop intimate "conversation post-dinner."

☑ Russia House Restaurant *Russian*   27 | 23 | 25 | $51

Herndon | 790 Station St. (bet. Elden St. & Park Ave.), VA | 703-787-8880 | www.russiahouserestaurant.com

"Someone in the kitchen truly knows how to cook" say fans of this high-end Herndon spot's "superb" French-influenced Russian specialties that naturally don't come cheap; cocktails get a boost from the "welcoming" owners' "excellent stash of Russian vodka" ("flavored shots" work too), enhancing the "unique charm" of a "delightful" meal in formal surroundings.

Rustico *American*   22 | 21 | 20 | $30

Greater Alexandria | 827 Slaters Ln. (Potomac Greens Dr.) | Alexandria, VA | 703-224-5051
Ballston | Liberty Ctr. | 4075 Wilson Blvd. (Randolph St.) | Arlington, VA | 571-384-1820
www.rusticorestaurant.com

"They're passionate about beer" at these "value"-priced "neighborhood haunts" in Alexandria and Ballston, where "small-batch and hard-to-find" brews whet the appetite for "tasty" wood-fired pizza and seasonal "upscale" American "tavern fare"; "knowledgeable", "low-key" staff creates a "relaxed" atmosphere at both locations, while Alexandria has a "funkier vibe", and Ballston is "bigger" with "lots of tables in the bar."

Rustik Tavern *American/Eclectic*   ∇ 23 | 20 | 23 | $20

Bloomingdale | 84 T St. NW (bet. 1st St. & Rhode Island Ave.) | 202-290-2936 | www.rustikdc.com

"Delicious" wood-fired pizzas (you'll hear the "squeaky wheel that fires" the oven) and a whole range of Eclectic-American fare beckons "local foodies" to this "always welcoming", "fairly priced" Bloomingdale spot that's "cozy on the inside" (exposed brick, an eye-catching mural) with a "relaxing" outdoor patio; the whole place is under the radar, but a small cadre says the "real secret" is the weekend brunch.

☑ Ruth's Chris Steak House *Steak*   26 | 24 | 26 | $67

Penn Quarter | 724 Ninth St. NW (bet. G & H Sts.) | 202-393-4488
Dupont Circle | 1801 Connecticut Ave. NW (S St.) | 202-797-0033
Bethesda | 7315 Wisconsin Ave. (Elm St.), MD | 301-652-7877
Crystal City | Crystal Park | 2231 Crystal Dr., 11th fl. (23rd St.) | Arlington, VA | 703-979-7275
Fairfax | 4100 Monument Corner Dr. (Monument Dr.), VA | 703-266-1004
Vienna | 8521 Leesburg Pike (Spring Hill Rd.), VA | 703-848-4290
www.ruthschris.com

You always "know what you're getting" at this eminently "reliable", "classy" steakhouse chain: "superior" chops smothered in "buttery excellence" that "melt in your mouth" after "sizzling" all the way to the table via "unobtrusive", "top-of-the-line" servers; in short, go for a "truly prime" time – just "bring your wallet", because the bill is "hefty."

Sabai Sabai Simply Thai *Thai*

26 | 20 | 21 | $27

Germantown | 19847 Century Blvd. (Middlebrook Rd.), MD | 301-528-1400 | www.sabaisimplythai.com

"Sensational, traditional" Thai cuisine employing "fresh ingredients with just enough spice" is the hallmark of this midpriced Germantown Siamese, but it also appeals for its "interesting mix of street food", reflected in photos of Thai street life that dot the walls; a "tasteful" interior of stone and earth tones heightens the "soothing" experience, as does an unexpectedly "worthwhile wine list."

Sakana ⑤ *Japanese*

∇ 23 | 14 | 17 | $29

Dupont Circle | 2026 P St. NW (bet. 20th & 21st Sts.) | 202-887-0900

"Like the smart girl next door" ("not the 'it girl' of the moment"), this Dupont Circle Japanese spot is an understated "gem" delivering "quality" sushi and other dishes that are "consistently very good without being showy"; "best-value" prices and adept service make up for a "plain" space that "hustles" on weekend nights.

Sakoontra *Thai*

23 | 20 | 20 | $23

Fairfax | Costco Plaza | 12300 Costco Plaza (W. Ox Rd.), VA | 703-818-8886 | www.sakoontra.com

This "classic" "neighborhood" Thai in Fairfax impresses with affordable standards and house specialties (both the 'yum watercress' salad and the namesake duck come recommended); the contemporary space is aswirl with eye-popping colors and includes playful touches (the centerpiece is a parked tuk-tuk), and "quick", "efficient" service plays well in the chain-heavy Costco Plaza.

NEW Sakuramen Ⓜ *Noodle Shop*

- | - | - | I

Adams Morgan | 2441 18th St. NW (bet. Columbia & Kalorama Rds.) | 202-656-5285 | www.sakuramen.net

Amid the bar-heavy Adams Morgan scene, this noodle shop is a welcome addition, serving wallet-friendly Asian fusion ramens (even letting diners customize their own brothy bowl), perfect for soaking up booze; tucked away in a basement, the compact digs feature a communal table and an arresting mural of guardian spirit Shoki on the wall.

Samantha's *Pan-Latin*

24 | 17 | 22 | $29

Silver Spring | 631 E. University Blvd. (Piney Branch Rd.), MD | 301-445-7300 | www.samanthasrestaurant.net

This "delightful" Pan-Latin in Silver Spring might look "like a hole-in-the-wall", but it's "nicer" inside, with white tablecloths and mood lighting, and the midpriced food is "out of this world" say "repeat customers"; "veteran" servers "know the menu well", and despite the "tight" parking, it's "worth it if you're in the neighborhood."

Scion Restaurant *American*

∇ 19 | 17 | 20 | $32

Dupont Circle | 2100 P St. NW (21st St.) | 202-833-8899 | www.scionrestaurant.com

"Bring your hangover" to this New American "neighborhood staple" in Dupont Circle for the bottomless liquid brunch that draws a "young" crowd at "the crack of noon" on Sunday – though it's also "worth a stop" at other days and times for a "nice mix" of "basics and more adventurous dishes"; other niceties include a "kind" staff, "reasonable" tabs and a year-round patio.

Sea Catch 🗷 Seafood

23 | 22 | 21 | $48

Georgetown | Canal Sq. | 1054 31st St. NW (bet. K & M Sts.) | 202-337-8855 | www.seacatchrestaurant.com

"Oyster happy hour rules" ($1 bivalves and half-priced wine) at this Georgetown seafooder where the mollusks are accompanied by a geographic "guide" from "aim-to-please" servers who also traffic in other aquatic "delights" like "delicious" grilled fish and "perfect" crab cakes; for most, a "romantic dinner" on the porch overlooking the C&O Canal, or fireside in winter, is worth the costly tabs.

Sea Pearl American/Californian

23 | 25 | 23 | $40

Merrifield | Merrifield Town Ctr. | 8191 Strawberry Ln. (bet. Gallows Rd. & Lee Hwy.), VA | 703-372-5161 | www.seapearlrestaurant.com

An "elegant and peaceful" "ocean oasis" (maritime hues, capiz-shell curtains, waveform wall) awaits at this Merrifield Cal-American where "personalized" hospitality hooks diners on seafood prepared with "Asian flavors that satisfy rather than overwhelm"; it's "not cheap", but there's a "lower-priced menu" for weeknight happy hour at the bar or in the lounge.

Sei Asian

26 | 25 | 22 | $51

Penn Quarter | 444 Seventh St. NW (bet. D & E Sts.) | 202-783-7007 | www.seirestaurant.com

"Extra flavor, sex and sizzle" dress up the "exceptional", "playful" sushi and "inventive" Asian-fusion small plates at this "sleek and shiny" Penn Quarter beauty queen where white-on-white surroundings "feel more like South Beach than DC"; costs can add up, but happy-hour specials keep it manageable, and "excellent" service makes it a lock for "date night" or pre-theater noshes before Woolly Mammoth or Shakespeare shows.

Senart's Oyster &
Chop House Seafood/Steak

24 | 23 | 21 | $37

Capitol Hill | 520 Eighth St. SE (bet. E & G Sts.) | 202-544-1168 | www.senartsdc.com

A "charming", "modern version of an old-time East Coast oyster house" centered on a 50-ft. marble bar, this "upscale" American seafooder on Capitol Hill wins accolades for "high-quality" surf 'n' turf and a "top-shelf" raw bar happy hour from 4–6:30 PM daily; the bartenders "know what they're doing", which makes for a "lively" atmosphere, and "prices are low" for what you get.

Sequoia American

17 | 24 | 18 | $46

Georgetown | Washington Harbour | 3000 K St. NW (Thomas Jefferson St.) | 202-944-4200 | www.arkrestaurants.com

With a "stunning waterfront" setting on the Potomac in Georgetown, this American venue proves "lovely at sunset" from the "cruise-ship" interior or the multilevel outdoor terrace with a "vibrant" bar scene; service is solid, but if the "expensive", "marginal" fare doesn't float your boat, most insist it's still worth going for "drinks", "excellent" people-watching and the "outta-this-world" view.

Serendipity 3 *American/Dessert* | 21 | 21 | 18 | $28 |

Georgetown | 3150 M St. NW (Wisconsin Ave.) | 202-333-5193 | www.serendipity3dc.com

"Save room for dessert" at this "just plain fun" American "fantasyland" in Georgetown, where signature frozen hot chocolate follows "above-average" "artery-clogging" favorites like burgers and fries, at middling prices; service is "friendly", though you'll still "wait to order, wait for ice cream, wait for the check", but while you do there's plenty to ogle, like "Tiffany lamps galore" and knickknacks "your crazy aunt stole."

Sergio Ristorante Italiano ⊠ *Italian* | ▽ 27 | 19 | 25 | $33 |

Silver Spring | Doubletree by Hilton Hotel – Silver Spring | 8727 Colesville Rd. (bet. Fenton & Spring Sts.), MD | 301-585-1040 | www.hilton.com

A "very loyal customer base" says there's "no better bargain in these down economic times" than an "authentic" Italian meal in the Silver Spring Hilton's basement in a "homey" but "windowless" space; that's where chef-owner Sergio Toni can be found not only preparing the "wonderful" food, but also "seating guests and singing Italian tunes" alongside his "experienced" staff.

Sette Osteria *Italian* | 21 | 17 | 17 | $37 |

Dupont Circle | 1666 Connecticut Ave. NW (R St.) | 202-483-3070 | www.setteosteria.com

"Reliable", "better-than-most" pizzas, pastas and more are the draws at this "popular" midpriced Dupont Circle "cafe-type" Italian where "waiters in a hurry" "cater to after-work and weekend" crowds; in nice weather, outdoor seats are in demand, while inside the "large", window-walled space, wood tables and terra-cotta tiles add rusticity.

701 *American* | 23 | 24 | 24 | $54 |

Penn Quarter | 701 Pennsylvania Ave. NW (7th St.) | 202-393-0701 | www.701restaurant.com

"Classy with a hip feel to it", this "adventurous" New American in Penn Quarter is prized for "civilized" business lunches ("professional" staff serves the "widely spaced" tables) and dinners that feel "like special occasions, even in jeans" ("candlelight" dots the "suave" setting); extras include "good-value" pre-theater and bar menus, "easy jazz" Thursday–Saturday and a "lovely" terrace with a view of the Navy Memorial.

Seven Seas *Chinese/Japanese* | 22 | 14 | 19 | $23 |

College Park | 8503 Baltimore Ave. (Quebec St.), MD | 301-345-5808 | www.sevenseascp.com

Rockville | Federal Plaza | 1776 E. Jefferson St. (bet. Montrose Rd. & Rollins Ave.), MD | 301-770-5020 | www.sevenseasrestaurant.com

This "good-value" Chinese-Japanese duo in College Park and Rockville specializes in "fresh seafood live from the tanks" and other "consistently good" fare; the "nothing-fancy" setups are "adequate", and the staff "treats you right"; P.S. College Park has a "cheap" lunch buffet.

☑ 1789 *American* 26 | 25 | 26 | $70

Georgetown | 1226 36th St. NW (Prospect St.) | 202-965-1789 | www.1789restaurant.com

"White gloves and pearls" might suit this "distinguished" Georgetown "classic" with a "refined", "historic" townhouse setting and "expertly prepared" "farm-to-table" New American cooking that together make it a "special place to impress or luxuriate"; politicians and parents visiting their kids at the university mean that the "people-watching" (and "eavesdropping") is as good as the food, while a "personable" wait staff makes diners feel so like "landed gentry" that it's "worth every penny" of its very contemporary prices.

Seventh Hill Pizza Ⓜ *Pizza* 25 | 14 | 20 | $19

Capitol Hill | 327 Seventh St. SE (Pennsylvania Ave.) | 202-544-1911 | www.montmartredc.com

Pizzaiolos "toss dough into the rafters", showing kids "a great time" at this Capitol Hill wood-fired-oven pizzeria, a bargain offshoot of Gallic bistro Montmartre next door, while more mature crustafarians go in for "artisanal" toppings ("goat cheese and tapenade", "brilliant") and "interesting" beers; though there's "little seating" in the bright, airy space, that's about to change with an upcoming expansion.

Shake Shack *Burgers* 21 | 15 | 17 | $15

Dupont Circle | 1216 18th St. NW (bet. Connecticut Ave. & Jefferson Pl.) | 202-683-9922
SW | Nationals Park | 1500 S. Capitol St. SE (P St.)
www.shakeshack.com

"You may have to wait", but the "addictive" burgers and "life-changing" 'concretes' ("milkshakes on steroids") are "worth it" say fans of this "friendly" counter-serve NYC import from Danny Meyer; a few dissenters dis "meh" crinkle-cut fries and "kinda pricey" tabs, but that doesn't stop the masses from shacking up at the wood-heavy Dupont Circle stop or Nationals Park stand (open during games only).

Shamshiry *Persian* ▽ 27 | 14 | 19 | $22

Tysons Corner | 8607 Westwood Center Dr. (Leesburg Pike) | Vienna, VA | 703-448-8883 | www.shamshiry.com

"Patrons speaking Farsi" and "totally enjoying themselves" signal that you're "in for a treat" at this "hard-to-find" eatery in a Tysons Corner office park, serving "delicious", "authentic" Persian cuisine – you can't go wrong with the "excellent" kebabs and rice dishes – in a utilitarian setting with solid service; plus portions are "great for the price" (folks "always have leftovers").

NEW Shophouse Southeast Asian Kitchen *SE Asian* 22 | 16 | 19 | $12

Dupont Circle | 1516 Connecticut Ave. NW (bet. Dupont Circle & Q St.) | 202-232-4141 | www.shophousekitchen.com

Chipotle's "great new concept" – Southeast Asian–inspired "assembly-line fast food" – recently debuted in Dupont Circle, where "flavorful" meals of rice/noodle bowls with "spicy" sauces are served up "cheap", "quick and with a smile"; "daunting" crowds can feel "like vultures hovering" to nab your seat in the narrow, wood-lined space, but early-adopters "overlook" these obstacles; P.S. a Georgetown outlet opens late 2012.

Shula's Steak House *Steak*
▽ 22 | 21 | 20 | $68

Tysons Corner | Marriott Tysons Corner | 8028 Leesburg Pike (Towers Crescent Dr.) | Vienna, VA | 703-506-3256 | www.donshula.com

They "know how to cook steaks" at this Marriott Tysons Corner chain steakhouse with "nice" dark-wood-and-leather environs and "friendly" service; a few feel it's "kind of expensive", but football fans usually enjoy scoping the famed coach's Dolphins ephemera while polishing off the signature porterhouse and, perhaps, a few martinis.

Sichuan Jin River *Chinese*
▽ 25 | 15 | 19 | $19

Rockville | 410 Hungerford Dr. (Beall Ave.), MD | 240-403-7351 | www.scpavilion.com

"Go with a big group" to sample the "massive" menu of "stunningly authentic" Sichuan fare at this Rockville strip-mall joint – and "don't be afraid to tell the waiters 'spicy'" for the "real experience"; the egg-noodle-hued digs are unassuming, but solid service and a low price further enamor fans.

Siroc *Italian*
24 | 20 | 23 | $50

Downtown | 915 15th St. NW (bet. I & K Sts.) | 202-628-2220 | www.sirocrestaurant.com

"Everything works" – from "business lunch" to "date night" – at this spendy Downtown Italian with an "elegant yet relaxed" interior and an outdoor cafe overlooking McPherson Square, offering "delicately handmade" pasta, "extensive" seafood and "excellent" wines via a "terrific", "no-attitude" staff; it's seemingly "tucked away where no one will notice – except many have", so reserve ahead.

Smith & Wollensky *Steak*
25 | 22 | 24 | $65

Golden Triangle | 1112 19th St. NW (bet. L & M Sts.) | 202-466-1100 | www.smithandwollensky.com

"Awesome" steaks, "quality" sides and "strong" drinks draw carnivores to this über-"reliable" NYC chain link with a "macho", "old-school" vibe in the Golden Triangle; the "wonderful" servers that will "go the extra mile" boost egos ("you'll feel like royalty"), but of course it's always "better if on someone else's tab."

Smith Commons *American*
▽ 22 | 25 | 21 | $35

Atlas District | 1245 H St. NE (bet. 12th & 13th Sts.) | 202-396-0038 | www.smithcommonsdc.com

A "gorgeous" triplex in a onetime carpet warehouse in the Atlas District is a chicly rough-hewn backdrop to a "good selection of small-brewery beers", "delicious" (if "hefty"-priced) cocktails and "inventive" New American plates; an "always-relaxed vibe" and "amazing bartenders" help make it a "highlight of H Street."

	FOOD	DECOR	SERVICE	COST

NEW Smoke & Barrel *American/BBQ* ▽ 20 | 19 | 19 | $23

Adams Morgan | 2471 18th St. NW (bet. Belmont & Columbia Rds.) | 202-319-9353 | www.smokeandbarreldc.com

"Pretty decent BBQ for a city that doesn't do it well" is the judgment on this "friendly", midpriced Adams Morgan entry, whose rustic, rough-hewn digs offer a pleasant "oasis" from the neighborhood's "post-college mess" of a scene; but where it really has fans over a barrel is with its "killer" beer list (think: "rare smoked" brews) and "magical" meatless 'cue options.

NEW Society Fair *American* ▽ 24 | 26 | 25 | $33

Old Town | 277 S. Washington St. (Duke St.) | Alexandria, VA | 703-683-3247 | www.societyfair.net

An "amazing concept" from Cathal Armstrong (Restaurant Eve), this "wonderful, sparkly" new Victorian-themed gourmet market/ eatery in Old Town tended by "attentive" staffers lets diners go shopping, then "sit down and have a nice wine" paired with cheese, charcuterie or other light fare in the wine room, or pick something from the bakery/cafe; prices are moderate, and for a "special treat", chef demos and classes in the showcase kitchen evolve into prix fixe dinners.

Sonoma Restaurant & Wine Bar *American* 21 | 20 | 20 | $40

Capitol Hill | 223 Pennsylvania Ave. SE (bet. 2nd & 3rd Sts.) | 202-544-8088 | www.sonomadc.com

Uncorking lots of "great" vino to complement its "tempting" New American small and large plates, this California-inspired venue is favored for "lunch on the Hill", with its solid service and moderate tabs; the narrow, brick-walled dining room sports a looong bar, and there's a "super-chill" lounge upstairs, and though it might "not pass muster in its namesake wine town", it's certainly "worth crossing the street for."

Sorriso *Italian* ▽ 22 | 19 | 24 | $34

Cleveland Park | 3518 Connecticut Ave. NW (bet. Ordway & Porter Sts.) | 202-537-4800

"Spot-on" service with a "smile" is the specialty of this "family-run" Cleveland Park Italian whose "cozy", sunny storefront space "has real personality" swear its coterie; for some, the Treviso-style pizza is "the best part" of the "homestyle" menu, while wine from the family vineyards "is an absolute have-to-have" – all told, given the "attractive prices", there are very few frowns.

The Source ⊠ *Asian* 27 | 24 | 24 | $68

Penn Quarter | Newseum | 575 Pennsylvania Ave. NW (6th St.) | 202-637-6100 | www.wolfgangpuck.com

"Brilliant East-meets-West fare" is the lead story (with a sidebar on "outstanding" bar bites) at this "hip" Wolfgang Puck destination adjacent to Penn Quarter's Newseum, sporting a "sleek" multilevel setting; "friendly but not intrusive" servers are another reason why subscribers place it in the "expensive-but-worth-it" column.

FOOD DECOR SERVICE COST

Sou'Wester *American*

21 | 23 | 21 | $49

SW | Mandarin Oriental | 1330 Maryland Ave. SW (12th St.) |
202-787-6990 | www.mandarinoriental.com
"Ask for a window table", and take in the "lovely view" at this American
resident of the Mandarin Oriental, serving "creative", "classy" inter-
pretations of Southern-accented down-home favorites that make for
"luxurious breakfasts" and "yummy lunches"; it's a bit "expensive",
but "terrific" help monitors the "swanky" earth-toned, wood-paneled
dining room (there's also a terrace), keeping the vibe "casual."

Spices *Asian*

21 | 16 | 20 | $29

Cleveland Park | 3333 Connecticut Ave. NW (bet. Macomb &
Ordway Sts.) | 202-686-3833 | www.spicesdc.com
"When you can't decide what kind of Asian food to get", this Cleveland
Park "neighborhood place" does it "all well" (including "tasty" sushi) at a "more than right" price; the orange-and-gray Zen setting is
also a "great spot for large groups" on account of many communal
tables and "quick" service from "sweet and endearing" servers.

Spice Xing *Indian*

22 | 22 | 22 | $28

Rockville | Rockville Town Sq. | 100 Gibbs St. (Middle Ln.), MD |
301-610-0303 | www.spicexing.com
"Inventive" Indian with international accents adds "creative fusion"
to subcontinental staples and "tapas-style" plates at this Rockville
spot – and at fair prices, particularly for the "bargain" lunch buffet;
"conscientious" service complements the "lovely", colorful space
complete with a billowy, variegated silk ceiling, and for a change of
pace, "curryoke" (curry plus karaoke) happens most Friday nights.

Standard ● Ⓜ *BBQ*

- | - | - | I

Logan Circle | 1801 14th St. NW (S St.) | www.standarddc.com
Hopping when the weather's nice, this mostly outdoor BBQ/beer
garden smack on a trendy stretch of 14th Street NW adds foodie-
friendly twists to its thrifty lineup, with unusual cuts and local vege-
table offerings, capped with German and American craft beers; the
game plan changes at the owners' inspiration (feel like barbecued
pig's head? – it just might be available); P.S. closed in winter.

Star & Shamrock ● *Deli/Pub Food*

19 | 17 | 20 | $20

Atlas District | 1341 H St. NE (bet. 13th & 14th Sts.) | 202-388-3833 |
www.starandshamrock.com
"A New York deli" walks into an "Irish pub" – it's no joke at this Atlas
District "marriage" of "two culinary cultures" serving "nothing-
fancy" grub, like 'paddy melts' and bagel pizza, that makes "perfect
drunk food", plus "unique beer choices"; what's more, the price is
right, the service is solid and the woody, taverny digs are cozy.

Station 4 *American*

21 | 24 | 18 | $40

SW Waterfront | 1101 Fourth St. SW (M St.) | 202-488-0987 |
www.station4dc.com
A "sexy, Miami-inspired setting" injects "a much-needed infusion of
swank" into the Southwest Waterfront at this New American with a

"tasty" menu of "creative" entrees and pizzas; yes, it "can get pricey", but the service is "pleasant", and most are just jazzed there's finally "a decent restaurant within easy walking distance of Arena Stage."

Sticky Rice *Asian/Eclectic* | 23 | 19 | 19 | $26 |

Atlas District | 1224 H St. NE (bet. 12th & 13th Sts.) | 202-397-7655 | www.stickyricedc.com

An "odd" but "delicious" mix of "sushi and tater tots" plus noodle dishes and "interesting" cocktails keeps this inexpensive Atlas District Asian-Eclectic "hopping" with a "young, hip" throng, especially on weekends; a few say the help can be "friendly but a little too cool", but it remains "quirky and fun" on account of the nightly happenings, e.g. karaoke, speed bingo and such.

Stoney's Lounge ❶ *Pub Food* | ▽ 18 | 13 | 18 | $21 |

Logan Circle | 1433 P St. NW (bet. 14th & 15th Sts.) | 202-234-1818

"Stick with the basics and you can't go wrong" at Logan Circle's "great local dive", a narrow, tin-ceilinged space that's a "pleasant" place to "enjoy time out with friends" over low-tabbed bar food (some say the "best grilled-cheese sandwich in DC") and a "surprisingly nice" selection of microbrews; it's also perfectly situated to grab a bite "before heading to nearby Studio Theatre."

NEW Sugo Cicchetti *Italian/Pizza* | - | - | - | M |

Potomac | Potomac Park | 12505 Park Potomac Ave. (Seven Locks Rd.), MD | 240-386-8080 | www.eatsugo.com

The Cava team's new Italian-inspired taperia/pizzeria outlet in Potomac has been buzzing since day one and boasts an open industrial-mod design, with a touch of luncheonette informality in the overstuffed red-leather booths; a wood-fired pizza oven sends out interestingly topped pies, while pastas, charcuterie and hot and cold *cicchetti* (small plates) provide plenty of options for moderately priced sampling and sharing – plus cotton candy for dessert.

Sunflower Vegetarian | 25 | 17 | 25 | $18 |
Restaurant *Asian/Vegetarian*

Falls Church | 6304 Leesburg Pike (Arlington Blvd.), VA | 703-237-3888
Vienna | 2531 Chain Bridge Rd. (Nutley St.), VA | 703-319-3888
www.crystalsunflower.com

Even "strict carnivores" may "forget they're in a vegetarian place" thanks to the "delicious" Asian-inspired fare with "lots of flavor" that shines "without emptying your billfold" at these eateries in Falls Church and Vienna; the "cheerful" decor is "cute if you like sunflowers", and the "family-friendly" service is "polite."

Surfside *Californian/Mexican* | 21 | 13 | 14 | $21 |

Glover Park | 2444 Wisconsin Ave. NW (Calvert St.) | 202-337-0004 | www.surfsidedc.com

Like a "seaside taco shack" (but bigger), this Glover Park Cal-Mex serves "spicy" fish tacos and other "exciting" eats to a company of "hipsters", "neighborhood singles" and families with "kids"; "cafeteria-style" service means "you're your own waiter, which can get hectic" in the narrow, "crowded" industrial room, so decamp to the rooftop with an icy margarita – "awesome on a hot summer day"; P.S. for food on the run, check online for the taco truck's location.

Sushi Damo *Japanese*

25 | 23 | 21 | $38

Rockville | Rockville Town Sq. | 36 Maryland Ave. (bet. Jefferson St. & Montgomery Ave.), MD | 301-340-8010 | www.sushidamo.com

"Sushi nirvana" is reached in Rockville at this NYC Japanese import via "layer upon layer of flavors" in the "beautifully presented", "innovative takes on old favorites" that appeal to the purist and modernminded alike (there are cooked items too); factor in "ultrachic" yet "comfortable" digs and a "personable", "sincere" crew, and it's deemed "worth" the "not-cheap" price.

Sushiko *Japanese*

24 | 18 | 21 | $45

Glover Park | 2309 Wisconsin Ave. NW (Calvert St.) | 202-333-4187
Chevy Chase | 5455 Wisconsin Ave. (Western Ave.), MD | 301-961-1644
www.sushikorestaurant.com

"Serious sushi eaters" consider this "pricey" Glover Park and Chevy Chase Japanese pair "essential" for its "very-high-quality" raw fish plus "inventive" East-meets-West small plates inspiringly paired with "outstanding" Burgundy wines; the DC original looks "rather plain", while Maryland's "hip", "modern" setting boasts a "vibrant bar scene" – and both keep attracting crowds on account of "attentive" service and "delicious" specials.

Sushi Taro 🅢 *Japanese*

26 | 22 | 24 | $65

Dupont Circle | 1503 17th St. NW (P St.) | 202-462-8999 |
www.sushitaro.com

For "divine" "classical sushi", piscine purists head to this "memorable" Dupont Circle Japanese where chefs who "know their stuff" present an "outstanding" omakase procession at the counter, while "exquisite" servers ferry "finely crafted" "traditional" dishes in a multicourse kaiseki to tables; "simple", "serene" surroundings contribute to a "calm" vibe despite "high" prices; P.S. bento box lunches offer a "real deal."

Sweet Ginger *Asian*

25 | 19 | 25 | $27

Vienna | Danor Plaza | 120 Branch Rd. SE (Maple Ave.), VA |
703-319-3922

Vienna's "beloved" Asian sweetheart attracts suitors with "wonderful sushi" and other "delicious" "comfort food" from China, Malaysia, Thailand et al., delivered by an "attentive" staff; although these charms are hidden in a "strip mall", her black, white and red dress is thoroughly modern, and everything comes together at a "decent price" that makes you want to commit.

Sweetgreen *Health Food*

22 | 15 | 18 | $13

Capitol Hill | 221 Pennsylvania Ave. SE (bet. 2nd & 3rd Sts.) |
202-547-9338
Dupont Circle | 1512 Connecticut Ave. NW (bet. Dupont Circle & Q St.) | 202-387-9338

(continued)

Sweetgreen

NEW **Foggy Bottom** | 2221 I St. NW (bet. 22nd & 23rd Sts.) | 202-507-8357

Georgetown | 3333 M St. NW (bet. 33rd & 34th Sts.) | 202-337-9338

Logan Circle | 1471 P St. NW (bet. 14th & 15th Sts.) | 202-234-7336

Bethesda | 4831 Bethesda Ave. (bet. Arlington Rd. & Woodmont Ave.), MD | 301-654-7336

Ballston | 4075 Wilson Blvd. (Randolph St.) | Arlington, VA | 703-522-2016

Reston | Reston Town Ctr. | 11935 Democracy Dr. (Library St.), VA | 571-203-0082

www.sweetgreen.com

Feel "virtuous" "stuffing your face" at this eco-chic, "Nouvelle salad bar" chain sourcing organic, local components for "creative pre-fab salads" or bowls "made to your specifications", plus soups and "amazing" frozen yogurts; there's almost "always a line", but there's also a "quick turnaround", so while some call it "a little pricey for some greens", most judge "the 'I-saved-the-world' vibe" "worth it."

☑ Sweetwater Tavern   *Southwestern*   26 | 23 | 24 | $29

Merrifield | 3066 Gatehouse Plaza (Rte. 50), VA | 703-645-8100

Centreville | 14250 Sweetwater Ln. (Multiplex Dr.), VA | 703-449-1100

Sterling | 45980 Waterview Plaza (Loudon Tech Dr.), VA | 571-434-6500

www.greatamericanrestaurants.com

"Always crowded", this "cowboy-themed" Southwestern microbrewery chain in NoVa "never disappoints" – whether for "splendid" eats like the "beyond-delicious" rolls and "to-die-for" drunken rib-eye or the "awesome" fresh-brewed beer and root beer; the only bitter notes are sounded by some who cite "ear-shattering" noise and the no-reservations policy ("call ahead . . . way ahead"), though "prompt" service and "reasonable" prices more than make up for it.

Tabaq Bistro ⏺ *Mediterranean*   ∇ 20 | 22 | 20 | $32

U Street Corridor | 1336 U St. NW (bet. 13th & 14th Sts.) | 202-265-0965 | www.tabaqdc.com

The "awesome" 360-degree view of DC's skyline from the roof deck of this U Street Med is a "favorite" backdrop for brunch or cocktails that "get the job done", while downstairs is "sexy" and "chill"; some say the food is "average" and "a bit pricey", and service can swing from "on point" to "inattentive", but the venue works for parties or a "night on the town" when "ambiance" matters.

Tabard Inn   *American*   25 | 23 | 22 | $47

Dupont Circle | Hotel Tabard Inn | 1739 N St. NW (bet. 17th & 18th Sts.) | 202-331-8528 | www.tabardinn.com

"DC's (not-so-well-kept) secret treasure" tucked in a "quaint" inn off Dupont Circle "keeps earning its reputation" with "innovative" New American cooking and a "warm", "knowledgeable" staff that's there to help explain the seasonally changing menu and "excellent" wine list; a true "romantic's place", it's a perfect "rendezvous" for dinner in the "intimate" main room, "cozy" drinks by the fire or a "wonderful" reservation-worthy brunch in the "hidden" garden – and for all that, it's "still not a wallet-buster."

Tachibana *Japanese*

24 | 14 | 20 | $37

McLean | 6715 Lowell Ave. (Emerson Ave.), VA | 703-847-1771 | www.tachibana.us

Regulars flock to the sushi counter at this well-"established" McLean Japanese for the "quality" fin fare at "quite reasonable" prices; a "caring" staff tends to customers who acknowledge the "tired" interior "is simply not the point", as evidenced by the fact that it's often "crowded."

Tackle Box *Seafood*

18 | 13 | 15 | $23

Georgetown | 3245 M St. NW (bet. 33rd St. & Wisconsin Ave.) | 202-337-8269 | www.tackleboxrestaurant.com

Lured by "fresh fish served quickly" and on the "cheap", seafood-seekers catch what they're craving at this "airy", industrial "sea shack" in Georgetown, ordering "fast-food" style, plonking their trays on communal "indoor picnic" tables and digging into lobster rolls that are "worth it, even if they leave you longing for seconds"; they also offer full lobster-pot dinners to go, and there are drinks and snacks upstairs at Crackle Bar.

Tako Grill *Japanese*

24 | 18 | 20 | $33

Bethesda | 7756 Wisconsin Ave. (Cheltenham Dr.), MD | 301-652-7030 | www.takogrill.com

The "consistently high standard" of sushi, robatayaki and other cooked specialties appeals to supporters of this longtime mid-priced Bethesda Japanese that also boasts a "strong sake selection"; the "pleasant" contemporary space is "large" enough that "you can usually get a table anytime" and promptly relax in the hands of "friendly", "efficient" servers; P.S. some nonpurists "love the brown-rice sushi" option.

Tallula/EatBar *American*

24 | 20 | 22 | $40

Clarendon | 2761 Washington Blvd. (Pershing Dr.), VA | 703-778-5051 | www.tallularestaurant.com

There's "funky decor but serious food" at these side-by-side Clarendon New Americans, where "creativity in the kitchen" means "an exciting mix of flavors" whether you're in the mood for the higher-priced seasonal offerings in the formal main dining room or just wanna "share some appetizers" in the relaxed gastropub; both sides can get a bit "noisy" but offer the same "accommodating" service and "excellent", "affordable" wine menu.

Tandoori Nights *Indian*

24 | 22 | 21 | $30

NEW **Bethesda** | 7236 Woodmont Ave. (Elm St.), MD | 301-656-4002
Gaithersburg | 106 Market St. (Kentlands Blvd.), MD | 301-947-4007
Clarendon | 2800 Clarendon Blvd. (Edgewood St.), VA | 703-248-8333
www.tandoorinights.com

Sign up for "North Indian Food 101" at these tandoori night schools where "tasty" subcontinental fare "prepared for American tastes" runs "lighter than the more traditional styles"; the "Bollywood feel" of "modern" dining rooms renders a "trendy" backdrop for "attentive" service, and moderate tabs seal the deal.

Taqueria Distrito Federal *Mexican* ∇ 22 | 11 | 17 | $13

Columbia Heights | 3463 14th St. NW (Oak St.) | 202-276-7331
Petworth | 805 Kennedy St. NW (8th St.) | 202-545-6990
www.taqueriadf.com

The "fantastic" "street tacos" might be "the best you'll find north of the Rio Grande" at these "tiny" Columbia Heights and Petworth "joints" where photos of Latin movie stars and "obligatory fútbol paraphernalia" make amigos feel like they're "in Mexico"; *sí*, the service is only "ok", but with prices as sweet as the "multiple" aguas frescas, most "look forward to going back."

Taqueria Nacional ⓩ *Mexican* ∇ 23 | 8 | 16 | $12

Capitol Hill | Hall of the States | 400 N. Capitol St. NW (Louisiana Ave.) | 202-737-7070 | www.taquerianational.com

"Yes, the tacos are small, but they pack quite a punch" at this "quick", "incredibly priced" weekday breakfast-and-lunch "hole-in-the-wall" behind big *papi* Johnny's Half Shell on Capitol Hill, which mostly packs things for "takeout"; wishes for more seats and longer hours will come true winter 2012/13, when it is set to relocate and become a full-service restaurant and bar at 1409 T Street NW.

Taqueria Poblano *Mexican* 22 | 15 | 20 | $21

Del Ray | 2400 Mt. Vernon Ave. (Oxford Ave.) | Alexandria, VA | 703-548-8226
NEW Arlington | 2401 Columbia Pike (Adams St.), VA | 703-271-8979
Arlington | 2503 N. Harrison St. (Lee Hwy.), VA | 703-237-8250
www.taqueriapoblano.com

"Swimmingly good" fish tacos are the lure at these "sunny" California-inspired Mexican joints in Arlington and Del Ray that also draw accolades for "good" salsa that hits the table "almost immediately" and "zippy" 'ritas "(no margarita mix here)"; "efficient", family-friendly service and "low prices" please an "enthusiastic crowd."

Tara Thai *Thai* 20 | 19 | 19 | $25

Upper NW | Spring Valley Shopping Ctr. | 4849 Massachusetts Ave. NW (49th St.) | 202-363-4141
Bethesda | 4828 Bethesda Ave. (bet. Arlington Rd. & Woodmont Ave.), MD | 301-657-0488
Gaithersburg | Rio Entertainment Ctr. | 9811 Washingtonian Blvd. (Rio Blvd.), MD | 301-947-8330
NEW Hyattsville | 5501 Baltimore Ave. (Jefferson St.), MD | 301-277-7888
Rockville | Montrose Crossing | 12071 Rockville Pike (Montrose Rd.), MD | 301-231-9899
Falls Church | 7501 Leesburg Pike (Pimmit Dr.), VA | 703-506-9788
Herndon | 13021 Worldgate Dr. (Centreville Rd.), VA | 703-481-8999
Vienna | 226 Maple Ave. W. (bet. Lawyers Rd. & Nutley St.), VA | 703-255-2467
www.tarathai.com

A "cute" "undersea vibe" sets a "relaxing" tone at this chainlet serving "reliably good" "standard-issue" Thai with a "focus on fish" for "relatively cheap; service is "efficient", especially at lunch, and many count it as an "around-the-corner" "favorite.""

Taste of Burma ⓜ Burmese   ∇ 26 | 19 | 20 | $20

Sterling | Countryside Shopping Ctr. | 126 Edds Ln. (Cromwell Rd.), VA | 703-444-8510 | www.tasteofburma.com

Families enjoy "trying new things out" on the "exotic" 100-item menu at this Sterling Burmese that knows "how to do spicy right"; golden embroidered panels jazz up the otherwise simple setting, and the "relaxed" service and modest tabs solidify it as a "neighborhood favorite."

Taste of Morocco Moroccan   ∇ 23 | 20 | 23 | $36

Clarendon | 3211 N. Washington Blvd. (Wilson Blvd.), VA | 703-527-7468 | www.atasteofmorocco.com

There's no end to the "old-school, authentic" Moroccan experience at this "breath of fresh air in Clarendon" that offers the option of a traditional multicourse dinner capped with mint tea and has a belly dancer Wednesday–Sunday; a recent Mediterranean-tinged redecoration may outdate the Decor score, but the "sincere", "generous" staff and moderate prices remain intact.

Taste of Saigon Vietnamese   22 | 21 | 22 | $28

Rockville | Rockville Town Sq. | 20 Maryland Ave. (I-270), MD | 301-424-7222
Tysons Corner | 8201 Greensboro Dr. (International Dr.) | McLean, VA | 703-790-0700
www.tasteofsaigon.com

"Not your usual pho joints", these "good-value" Vietnamese venues in Rockville and Tysons Corner bring a French influence to bear on the "consistently excellent", "authentic dishes of Saigon"; service is "extraordinarily friendly", and the atmosphere is "airy" and "attractive", adding up to a "pleasant" experience.

❷ Tasting Room ⓢ American   27 | 23 | 26 | $48

Frederick | 101 N. Market St. (Church St.), MD | 240-379-7772 | www.tastetr.com

Floor-to-ceiling windows bordering a "bright, contemporary interior" mean this "sophisticated" Frederick "favorite" is literally "a place to see and be seen" while partaking of "wonderful", "well-executed" New American fare, "superb martinis" and an "extensive" wine list; it's a "splurge" and can be "crowded", but with "exceptional" service, it's suited to a "special occasion."

Tavira Portuguese   25 | 20 | 24 | $47

Chevy Chase | Chevy Chase Bank Bldg. | 8401 Connecticut Ave. (Chevy Chase Lake Dr.), MD | 301-652-8684 | www.tavirarestaurant.com

"So what" if it's in the "basement of a bank" – where else to keep a "neighborhood treasure" ask acolytes of this "wonderful" Portuguese "hideaway" in Chevy Chase, where "magicians with fish" and meat make "outstanding" dishes appear from the kitchen; the "attentive" staff suggests Med wines for a "white-tablecloth" meal in an "old-world" setting complete with "high" prices (bargain-hunters suggest the three-course daily prix fixe).

	FOOD	DECOR	SERVICE	COST

Taylor Gourmet *Deli/Italian* | 22 | 16 | 17 | $14 |

Atlas District | 1116 H St. NE (bet. 11th & 12th Sts.) | 202-684-7001
Dupont Circle | 1200 19th St. NW (M St.) | 202-775-2005
Mt. Vernon Square/Convention Center | 485 K St. NW (bet. 4th & 5th Sts.) | 202-289-8001
NEW Logan Circle | 1910 14th St. NW (bet. T & U Sts.) | 202-588-7117
Bethesda | Bethesda Row | 7280 Woodmont Ave. (Elm St.), MD | 301-951-9001
www.taylorgourmet.com

With "fresh", "zesty" ingredients piled high on "perfect seeded" bread, expats from the City of Brotherly Love feel like they've returned "home" at these Philly-inspired delis where the "criminally good" Italian-style hoagies are made to order by "friendly" crews; low tabs match the "simple" industrial setups.

Teaism *Tearoom* | 20 | 16 | 17 | $17 |

Penn Quarter | 400 Eighth St. NW (D St.) | 202-638-6010
Dupont Circle | 2009 R St. NW (Connecticut Ave.) | 202-667-3827
Golden Triangle | 800 Connecticut Ave. NW (H St.) | 202-835-2233 **⑤**
NEW Greater Alexandria | 682 N. St. Asaph St. (bet. Pendleton & Wythe Sts.) | Alexandria, VA | 703-684-7777
www.teaism.com

"Linger over your tea" at this "quick", "casual" chain-coffeeshop "alternative" serving "wonderful" leafy brews alongside "tasty" "Eastern-flavored" bento boxes and sandwiches plus salty oat cookies that "can improve any dreary day"; "inexpensive" tabs and "tasteful" "Zen" decor contribute to the sense of "serenity", which you can even take home (they have "nice tea-related gifts").

Ted's Bulletin *American* | 23 | 23 | 21 | $26 |

Capitol Hill | 505 Eighth St. SE (bet. E & G Sts.) | 202-544-8337 | www.tedsbulletin.com

This retro Capitol Hill "throwback" puts "twists" on its midpriced American "favorites" in an upscale luncheonette setting with authentic "art deco" details and "classic B&W movies" screened on the wall; fans warn the "only downside is long wait times", but say you'll be "delighted" once installed at the counter stools or comfy booths.

NEW Tel'Veh Café & Wine Bar ❶ *Mediterranean* | - | - | - | M |

Mt. Vernon Square/Convention Center | 401 Massachusetts Ave. NW (4th St.) | 202-241-9696

In the burgeoning Convention Center area is this newly minted Mediterranean from the team behind Agora, serving midpriced eats alongside a 300-label wine list; full-height windows flood the wavy, nautical-chic space with light during the day, while the rope-lined bar fills with punched-out office workers come evening.

Tempo *French/Italian* | 24 | 20 | 23 | $36 |

Greater Alexandria | 4231 Duke St. (Gordon St.) | Alexandria, VA | 703-370-7900 | www.temporestaurant.com

"You'd never believe it's a converted gas station" say advocates who appreciate this "upscale" "neighborhood treasure" in Alexandria for its "excellent" French-Italian fare and "bargain" wines; service comes "with a personal touch" in the white, airy, art-filled space, and the "reasonable" prices are often lower than what you pay at the pump.

Thai at Silver Spring *Thai*

24 | 18 | 21 | $22

Silver Spring | Downtown Silver Spring | 921 Ellsworth Dr. (bet. Fenton St. & Georgia Ave.), MD | 301-650-0666 | www.thaiatsilverspring.com

With a "convenient location" in the Downtown Silver Spring complex, inexpensive tabs and a "sophisticated" look, this "consistent, delicious" Thai eatery is an attractive option; "fast" service is "accommodating" of children and suitable "if you are in a hurry to see a movie" at the nearby multiplex.

Thai Basil *Thai*

26 | 15 | 21 | $21

Chantilly | 14511 Lee Jackson Memorial Hwy. (Airline Pkwy.), VA | 703-631-8277 | www.thaibasilchantilly.com

Chef-owner Nonkgran Daks' Thai dishes are an "unexpectedly excellent" surprise given the "unremarkable" setting in a Chantilly shopping center, where this "diamond in the rough" is "always busy" (especially at lunch), and the popular cooking classes are always booked; with solid service and "bargain" prices, for those sweet on Siam, it's "nirvana."

T.H.A.I. in Shirlington *Thai*

25 | 22 | 23 | $24

Shirlington | Village at Shirlington | 4029 Campbell Ave. (Randolph St.) | Arlington, VA | 703-931-3203 | www.thaiinshirlington.com

"Consistently Thai-rific" cuisine "that's not dumbed down for Western palates" gets Shirlington tongues wagging "tasty, spicy, nicey" at this area "go-to" sporting a "subdued" Eastern-accented space; "fair" prices, especially at lunch when service is suitably "speedy", please wallet-watchers.

Thaiphoon *Thai*

21 | 18 | 19 | $24

Dupont Circle | 2011 S St. NW (bet. Connecticut Ave. & 20th St.) | 202-667-3505

Pentagon City | Pentagon Row | 1301 S. Joyce St. (Army Navy Dr.) | Arlington, VA | 703-413-8200

www.thaiphoon.com

Locals are "happy with the quality" of the "traditional" Thai eats at this Pentagon City and Dupont Circle duo, with nine-to-fivers especially appreciative of the "fast lunch service"; "extraordinarily reasonable" prices mean the "modern" environs "can get packed" (especially on weekends at the S Street locale).

Thai Square *Thai*

26 | 14 | 20 | $25

Arlington | 3217 Columbia Pike (Highland St.), VA | 703-685-7040 | www.thaisquarerestaurant.com

"Enjoy the spices and the prices" at this "authentic", "consistently excellent" Thai in Arlington, where the dishes may be "simple", but the taste is "complex"; if a few fret that there's "not much to look at" in the "cozy", "rather minimal" space, most prefer to focus on the "cheerful" service or opt for takeout.

Thai Tanic *Thai*   23 | 17 | 18 | $23

Columbia Heights | 3462 14th St. NW (Newton St.) | 202-387-0882
Logan Circle | 1326 14th St. NW (bet. N St. & Rhode Island Ave.) |
202-588-1795
www.thaitanic.us

All aboard these "good, cheap and fast" Siamese twins in Logan
Circle and Columbia Heights for "flavor-packed" fare, notably
some "fire-hot" specialties begging to be cooled down with a
"mean mai tai"; "efficient" crews keep everything running ship-
shape in the "sleek", "colorful" quarters as well as offer an "always
dependable" delivery service.

Thunder Burger & Bar ☻ *Burgers*   24 | 21 | 20 | $22

Georgetown | 3056 M St. NW (bet. 30th & 31st Sts.) | 202-333-2888 |
www.thunderburger.com

"Gourmet" "build-your-own" burgers with "creative" toppings and
"tip-top" fries impress at this Georgetown spot whose "funky", glitzy
rock-themed interior looks like something off of "VH1"; prices and
service are perfectly solid – more striking, perhaps, is the "truly exceptional" draft beer list and happy hour.

Toki Underground *Noodle Shop/Taiwanese*   26 | 22 | 24 | $22

Atlas District | 1234 H St. NE (bet. 12th & 13th Sts.) | 202-388-3086 |
www.tokiunderground.com

"Come hungry, leave sloshy-full" of the "modern takes" on Taiwanese
"comfort food", like "out-of-this-world" steamed dumplings, dished
by this Atlas District "heavy-metal ramen shop"; it's a wallet-friendly
"cool scene" (with a decorative skateboard ramp on the ceiling)
where the "out-of-control" waits for its few seats after ordering at
the counter are deemed part of the "unique" experience.

Tonic *American*   17 | 17 | 16 | $23

Foggy Bottom | Quigley's Pharmacy | 2036 G St. NW (bet. 20th &
21st Sts.) | 202-296-0211
Mt. Pleasant | 3155 Mt. Pleasant St. NW (bet. Kenyon St. &
Kilbourne Pl.) | 202-986-7661 ☻
www.tonicrestaurant.com

You've "got to have the tater tots" at this American duo slinging
"decent" "upscale comfort" fare washed down by plenty of suds
at bargain rates; service is fair for places that are "always crowded",
and a "welcoming" atmosphere pleases "State Department
types, Fed bankers and GWU students" at the three-story Foggy
Bottom location, while the bi-level Mt. Pleasant branch acts as
a "neighborhood *Cheers.*"

Tono Sushi *Japanese*   ▽ 22 | 15 | 24 | $25

Woodley Park | 2605 Connecticut Ave. NW (Calvert St.) | 202-332-7300 |
www.tonosushi.com

"Affordable", "creative" sushi is the name of the game at this Woodley
Parker that also offers cooked Japanese and Thai standards to locals
and "name-tagged convention-goers" from nearby hotels; the setting is simple (brick walls, sushi counter), but a "friendly" staff will

even keep "young children entertained", and the daily $1 sushi happy hour has acolytes professing their "love."

Tony Cheng's *Chinese* | 22 | 17 | 19 | $27

Chinatown | 619 H St. NW (bet. 6th & 7th Sts.) | 202-842-8669 | www.tonychengrestaurant.com

A Chinatown "institution", this Asian triple play offers diners three options: upstairs, a "complex" Chinese menu, plus "quality" daily dim sum (although carts roll only on the weekends), and downstairs, an "authentic", "way-to-go" Mongolian BBQ buffet; service is professional in accord with the (some say "dated") white-tablecloth look, though tabs are positively Formican.

Z Tosca *Ⓩ Italian* | 27 | 24 | 26 | $68

Penn Quarter | 1112 F St. NW (bet. 11th & 12th Sts.) | 202-367-1990 | www.toscadc.com

"Fine dining gets no finer" say fans, than at this "sophisticated" Penn Quarter Italian where the "flawless", uniformed waiters deliver near-"perfect" food as "ex-senators and lobbyists swap business cards" in the "elegant" neutral-toned setting; it's a perfect place for observing "how Washington really works", and the relatively "affordable" pre-theater dinner menu is ideal "for those not on an expense account."

Toscana Café *Deli/Italian* | ▽ 25 | 20 | 25 | $42

Capitol Hill | 601 Second St. NE (F St.) | 202-525-2693 | www.toscanacafedc.com

Chef-owner Daniele Catalani evokes his native Tuscany in a "rustic" Capitol Hill townhouse, hidden behind Union Station, where "outstanding" housemade pastas, pizza and focaccia sandwiches are doled out in a first-floor counter-serve at lunch, while in the evening "fabulous" dinners are set in the trim upstairs dining room; relatively "reasonable" prices, "fast" service and an outdoor patio are highlights of this "funky" trattoria.

Town Hall *American* | ▽ 23 | 19 | 22 | $27

Glover Park | 2340 Wisconsin Ave. NW (bet. Calvert & Hall Sts.) | 202-333-5640 | www.townhalldc.com

Glover Park's young set gravitates to this all-American neighborhood "mecca" for "food, drinks and good times"; a recent move up the street to "bigger and better" digs results in a rustic, art-filled dining room in which to scarf down midpriced quality fare like grilled cheese, burgers and salads – and there's a breezy garden patio and sundeck that's ideal for a "cool cocktail."

Tragara *Italian* | 22 | 21 | 23 | $53

Bethesda | 4935 Cordell Ave. (bet. Norfolk Ave. & Old Georgetown Rd.), MD | 301-951-4935 | www.tragara.com

A Bethesda fixture for a quarter-century, this "high-end" Italian dishes up "well-prepared" "old-school" classics served by a "nice", "helpful" staff in an "upscale", formal setting straight out of a "hotel"; it really excels as an venue for "large parties" celebrating "memorable occasions", so consider it for "a bar/bat mitzvah or wedding"; P.S. free valet parking at dinner in this "busy part of Bethesda" is "appreciated."

	FOOD	DECOR	SERVICE	COST

Trummer's On Main Ⓜ American 24 | 26 | 24 | $71

Clifton | 7134 Main St. (bet. Chapel St. & Clifton Creek Dr.), VA | 703-266-1623 | www.trummersonmain.com

Take a "culinary journey" to "bucolic" Clifton, VA, for "inspired" New American fare so "memorable", diners leave giddy over "delicious" dishes and "divine" wine pairings; the "beautiful, bright", "richly" appointed main dining room and buzzing bar, overseen by a "top-notch" staff, make for a "perfect" evening that's "pricey but worth every cent" – plus, the three-course "Sunday supper is a great deal."

Tryst ◑ Coffeehouse 21 | 22 | 19 | $17

Adams Morgan | 2459 18th St. NW (bet. Belmont & Columbia Rds.) | 202-232-5500 | www.trystdc.com

"Thick-rimmed glasses" and "laptops" are the must-have accessories at Adams Morgan's "packed" answer to a "Berkeley" coffeehouse, where "comfy", "unhomologous" furniture and "great" music (recorded by day, live by night) invite "hipsters" to "hang out" nursing a latte or noshing on "reasonably priced" "sandwiches and sweets"; "friendly" service matches the "relaxed" groove – speaking of which, wine, beer and cocktails offer further opportunities to "chill."

Tuscarora Mill American 25 | 25 | 25 | $45

Leesburg | Market Station | 203 Harrison St. SE (Loudoun St.), VA | 703-771-9300 | www.tuskies.com

Set in a restored old mill and affectionately known as 'Tuskie's' by its tony "horse-country" clientele, this longtime Leesburger features "superb", "creative" American fare complemented by Virginia wines and served in a "romantic" dining room, "rustic" bar or pink-"chintz" garden room; "polished" service matches the "expensive" price tag (the cafe menu is cheaper), providing grist for those who claim it's the area's "finest white-tablecloth restaurant."

Tutto Bene Italian/S American ▽ 23 | 18 | 20 | $27

Ballston | 501 N. Randolph St. (Glebe Rd.) | Arlington, VA | 703-522-1005 | www.tuttobeneitalian.com

Few know that this "old-school Italian banquet hall" in Ballston, frequented by an "older crowd", lives a double life on the weekends when it serves "authentic" food from the Bolivian Highlands (the popular *salteñas*, which resemble baked empanadas, are available daily); service is solid and fare midpriced, so everything is, indeed, *tutto bene*.

❷ 2941 Restaurant Ⓢ American 27 | 27 | 26 | $70

Falls Church | 2941 Fairview Park Dr. (I-495), VA | 703-270-1500 | www.2941.com

This "French-meets-American" "oasis" "hidden" in a Falls Church office park recently "reinvented" itself with a "casually elegant" bistro look (possibly outdating its Decor rating) to match chef Bertrand Chemel's new menu, which includes a larger number of offerings like small plates and pastas at "reasonable" prices; longtime loyalists say the "focused" staff and "stunning" setting – with floor-to-ceiling windows showcasing "beautifully landscaped" grounds – remain as some of the "2,941 reasons to love this place."

	FOOD	DECOR	SERVICE	COST

2100 Prime *American*   24 | 23 | 22 | $56

Dupont Circle | The Fairfax at Embassy Row Hotel |
2100 Massachusetts Ave. NW (21st St.) | 202-835-2100 |
www.2100prime.com

Formerly home of the "classic" Jockey Club, this storied Dupont
Circle hotel dining room has been reborn, and now features an
"excellent" slate of "elegant [American] comfort" food served
with "attention to detail"; "prime" pricing goes with the "upscale"
private-club vibe that emanates from its wood-paneled walls and
equestrian-themed art.

Twisted Vines Bottleshop &   ▽ 20 | 21 | 23 | $26
Bistro *Eclectic*

Arlington | 2803 Columbia Pike (Walter Reed Dr.), VA | 571-482-8581 |
www.twisted-vines.com

They're "helpful about explaining" Cabs and Chards at this triple
threat in South Arlington – part "great little wine bar", part bottle
shop with an "eclectic selection" and part bistro with a "small",
"well-priced" menu of "interesting" cheeses, charcuterie, entrees and flatbreads; a mod yet "cozy atmosphere" with window
seats and a sinuous bar, combined with "fun" tasting events, have
area oenophiles "thrilled."

Z 2 Amys *Pizza*   25 | 17 | 20 | $25

Cleveland Park | 3715 Macomb St. NW (Wisconsin Ave.) |
202-885-5700 | www.2amyspizza.com

"Dough my god, the crust!" gush groupies wowed by the "ambro-
sial" DOC-certified Neapolitan pies at this "popular" Cleveland Park
pizzeria (some tout the "exceptional" small plates too); the scene
inside the "sunny", white-tiled premises can be "mayhem" – it's a
"yuppies-with-kids" magnet – but once the "friendly" staff delivers
the "excellent-for-the-price" food, most "everyone is happy" – especially after swigging one of the "treasures on tap" or something from
the quieter wine bar's "adventurous selection."

Ulah Bistro *American*   20 | 20 | 20 | $31

U Street Corridor | 1214 U St. NW (bet. 12th & 13th Sts.) |
202-234-0123 | www.ulahbistro.com

The "tasty", "reliable" menu at this "rustic-chic" bi-level U Street
American bistro trades on its "variety" – both in its offerings (pizza,
sandwiches, pastas, chops, pub grub and more) and its "good range
of prices"; the "easy-going" crowd also appreciates a "low-key" vibe
from the "friendly" staff and the flowing "libations."

Z Uncle Julio's *Tex-Mex*   21 | 19 | 20 | $26

Bethesda | 4870 Bethesda Ave. (Arlington Rd.), MD | 301-656-2981
Gaithersburg | 231 Rio Blvd. (Washingtonian Blvd.), MD | 240-632-2150
Ballston | 4301 N. Fairfax Dr. (bet. Taylor & Utah Sts.) | Arlington,
VA | 703-528-3131
Fairfax | 4251 Fairfax Corner Ave. (Monument Dr.), VA | 703-266-7760
Reston | Reston Town Ctr. | 1827 Library St. (New Dominion Pkwy.),
VA | 703-904-0703

	FOOD	DECOR	SERVICE	COST

(continued)

Uncle Julio's

Woodbridge | Stonebridge at Potomac Town Ctr. | 14900 Potomac Town Pl. (Neabsco Mills Rd.), VA | 703-763-7322
www.unclejulios.com

Believers say *"bueno"* to "absolutely huge portions" of this Dallas-based chain's midpriced "Texican" grub, with the "endless" chips and salsa scooping up mucho praise, along with the "obligatory 'swirl'" (a drink of layered frozen margarita and sangria), all served "quick" in a colorful hacienda-style setting; that parents can bring children and "never feel nervous about them being too loud" has some quipping it's the "Chuck E. Cheese's of Mexican" eateries.

NEW Unum *American* — | — | — | E

Georgetown | 2917 M St. NW (bet. 29th & 30th Sts.) | 202-621-6959 | www.unumdc.com

Culinary and political worlds meet at this fresh face in Georgetown owned by chef Phillip Blane (ex Equinox) and his wife, Laura Schiller (Barbara Boxer's chief of staff), where high-end, creative takes on America's many culinary traditions are presented within intimate, modern rusticity; there's also an inviting bar with cheese and charcuterie to pair smartly with cocktails, craft beer and international wines.

Urbana *French/Italian* 21 | 22 | 21 | $44

Dupont Circle | Hotel Palomar | 2121 P St. NW (bet. 21st & 22nd Sts.) | 202-956-6650 | www.urbanadc.com

Step down into a "sexy", "cool" enclave for "consistently good" French-Italian fare in Dupont Circle's Hotel Palomar, where a "young" crowd gives it a "local hangout" vibe; bar noshes and "friendly" bartenders keep happy hour "frenetic", but dinner can be great for an intimate "date", thanks in part to "perfectly selected" "wine pairings."

Urban Bar-B-Que Company *BBQ* 24 | 16 | 19 | $18

Rockville | 2007 Chapman Ave. (Twinbrook Pkwy.), MD | 240-290-4827
Rockville | Rock Creek Village Ctr. | 5566 Norbeck Rd. (Bauer Dr.), MD | 301-460-0050
Sandy Springs | 805 Olney Sandy Spring Rd. (Rte. 650), MD | 301-570-3663
Silver Spring | Hillandale | 10163 New Hampshire Ave. (Powder Mill Rd.), MD | 301-434-7427
NEW Ashburn | Ashburn Shopping Plaza |
44050 Ashburn Shopping Plaza (Christiana Dr.), VA | 703-858-7226 | www.urbanbbqco.com

Be prepared to "get dirty" digging into the "juicy", "tender", "smoky" meat at these "down-to-earth" suburban Maryland BBQ havens guaranteed to "fatten you up" on the "cheap"; "takeout is big" at the counter-serve operations, while other locations boast table service and bars, but all of them are "friendly" and plastered with "kitschy" bumper stickers and the like.

Vapiano *Italian* 20 | 20 | 17 | $20

Chinatown | 625 H St. NW (bet. 6th & 7th Sts.) | 202-621-7636
(continued)

(continued)

Vapiano

Golden Triangle | 1800 M St. NW (18th St.) | 202-640-1868
Bethesda | 4900 Hampden Ln. (Woodmont Ave.), MD | 301-215-7013
Ballston | 4401 Wilson Blvd. (Glebe Rd.) | Arlington, VA | 703-528-3113
Reston | Reston Town Ctr. | 1871 Explorer St. (Market St.), VA | 571-281-2893
Sterling | Dulles Town Ctr. | 21100 Dulles Town Circle (Nokes Blvd.), VA | 703-574-4740
www.vapiano.com

"A swanky cafeteria with made-to-order food", this international Italian chain does things differently with a card system for "DIY" ordering ("convenient for large groups", although a few find it "complicates dining") and "solid" pasta, pizza and salad stations staffed with "delightful" chefs; so what if you "bus your own table", "the price is right", and many "love" the "fresh potted herbs" throughout the space.

Vaso's Kitchen Ⓢ *Greek*

26 | 17 | 24 | $30

Old Town | 1225 Powhatan St. (Bashford Ln.) | Alexandria, VA | 703-548-2747

The "historic BBQ pig" neon sign on the roof of this Old Town "gem" offers no clues as to the "excellent" Greek "comfort food" within; and talk about Southern (Peloponnese, that is) hospitality: expect to be treated "with real warmth" in the "cute, little" dining room or the "nice" patio, so with "moderate" prices ("rare in this area"), it's a "must-try."

Vegetable Garden *Chinese/Vegetarian*

24 | 14 | 22 | $21

White Flint | 11618 Rockville Pike (bet. Nicholson Ln. & Old Georgetown Rd.) | Rockville, MD | 301-468-9301 | www.thevegetablegarden.com

Find out "just how great all-vegetarian, vegan food can be" at this White Flint Chinese, and "never miss a cow again", thanks to an "extensive" menu of dishes so "delicious and inventive", even "omnivores will find something to their tastes"; while some gripe the low-frills space could "use an update", longtime fans "go out of their way" for the "decent" prices and "attentive" service.

Vermilion *American*

26 | 22 | 24 | $51

Old Town | 1120 King St. (bet. Fayette & Henry Sts.) | Alexandria, VA | 703-684-9669 | www.vermilionrestaurant.com

Old Town's "farm-to-table" "jewel" glimmers with a "constantly changing" menu of "wonderfully prepared" New American fare, offered in a "hip", "chic" atmosphere ("romantic" dining room or "lively" bar) where "foodies" rave over the "awesome" tasting menu with wine pairings served by a "fabulous" staff; "terrific lunch deals" and happy-hour specials satisfy those who worry that "prices are a bit high."

Vidalia *Southern*

26 | 24 | 25 | $63

Golden Triangle | 1990 M St. NW (bet. 19th & 20th Sts.) | 202-659-1990 | www.vidaliadc.com

"Southern roots" sprout "undeniably cosmopolitan" blossoms on the "inspired" New American menu at this fine-dining "favorite" in Golden Triangle, where the "impeccable" staff makes each meal "an event in itself"; hidden underground, the "comfortably" "elegant" setting is "just right" for "intimate moments" and "special events", with "witty" cocktails and happy-hour specials in the lounge; P.S. for around $20, the three-course lunch is a "fantastic deal."

Village Bistro *European* ▽ 26 | 20 | 24 | $38

Courthouse | Colonial Vill. | 1723 Wilson Blvd. (bet. Quinn & Rhodes Sts.) | Arlington, VA | 703-522-0284 | www.villagebistro.com

A wide range of "European-style" cuisine that's "excellent for the price" has long been the draw at this Arlington Courthouse "gem" with a French-leaning wine list and "small-town" feel; the "friendliest" staff tends to a cozy, tin-ceilinged bistro-style room "crowded" with everyone from "groups" to "dates."

Villa Mozart ⧄ *Italian* 26 | 21 | 25 | $49

Fairfax | 4009 Chain Bridge Rd. (Main St.), VA | 703-691-4747 | www.villamozartrestaurant.com

Chef-owner Andrea Pace brings a "delicate balance" of "inventive", "delicious" Northern Italian flavors to his "classically elegant" Fairfax ristorante where the "polished" service and "formal yet not intimidating" grayscale environs say "special event"; the "small, quiet" space (perfect for eavesdroppers) encourages reservations, and the prix fixe menus are a welcome option for those who cry "expensive."

Vinifera Wine Bar & Bistro *American* ▽ 23 | 22 | 22 | $45

Reston | Westin Reston Heights | 11750 Sunrise Valley Dr. (Reston Pkwy.), VA | 703-234-3550 | www.viniferabistro.com

"Tucked away" in the Westin Reston Heights, this New American harbors a "vast" vino vault to go with its "ambitious" seasonal menu that includes "little bites with big flavor" in its small plates; the "soothing", glam environment, including a nightclubby lounge and a patio with fire pits, "invites you to get cozy", as do "accommodating" staffers.

Vinoteca *Eclectic* 22 | 21 | 21 | $35

U Street Corridor | 1940 11th St. NW (U St.) | 202-332-9463 | www.vinotecadc.com

It's "fun to eat, drink and socialize" at this "hip" U Street wine bar/bistro with "knowledgeable" servers uncorking "lovely" vintages to match its "tasty" Eclectic "nosh" (though "bottomless mimosas" are the tipple of choice during its "awesome" brunch); pops of red punctuate the "chic", "romantic" interior, and with bocce on the "back patio", "how could you go wrong?"

Virtue Feed & Grain *American* 19 | 23 | 20 | $38

Old Town | 106 S. Union St. (bet. King & Prince Sts.) | Alexandria, VA | 571-970-3669 | www.virtuefeedandgrain.com

A "hip" crowd coalesces in the "rustic"-meets-"urban" confines of this 18th-century granary in Old Town, a "younger bar-scene answer to Restaurant Eve", for midpriced, "elevated" pub grub – though a "disappointed" delegation says it's "not up to the standards" of an Armstrong establishment; still, "hoptails" mixed by "well-trained" bartenders" keep the bar "lively" and fuel the competitive "buzz" upstairs in the game room.

	FOOD	DECOR	SERVICE	COST

🅩 Volt Ⓜ American   28 | 26 | 28 | $104

Frederick | Houck Mansion | 228 N. Market St. (bet. 2nd & 3rd Sts.), MD | 301-696-8658 | www.voltrestaurant.com

An "evening in foodie heaven" awaits at this true "dining destination" in a "beautiful", contemporized 1890s mansion in Frederick, where chef/co-owner Bryan Voltaggio "evokes a sense of wonder" with his "exotically scrumptious" New American meals based on seasonal ingredients; choose from several prix fixe options for dinner, including a "well-choreographed" 21-course "culinary adventure", then let the "incredibly friendly", "top-notch" servers take it from there; "is it expensive? yes – is it really worth it? yes."

Watershed American/Seafood   ∇ 23 | 19 | 23 | $49
(aka Todd Gray's Watershed)

NoMa | Hilton Garden Inn | 1225 First St. NE (bet. M & N Sts.) | 202-534-1350 | www.toddgrayswatershed.com

Todd Gray's "gourmet touch" is on display in the "casual" seafood with a "Southern twist" at this Hilton venue in NoMa, though a mid-Survey chef change and partnership with a management company may outdate the Food rating; a few label the setting "corporate", but many area workers enjoy eating, drinking and "chatting with the bartenders" in the bar/lounge and find its spacious courtyard a "summer treat."

Westend Bistro by Eric Ripert American   22 | 21 | 22 | $57

West End | Ritz-Carlton, Washington DC | 1190 22nd St. NW (M St.) | 202-974-4900 | www.westendbistrodc.com

At chef/author/TV personality Eric Ripert's New American bistro in the Ritz-Carlton, "lovely combinations" of "local", "seasonal" food that "awaken the taste buds" are ferried by a pro crew in a "sleek" and "lively" setting warmed by orange accents; a vocal minority complain it's "overpriced" and "below expectations", but most say it "does not disappoint" and also praise "wonderful" cocktails and happy-hour deals that make the bar a "highlight" for the "ultracool" crowd.

We the Pizza Ⓩ Pizza   22 | 15 | 17 | $16

Capitol Hill | 305 Pennsylania Ave. SE (bet. 3rd & 4th Sts.) | 202-544-4008 | www.wethepizza.com

Spike Mendelsohn's "superb" take on NY-style pizza "could lead to consensus between even the most contentious political opponents" say partisans of his cheap, "no-frills but cute" joint on Capitol Hill (next to his Good Stuff Eatery); beyond slices and pies, "grand-slam" subs and "incredible" jerked sodas are also a draw, so though it's "crowdy" ("all interns, all the time"), most keep "coming back for more."

Wildfire Seafood/Steak   22 | 21 | 22 | $42

Tysons Corner | Tysons Galleria | 1714 International Dr. (Chain Bridge Rd.) | McLean, VA | 703-442-9110 | www.wildfirerestaurant.com

You almost expect to rub shoulders with "gentlemen in three-piece suits and fedoras" in the "dark" and "sophisticated" expanses of this "pricey" Chicago-born surf 'n' turfer with a "1940s" supper club vibe at the Tysons Galleria; "consistent" staffers ferry "large" portions of "delicious" eats and "perfect" martinis through the "bustle" to

FOOD | DECOR | SERVICE | COST

guys and dolls who call it a "great date place"; P.S. the gluten-free options are "fantastic."

Wild Tomato ⬛ *American*

| 22 | 13 | 17 | $28 |

Potomac | 7945 MacArthur Blvd. (Seven Locks Rd.), MD | 301-229-0680 | www.wildtomatorestaurant.com

An "oasis in a food desert", this "sorely needed" Potomac bistro turns out "enjoyable" pizza and other "all-American" "genuine comfort" fare that will "satisfy almost anyone" – and for a "reasonable price"; despite the "informal", "plain" setting, it's often "jammed", though the "young" servers are nevertheless "attentive."

NEW William Jeffrey's Tavern ● *American*

| ▽ 20 | 22 | 18 | $25 |

Arlington | 2301 Columbia Pike (bet. S. Adams & Wayne Sts.), VA | 703-746-6333 | www.williamjeffreystavern.com

This "welcoming" American, a "nice addition to the 'Pike'" in South Arlington, satisfies with a "creative, affordable" tavern menu and an "extensive" craft-beer list; "classy" digs that are part prohibition (speakeasy murals, tin ceilings), part exhibition (flat-screen TVs, communal high-tops) leave most declaring it "a winner."

Willow ⬛ *American*

| 24 | 22 | 22 | $50 |

Ballston | 4301 N. Fairfax Dr. (bet. Taylor & Utah Sts.) | Arlington, VA | 703-465-8800 | www.willowva.com

"Culinary art", in the form of contemporary Americana, awaits at this "fine-dining" bastion in Ballston's "concrete jungle", where "attentive" servers suggest "excellent wine pairings" to accompany the "beautifully presented" seasonal dishes; a "grown-up" crowd appreciates the "relaxed", "elegant" atmosphere (mood lighting, jewel tones, mahogany), a patio with "real trees" (though not willows) and a "clubby" bar serving small plates.

Wine Kitchen ⬛ *American*

| 26 | 24 | 25 | $34 |

NEW Frederick | 50 Carroll Creek Way (Market St.), MD | 301-663-6968
Leesburg | 7 S. King St. (Market St.), VA | 703-777-9463
www.thewinekitchen.com

In Leesburg and Frederick, these New American wine bars "tickle the taste buds" with flights from their "dynamic" vino selection and "phenomenal" "matching" fare, featuring "unusual combinations that work" via small and large plates; the urbanely countrified premises are patrolled by a "friendly" staff, and "reasonable" prices seal the deal.

Wings To Go *Chicken*

| 25 | 16 | 22 | $18 |

Northeast | 3502 12th St. NE (Monroe St.) | 202-529-7619 | www.wingstogodc.com

There's "no atmosphere, but who cares" with such "excellent" wings and so "many different types of sauces" at this Northeast take-out "staple for the college kids and neighborhood folks", which also serves pizza and subs; bonus: the "not-expensive" fare comes "quick" and "friendly."

Woodlands Restaurant *Indian/Vegetarian* | 24 | 15 | 20 | $20 |

Hyattsville | 8046 New Hampshire Ave. (Lebanon St.), MD |
301-434-4202 | www.woodlandsrestaurants.com

"Authentic and delicious" South Indian vegetarian fare is the "main
attraction" at this subcontinental survivor that's also valued by the
Hyattsville hoi polloi for its "cheap, cheap, cheap" prices, especially
during its "excellent" lunch buffet; if the storefront space is "without
a lot of ambiance", it's made up for by "very friendly" service.

Woo Lae Oak *Korean* | 23 | 21 | 18 | $36 |

Tysons Corner | 8240 Leesburg Pike (Chain Bridge Rd.) | Vienna, VA |
703-827-7300 | www.woolaeoak.com

Most give "two thumbs-up" to this "upscale Korean" banquet hall in
Tysons Corner, serving "premium-quality" barbecue (plus other
standards and sushi) in a "vibrant", "elegant" setting that's a "marriage of modern and traditional" Asian decor; "rooftop parking" is
another perk beyond the "attentive" service and moderate prices.

Woomi Garden ◑ *Korean* | 20 | 15 | 19 | $27 |

Wheaton | 2423 Hickerson Dr. (bet. Elkin St. & Rte. 97), MD |
301-933-0100 | www.woomigarden.com

"Get an education" in bibimbop, bulgogi and other Korean staples at
this no-frills Wheaton emissary known for its lunch buffet "bargain", pricier "grill-your-own" barbecue and even sushi from a small
Japanese menu; "pleasant" service helps keep it "jammed", so if you
hate crowds, chill out with a cold sake, or come for a "late" dinner.

X.O. Taste *Chinese* | 24 | 14 | 17 | $24 |

NEW **Germantown** | Middlebrook Vill. | 11542 Middlebrook Rd.
(Frederick Rd.), MD | 240-686-3560
Falls Church | 6124 Arlington Blvd. (Patrick Henry Dr.), VA |
703-536-1630 ◑

Falls Church and Germantown locals challenge their palates with
"outstanding" Hong Kong–style choices from a menu as "huge" as the
portions at this Cantonese pair; there's not "much to look at" (aside
from the lobster tanks), but with service so "friendly" you trust their
suggestions, you're in for "one of the best Chinese meals" around.

Yama *Japanese* | 25 | 18 | 23 | $27 |

Vienna | Jade Plaza | 328 Maple Ave. W. (Nutley St.), VA | 703-242-7703 |
www.sushiyamava.com

"Sit at the bar" and "watch the artistry" unfold at what's an "amazing sushi place for a Vienna strip mall" and that delivers "yummy"
Japanese fare of all stripes (tempura, katsu, noodles) in a minimalist
space; it's a "value for the money", servers are "warm and responsive" and "reservations on weekends" are suggested.

Yamazato *Japanese* | 25 | 18 | 22 | $29 |

Greater Alexandria | Beauregard Sq. | 6303 Little River Tpke.
(Beauregard St.) | Alexandria, VA | 703-914-8877 |
www.yamazato.net

The "perfect balance between modern Western style and [tradi-
tional] Japanese spirit" can be found at this "always consistent" su-

shi spot in Alexandria known for its "fresh, innovative" take on raw fish, "superb" cooked Japanese fare and even a few "delicious" Thai dishes, all at a "great price"; "trendy" green-and-orange decor and an "über-friendly" staff help keep it on rotation as a local "favorite."

Yechon ● *Japanese/Korean* | 22 | 16 | 18 | $23 |

Annandale | 4121 Hummer Rd. (Little River Tpke.), VA | 703-914-4646
"They've got it all" at this budget Annandale Japanese-Korean, from "authentic" barbecue "prepared at your table" to "good" sushi, and "the best part might be" the "little dishes you get before you even or-der" (aka banchan); a low-frills, "hustle-bustle ambiance" requires patience "if you arrive at the peak time", but service from tradition-ally dressed staff is "quick"; P.S. the 24/7 hours are "an added plus."

Yosaku *Japanese* | 21 | 14 | 23 | $29 |

Upper NW | 4712 Wisconsin Ave. NW (Chesapeake St.) | 202-363-4453 | www.yosakusushi.com
The "staff treats everyone like a returning customer" at this Tenleytown "old favorite" dating from "before there was sushi in the grocery store"; it's traditionally "nondescript", but offers a "huge value" on "traditional" and "creative" raw fish and other Japanese dishes, in particular the "bargain lunch and "deal" of a happy hour.

Yuan Fu *Chinese/Vegetarian* | 25 | 16 | 23 | $20 |

Rockville | 798 Rockville Pike (Wootton Pkwy.), MD | 301-762-5937 | www.yuanfuvegetarian.com
Converts report they went in "skeptical" and "came out a true be-liever" thanks to an "incredible menu" of "mock meats" that'll make "you wonder 'how'd they do it?'" at this reasonably priced Chinese vegan haven in Rockville; it "doesn't look like much from the out-side", and inside it's "tight quarters", but the "warm" service has ha-bitués feeling "like family."

Yves Bistro *French* | 25 | 21 | 21 | $27 |

Old Town | 235 Swamp Fox Rd. (Eisenhower Ave.) | Alexandria, VA | 703-329-1010 | www.yvesbistrova.com
For a "warm", "down-to-earth" French dining experience, this "charming" peach-colored bistro/cafe in Old Town (across from the Eisenhower Avenue Metro stop and AMC cinema) has connoisseurs raving about its "excellent" "home-cooked" provincial fare; it's an "outstanding value" for the "quality", from breakfast through dinner, and the "friendly" owner "seems to be working at all times."

🅩 Zaytinya *Mediterranean/Mideastern* | 26 | 24 | 22 | $43 |

Penn Quarter | Pepco Bldg. | 701 Ninth St. NW (G St.) | 202-638-0800 | www.zaytinya.com
"Who can resist" the "wonders" of chef José Andrés' "unbelievably tasty" Eastern Mediterranean meze, especially when paired with "phenomenal" regional wines in a "beautiful, light and airy" setting close to everything in the Penn Quarter; the city's "enduring" "love affair" with this "crazy, loud" stunner means reservations are "highly recommended", but once your "culinary tour" is booked, a "helpful

FOOD | DECOR | SERVICE | COST

staff" will be your "guide" – just beware: it's "hard to keep the bill down with so many tempting small plates."

Zeffirelli Ristorante *Italian*   24 | 21 | 25 | $43
Herndon | 728 Pine St. (Station St.), VA | 703-318-7000 |
www.zeffirelliristorante.com

"It's hard to resist" the "wonderful" signature veal chop say longtime customers who look to this Herndon Italian mainstay as a setting for a "special occasion" or "romantic evening", with its "pleasant" candlelit setting; it's expensive, but the "extensive" wine list and "warm", family-owned atmosphere make it a comfortable fit, time and again.

Zengo *Asian/Pan-Latin*   22 | 23 | 20 | $41
Chinatown | Gallery Pl. | 781 Seventh St. NW (bet. F & H Sts.) |
202-393-2929 | www.richardsandoval.com

This Chinatown outpost of Richard Sandoval's Asian-Latin fusion concept is "always buzzing" with groups of "adventuresome" friends sampling "creative", if "somewhat pricey", small plates ferried by a professional crew; the "sexy", "Vegasy vibe" appeals to PYTs who take full advantage of the "terrific", "heavy-on-the-booze" cocktails and "great" happy hour.

Zentan *Asian*   22 | 22 | 20 | $43
Downtown | Donovan Hse. | 1155 14th St. NW (Massachusetts Ave.) |
202-379-4366 | www.zentanrestaurant.com

"Trendsetting cocktails" draw a "wild, fun" bar crowd to this "hip" Downtown hotel resto-lounge where diners feast on "delicious" dishes from "celebrity" chef Susur Lee's Asian repertoire, most notably his "addictive" Singapore slaw and "fresh, innovative" sushi; it's "pricey", and service is just "ok", but most find it "delightful" chilling in the "sleek", sexy "black-lacquered" digs.

Zest, An American Bistro *American*   21 | 18 | 22 | $32
Capitol Hill | 735 Eighth St. SE (bet. G & I Sts.) | 202-544-7171 |
www.zestbistro.com

"Easy to miss" on Capitol Hill's Barracks Row, this "solid", "moderately" priced New American bistro charms neighborhood denizens with its "tasty sandwiches", Tuesday nights' half-off wine bottles ("just have a ride ready") and a "cheerful" staff; a "nice mix of couples, groups and families" fills the "small but bustling" brick-walled space, although it's "lovely to sit outside on a fine day."

Zorba's Cafe ● *Greek*   23 | 16 | 20 | $20
Dupont Circle | 1612 20th St. NW (Hillyer Pl.) | 202-387-8555 |
www.zorbascafe.com

This "cheap Greek stays the same" say Dupont Circle denizens who appreciate the perennial nature of the bi-level blue-and-white "hole-in-the-wall" where you "order at the counter" and "lug your pungent kebabs or salty-good salad" outside for "people-watching" and Hellenic "background music" or upstairs for "nice views"; solid service aids in its forte: a "quick, casual meal."

BALTIMORE, ANNAPOLIS AND THE EASTERN SHORE

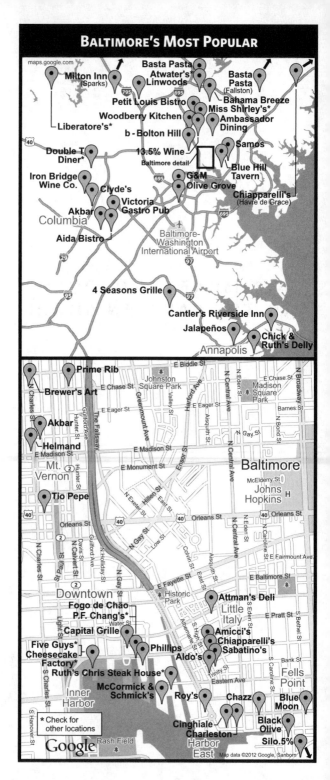

BALTIMORE'S MOST POPULAR

maps.google.com

Milton Inn (Sparks)
Basta Pasta
Atwater's*
Linwoods
Basta Pasta (Fallston)
Petit Louis Bistro
Bahama Breeze
Miss Shirley's*
Woodberry Kitchen
Ambassador Dining
Liberatore's*
b - Bolton Hill
13.5% Wine
Baltimore detail
Samos
Double T Diner*
Blue Hill Tavern
Iron Bridge Wine Co.
G&M
Olive Grove
Chiapparelli's (Havre de Grace)
Clyde's
Victoria Gastro Pub
Akbar
Columbia
Aida Bistro
Baltimore-Washington International Airport
4 Seasons Grille
Cantler's Riverside Inn
Jalapeños
Chick & Ruth's Delly
Annapolis

Prime Rib
Brewer's Art
E Biddle St
Johnston Square Park
E Chase St
Madison Square Park
E Eager St
E Chase St
E Eager St
Barnes St
Akbar
Helmand
Mt. Vernon
E Madison St
E Monument St
Baltimore
McElderry St
Johns Hopkins
Tio Pepe
Orleans St
Orleans St
Downtown
E Fayette St
Historic Park
Little Italy
Attman's Deli
E Pratt St
Fogo de Chao
P.F. Chang's*
Capital Grille
Amicci's
Chiapparelli's
Sabatino's
Phillips
Aldo's
Five Guys*
Cheesecake Factory*
Ruth's Chris Steak House*
Fells Point
McCormick & Schmick's
Roy's
Chazz
Blue Moon
Inner Harbor
★ Check for other locations
Cinghiale
Charleston
Black Olive
Silo.5%
Rash Field
Google
Harbor East
Map data ©2012 Google, Sanborn

Baltimore's Most Popular

All restaurants are in the Baltimore area unless otherwise noted (A=Annapolis and E=Eastern Shore). When a restaurant has locations both inside and out of the city limits, we include the notation BA as well.

1. Woodberry Kitchen | *American*
2. Double T Diner/A/BA | *Diner*
3. Prime Rib | *Steak*
4. Charleston | *American*
5. G&M | *Seafood*
6. Miss Shirley's/A/BA | *American*
7. 4 Seasons Grille | *Eclectic/Med.*
8. Tio Pepe | *Continental/Spanish*
9. Cinghiale | *Italian*
10. Sabatino's | *Italian*
11. Brewer's Art | *American*
12. Liberatore's | *Italian*
13. Petit Louis Bistro | *French*
14. Clyde's | *American*
15. Chiapparelli's | *Italian*
16. 13.5% Wine Bar/Silo | *American*
17. Linwoods | *American*
18. Helmand | *Afghan*
19. Aldo's | *Italian*
20. Black Olive | *Greek/Seafood*
21. Jalapeños/A | *Mexican/Spanish*
22. Blue Moon Cafe | *American*
23. Phillips | *Seafood*
24. Atwater's | *Bakery*
25. Iron Bridge Wine Co. | *Amer.*
26. Samos | *Greek*
27. Attman's Delicatessen | *Deli*
28. Amicci's | *Italian*
29. Akbar | *Indian*
30. Blue Hill Tavern | *American*
31. Cantler's Riverside/A | *Crab Hse.*
32. Victoria Gastro Pub | *Eclectic*
33. Olive Grove | *Italian*
34. Chick & Ruth's Delly/A | *Diner*
35. b – Bolton Hill Bistro | *Amer.*
36. Basta Pasta | *Italian*
37. Ambassador Dining | *Indian*
38. Chazz: A Bronx Orig. | *Ital./Pizza*
39. Aida Bistro & Wine Bar | *Italian*
40. Milton Inn | *American*

Many of the above restaurants are among the Baltimore area's most expensive, but if popularity were calibrated to price, a number of other restaurants would surely join their ranks. To illustrate this, we have added two lists comprising 60 Best Buys on page 232.

MOST POPULAR CHAINS

1. Cheesecake/A/BA | *Amer.*
2. Five Guys/A/BA | *Burgers*
3. P.F. Chang's/A/BA | *Chinese*
4. Ruth's Chris/A/BA/E | *Steak*
5. Fogo de Chão | *Braz./Steak*
6. Bahama Breeze | *Caribbean*
7. Capital Grille | *Steak*
8. Roy's | *Hawaiian*
9. McCormick/A/BA | *Seafood*
10. Fleming's Prime | *Steak*

KEY NEWCOMERS

Our editors' picks among this year's arrivals. See full list at p. 236.

Artifact Coffee | *Coffeehouse*

Earth, Wood & Fire | *Pizza*

Food Market | *Amer.*

Fork & Wrench | *Amer.*

Heavy Seas | *Pub Food*

Hersh's Pizza | *Pizza*

Of Love & Regret | *Amer.*

Pabu | *Japanese*

Thames St. | *Seafood*

Wit & Wisdom | *Amer.*

Top Food

29 | Charleston | *American*

28 | Di Pasquale's | *Italian*
Samos | *Greek*
Vin 909/A | *American*
Bartlett Pear Inn/E | *American*
Prime Rib | *Steak*
Tersiguel's | *French*
Out of the Fire/E | *Amer./Eclec.*
Sushi King | *Japanese*
Milton Inn | *American*
Aldo's | *Italian*
Lewnes' Steak/A | *Steak*

Scossa/E | *Italian*

27 | Koco's | *Pub Food*
Osteria 177/A | *Italian*
Mekong Delta | *Viet.*
R & R Taqueria | *Mexican*
Linwoods | *American*
Peter's Inn | *American*
Salt | *American*
Bon Fresco | *Sandwiches*
Black Olive | *Greek/Seafood*
Woodberry Tavern | *American*
Broom's Bloom | *Ice Cream*
Chicken Rico | *Peruvian*

BY CUISINE

AMERICAN (NEW)

29 | Charleston
28 | Vin 909/A
Bartlett Pear Inn/E
Out of the Fire/E
Milton Inn

AMERICAN (TRAD.)

26 | Miss Shirley's/A/BA
25 | Friendly Farm
Harry Browne's/A
24 | Stanford Grill
Open Door

CHINESE

26 | Red Pearl
Szechuan House
25 | Grace's Fortune
David Chu's
23 | Hunan Manor

CRAB HOUSES

26 | Faidley's
25 | Costas Inn
24 | Harris Crab/E
Cantler's Riverside/A
23 | Gunning's Seafood

FRENCH

28 | Tersiguel's
27 | Les Folies/A
Antrim 1844
26 | Petit Louis
25 | Café Normandie/A

GREEK

28 | Samos
27 | Black Olive

25 | Paul's Homewood/A
24 | Olive Room▽
23 | Ikaros

INDIAN

25 | Ambassador Dining
24 | Akbar
23 | House of India

ITALIAN

28 | Di Pasquale's
Aldo's
Scossa/E
27 | Osteria 177/A
Ava's/E

JAPANESE

28 | Sushi King
27 | Joss Cafe/A/BA
Sushi Sono
Kobe
26 | Sushi Hana

MEXICAN/SPANISH

27 | R & R Taqueria
Jalapeños/A
26 | Tio Pepe
25 | Mari Luna Latin Grill
24 | Mari Luna Mexican Grill

PIZZA

27 | Johnny Rad's
Iggies
Ava's/E
Matthew's Pizza
24 | Joe Squared

---

*Indicates a tie with restaurant above; excludes places with low votes

PUB FOOD

27 Koco's
   Johnny Rad's
24 Hamilton Tavern
   Galway Bay/A
23 McCabe's

SEAFOOD

27 Black Olive
26 Jerry's Seafood
   Faidley's
   Seaside Restaurant
   Catonsville Gourmet

STEAKHOUSES

28 Prime Rib
   Lewnes' Steak/A
26 Capital Grille
   Ruth's Chris/A/BA/E
   Morton's

THAI

26 Thai Arroy
25 Lemongrass/A
23 Bân Thai

BY SPECIAL FEATURE

BREAKFAST

26 Miss Shirley's/A/BA
25 Blue Moon
   Main Ingredient/A
   Goldberg's
24 Open Door

BRUNCH

26 b – Bolton Hill Bistro
   Orchard Mkt.
24 Harryman Hse.
23 City Cafe
22 Gertrude's

BUSINESS DINING

29 Charleston
28 Lewnes' Steak/A
27 Linwoods
   Roy's
26 Capital Grille

HOTEL DINING

28 Bartlett Pear Inn/E
27 Antrim 1844
26 Ruth's Chris (Sheraton Pier 5)
   Morton's
   (Sheraton Inner Harbor)
25 Salter's Tavern/E
   (Robert Morris)

MEET FOR A DRINK

28 Out of the Fire/E
   Lewnes' Steak/A
26 Cinghiale
24 Victoria Gastro Pub
23 B&O

NEWCOMERS (RATED)

23 Wit & Wisdom
22 Waterfront Kit.
19 Bond St. Social

POWER SCENES

29 Charleston
28 Prime Rib
   Lewnes' Steak/A
27 Linwoods
   Woodberry Kitchen

QUICK BITES

28 Samos
27 R & R Taqueria
   Bon Fresco
   Attman's Deli
26 Faidley's

TRENDY

28 Out of the Fire/E
27 Osteria 177/A
24 Chazz
22 13.5% Wine Bar/Silo
19 Bond St. Social

WATERSIDE

24 Cantler's Riverside/A
23 Carrol's Creek/A
   Wit & Wisdom
22 Rusty Scupper
   Waterfront Kitchen

WORTH A TRIP

28 Lewnes' Steak/A (Eastport)
27 Broom's Bloom (Bel Air)
   Antrim 1844 (Taneytown)
26 O'Learys/A (Eastport)
25 Salter's Tavern/E (Oxford)

BY LOCATION

ANNAPOLIS

28 Vin 909
27 Osteria 177
Joss Cafe
Les Folies Brasserie
Jalapeños

COLUMBIA

28 Sushi King
27 Bon Fresco
Sushi Sono
26 Red Pearl
25 Iron Bridge Wine Co.

EASTERN SHORE

28 Bartlett Pear Inn
Out of the Fire
Scossa
27 Ava's
26 Ruth's Chris

EASTPORT

28 Lewnes' Steak
26 Ruth's Chris
O'Learys Seafood
23 Carrol's Creek
22 Boatyard Bar & Gril

FELLS POINT

27 Peter's Inn
Salt
Black Olive
Johnny Rad's
25 Kali's Court

HAMPDEN

26 Dogwood
25 Grano Pasta Bar
24 Corner BYOB
23 McCabe's
Alchemy

HARBOR EAST

29 Charleston
27 Roy's
26 Cinghiale

25 Pazo
Fleming's Prime

INNER HARBOR

27 Fogo de Chão
26 Capital Grille
Ruth's Chris
Morton's
Miss Shirley's

LITTLE ITALY

28 Aldo's
26 La Tavola
La Scala
25 Da Mimmo
24 Amicci's

LUTHERVILLE/
TIMONIUM

26 Sushi Hana
Szechuan House
24 Liberatore's
Edo Sushi
23 BlueStone

MT. VERNON

28 Prime Rib
27 Joss Cafe
Helmand
26 Sotto Sopra
Tio Pepe

SOUTH BALTIMORE

26 Thai Arroy
24 Bluegrass
23 Regi's
Mr. Rain's Fun House
22 Blue Agave

TOWSON

26 Sushi Hana
Orchard Mkt.
25 Atwater's
24 Five Guys
Pho Dat Thanh

Top Decor

29 Charleston	Aldo's
	Ambassador Dining
27 Antrim 1844	Prime Rib
Pazo	Scossa/E
Wit & Wisdom	Kali's Court
Elkridge Furnace Inn	Oregon Grille
26 Milton Inn	
Mr. Rain's Fun House	25 Reynolds Tavern/A
Linwoods	Severn Inn/A
Cinghiale	Blue Hill Tavern
Woodberry Kitchen	Vin 909/A

OUTDOORS

Ambassador Dining	Mr. Rain's Fun House
Bartlett Pear Inn/E	Olive Room
b – Bolton Hill Bistro	Oregon Grille
Carrol's Creek	Tapas Teatro
Gertrude's	13.5% Wine/Silo (Locust Pt.)
Kali's Court	Wine Market

ROMANCE

Aldo's	Linwoods
Ambassador Dining	Milton Inn
Antrim 1844	Narrows/E
Charleston	Scossa/E
Elkridge Furnace Inn	Sotto Sopra
Kali's Court	Tersiguel's

ROOMS

Bond St. Social	Linwoods
Charleston	Oceanaire
Cinghiale	Prime Rib
Della Notte	Sotto Sopra
Fork & Wrench	Wit & Wisdom
Kali's Court	Woodberry Kitchen

VIEWS

Broom's Bloom	Severn Inn/A
Carrol's Creek/A	Tabrizi's
Friendly Farm	13.5% Wine/Silo (Locust Pt.)
Kentmorr	Tidewater Grille
Olive Room	Waterfront Kitchen
Rusty Scupper	Wit & Wisdom

Top Service

Best Buys

In order of rating.

OTHER GOOD VALUES

BALTIMORE & ENVIRONS
OTHER USEFUL LISTS*

---

* These lists include low vote places that do not qualify for top lists.

Special Features

Listings cover the best in each category and include names, locations and Food ratings. Multi-location restaurants' features may vary by branch.

BREAKFAST

(See also Hotel Dining)

Miss Shirley's | **multi.**	26
Blue Moon | **Fells Pt**	25
Main Ingredient | **Annap**	25
Goldberg's | **Pikesville**	25
Breakfast Shoppe | **Severna Pk**	25
Open Door | **Bel Air**	24
Stone Mill | **Brook'ville**	24
Chick/Ruth's | **Annap**	22
Double T | **multi.**	20
Baugher's | **Westminster**	20
Jimmy's | **Fells Pt**	20
NEW Artifact Coffee | **Clipper Mill**	–

BRUNCH

b | **Bolton Hill**	26
Orchard Mkt. | **Towson**	26
Main Ingredient | **Annap**	25
Ambassador | **Homewood**	25
Harryman Hse. | **Reist'town**	24
Woman's Industrial | **Mt. Vernon**	24
Regi's | **S Balt**	23
Carrol's Creek | **Annap**	23
Jesse Wong's Asean | **Columbia**	23
Ze Mean Bean | **Fells Pt**	23
City Cafe | **Mt. Vernon**	23
Gertrude's | **Charles Vill**	22
Bertha's | **Fells Pt**	22
Clyde's | **Columbia**	22
Jesse Wong's Kit. | **Hunt Valley**	20

BUSINESS DINING

Charleston | **Harbor E**	29
Lewnes' Steak | **Annap**	28
Linwoods | **Owings Mills**	27
Roy's | **Harbor E**	27
Capital Grille | **Inner Harbor**	26
Ruth's Chris | **Inner Harbor**	26
Morton's | **Inner Harbor**	26
Cinghiale | **Harbor E**	26
Sullivan's Steak | **Inner Harbor**	25
Carpaccio | **Annap**	25
Fleming's Steak | **Harbor E**	25
Harry Browne | **Annap**	25
Oceanaire | **Harbor E**	24
La Famiglia | **Homewood**	22
Clyde's | **Columbia**	22
Greystone Grill | **Ellicott City**	19

BYO

Spice & Dice | **Towson**	29
Samos | **Gr'town**	28
Mekong Delta | **D'town W**	27
R & R Taqueria | **Elkridge**	27
Iggies | **Mt. Vernon**	27
Sushi Hana | **Timonium**	26
Thai Arroy | **S Balt**	26
Catonsville Gourm. | **Catonsville**	26
Andy Nelson's | **Cockeysville**	26
Orchard Mkt. | **Towson**	26
Blue Moon | **Fells Pt**	25
Atwater's | **multi.**	25
Grano | **Hampden**	25
Sofi's Crepes | **York Rd Corr**	24
Edo Sushi | **multi.**	24
Corner BYOB | **Hampden**	24
Woman's Industrial | **Mt. Vernon**	24
Regions | **Catonsville**	23
Wild Orchid | **Annap**	23
Havana Rd. | **Towson**	21
Meet 27 | **Charles Vill**	21
NEW Poor Boy | **Severna Pk**	–

CHILD-FRIENDLY

(Alternatives to the usual fast-food places; * children's menu available)

Woodberry Kit.* | **Clipper Mill**	27
Broom's Bloom | **Bel Air**	27
b* | **Bolton Hill**	26
Friendly Farm* | **Upperco**	25
Ann's Dari* | **Glen Burnie**	25
Open Door* | **Bel Air**	24
Five Guys* | **multi.**	24
Hunan Manor | **Columbia**	23
P.F. Chang's | **Columbia**	23
Grilled Cheese* | **multi.**	22
Chick/Ruth's* | **Annap**	22
Red Hot/Blue* | **Laurel**	22
Clyde's* | **Columbia**	22
Double T* | **multi.**	20
Baugher's* | **Westminster**	20
Cafe Hon* | **Hampden**	16

DESSERT SPECIALISTS

Broom's Bloom | **Bel Air**	27
Main Ingredient | **Annap**	25
Paul's Homewood | **Annap**	25
Cheesecake | **Inner Harbor**	24
Stone Mill | **Brook'ville**	24

Gunning's Seafood | **multi.**	23
City Cafe | **Mt. Vernon**	23
NEW Wit/Wisdom | **Harbor E**	23
Teavolve | **Harbor E**	23
Chick/Ruth's | **Annap**	22
Crêpe du Jour | **Mt. Wash**	21
Dangerously Delicious | **Canton**	21
Baugher's | **Westminster**	20
Cafe Hon | **Hampden**	16

ENTERTAINMENT

(Call for days and times of performances)

Sotto Sopra | opera | **Mt. Vernon**	26
Joe Squared | live music | **D'town N**	24
Germano's | cabaret | **Little Italy**	24
Jesse Wong's Asean | jazz | **Columbia**	23
Ze Mean Bean | jazz | **Fells Pt**	23
Gertrude's | jazz | **Charles Vill**	22
Bertha's | blues/jazz | **Fells Pt**	22
49 West | live music | **Annap**	22
Boatyard B&G | live music | **Annap**	22
Tabrizi's | piano | **S Balt**	21
Rockfish | acoustic/jazz | **Annap**	20

FIREPLACES

Bartlett Pear | **E Shore**	28
Milton Inn | **Sparks**	28
Cafe Bretton | **Severna Pk**	27
Antrim 1844 | **Taneytown**	27
Jalapeños | **Annap**	27
Mason's | **E Shore**	26
Petit Louis | **Roland Pk**	26
Elkridge Furnace | **Elkridge**	25
Kentmorr | **E Shore**	25
Café Normandie | **Annap**	25
Salter's Tav. | **E Shore**	25
Oregon Grille | **Hunt Valley**	25
Iron Bridge Wine | **Columbia**	25
Harry Browne | **Annap**	25
Ambassador | **Homewood**	25
Da Mimmo | **Little Italy**	25
Stanford Grill | **Columbia**	24
Kings Contrivance | **Columbia**	24
Liberatore's | **Eldersburg**	24
Harryman Hse. | **Reist'town**	24
Manor Tav. | **Monkton**	24
Regi's | **S Balt**	23
Pappas | **NE Balt**	23
Ze Mean Bean | **Fells Pt**	23
Langermann's | **Canton**	22
Patrick's | **Cockeysville**	22
Ciao Bella | **Little Italy**	22
La Famiglia | **Homewood**	22

Tidewater | **Havre de Grace**	22
Tabrizi's | **S Balt**	21
Sammy's Tratt. | **Mt. Vernon**	21
Peerce's | **Phoenix**	21
NEW Bond St. Social | **Fells Pt**	19
Theo's | **E Shore**	-

HISTORIC PLACES

(Year opened; * building)

1710 | Salter's Tav.* | **E Shore**	25
1740 | Milton Inn* | **Sparks**	28
1744 | Elkridge Furnace* | **Elkridge**	25
1747 | Reynolds Tav.* | **Annap**	23
1772 | Faidley's* | **D'town W**	26
1799 | Peter's Inn* | **Fells Pt**	27
1820 | Bertha's* | **Fells Pt**	22
1844 | Antrim 1844* | **Taneytown**	27
1865 | Henninger's* | **Fells Pt**	25
1880 | Pope's Tav.* | **E Shore**	27
1880 | Woman's Industrial* | **Mt. Vernon**	24
1886 | Mason's* | **E Shore**	26
1890 | Lewnes' Steak* | **Annap**	28
1890 | Petit Louis* | **Roland Pk**	26
1900 | Kings Contrivance* | **Columbia**	24
1905 | Annabel Lee* | **Hi'town**	26
1905 | Brewer's Art* | **Mt. Vernon**	25
1914 | Di Pasquale's | **E Balt**	28
1915 | Attman's Deli | **E Balt**	27
1920 | Josef's* | **Fallston**	25
1920 | Hamilton Tav.* | **NE Balt**	24
1940 | Chiapparelli's | **Little Italy**	24
1943 | Matthew's Pizza | **Hi'town**	27
1947 | Jimmy's | **Fells Pt**	20
1948 | Baugher's | **Westminster**	20
1949 | Paul's Homewood | **Annap**	25

HOTEL DINING

Antrim 1844	
Antrim 1844 Smokehouse | **Taneytown**	27
Bartlett Pear Inn	
Bartlett Pear | **E Shore**	28
Four Seasons Baltimore	
NEW Wit/Wisdom | **Harbor E**	23
NEW Pabu | **Harbor E**	-
Inn at Black Olive	
Olive Rm. | **Fells Pt**	24
Monaco	
B&O | **D'town**	23
Oxford Inn	
Pope's Tav. | **E Shore**	27
Pier 5	
Ruth's Chris | **Inner Harbor**	26

McCormick/Schmick | **Inner Harbor** — 23

Reynolds Tavern
Reynolds Tav. | **Annap** — 23

Robert Morris Inn
Salter's Tav. | **E Shore** — 25

Sheraton Inner Harbor
Morton's | **Inner Harbor** — 26

LATE DINING

(Weekday closing hour)

Johnny Rad's | 2 AM | **Fells Pt** — 27
Jalapeños | 12 AM | **Annap** — 27
Annabel Lee | 12:30 AM | **Hi'town** — 26
Szechuan Hse. | 12 AM | **Lutherville** — 26
Costas Inn | 1 AM | **Dundalk** — 25
Tsunami | 1 AM | **Annap** — 25
Tapas Teatro | 12 AM | **D'town N** — 24
Joe Squared | 12 AM | **D'town** — 24
Sabatino's | varies | **Little Italy** — 24
Talara | 12 AM | **Harbor E** — 24
Michael's Café | 2 AM | **Timonium** — 23
Honey Pig | 24 hrs. | **Ellicott City** — 23
Alewife | 1 AM | **D'town W** — 22
Ale Marys | 2 AM | **Fells Pt** — 22
Kooper's | 2 AM | **Fells Pt** — 22
Nacho Mama's | 2 AM | **Canton** — 22
Clyde's | 12 AM | **Columbia** — 22
49 West | 12 AM | **Annap** — 22
🆕 Waterfront Kit. | 2 AM | **Fells Pt** — 22
Towson Diner | 24 hrs. | **Towson** — 21
Rocket/Venus | 2 AM | **Hampden** — 20
Double T | varies | **multi.** — 20
Rockfish | varies | **Annap** — 20
Dizz | 2AM | **Hampden** — 19
🆕 Bond St. Social | 2 AM | **Fells Pt** — 19
Sip & Bite | 24 hrs. | **Fells Pt** — 19
🆕 Heavy Seas | 12 AM | **Harbor E** — 19
🆕 Food Market | 2 AM | **Hampden** — ⌐
🆕 Fork & Wrench | 2 AM | **Canton** — ⌐
🆕 Kettle Hill | 12 AM | **D'town** — ⌐
🆕 Museum | 2 AM | **Mt. Vernon** — ⌐
🆕 Of Love/Regret | 2 AM | **Canton** — ⌐
🆕 Plug Ugly's | 2 AM | **Canton** — ⌐
🆕 Townhouse | 2 AM | **Harbor E** — ⌐

MEET FOR A DRINK

Out of the Fire | **E Shore** — 28
Lewnes' Steak | **Annap** — 28
Capital Grille | **Inner Harbor** — 26
Annabel Lee | **Hi'town** — 26
Cinghiale | **Harbor E** — 26
Henninger's | **Fells Pt** — 25
Carpaccio | **Annap** — 25
Iron Bridge Wine | **Columbia** — 25
Pazo | **Harbor E** — 25
Brewer's Art | **Mt. Vernon** — 25
Bistro Rx | **Hi'town** — 25
Galway Bay | **Annap** — 24
Wine Mkt. | **Locust Pt** — 24
Café de Paris | **Columbia** — 24
🆕 Thames St. | **Fells Pt** — 24
Liberatore's | **multi.** — 24
Aida | **Columbia** — 24
Victoria Gastro | **Columbia** — 24
Talara | **Harbor E** — 24
Chazz | **Harbor E** — 24
Manor Tav. | **Monkton** — 24
B&O | **D'town** — 23
City Cafe | **Mt. Vernon** — 23
Azul 17 | **Columbia** — 23
One-Eyed Mike | **Fells Pt** — 23
Crush | **York Rd Corr** — 23
🆕 Wit/Wisdom | **Harbor E** — 23
Teavolve | **Harbor E** — 23
Banning's | **E Shore** — 22
Clyde's | **Columbia** — 22
Porters | **S Balt** — 22
Vino Rosina | **Harbor E** — 22
13.5%/Silo | **Hampden** — 22
Brass. Brightwell | **E Shore** — 21
Tark's Grill | **Brook'ville** — 21
Rocket/Venus | **Hampden** — 20
John Steven | **Fells Pt** — 20
🆕 Bond St. Social | **Fells Pt** — 19
🆕 Heavy Seas | **Harbor E** — 19
🆕 Earth/Wood/Fire | **N Balt** — ⌐
🆕 Food Market | **Hampden** — ⌐
🆕 Fork & Wrench | **Canton** — ⌐
🆕 Kettle Hill | **D'town** — ⌐
🆕 Of Love/Regret | **Canton** — ⌐
🆕 Townhouse | **Harbor E** — ⌐

NEWCOMERS

Ten Ten | **Harbor E** — 25
Thames St. | **Fells Pt** — 24
Stang/Siam | **Mt. Vernon** — 23
Wit/Wisdom | **Harbor E** — 23
Waterfront Kit. | **Fells Pt** — 22
Bond St. Social | **Fells Pt** — 19

Heavy Seas	**Harbor E**	19
Adam's Eve	**Canton**	-
Artifact Coffee	**Clipper Mill**	-
Clementine/Creative	**Hi'town**	-
Dempsey's Brew	**Camden Yds**	-
Earth/Wood/Fire	**N Balt**	-
Food Market	**Hampden**	-
Fork & Wrench	**Canton**	-
Hersh's Pizza	**S Balt**	-
Kettle Hill	**D'town**	-
Museum	**Mt. Vernon**	-
Of Love/Regret	**Canton**	-
Pabu	**Harbor E**	-
Plug Ugly's	**Canton**	-
Poor Boy	**Severna Pk**	-
Theo's	**E Shore**	-
Townhouse	**Harbor E**	-
208 Talbot	**E Shore**	-

OUTDOOR DINING

Charleston	**Harbor E**	29
Bartlett Pear	**E Shore**	28
Prime Rib	**Mt. Vernon**	28
Tersiguel's	**Ellicott City**	28
Milton Inn	**Sparks**	28
Linwoods	**Owings Mills**	27
Peter's Inn	**Fells Pt**	27
Sotto Sopra	**Mt. Vernon**	26
Mason's	**E Shore**	26
Cinghiale	**Harbor E**	26
b	**Bolton Hill**	26
Kali's Ct.	**Fells Pt**	25
Mari Luna Latin	**Pikesville**	25
Kentmorr	**E Shore**	25
Oregon Grille	**Hunt Valley**	25
Ambassador	**Homewood**	25
Oceanaire	**Harbor E**	24
Wine Mkt.	**Locust Pt**	24
Tapas Teatro	**D'town N**	24
Harris Crab	**E Shore**	24
Mari Luna Mex.	**multi.**	24
Stone Mill	**Brook'ville**	24
Cantler's Riverside	**Annap**	24
Reynolds Tav.	**Annap**	23
Carrol's Creek	**Annap**	23
BlueStone	**Timonium**	23
McCormick/Schmick	**Inner Harbor**	23
City Cafe	**Mt. Vernon**	23
Wild Orchid	**Annap**	23
Gertrude's	**Charles Vill**	22
Crab Claw	**E Shore**	21
Tabrizi's	**S Balt**	21
Crêpe du Jour	**Mt. Wash**	21
Tark's Grill	**Brook'ville**	21

Carlyle Club	**Homewood**	21
John Steven	**Fells Pt**	20
NEW Plug Ugly's	**Canton**	-

PEOPLE-WATCHING

Faidley's	**D'town W**	26
Pazo	**Harbor E**	25
Harry Browne	**Annap**	25
Sabatino's	**Little Italy**	24
Victoria Gastro	**Columbia**	24
Honey Pig	**Ellicott City**	23
Chick/Ruth's	**Annap**	22
Jimmy's	**Fells Pt**	20
NEW Dempsey's Brew	**Camden Yds**	-
NEW Food Market	**Hampden**	-
NEW Museum	**Mt. Vernon**	-

POWER SCENES

Charleston	**Harbor E**	29
Prime Rib	**Mt. Vernon**	28
Lewnes' Steak	**Annap**	28
Linwoods	**Owings Mills**	27
Woodberry Kit.	**Clipper Mill**	27
Capital Grille	**Inner Harbor**	26
Miss Shirley's	**multi.**	26
Harry Browne	**Annap**	25
Banning's	**E Shore**	22

PRIVATE ROOMS

(Restaurants charge less at off times; call for capacity)

Charleston	**Harbor E**	29
Tersiguel's	**Ellicott City**	28
Milton Inn	**Sparks**	28
Lewnes' Steak	**Annap**	28
Broom's Bloom	**Bel Air**	27
Antrim 1844	**Taneytown**	27
Capital Grille	**Inner Harbor**	26
Morton's	**Inner Harbor**	26
Cinghiale	**Harbor E**	26
O'Learys	**Annap**	26
Elkridge Furnace	**Elkridge**	25
Kali's Mezze	**Fells Pt**	25
Oregon Grille	**Hunt Valley**	25
Pazo	**Harbor E**	25
Fleming's Steak	**Harbor E**	25
Harry Browne	**Annap**	25
Kings Contrivance	**Columbia**	24
Sabatino's	**Little Italy**	24
Ikaros	**Gr'town**	23
Portalli's	**Ellicott City**	22
La Famiglia	**Homewood**	22
Clyde's	**Columbia**	22
Greystone Grill	**Ellicott City**	19

BALTIMORE AREA

SPECIAL FEATURES

Cafe Hon | **Hampden** 16
NEW Museum | **Mt. Vernon** -
NEW Pabu | **Harbor E** -

PRIX FIXE MENUS

(Call for prices and times)
Charleston | **Harbor E** 29
Tersiguel's | **Ellicott City** 28
Milton Inn | **Sparks** 28
Antrim 1844 | **Taneytown** 27
Petit Louis | **Roland Pk** 26
Café de Paris | **Columbia** 24
Wild Orchid | **Annap** 23
Luna Blu | **Annap** 22
Tabrizi's | **S Balt** 21
Jesse Wong's Kit. | **Hunt Valley** 20

QUIET CONVERSATION

Dogwood | **Hampden** 26
Paul's Homewood | **Annap** 25
Little Spice | **Hanover** 25
Ambassador | **Homewood** 25
Great Sage | **Clarksville** 24
Mari Luna Mex. | **Mt. Vernon** 24
Woman's Industrial | **Mt. Vernon** 24
Bân Thai | **Mt. Vernon** 23
Teavolve | **Harbor E** 23
Havana Rd. | **Towson** 21
Meet 27 | **Charles Vill** 21
NEW Pabu | **Harbor E** -

ROMANTIC PLACES

Charleston | **Harbor E** 29
Tersiguel's | **Ellicott City** 28
Milton Inn | **Sparks** 28
Aldo's | **Little Italy** 28
Scossa | **E Shore** 28
Linwoods | **Owings Mills** 27
Pope's Tav. | **E Shore** 27
Chameleon | **NE Balt** 27
Antrim 1844 | **Taneytown** 27
Sotto Sopra | **Mt. Vernon** 26
Petit Louis | **Roland Pk** 26
Dogwood | **Hampden** 26
Elkridge Furnace | **Elkridge** 25
Kali's Ct. | **Fells Pt** 25
Narrows | **E Shore** 25
Paul's Homewood | **Annap** 25
Ambassador | **Homewood** 25

SINGLES SCENES

Mama's/Half Shell | **Canton** 26
Sullivan's Steak | **Inner Harbor** 25

Tsunami | **Annap** 25
Pazo | **Harbor E** 25
Brewer's Art | **Mt. Vernon** 25
Liberatore's | **multi.** 24
B&O | **D'town** 23

SLEEPERS

(Good food, but little known)
Spice & Dice | **Towson** 29
Grace Gdn. | **Odenton** 28
Bistro Poplar | **E Shore** 28
Umi Sake | **Cockeysville** 28
Tratt. Alberto | **Glen Burnie** 28
Piedigrotta | **Harbor E** 28
Cafe Bretton | **Severna Pk** 27
Schultz's Crab | **Essex** 27
Pope's Tav. | **E Shore** 27
Pho Nam | **Catonsville** 27
Laurrapin | **Havre de Grace** 26
Mr. Bill's | **Essex** 26
Chiyo Sushi | **Mt. Wash** 26
San Sushi | **Cockeysville** 26
Kentmorr | **E Shore** 25
Henninger's | **Fells Pt** 25
Rustico | **E Shore** 25
Breakfast Shoppe | **Severna Pk** 25
Little Spice | **Hanover** 25
Grano | **Hampden** 25
Bistro Rx | **Hi'town** 25

TRENDY

Out of the Fire | **E Shore** 28
Osteria 177 | **Annap** 27
Bistro Blanc | **Glenelg** 26
Pazo | **Harbor E** 25
Brewer's Art | **Mt. Vernon** 25
Olive Rm. | **Fells Pt** 24
NEW Thames St. | **Fells Pt** 24
Talara | **Harbor E** 24
Chazz | **Harbor E** 24
Corner BYOB | **Hampden** 24
Alchemy | **Hampden** 23
Crush | **York Rd Corr** 23
Honey Pig | **Ellicott City** 23
NEW Waterfront Kit. | **Fells Pt** 22
13.5%/Silo | **Hampden** 22
Rocket/Venus | **Hampden** 20
NEW Bond St. Social | **Fells Pt** 19
NEW Heavy Seas | **Harbor E** 19
NEW Clementine/Creative | **Hi'town** -
NEW Food Market | **Hampden** -
NEW Fork & Wrench | **Canton** -
NEW Of Love/Regret | **Canton** -
NEW Pabu | **Harbor E** -

VALET PARKING

Charleston | **Harbor E**	29
Prime Rib | **Mt. Vernon**	28
Aldo's | **Little Italy**	28
Osteria 177 | **Annap**	27
Black Olive | **Fells Pt**	27
Woodberry Kit. | **Clipper Mill**	27
Roy's | **Harbor E**	27
Capital Grille | **Inner Harbor**	26
Sotto Sopra | **Mt. Vernon**	26
Ruth's Chris | **multi.**	26
La Tavola | **Little Italy**	26
Morton's | **Inner Harbor**	26
La Scala | **Little Italy**	26
Cinghiale | **Harbor E**	26
Kali's Ct. | **Fells Pt**	25
Mari Luna Latin | **Pikesville**	25
Sullivan's Steak | **Inner Harbor**	25
Carpaccio | **Annap**	25
Kali's Mezze | **Fells Pt**	25
Pazo | **Harbor E**	25
Fleming's Steak | **Harbor E**	25
Harry Browne | **Annap**	25
Ambassador | **Homewood**	25
Blue Hill Tav. | **Canton**	25
Oceanaire | **Harbor E**	24
Bluegrass | **S Balt**	24
Sabatino's | **Little Italy**	24
Talara | **Harbor E**	24
Facci | **Laurel**	24
Chazz | **Harbor E**	24
Cheesecake | **multi.**	24
Chiapparelli's | **Little Italy**	24
Germano's | **Little Italy**	24
Regi's | **S Balt**	23
Café Troia | **Towson**	23
Tapas Adela | **Fells Pt**	23
Lebanese Tav. | **Harbor E**	23
McCormick/Schmick | **Inner Harbor**	23
City Cafe | **Mt. Vernon**	23
Meli | **Fells Pt**	23
Caesar's Den | **Little Italy**	23
NEW Wit/Wisdom | **Harbor E**	23
Yellowfin | **Annap**	23
Bahama Breeze | **Towson**	23
P.F. Chang's | **Annap**	23
Langermann's | **Canton**	22
Ciao Bella | **Little Italy**	22
Portalli's | **Ellicott City**	22
La Famiglia | **Homewood**	22
Crêpe du Jour | **Mt. Wash**	21
NEW Pabu | **Harbor E**	–
NEW Townhouse | **Harbor E**	–

VIEWS

Charleston | **Harbor E**	29
Pope's Tav. | **E Shore**	27
Broom's Bloom | **Bel Air**	27
Sushi Sono | **Columbia**	27
Antrim 1844 | **Taneytown**	27
Red Pearl | **Columbia**	26
Cinghiale | **Harbor E**	26
Kentmorr | **E Shore**	25
Salter's Tav. | **E Shore**	25
Narrows | **E Shore**	25
Friendly Farm | **Upperco**	25
Mango Grove | **Columbia**	24
Olive Rm. | **Fells Pt**	24
Harris Crab | **E Shore**	24
Edo Sushi | **Inner Harbor**	24
Cheesecake | **Inner Harbor**	24
Cantler's Riverside | **Annap**	24
Carrol's Creek | **Annap**	23
McCormick/Schmick | **Inner Harbor**	23
NEW Wit/Wisdom | **Harbor E**	23
Yellowfin | **Annap**	23
Gertrude's | **Charles Vill**	22
Severn Inn | **Annap**	22
Clyde's | **Columbia**	22
Rusty Scupper | **S Balt**	22
NEW Waterfront Kit. | **Fells Pt**	22
13.5%/Silo | **Locust Pt**	22
Boatyard B&G | **Annap**	22
Tidewater | **Havre de Grace**	22
Crab Claw | **E Shore**	21
Tabrizi's | **S Balt**	21
John Steven | **Fells Pt**	20
NEW Pabu | **Harbor E**	–

WINNING WINE LISTS

Charleston | **Harbor E**	29
Tersiguel's | **Ellicott City**	28
Out of the Fire | **E Shore**	28
Antrim 1844 | **Taneytown**	27
Capital Grille | **Inner Harbor**	26
Petit Louis | **Roland Pk**	26
Cinghiale | **Harbor E**	26
Bistro Blanc | **Glenelg**	26
Oregon Grille | **Hunt Valley**	25
Iron Bridge Wine | **Columbia**	25
Pazo | **Harbor E**	25
Fleming's Steak | **Harbor E**	25
Wine Mkt. | **Locust Pt**	24
Café de Paris | **Columbia**	24
Della Notte | **Little Italy**	24
Vino Rosina | **Harbor E**	22
13.5%/Silo | **multi.**	22

WORTH A TRIP

Cuisines

Includes names, locations and Food ratings.

AFGHAN

Helmand | **Mt. Vernon** 27

AMERICAN

Charleston	**Harbor E**	29
Vin 909	**Annap**	28
Bartlett Pear	**E Shore**	28
Out of the Fire	**E Shore**	28
Milton Inn	**Sparks**	28
Linwoods	**Owings Mills**	27
Peter's Inn	**Fells Pt**	27
Salt	**Fells Pt**	27
Pope's Tav.	**E Shore**	27
Woodberry Kit.	**Clipper Mill**	27
Chameleon	**NE Balt**	27
Antrim 1844	**Taneytown**	27
Attman's Deli	**E Balt**	27
Mason's	**E Shore**	26
Annabel Lee	**Hi'town**	26
Laurrapin	**Havre de Grace**	26
Dogwood	**Hampden**	26
Miss Shirley's	**multi.**	26
b	**Bolton Hill**	26
Bistro Blanc	**Glenelg**	26
Elkridge Furnace	**Elkridge**	25
Kentmorr	**E Shore**	25
Henninger's	**Fells Pt**	25
Blue Moon	**Fells Pt**	25
Main Ingredient	**Annap**	25
Clementine	**NE Balt**	25
Oregon Grille	**Hunt Valley**	25
NEW Ten Ten	**Harbor E**	25
Friendly Farm	**Upperco**	25
Breakfast Shoppe	**Severna Pk**	25
Iron Bridge Wine	**Columbia**	25
Paul's Homewood	**Annap**	25
Harry Browne	**Annap**	25
Brewer's Art	**Mt. Vernon**	25
Bistro Rx	**Hi'town**	25
Blue Hill Tav.	**Canton**	25
Ann's Dari	**Glen Burnie**	25
Bluegrass	**S Balt**	24
Galway Bay	**Annap**	24
Level	**Annap**	24
Wine Mkt.	**Locust Pt**	24
Stanford Grill	**Columbia**	24
Kings Contrivance	**Columbia**	24
Open Door	**Bel Air**	24
Sascha's 527	**Mt. Vernon**	24
Harryman Hse.	**Reist'town**	24
Manor Tav.	**Monkton**	24

Cheesecake	**multi.**	24
Woman's Industrial	**Mt. Vernon**	24
Regi's	**S Balt**	23
Pappas	**multi.**	23
Reynolds Tav.	**Annap**	23
BlueStone	**Timonium**	23
B&O	**D'town**	23
McCabe's	**Hampden**	23
Paladar	**Annap**	23
Crush Winehouse	**Annap**	23
Alchemy	**Hampden**	23
City Cafe	**Mt. Vernon**	23
Meli	**Fells Pt**	23
Metropolitan Coffee	**S Balt**	23
Wild Orchid	**Annap**	23
Christopher Daniel	**Timonium**	23
Crush	**York Rd Corr**	23
Mr. Rain's Fun Hse.	**S Balt**	23
NEW Wit/Wisdom	**Harbor E**	23
Yellowfin	**Annap**	23
Michael's Café	**Timonium**	23
Peppermill	**Lutherville**	23
Teavolve	**Harbor E**	23
Severn Inn	**Annap**	22
Alewife	**D'town W**	22
Patrick's	**Cockeysville**	22
Ale Marys	**Fells Pt**	22
Kooper's	**Fells Pt**	22
Banning's	**E Shore**	22
Clyde's	**Columbia**	22
49 West	**Annap**	22
Porters	**S Balt**	22
Vino Rosina	**Harbor E**	22
NEW Waterfront Kit.	**Fells Pt**	22
13.5%/Silo	**multi.**	22
M&S Grill	**Inner Harbor**	22
BGR	**Columbia**	22
Tidewater	**Havre de Grace**	22
First Watch	**Pikesville**	21
Eggspectation	**Ellicott City**	21
Brass. Brightwell	**E Shore**	21
Meet 27	**Charles Vill**	21
Tark's Grill	**Brook'ville**	21
Big Pickle Food	**E Shore**	21
Peerce's	**Phoenix**	21
Dangerously Delicious	**Canton**	21
Double T	**multi.**	20
Baugher's	**Westminster**	20
John Steven	**Fells Pt**	20
Rockfish	**Annap**	20
Garry's Grill	**Severna Pk**	20

Dizz	**Hampden**	19
NEW Heavy Seas	**Harbor E**	19
Cafe Hon	**Hampden**	16
NEW Adam's Eve	**Canton**	-
NEW Artifact Coffee	**Clipper Mill**	-
NEW Clementine/Creative	**Hi'town**	-
NEW Food Market	**Hampden**	-
NEW Fork & Wrench	**Canton**	-
NEW Kettle Hill	**D'town**	-
NEW Of Love/Regret	**Canton**	-
NEW Townhouse	**Harbor E**	-
NEW 208 Talbot	**E Shore**	-

ASIAN

Tsunami	**Annap**	25
Jesse Wong's Asean	**Columbia**	23
Jesse Wong's Kit.	**Hunt Valley**	20

BAKERIES

Piedigrotta	**Harbor E**	28
Bon Fresco	**Columbia**	27
Main Ingredient	**Annap**	25
Goldberg's	**Pikesville**	25
Atwater's	**multi.**	25
Greg's Bagels	**York Rd Corr**	24
Stone Mill	**Brook'ville**	24
Dangerously Delicious	**Canton**	21

BARBECUE

Chaps Pit Beef	**E Balt**	27
Andy Nelson's	**Cockeysville**	26
Big Bad Wolf	**NE Balt**	26
Red Hot/Blue	**multi.**	22
Kloby's Smokehse.	**Laurel**	21

BRAZILIAN

Fogo de Chão	**Inner Harbor**	27

BRITISH

Reynolds Tav.	**Annap**	23

BURGERS

Linwoods	**Owings Mills**	27
Hamilton Tav.	**NE Balt**	24
Five Guys	**multi.**	24
Kooper's	**Location Varies**	22
Gino's	**multi.**	22
Clyde's	**Columbia**	22
BGR	**Columbia**	22

CARIBBEAN

Paladar	**Annap**	23
Bahama Breeze	**Towson**	23

CHESAPEAKE

Salter's Tav.	**E Shore**	25
Narrows	**E Shore**	25
Gertrude's	**Charles Vill**	22

CHICKEN

Chicken Rico	**Hi'town**	27
Gino's	**Perry Hall**	22
Nando's	**Annap**	22

CHINESE

Grace Gdn.	**Odenton**	28
Red Pearl	**Columbia**	26
Szechuan Hse.	**Lutherville**	26
Grace's	**Bowie**	25
David Chu's	**Pikesville**	25
Hunan Manor	**Columbia**	23
P.F. Chang's	**multi.**	23
Cafe Zen	**York Rd Corr**	22

COFFEEHOUSES

City Cafe	**Mt. Vernon**	23
Metropolitan Coffee	**S Balt**	23
49 West	**Annap**	22
One World	**Homewood**	22
NEW Artifact Coffee	**Clipper Mill**	-

CONTINENTAL

Tio Pepe	**Mt. Vernon**	26
Josef's	**Fallston**	25
Corner BYOB	**Hampden**	24

CRAB HOUSES

Schultz's Crab	**Essex**	27
Mr. Bill's	**Essex**	26
Faidley's	**D'town W**	26
Kentmorr	**E Shore**	25
Costas Inn	**Dundalk**	25
Harris Crab	**E Shore**	24
Cantler's Riverside	**Annap**	24
Gunning's Seafood	**Hanover**	23
Crab Claw	**E Shore**	21

CRÊPES

Sofi's Crepes	**multi.**	24
Crêpe du Jour	**Mt. Wash**	21

CUBAN

Havana Rd.	**Towson**	21

DELIS

Attman's Deli	**E Balt**	27
Chick/Ruth's	**Annap**	22
Suburban Hse.	**Pikesville**	19

DINERS

Chick/Ruth's	**Annap**	22
Towson Diner	**Towson**	21
Double T	**multi.**	20
Jimmy's	**Fells Pt**	20
Cafe Hon	**Hampden**	16

EASTERN EUROPEAN

Ze Mean Bean	**Fells Pt**	23

ECLECTIC

Out of the Fire | **E Shore**	28
Jack's Bistro | **Canton**	27
4 Seasons Grille | **Gambrills**	25
Tsunami | **Annap**	25
Great Sage | **Clarksville**	24
Tapas Teatro | **D'town N**	24
Victoria Gastro | **Columbia**	24
Regions | **Catonsville**	23
Boatyard B&G | **Annap**	22
Golden West | **Hampden**	21
Rocket/Venus | **Hampden**	20
NEW Bond St. Social | **Fells Pt**	19
NEW Museum | **Mt. Vernon**	-‌

ETHIOPIAN

Dukem | **Mt. Vernon**	24

FRENCH

Tersiguel's | **Ellicott City**	28
Cafe Bretton | **Severna Pk**	27
Les Folies | **Annap**	27
Antrim 1844 | **Taneytown**	27
Sofi's Crepes | **D'town N**	24

FRENCH (BISTRO)

Bistro Poplar | **E Shore**	28
Petit Louis | **Roland Pk**	26
Café Normandie | **Annap**	25
Café de Paris | **Columbia**	24
Marie Louise | **Mt. Vernon**	22
Crêpe du Jour | **Mt. Wash**	21
Brass. Brightwell | **E Shore**	21

GASTROPUBS

Victoria Gastro | Eclectic | **Columbia**	24
Alewife | Amer. | **D'town W**	22
Porters | Amer. | **S Balt**	22
NEW Heavy Seas | Amer. | **Harbor E**	19
NEW Adam's Eve | Amer. | **Canton**	-‌
NEW Fork & Wrench | Amer. | **Canton**	-‌

GREEK

Samos | **Gr'town**	28
Black Olive | **Fells Pt**	27
Paul's Homewood | **Annap**	25
Olive Rm. | **Fells Pt**	24
Ikaros | **Gr'town**	23

HAWAIIAN

Roy's | **Harbor E**	27

HOT DOGS

Ann's Dari | **Glen Burnie**	25

ICE CREAM PARLORS

Broom's Bloom | **Bel Air**	27

INDIAN

Ambassador | **Homewood**	25
Mango Grove | **Columbia**	24
Akbar | **multi.**	24
House of India | **Columbia**	23
Carlyle Club | **Homewood**	21

IRISH

Galway Bay | **Annap**	24

ITALIAN

(N=Northern; S=Southern)

Di Pasquale's | **E Balt**	28
Tratt. Alberto | N | **Glen Burnie**	28
Aldo's | S | **Little Italy**	28
Scossa | N | **E Shore**	28
Piedigrotta | **Harbor E**	28
Osteria 177 | **Annap**	27
Ava's | **E Shore**	27
Pasta Plus | **Laurel**	26
Sotto Sopra | N | **Mt. Vernon**	26
La Tavola | **Little Italy**	26
La Scala | S | **Little Italy**	26
Cinghiale | **Harbor E**	26
Rustico | S | **E Shore**	25
Carpaccio | N | **Annap**	25
Grano | **Hampden**	25
Grano | **Hampden**	25
Da Mimmo | **Little Italy**	25
Joe Squared | **multi.**	24
Amicci's | **Little Italy**	24
Liberatore's | S | **multi.**	24
Aida | **Columbia**	24
Della Notte | **Little Italy**	24
Sabatino's | **Little Italy**	24
Facci | **Laurel**	24
Chazz | S | **Harbor E**	24
Olive Grove | **Linthicum**	24
Chiapparelli's | **multi.**	24
Germano's | N | **Little Italy**	24
Café Troia | **Towson**	23
Caesar's Den | S | **Little Italy**	23
Ledo Pizza | N | **Lanham**	23
Café Gia | S | **Little Italy**	22
Ciao Bella | **Little Italy**	22
Portalli's | **Ellicott City**	22
La Famiglia | N | **Homewood**	22
Luna Blu | S | **Annap**	22
Mamma Lucia | **Elkridge**	22
Chef Paolino | **Catonsville**	21
Sammy's Tratt. | S | **Mt. Vernon**	21
Basta Pasta | **multi.**	21

JAMAICAN

Negril | multi. — 24

JAPANESE

(* sushi specialist)

Umi Sake*	**Cockeysville**	28
Sushi King*	**Columbia**	28
Joss Cafe/Sushi*	**multi.**	27
Sushi Sono*	**Columbia**	27
Kobe	**multi.**	27
Sushi Hana*	**multi.**	26
Chiyo Sushi*	**Mt. Wash**	26
San Sushi*	**Cockeysville**	26
Minato*	**Mt. Vernon**	24
Ra Sushi*	**Harbor E**	24
Matsuri*	**S Balt**	24
Edo Sushi*	**multi.**	24
San Sushi/Thai*	**multi.**	21
NEW Pabu	**Harbor E**	–

JEWISH

Goldberg's	**Pikesville**	25
Suburban Hse.	**Pikesville**	19

KOREAN

(* barbecue specialist)

Honey Pig*	**Ellicott City**	23
Shin Chon*	**Ellicott City**	22

KOSHER

David Chu's	**Pikesville**	25
Goldberg's	**Pikesville**	25

LEBANESE

Lebanese Tav. | **multi.** — 23

MEDITERRANEAN

Kali's Ct.	**Fells Pt**	25
Kali's Mezze	**Fells Pt**	25
4 Seasons Grille	**Gambrills**	25
Pazo	**Harbor E**	25
Tapas Teatro	**D'town N**	24
Marie Louise	**Mt. Vernon**	22
Tabrizi's	**S Balt**	21

MEXICAN

R & R Taqueria	**multi.**	27
Jalapeños	**Annap**	27
Mari Luna Latin	**Pikesville**	25
Mari Luna Mex.	**multi.**	24
Azul 17	**Columbia**	23
Nacho Mama's	**Canton**	22
Blue Agave	**S Balt**	22
Miguel's Cocina	**Locust Pt**	20

MIDDLE EASTERN

Tabrizi's | **S Balt** — 21

NEW MEXICAN

Golden West | **Hampden** — 21

NUEVO LATINO

Talara | **Harbor E** — 24

PAN-LATIN

Mari Luna Latin	**Pikesville**	25
Mari Luna Mex.	**multi.**	24
Paladar	**Annap**	23

PERSIAN

Orchard Mkt. | **Towson** — 26

PERUVIAN

Chicken Rico | **Hi'town** — 27

PIZZA

Johnny Rad's	**Fells Pt**	27
Iggies	**Mt. Vernon**	27
Ava's	**E Shore**	27
Matthew's Pizza	**Hi'town**	27
Pasta Plus	**Laurel**	26
Joe Squared	**D'town N**	24
Facci	**Laurel**	24
Chazz	**Harbor E**	24
Bagby Pizza	**Harbor E**	23
Coal Fire	**multi.**	22
Chef Paolino	**Catonsville**	21
NEW Earth/Wood/Fire	**N Balt**	–
NEW Hersh's Pizza	**S Balt**	–

PUB FOOD

Koco's	**NE Balt**	27
Johnny Rad's	**Fells Pt**	27
Hamilton Tav.	**NE Balt**	24
Galway Bay	**Annap**	24
McCabe's	**Hampden**	23
One-Eyed Mike	**Fells Pt**	23
Ale Marys	**Fells Pt**	22
Clyde's	**Columbia**	22
Boatyard B&G	**Annap**	22
Du-Claw	**multi.**	21
NEW Dempsey's Brew	**Camden Yds**	–
NEW Plug Ugly's	**Canton**	–

SANDWICHES

(See also Delis)

Bon Fresco	**Columbia**	27
Broom's Bloom	**Bel Air**	27
Attman's Deli	**E Balt**	27
Goldberg's	**Pikesville**	25
Atwater's	**multi.**	25
Greg's Bagels	**York Rd Corr**	24
Stone Mill	**Brook'ville**	24
Grilled Cheese	**multi.**	22
Chick/Ruth's	**Annap**	22

SEAFOOD

(See also Crab Houses)

Schultz's Crab | **Essex**	27
Black Olive | **Fells Pt**	27
Jerry's Seafood | **multi.**	26
Mr. Bill's | **Essex**	26
Faidley's | **D'town W**	26
Seaside Rest. | **Glen Burnie**	26
Catonsville Gourm. | **Catonsville**	26
Mama's/Half Shell | **Canton**	26
O'Learys | **Annap**	26
Kali's Ct. | **Fells Pt**	25
Kentmorr | **E Shore**	25
Salter's Tav. | **E Shore**	25
Oregon Grille | **Hunt Valley**	25
Narrows | **E Shore**	25
Oceanaire | **Harbor E**	24
G&M | **Linthicum**	24
Harris Crab | **E Shore**	24
NEW Thames St. | **Fells Pt**	24
Cantler's Riverside | **Annap**	24
Pappas | **multi.**	23
Carrol's Creek | **Annap**	23
Gunning's Seafood | **multi.**	23
BlueStone | **Timonium**	23
McCormick/Schmick | **Inner Harbor**	23
Timbuktu | **Hanover**	23
Yellowfin | **Annap**	23
Michael's Café | **Timonium**	23
Gertrude's | **Charles Vill**	22
Severn Inn | **Annap**	22
Bertha's | **Fells Pt**	22
Rusty Scupper | **S Balt**	22
M&S Grill | **Inner Harbor**	22
Tidewater | **Havre de Grace**	22
Crab Claw | **E Shore**	21
John Steven | **Fells Pt**	20
Rockfish | **Annap**	20
Phillips | **Inner Harbor**	20

SMALL PLATES

(See also Spanish tapas specialist)

Kali's Mezze | Med. | **Fells Pt**	25
Iron Bridge Wine | Amer. | **Columbia**	25
Pazo | Med. | **Harbor E**	25
Level | Amer. | **Annap**	24
Tapas Teatro | Eclectic | **D'town N**	24
Aida | Italian | **Columbia**	24
Talara | Nuevo Latino | **Harbor E**	24
B&O | Amer. | **D'town**	23
Crush Winehouse | Amer. | **Annap**	23
City Cafe | Amer. | **Mt. Vernon**	23

NEW Bond St. Social | Eclectic | **Fells Pt**	19
NEW Hersh's Pizza | Pizza | **S Balt**	-

SOUTHERN

Miss Shirley's | **Annap**	26
Carolina Kit. | **Largo**	25
Langermann's | **Canton**	22

SPANISH

(* tapas specialist)

Jalapeños* | **Annap**	27
Tio Pepe | **Mt. Vernon**	26
Tapas Adela* | **Fells Pt**	23

STEAKHOUSES

Prime Rib | **Mt. Vernon**	28
Lewnes' Steak | **Annap**	28
Fogo de Chão | **Inner Harbor**	27
Capital Grille | **Inner Harbor**	26
Ruth's Chris | **multi.**	26
Morton's | **Inner Harbor**	26
Sullivan's Steak | **Inner Harbor**	25
Oregon Grille | **Hunt Valley**	25
Fleming's Steak | **Harbor E**	25
Yellowfin | **Annap**	23
M&S Grill | **Inner Harbor**	22
Greystone Grill | **Ellicott City**	19
NEW Poor Boy | **Severna Pk**	-
Theo's | **E Shore**	-

TEAHOUSE

Teavolve | **Harbor E**	23

THAI

Spice & Dice | **Towson**	29
Thai Arroy | **S Balt**	26
Lemongrass | **Annap**	25
Little Spice | **Hanover**	25
Thai | **Charles Vill**	24
NEW Stang/Siam | **Mt. Vernon**	23
Bân Thai | **Mt. Vernon**	23
San Sushi/Thai | **multi.**	21

TURKISH

Cazbar | **Mt. Vernon**	24

VEGETARIAN

(* vegan)

Great Sage* | **Clarksville**	24
Mango Grove* | **Columbia**	24
One World* | **Homewood**	22

VIETNAMESE

Mekong Delta | **D'town W**	27
Pho Nam | **Catonsville**	27
Pho Dat Thanh | **multi.**	24
An Loi | **Columbia**	23

BALTIMORE AREA

CUISINES

Locations

Includes names, cuisines and Food ratings.

Baltimore

BARE HILLS/ MT. WASHINGTON

Sushi Hana | *Japanese*	26
Chiyo Sushi | *Japanese*	26
Atwater's | *Bakery*	25
Crêpe du Jour | *French*	21

BUSINESS DISTRICT/ CAMDEN YARDS/ CONVENTION CTR./ DOWNTOWN/ INNER HARBOR

Fogo de Chão | *Brazilian/Steak*	27
Capital Grille | *Steak*	26
Ruth's Chris | *Steak*	26
Morton's | *Steak*	26
Miss Shirley's | *Amer.*	26
b | *Amer.*	26
Sullivan's Steak | *Steak*	25
Joe Squared | *Italian/Pizza*	24
Five Guys | *Burgers*	24
Edo Sushi | *Japanese*	24
Cheesecake | *Amer.*	24
B&O | *Amer.*	23
McCormick/Schmick | *Seafood*	23
P.F. Chang's | *Chinese*	23
M&S Grill | *Seafood/Steak*	22
Phillips | *Seafood*	20
NEW Dempsey's Brew | *Pub*	-
NEW Kettle Hill | *Amer.*	-

CANTON

Jack's Bistro | *Eclectic*	27
Mama's/Half Shell | *Seafood*	26
Blue Hill Tav. | *Amer.*	25
Five Guys | *Burgers*	24
Langermann's | *Southern*	22
Nacho Mama's | *Mex.*	22
San Sushi/Thai | *Japanese/Thai*	21
Dangerously Delicious | *Amer./Bakery*	21
NEW Adam's Eve | *Amer.*	-
NEW Fork & Wrench | *Amer.*	-
NEW Of Love/Regret | *Amer.*	-
NEW Plug Ugly's | *Pub*	-

CHARLES VILLAGE

Thai | *Thai*	24
Gertrude's | *Chesapeake*	22
Meet 27 | *Amer.*	21

DOWNTOWN NORTH/ CHARLES ST./ MT. VERNON

Prime Rib | *Steak*	28
Iggies | *Pizza*	27
Joss Cafe/Sushi | *Japanese*	27
Helmand | *Afghan*	27
Sotto Sopra | *Italian*	26
Tio Pepe | *Continental/Spanish*	26
Brewer's Art | *Amer.*	25
Minato | *Japanese*	24
Tapas Teatro | *Eclectic/Med.*	24
Joe Squared | *Italian/Pizza*	24
Akbar | *Indian*	24
Sofi's Crepes | *Crêpes*	24
Sascha's 527 | *Amer.*	24
Dukem | *Ethiopian*	24
Mari Luna Mex. | *Mex./Pan-Latin*	24
Cazbar | *Turkish*	24
Woman's Industrial | *Amer.*	24
City Cafe | *Amer.*	23
NEW Stang/Siam | *Thai*	23
Bân Thai | *Thai*	23
Marie Louise | *French/Med.*	22
Sammy's Tratt. | *Italian*	21
NEW Museum | *Eclectic*	-

EAST BALTIMORE

Di Pasquale's | *Italian*	28
Attman's Deli | *Deli*	27
Chaps Pit Beef | *BBQ*	27

FELLS POINT

Peter's Inn | *Amer.*	27
Salt | *Amer.*	27
Black Olive | *Greek/Seafood*	27
Johnny Rad's | *Pizza*	27
Kali's Ct. | *Med./Seafood*	25
Henninger's | *Amer.*	25
Blue Moon | *Amer.*	25
Kali's Mezze | *Med.*	25
Olive Rm. | *Greek*	24
NEW Thames St. | *Seafood*	24
Tapas Adela | *Spanish*	23
Ze Mean Bean | *E Euro.*	23
Meli | *Eclectic*	23
One-Eyed Mike | *Pub*	23
Ale Marys | *Pub*	22
Kooper's | *Amer.*	22
Bertha's | *Seafood*	22
NEW Waterfront Kit. | *Amer.*	22

John Steven	*Seafood*	20
Jimmy's	*Diner*	20
NEW Bond St. Social	*Eclectic*	19
Sip & Bite	*Diner*	19

HAMPDEN/
ROLAND PARK

(Including Clipper Mill)

Woodberry Kit.	*Amer.*	27
Petit Louis	*French*	26
Dogwood	*Amer.*	26
Miss Shirley's	*Amer.*	26
Grano	*Italian*	25
Grano	*Italian*	25
Corner BYOB	*Continental*	24
McCabe's	*Pub*	23
Alchemy	*Amer.*	23
13.5%/Silo	*Amer.*	22
Golden West	*Eclectic/New Mex.*	21
Rocket/Venus	*Eclectic*	20
Dizz	*Amer.*	19
Cafe Hon	*Amer.*	16
NEW Artifact Coffee	*Coffee*	-
NEW Food Market	*Amer.*	-

HARBOR EAST/
LITTLE ITALY

Charleston	*Amer.*	29
Aldo's	*Italian*	28
Piedigrotta	*Bakery/Italian*	28
Roy's	*Hawaiian*	27
La Tavola	*Italian*	26
La Scala	*Italian*	26
Cinghiale	*Italian*	26
NEW Ten Ten	*Amer.*	25
Pazo	*Med.*	25
Fleming's Steak	*Steak*	25
Da Mimmo	*Italian*	25
Oceanaire	*Seafood*	24
Amicci's	*Italian*	24
Della Notte	*Italian*	24
Ra Sushi	*Japanese*	24
Sabatino's	*Italian*	24
Talara	*Nuevo Latino*	24
Chazz	*Italian/Pizza*	24
Chiapparelli's	*Italian*	24
Germano's	*Italian*	23
Lebanese Tav.	*Lebanese*	23
Bagby Pizza	*Pizza*	23
Caesar's Den	*Italian*	23
NEW Wit/Wisdom	*Amer.*	23
Teavolve	*Amer./Tea*	23
Café Gia	*Italian*	22

Ciao Bella	*Italian*	22
Vino Rosina	*Amer.*	22
NEW Heavy Seas	*Amer.*	19
NEW Pabu	*Japanese*	-
NEW Townhouse	*Amer.*	-

HIGHLANDTOWN/
GREEKTOWN

Samos	*Greek*	28
Chicken Rico	*Chicken/Peruvian*	27
Matthew's Pizza	*Pizza*	27
Annabel Lee	*Amer.*	26
Bistro Rx	*Amer.*	25
Ikaros	*Greek*	23
NEW Clementine/Creative	*Amer.*	-

HOMEWOOD

Ambassador	*Indian*	25
La Famiglia	*Italian*	22
One World	*Veg.*	22
Carlyle Club	*Indian*	21

LOCUST POINT

Wine Mkt.	*Amer.*	24
13.5%/Silo	*Amer.*	22
Miguel's Cocina	*Mex.*	20

NORTH BALTIMORE/
YORK ROAD CORRIDOR

Atwater's	*Bakery*	25
Greg's Bagels	*Bakery*	24
Sofi's Crepes	*Crêpes*	24
Crush	*Amer.*	23
Cafe Zen	*Chinese*	22
NEW Earth/Wood/Fire	*Pizza*	-

SOUTH BALTIMORE

(Including Federal Hill)

Thai Arroy	*Thai*	26
Bluegrass	*Amer.*	24
Matsuri	*Japanese*	24
Regi's	*Amer.*	23
Metropolitan Coffee	*Amer.*	23
Mr. Rain's Fun Hse.	*Amer.*	23
Grilled Cheese	*Sandwiches*	22
Blue Agave	*Mex.*	22
Rusty Scupper	*Seafood*	22
Porters	*Amer.*	22
Tabrizi's	*Med./Mideast.*	21
NEW Hersh's Pizza	*Pizza*	-

WEST BALTIMORE

Mekong Delta	*Viet.*	27
Faidley's	*Seafood*	26
Alewife	*Amer.*	22

Outer Baltimore

ABERDEEN/ HARFORD COUNTY/ HAVRE DE GRACE

(Including White Marsh)

R & R Taqueria	*Mex.*	27
Broom's Bloom	*Ice Cream*	27
Kobe	*Japanese*	27
Laurrapin	*Amer.*	26
Josef's	*Continental*	25
Open Door	*Amer.*	24
Five Guys	*Burgers*	24
Liberatore's	*Italian*	24
Chiapparelli's	*Italian*	24
P.F. Chang's	*Chinese*	23
Tidewater	*Amer.*	22
Du-Claw	*Pub*	21
Basta Pasta	*Italian*	21
Double T	*Diner*	20

BOWIE/LAUREL

Pasta Plus	*Italian*	26
Jerry's Seafood	*Seafood*	26
Grace's	*Chinese*	25
Five Guys	*Burgers*	24
Negril	*Jamaican*	24
Facci	*Italian/Pizza*	24
Red Hot/Blue	*BBQ*	22
Kloby's Smokehse.	*BBQ*	21
Du-Claw	*Pub*	21

BROOKLANDVILLE

Stone Mill	*Bakery*	24
Tark's Grill	*Amer.*	21

BWI/ELKRIDGE/ HANOVER/LINTHICUM

R & R Taqueria	*Mex.*	27
Elkridge Furnace	*Amer.*	25
Little Spice	*Thai*	25
G&M	*Seafood*	24
Five Guys	*Burgers*	24
Olive Grove	*Italian*	24
Gunning's Seafood	*Seafood*	23
Timbuktu	*Seafood*	23
Mamma Lucia	*Italian*	22
Du-Claw	*Pub*	21

CATONSVILLE/ WOODLAWN

Pho Nam	*Viet.*	27
Catonsville Gourm.	*Seafood*	26
Atwater's	*Bakery*	25
Regions	*Eclectic*	23
Grilled Cheese	*Sandwiches*	22
Chef Paolino	*Italian/Pizza*	21

Double T	*Diner*	20

CLARKSVILLE/ GLENELG

Bistro Blanc	*Amer.*	26
Great Sage	*Vegan*	24

COLUMBIA/ ELLICOTT CITY/ HIGHLAND

Tersiguel's	*French*	28
Sushi King	*Japanese*	28
Bon Fresco	*Sandwiches*	27
Sushi Sono	*Japanese*	27
Red Pearl	*Chinese*	26
Iron Bridge Wine	*Amer.*	25
Mango Grove	*Indian*	24
Stanford Grill	*Amer.*	24
Kings Contrivance	*Amer.*	24
Café de Paris	*French*	24
Akbar	*Indian*	24
Aida	*Italian*	24
Victoria Gastro	*Eclectic*	24
Pho Dat Thanh	*Viet.*	24
Cheesecake	*Amer.*	24
Jesse Wong's Asean	*Pan-Asian*	23
Azul 17	*Mex.*	23
House of India	*Indian*	23
An Loi	*Viet.*	23
Hunan Manor	*Chinese*	23
P.F. Chang's	*Chinese*	23
Honey Pig	*Korean*	23
Coal Fire	*Pizza*	22
Portalli's	*Italian*	22
Clyde's	*Amer.*	22
Shin Chon	*Korean*	22
BGR	*Burgers*	22
Eggspectation	*Amer.*	21
Double T	*Diner*	20
Greystone Grill	*Steak*	19

ESSEX/DUNDALK

Schultz's Crab	*Crab*	27
Mr. Bill's	*Crab*	26
Costas Inn	*Crab*	25

GAMBRILLS

4 Seasons Grille	*Eclectic/Med.*	25
Coal Fire	*Pizza*	22

GLEN BURNIE/ ODENTON/ SEVERNA PARK

Grace Gdn.	*Chinese*	28
Tratt. Alberto	*Italian*	28
Cafe Bretton	*French*	27
Seaside Rest.	*Seafood*	26

Breakfast Shoppe	*Amer.*	25
Ann's Dari	*Hot Dogs*	25
Five Guys	*Burgers*	24
Pappas	*Amer./Seafood*	23
Gunning's Seafood	*Seafood*	23
Garry's Grill	*Amer.*	20
NEW Poor Boy	*Steak*	-

HUNT VALLEY/ NORTH BALTIMORE COUNTY

Milton Inn	*Amer.*	28
Oregon Grille	*Seafood/Steak*	25
Friendly Farm	*Amer.*	25
Manor Tav.	*Amer.*	24
Peerce's	*Amer.*	21
Jesse Wong's Kit.	*Asian*	20

LANHAM

Jerry's Seafood	*Seafood*	26
Ledo Pizza	*Pizza*	23

LARGO

Kobe	*Japanese*	27
Carolina Kit.	*Southern*	25

LUTHERVILLE/ COCKEYSVILLE/ TIMONIUM

Umi Sake	*Asian*	28
Sushi Hana	*Japanese*	26
Szechuan Hse.	*Chinese*	26
San Sushi	*Japanese*	26
Andy Nelson's	*BBQ*	24
Five Guys	*Burgers*	24
Liberatore's	*Italian*	24
Edo Sushi	*Japanese*	24
BlueStone	*Seafood*	23
Christopher Daniel	*Amer.*	23
Michael's Café	*Amer.*	23
Peppermill	*Amer.*	23
Patrick's	*Amer.*	22
Basta Pasta	*Italian*	21

MITCHELLVILLE

Negril	*Jamaican*	24

NORTHEAST BALTIMORE/ PERRY HALL

Koco's	*Pub*	27
Chameleon	*Amer.*	27
Big Bad Wolf	*BBQ*	26
Clementine	*Amer.*	25
Hamilton Tav.	*Pub*	24
Liberatore's	*Italian*	24
Pappas	*Amer./Seafood*	23
Gino's	*Burgers*	22

Double T	*Diner*	20

OWINGS MILLS/ REISTERSTOWN/ FINKSBURG

Linwoods	*Amer.*	27
Sofi's Crepes	*Crêpes*	24
Edo Sushi	*Japanese*	24
Harryman Hse.	*Amer.*	24

PASADENA

Seaside Rest.	*Seafood*	26
Double T	*Diner*	20

PIKESVILLE

Ruth's Chris	*Steak*	26
Mari Luna Latin	*Mex./Pan-Latin*	25
David Chu's	*Chinese/Kosher*	25
Goldberg's	*Bakery/Jewish*	25
Mari Luna Mex.	*Mex./Pan-Latin*	24
First Watch	*Amer.*	21
Suburban Hse.	*Deli*	19

TOWSON

Spice & Dice	*Thai*	29
Sushi Hana	*Japanese*	26
Orchard Mkt.	*Persian*	26
Atwater's	*Bakery*	25
Five Guys	*Burgers*	24
Pho Dat Thanh	*Viet.*	24
Cheesecake	*Amer.*	24
Café Troia	*Italian*	23
Bahama Breeze	*Carib.*	23
P.F. Chang's	*Chinese*	23
Gino's	*Burgers*	22
Havana Rd.	*Cuban*	21
San Sushi/Thai	*Japanese/Thai*	21
Towson Diner	*Diner*	21

WESTMINSTER/ ELDERSBURG/ SYKESVILLE/ TANEYTOWN

Antrim 1844	*Amer./French*	27
Five Guys	*Burgers*	24
Liberatore's	*Italian*	24
Grilled Cheese	*Sandwiches*	22
Baugher's	*Amer.*	20

Annapolis/ Anne Arundel

Vin 909	*Amer.*	28
Lewnes' Steak	*Steak*	28
Osteria 177	*Italian*	27

BALTIMORE AREA

LOCATIONS

Joss Cafe/Sushi | *Japanese*	27
Les Folies | *French*	27
Jalapeños | *Mex./Spanish*	27
Ruth's Chris | *Steak*	26
Miss Shirley's | *Amer.*	26
O'Learys | *Seafood*	26
Main Ingredient | *Amer.*	25
Café Normandie | *French*	25
Carpaccio | *Italian*	25
Lemongrass | *Thai*	25
Tsunami | *Asian*	25
Chop Hse. | *Steak*	25
Paul's Homewood | *Amer./Greek*	25
Harry Browne | *Amer.*	25
Galway Bay | *Pub*	24
Level | *Amer.*	24
Five Guys | *Burgers*	24
Sofi's Crepes | *Crêpes*	24
Cheesecake | *Amer.*	24
Cantler's Riverside | *Crab*	24
Reynolds Tav. | *Amer./British*	23
Carrol's Creek | *Seafood*	23
Paladar | *Carib./Pan-Latin*	23
Lebanese Tav. | *Lebanese*	23
Crush Winehouse | *Amer.*	23
Wild Orchid | *Amer.*	23
Yellowfin | *Amer.*	23
P.F. Chang's | *Chinese*	23
Severn Inn | *Amer.*	22

Chick/Ruth's | *Diner*	22
Red Hot/Blue | *BBQ*	22
49 West | *Coffee*	22
Luna Blu | *Italian*	22
Nando's | *Chicken*	22
Boatyard B&G | *Pub*	22
Double T | *Diner*	20
Rockfish | *Amer.*	20

Eastern Shore

Bistro Poplar | *French*	28
Bartlett Pear | *Amer.*	28
Out of the Fire | *Amer./Eclectic*	28
Scossa | *Italian*	28
Pope's Tav. | *Amer.*	27
Ava's | *Italian/Pizza*	27
Ruth's Chris | *Steak*	26
Mason's | *Amer.*	26
Kentmorr | *Crab*	25
Rustico | *Italian*	25
Salter's Tav. | *Amer./Seafood*	25
Narrows | *Seafood*	25
Harris Crab | *Crab*	24
Banning's | *Amer.*	22
Crab Claw | *Crab*	21
Brass. Brightwell | *Amer./French*	21
Big Pickle Food | *Amer.*	21
Theo's | *Steak*	-
NEW 208 Talbot | *Amer.*	-

BALTIMORE, ANNAPOLIS AND THE EASTERN SHORE RESTAURANT DIRECTORY

Baltimore

NEW Adam's Eve American

`-` `-` `-` `I`

Canton | 3328 Foster Ave. (Highland Ave.) | 443-619-0856 |
www.adamsevegastropub.com

This cheerful Canton gastropub features a New American farm-to-table menu of burgers, steaks, salads and crab cakes by Mark Littleton, who helped launch Annabel Lee Tavern; the vintage posters of '70s bands, free truffle-salt popcorn in the bar, local drafts and Maryland wines are aimed at an after-work crowd and grown-ups from the neighborhood in search of a sedate repast.

Aida Bistro & Wine Bar Ⓢ Italian

`24` `21` `23` `$44`

Columbia | 6741 Columbia Gateway Dr. (Rte. 175) | 410-953-0500 |
www.aidabistro.com

"Real homemade pasta" and "innovative" Italian small and large plates – plus a "top-notch" "wine-on-tap program" – make this bistro/wine bar with a "wide-open" contemporary setting in an "unexpected" business-park locale a Howard County favorite; if it strikes some as "a bit pricey", the owners "make it seem like you're eating at their house", and hard-core fans are willing to splurge on the chef's table to watch the cooking action.

Akbar Indian

`24` `18` `22` `$25`

Mt. Vernon | 823 N. Charles St. (bet. Madison & Read Sts.) |
410-539-0944
Columbia | Columbia Mktpl. | 9400 Snowden River Pkwy.
(bet. Carved Stone Way & Rustling Leaf) | 410-381-3600
www.akbar-restaurant.com

"Authentic" Indian dishes "fit for the raja" can be piled high at the "excellent-value" lunch buffets or served by the "attentive but not hovering" staffs at these subcontinental survivors occupying an "underground lair" in Mt. Vernon and a strip mall in Columbia; if the decor's somewhat "dated", few mind.

Alchemy Ⓜ American

`23` `21` `22` `$40`

Hampden | 1011 W. 36th St. (bet. Hickory & Roland Aves.) |
410-366-1163 | www.alchemyon36.com

Ever-present chef Michael Matassa's "inspired", moderately priced New American offerings are well paired with wine by the sommelier, his wife Debi, at this Hampdenite "right on the 'Avenue'"; the "enthusiastic and helpful" staff ably plays upstairs/downstairs in the bi-level space that's "snug" but "sleek."

Ⓩ Aldo's Italian

`28` `26` `27` `$57`

Little Italy | 306 S. High St. (Fawn St.) | 410-727-0700 |
www.aldositaly.com

"Splendid" "old-world Italian" cuisine is "served with class" by tuxedoed waiters at this venerable Little Italy "gem" that's "worth all the hype" (and the liras) thanks to chef-owners Aldo and Sergio Vitale, who "make you feel Italian"; a light-filled atrium is the centerpiece of the "serene", "elegant" dining room, which many deem the perfect place "to entertain clients, take a romantic date or just spoil yourself."

Ale Marys ❶ *Pub Food* <u>22</u> <u>19</u> <u>22</u> <u>$23</u>

Fells Point | 1939 Fleet St. (S. Washington St.) | 410-276-2044 | www.alemarys.com

There are "enough photos of nuns to make any lapsed Catholic feel guilty (or at least giggle)" mixed in with other "campy" religious ephemera at this late-night, "laid-back" "neighborhood" watering hole in Fells Point; the taps are loaded with "prime" suds and helmed by "personable" bartenders, and the cheap eats provide a "fun twist on classic pub fare" (multiple styles of tater tots, Krispy Kreme bread pudding).

Alewife ❶ *American* <u>22</u> <u>20</u> <u>21</u> <u>$30</u>

Downtown West | 21 N. Eutaw St. (Lombard St.) | 410-545-5112 | www.alewifebaltimore.com

Chef Chad Wells' "monstrously delicious" "smoke burger" tops a "meat-heavy" menu at this midpriced American gastropub in Downtown West housed in an "intriguingly" reimagined 1800s bank that retains a whiff of gaslight in its coffered ceilings and ye olde floors; it's also known for its "phenomenal" beer offerings, including 40 craft brews on tap, and a solid staff that's adept at getting ticket-holders to the nearby Hippodrome by curtain time.

Ambassador Dining Room *Indian* <u>25</u> <u>26</u> <u>25</u> <u>$41</u>

Homewood | Ambassador Apts. | 3811 Canterbury Rd. (bet. 39th St. & University Pkwy.) | 410-366-1484 | www.ambassadordining.com

A Homewood apartment building hides this "delicious" "time machine" to "Colonial India" that's "romantic" whether dining in the "gorgeous" garden in warm weather or in the "quiet and dignified" wood-beamed interior with fireplaces blazing in season; "thoughtful and timely" service contributes to the "expensive but worth it" designation, and free valet parking is a nice extra.

Amicci's *Italian* <u>24</u> <u>19</u> <u>23</u> <u>$29</u>

Little Italy | 231 S. High St. (bet. Fawn & Stiles Sts.) | 410-528-1096 | www.amiccis.com

There's "plenty of cheese and sauce to go around" at this "reasonably" priced, "family-friendly" Little Italy longtimer in a "simple" space decorated with vintage posters; thanks to the "attentive" staff and "huge" servings – like the "big-as-your-head" *pane rotundo,* a bread bowl stuffed with shrimp – "you won't go home hungry."

Andy Nelson's BBQ ⓩ *BBQ* <u>26</u> <u>14</u> <u>22</u> <u>$15</u>

Cockeysville | 11007 York Rd. (Wight Ave.) | 410-527-1226 | www.andynelsonsbbq.com

If you miss the "pink pig on the roof", follow your nose to this "venerable" Cockeysville "hole-in-the-wall", where "succulent" pulled pork "drenched" in "special sauce" "tastes as good as it smells"; besides, "you can't beat the price" or the sides with "kick", often served up by the eponymous "legendary" Baltimore Colts safety; P.S. the pigskin "memorabilia" appeals to sports fans.

An Loi *Vietnamese*

23 | 13 | 19 | $16

Columbia | 7104 Minstrel Way (Snowden River Pkwy.) | 410-381-3188

"Soul-warming" pho noodle soup bowls over connoisseurs at this "delicious" Columbia Vietnamese that also throws in some Korean specialties for good measure; some "don't think much of its plain decor and strip-mall location", but it's always "packed at lunch" on account of "prompt" service and "cheap" tabs.

Annabel Lee Tavern ●☒ *American*

26 | 24 | 23 | $27

Highlandtown | 601 S. Clinton St. (Fleet St.) | 410-522-2929 | www.annabelleetavern.com

This Edgar Allen Poe–themed tavern on the edge of Highlandtown near Canton is a favorite local "haunt" with its "killer" New American menu and moderate tabs; while the small place gets "crowded" and "enthusiastically noisy", Poe fans can sip "clever" cocktails and "read the writing on the walls – literally" (they're covered in excerpts), prompting one reviewer to quoth "I will dine here evermore."

☒ Ann's Dari Creme *Hot Dogs*

25 | 14 | 25 | $10

Glen Burnie | 7918 Ritchie Hwy. (Americana Circle) | 410-761-1231

"They don't make them" like this "kitschy" red, white and blue "Ritchie Highway landmark" anymore, a roadside stand beloved by several generations for its "top-notch deep-fried hot dog subs" and "scrumptious shakes" served by a "witty" staff that "never writes anything down and always gets your order right"; there are a few stools inside, but better to "eat in your car" or at a picnic table – "just don't tell your cardiologist."

☒ Antrim 1844's Smokehouse Restaurant *American/French*

27 | 27 | 27 | $89

Taneytown | Antrim 1844 | 30 Trevanion Rd. (Rte. 140) | 410-756-6812 | www.antrim1844.com

"A night of luxury" awaits at this "historic" Taneytown inn, where the "romantic" experience may start with "hand-passed hors d'oeuvres" "elegantly served" in the drawing room before moving to the dining room for a multicourse French-inspired New American feast that's "as stellar as the starlit sky" – best viewed via a "delightful" stroll through the formal gardens after dinner; it will add considerably to the "splurge", but "stay overnight for the full, unforgettable experience."

NEW Artifact Coffee *Coffeehouse*

- | - | - | I

Clipper Mill | 1500 Union Ave. (Buena Vista Ave.) | 410-449-2287 | www.artifactcoffee.com

Expanding on Woodberry Kitchen's long-brewing passion for caffeine comes this rustic new coffeehouse spin-off in a reclaimed stone factory building near Clipper Mill; a simple American menu of house-made pastries in the morning (with local preserves, natch) as well as local and seasonal lunch and dinner plates share the philosophy, though not the high prices, of the parental unit.

a "longtime favorite" for well-heeled suburbanites; service is "professional", but "be prepared to hand over your wallet" – unless it's Sunday, which is half-price wine night.

Cafe Zen *Chinese*
22 | 15 | 20 | $23

York Road Corridor | 438 E. Belvedere Ave. (York Rd.) | 410-532-0022 | www.cafezen.us

The "diverse menu" of "Chinese food with imagination" ("don't miss the string bean rolls") has made this "spare" but contemporary eatery a "North Baltimore mainstay"; "low" prices and "cordial" service make it an "excellent" dining option "before or after" a movie at the Senator nearby, though "carryout" works too.

Capital Grille *Steak*
26 | 25 | 26 | $62

Inner Harbor | 500 E. Pratt St. (Gay St.) | 443-703-4064 | www.thecapitalgrille.com

See review in the Washington, DC, Directory.

Carlyle Club *Indian*
▽ 21 | 22 | 23 | $37

Homewood | The Carlyle | 500 W. University Pkwy. (bet. 39th & 40th Sts.) | 410-243-5454 | www.carlyleclub.com

This "hidden" Indian "gem" (a sibling of Homewood's Ambassador), "nestled" just off the Johns Hopkins Homewood campus, specializes in coastal subcontinental cuisine that's "delicious", if pricey, and deftly served by a "great" staff; the "peaceful and intimate" space is "surprisingly romantic", with booths for two making it "ideal for dates."

Carolina Kitchen *Southern*
25 | 23 | 23 | $24

Largo | 800 Shoppers Way (Harry S. Truman Dr. N.) | 301-350-2929 | www.thecarolinakitchen.com

Southern "home cooking" "just like grandma's (except here the furniture and dishes actually match)" is the word on these Largo-Hyattsville comfort stations where you are "welcomed when you walk in the door"; they're "inviting" places, with polished wood and homey touches, offering "good value" that a local might visit "every Friday night."

Catonsville Gourmet *Seafood*
26 | 20 | 23 | $35

Catonsville | 829 Frederick Rd. (bet. Mellor & Newburg Aves.) | 410-788-0005 | www.catonsvillegourmet.com

"Not to be missed if you're in the western suburbs", this "fantastic find" in Catonsville nets fans with its "wonderful", "expertly prepared" seafood with occasional Asian touches; while the "noise level" is often high in the "classy"-"casual", nautically minded digs, BYO "helps to keep costs down" (the "knowledgeable" staff is happy to provide the "essentials"); P.S. no reservations means occasional "waits", but the in-house fish market is a "quick" take-out option.

Cazbar *Turkish*
24 | 21 | 21 | $29

Mt. Vernon | 316 N. Charles St. (Saratoga St.) | 410-528-1222 | www.cazbar.pro

A "delectable magic carpet ride" – woven from "elegantly spiced" kebabs, "dreamy" mezes and "Turkish coffee to die for" – is in store

FOOD | DECOR | SERVICE | COST

at this "cool", "dimly" lit Ottoman "hideaway" in Mt. Vernon tended by an "informed" staff; weekend belly dancers and DJs add to "value", and you can get your puff on in the upstairs hookah lounge.

Chameleon Cafe ⬛Ⓜ *American*   27 | 19 | 26 | $43

Northeast Baltimore | 4341 Harford Rd. (Montebello Terr.) | 410-254-2376 | www.thechameleoncafe.com

"Farm-to-table since before it was trendy", this Lauraville New American is still known for "casual but complex" menus "based on local, fresh" ingredients, though a returning chef is freshening the menu (possibly outdating the Food rating); the "humble-looking" exterior belies high tabs and hides an "intimate" dining room show-casing work by local artists and tended by "lovely, informal" servers, all adding to this "neighborhood gastronome's dream."

Chaps Pit Beef *BBQ*   27 | 10 | 23 | $12

East Baltimore | 5801 Pulaski Hwy. (Erdman Ave.) | 410-483-2379 | www.chapspitbeef.com

"Meat paired with meat with a side of meat" makes for "carni-vore heaven" at this "East Bawlmer" pit-beef stand that's famous for its "smoked deliciousness on a bun" – and where "the only green thing may be relish"; service is solid, and prices are low, but "prepare for lines" and the fact that it's located "in the parking lot of a strip club."

🇿 Charleston ⬛ *American*   29 | 28 | 28 | $99

Harbor East | 1000 Lancaster St. (Exeter St.) | 410-332-7373 | www.charlestonrestaurant.com

Cindy Wolf remains "at the top of her game", applying "world-class technique" to "Low Country" cuisine to create "phenomenal" New American masterpieces at her Harbor East "destination", which qualifies as "Baltimore's best restaurant" with its No. 1 ratings for Food, Decor and Service; "no detail goes unnoticed" by the "super-lative" staffers who "spoil" guests, plying them with selections from an "epic" wine list in a "stunningly beautiful" space; just "be pre-pared" for the multicourse menu's "sticker shock" – for many, it's a "once-every-few-years kind of place."

Chazz: A Bronx Original *Italian/Pizza*   24 | 25 | 23 | $32

Harbor East | 1415 Aliceanna St. (Central Ave.) | 410-522-5511 | www.chazzbronxoriginal.com

"Welcome to the Bronx", or as close as you can get to it in Harbor East, says the "authentic" decor (subway tiles, old-timey photo murals) at actor Chazz Palminteri's Arthur Avenue–Italian theme park that's "loads of fun"; the "excellent", midpriced menu, including "awesome" coal-fired pizza, is overseen by the Vitale family of Aldo's, prompting even "New Yorkers" to praise the food and "courteous" service.

🇿 Cheesecake Factory *American*   24 | 22 | 22 | $30

Inner Harbor | Harborplace Pratt Street Pavilion | 201 E. Pratt St. (South St.) | 410-234-3990
Columbia | Mall in Columbia | 10300 Little Patuxent Pkwy. (Wincopin Circle) | 410-997-9311

crab cakes, wings, nachos and bacon on a stick, washed down by proprietary beers brewed on-site; the old warehouse environs are festooned with baseball memorabilia, but if you want to ogle any of it on game days around game time, you must have a ticket.

Z Di Pasquale's Marketplace 🖺 *Italian*　28　15　22　$16

East Baltimore | 3700 Gough St. (Dean St.) | 410-276-6787 | www.dipasquales.com

"Bring your appetite" to this "old-fashioned" East Baltimore specialty store where Europhiles shop for "Italian staples" or sit in the cafe area for a quick meal of "homemade" soups and "big, fat" sandwiches heaped with "made-fresh-daily" mozzarella; staffers "make you feel at home", and though there is "no decor" to speak of, the "wonderful aromas" provide ambiance; P.S. closes at 6 PM.

The Dizz ◑ *American*　19　16　20　$20

Hampden | 300 W. 30th St. (Remington Ave.) | 443-869-5864 | www.thedizzbaltimore.com

"Baltimore in a bar" say adoptees of this "homey" Hampdenite with "mismatched" decor, a "mixed bag of patrons" and servers who "treat you like family"; the "big plates" of "well-made" American pub "standards" – burgers, wings and a few "fancy" specials – come at prices that are "hard to beat."

Dogwood *American*　26　19　24　$39

Hampden | 911 W. 36th St. (Roland Ave.) | 410-889-0952 | www.dogwoodbaltimore.com

The "social conscience" of chefs-owners Bridget and Galen Sampson is in full blossom at their midpriced Hampden American on the 'Avenue' – from the "applause"-worthy "reliance on local" ingredients in the "imaginative", "palate-pleasing" plates to employing staffers "who need a second chance" to provide the "excellent", "accommodating" service; the basement venue feels "cave"-like to a few, but most find it "funky", "colorful" and "fun", and cite a "very good price-value relationship."

Z Double T Diner *Diner*　20　16　21　$18

Bel Air | 543 Market Place Dr. (Veterans Memorial Hwy.) | 410-836-5591

White Marsh | 10741 Pulaski Hwy. (Ebenezer Rd.) | 410-344-1020 ◑

Catonsville | 6300 Baltimore National Pike (N. Rolling Rd.) | 410-744-4151 ◑

Ellicott City | 10055 Baltimore National Pike (Bethany Ln.) | 410-750-3300

Perry Hall | 4140 E. Joppa Rd. (Belair Rd.) | 410-248-0160 ◑

Pasadena | 1 Mountain Rd. (Ritchie Hwy.) | 410-766-9669 ◑
www.doubletdiner.com

For "sinful" breakfasts or "a quick bite anytime", eaters of "all ages" flock to this "always busy", "subtly Greek", retro-looking Maryland diner chain; the menu is "novel"-length, and the "tasty" grub and "phenomenal" desserts – served "lickety-split" by "courteous" staff – are a "great value for the money"; P.S. some locations are open 24/7.

	FOOD	DECOR	SERVICE	COST

Du-Claw *Pub Food*

21 | 20 | 20 | $24

Bel Air | 16 Bel Air S. Pkwy. (Veterans Memorial Hwy.) |
410-515-3222
Bowie | Bowie Town Ctr. | 4000 Town Center Blvd. (Collington Rd.) |
301-809-6943
Hanover | Arundel Mills | 7000 Arundel Mills Circle (Arundel Mills Dr.) |
410-799-1166
www.duclaw.com

"Crispy" wings, "go-to" burgers and other pub grub standards provide an inexpensive, "dependable" accompaniment to the "awesome" selection of beer at this microbrewery mini-chain; service is "energetic", and the "homey" spaces are "relaxing", plus there are occasional "fun" beer-release events.

Dukem *Ethiopian*

24 | 15 | 19 | $25

Mt. Vernon | 1100 Maryland Ave. (W. Chase St.) | 410-385-0318 |
www.dukemrestaurant.com
See review in the Washington, DC, Directory.

NEW Earth, Wood & Fire Ⓜ *Pizza*

- | - | - | I

North Baltimore | 1407 Clarkview Rd. (Falls Rd.) | 410-825-3473 |
www.earthwoodfire.com

A coal-burning oven that can crisp a pizza in just four minutes flat cranks out pies – with both traditional and creative toppings – at this new, inexpensive North Baltimore parlor; the modern-industrial decor of the former machine-parts factory provides an inviting backdrop for noshing and sampling from a well-edited selection of craft beers and wines.

Edo Sushi *Japanese*

24 | 20 | 23 | $29

Inner Harbor | Harborplace Pratt Street Pavilion | 201 E. Pratt St.
(South St.) | 410-843-9804
Timonium | Padonia Village Shopping Ctr. | 53 E. Padonia Rd. (York Rd.) |
410-667-9200

Edo Mae Sushi *Japanese*

Owings Mills | Boulevard Corporate Ctr. | 10995 Owings Mills Blvd.
(bet. Gwynnbrook Ave. & Reisterstown Rd.) | 410-356-6818

Edo Sushi II *Japanese*

Owings Mills | Garrison Forest Plaza | 10347 Reisterstown Rd.
(Rosewood Ln.) | 410-363-7720
www.edosushimd.com

"Dynamite!" say raw-raw supporters of this "local favorite" chain of sushi specialists, whose "fun chefs" craft "inventive rolls" that are "always super-fresh" and priced to move; service is "pleasant" and "polite", and the traditional blond-wood settings are "inviting" (the more contemporary Harborplace outpost commands a "wonderful view" of the water).

Eggspectation *American*

21 | 20 | 21 | $22

Ellicott City | Columbia Corporate Park 100 |
6010 University Blvd. (Waterloo Rd.) | 410-750-3115 |
www.eggspectations.com
See review in the Washington, DC, Directory.

	FOOD	DECOR	SERVICE	COST

Z Elkridge Furnace Inn M *American*   `25` `27` `27` `$49`

Elkridge | 5745 Furnace Ave. (bet. Main St. & Race Rd.) | 410-379-9336 |
www.elkridgefurnaceinn.com

"An elegance rarely seen in Elkridge" is the draw at this 18th-
century inn offering a "plush, Colonial" backdrop for an "excellent" New American repast that may include a few "unusual
offerings" like game in season; service is "impeccable", and
though it's "expensive", true "romantics" aver "that's how you tell
someone you care."

Facci *Italian/Pizza*   `24` `21` `21` `$30`

Laurel | Montpelier Shopping Ctr. | 7530 Montpelier Rd.
(Johns Hopkins Rd.) | 301-604-5555 | www.faccirestaurant.com

"Wildly popular" in Laurel, this "progressive Italian" features a "diverse, modern" menu that includes "fantastic" brick-oven pizza,
washed down by "impressive" wines, some dispensed by an Enomatic
machine; "parking can be a challenge", but the "casual-classy" atmosphere, "pleasant" service and "reasonable" prices make it worth
fighting for a space.

Z Faidley's Seafood S *Seafood*   `26` `10` `18` `$21`

Downtown West | Lexington Mkt. | 203 N. Paca St. (Lexington St.) |
410-727-4898 | www.faidleyscrabcakes.com

"True crab cake pilgrims" come from afar for the "incredible",
"softball-sized" delicacies "jam-packed with big chunks" of lump
meat at this "real Baltimore experience" in the "historic", circa-1886
Lexington Market on the "gritty" Westside; service is "quick", prices
are "low" and there are "no frills" (no chairs – you stand up to eat at
communal tables); P.S. fans swear by an "unsurpassed raw bar" and
oyster shuckers that are "the best in the business."

First Watch *American*   `21` `16` `22` `$14`

Pikesville | 1431 Reisterstown Rd. (Old Court Rd.) | 410-602-1595 |
www.firstwatch.com

As a "consistently good" breakfast-and-lunch option (sorry, no dinner), this chain cafe in Pikesville pleases with its "varied" menu (you
can be "healthy" or "bad") and "can't-beat" prices; the brand's "bright,
happy colors" go well with the "prompt and friendly" service, leading the families and business folks who frequent it to lament "too
bad" the hours are "so short."

Z Five Guys *Burgers*   `24` `14` `21` `$12`

Inner Harbor | Harborplace Pratt Street Pavilion | 201 E. Pratt St.
(South St.) | 410-244-7175
Canton | Shoppes at Brewers Hill | 3600 Boston St. (S. Conkling St.) |
410-522-1580
White Marsh | Shops at Nottingham Sq. | 5272 Campbell Blvd.
(Philadelphia Rd.) | 410-933-1017
Bowie | Bowie Town Ctr. | 3851 Town Center Blvd. (Emerald Way) |
301-464-9633
Hanover | Shops at Arundel Preserve | 7690 Dorchester Blvd.
(bet. Arundel Mills Blvd. & Wright Rd.) | 410-799-3933

(continued)

(continued)

Five Guys

Glen Burnie | Centre Mall of Glen Burnie | 6711 Ritchie Hwy.
(Ordnance Rd.) | 410-590-3933
Cockeysville | York Market Pl. | 10015 York Rd. (bet. Cranbrook &
Warren Sts.) | 410-667-0818
Towson | 936 York Rd. (Fairmount Ave.) | 410-321-4963
Westminster | 140 Village Shopping Ctr. | 596 Jermor Ln.
(Old Baltimore Rd.) | 410-751-9969
www.fiveguys.com
Additional locations throughout the Baltimore area
See review in the Washington, DC, Directory.

Fleming's Prime Steakhouse & Wine Bar *Steak*

25 | 24 | 25 | $61

Harbor East | 720 Aliceanna St. (President St.) | 410-332-1666 |
www.flemingssteakhouse.com
See review in the Washington, DC, Directory.

Fogo de Chão *Brazilian/Steak*

27 | 24 | 27 | $61

Inner Harbor | 600 E. Pratt St. (bet. Gay St. & Market Pl.) |
410-528-9292 | www.fogodechao.com
See review in the Washington, DC, Directory.

NEW Food Market ● *American*

- | - | - | M

Hampden | 1017 W. 36th St. (Roland Ave.) | 410-366-0606 |
www.thefoodmarketbaltimore.com
From the open kitchen of a former Hampden grocery store made
famous in John Waters' film *Pecker,* Chad Gauss dishes up an inventive menu of traditional Americana loaded with twists; the
sleek, modern interior with touches of rustic metal and wood,
plus a bar pouring cool cocktails until late, have made it a fast favorite on the 'Avenue.'

NEW Fork & Wrench ● *American*

- | - | - | M

Canton | 2322 Boston St. (Wagner St.) | 443-759-9360 |
www.theforkandwrench.com
The setting for this New American gastropub in Canton is designed
to evoke early 20th-century industry, with distressed zinc-covered
tables, retro fixtures and vintage tools and accoutrement throughout its many dark nooks; the midpriced, oft-changing farm-to-table
menu is likewise period themed – presented in categories like 'jars',
'flock and field' and 'herd and pen' – as is the cocktail list (how
about an Aviation?).

4 Seasons Grille *Eclectic/Mediterranean*

25 | 24 | 24 | $40

Gambrills | 2630 Chapel Lake Dr. (Crain Hwy.) | 410-451-5141 |
www.4seasonsgrille.com
A "bright little surprise" in a Gambrills strip mall, this midpriced
Mediterranean-Eclectic bistro "delivers" with its "excellent",
"healthy"-feeling cuisine and "wonderful" service; it's "warm and
inviting" and "just dark enough" for an "awesome" date night, and
there's a "popular" bar that's a "great place to meet friends."

Friendly Farm *American*

25 | 16 | 24 | $25

Upperco | 17434 Foreston Rd. (Mt. Carmel Rd.) | 410-239-7400 |
www.friendlyfarm.net

"Only real Hoovers leave" this "old-fashioned dining hall" on a
"picturesque" North Baltimore County farm "without a doggie bag"
of "1950s"-inspired Americana reminiscent of "Sunday dinner at
grandma's" (e.g. "excellent" fried chicken, "out-of-this-world" sugar
biscuits); the "service lives up to the name", and those waiting in
weekend lines can visit the gift shop or feed the ducks.

⬧ G&M *Seafood*

24 | 16 | 20 | $29

Linthicum | 804 N. Hammonds Ferry Rd. (Nursery Rd.) | 410-636-1777 |
www.gandmcrabcakes.com

"Bigger-than-your-head" crab cakes with "lots of lump meat" are the
reason travelers "take cabs from BWI" during layovers to visit this
"affordable" Linthicum "mecca", where the lengthy menu has Italian
and Greek eats, but the crustacean creations are the "real star"; the
simple, white-tablecloth setting is "pleasant" enough, and service is
"old-school", but really, it's all about "one thing" here.

Garry's Grill *American*

20 | 14 | 19 | $22

Severna Park | 553 Baltimore Annapolis Blvd. (bet. McKinsey Rd. &
Ritchie Hwy.) | 410-544-0499 | www.garrysgrill.com

"Homestyle cooking" "with a twist" makes this "casual" American fixture "hidden" in a Severna Park strip mall a "decent" "neighborhood"
option for a "nice, reasonable meal", especially at "breakfast"; the
comfortable, upscale-diner setup gets a boost from "friendly" service.

Germano's Trattoria *Italian*

24 | 21 | 23 | $35

Little Italy | 300 S. High St. (Fawn St.) | 410-752-4515 |
www.germanostrattoria.com

Owner Germano Fabiani "oversees all" at his long-standing Little Italy
mainstay, ensuring "excellent" service as diners sup on the "extremely
good" midpriced Tuscan fare; "fantastic Belle Époque art posters"
(yes, they're originals) are the highlight of the old-school interior,
though the musically minded "love" the upstairs cabaret, "a gem" that
features performances by local and far-flung acts Thursday–Sunday.

Gertrude's ⓜ *Chesapeake*

22 | 25 | 23 | $37

Charles Village | Baltimore Museum of Art | 10 Art Museum Dr.
(N. Charles St.) | 410-889-3399 | www.gertrudesbaltimore.com

"Manet and Cezanne would have stopped painting" to enjoy an alfresco meal "at the edge of the sculpture garden" or inside this "oasis" within the Baltimore Museum of Art say connoisseurs of John
Shields' "sassy, Southern", "Chesapeake Bay–oriented" menu presented by "knowledgeable" servers; prices are moderate, and $12
entrees on Tuesdays are "a great touch."

Gino's Burgers & Chicken *Burgers*

22 | 20 | 21 | $12

NEW **Perry Hall** | 5001 Honeygo Center Dr. (Honeygo Blvd.) |
410-870-2746

(continued)

(continued)

Gino's Burgers & Chicken

Towson | 8600 LaSalle Rd. (bet. E. Joppa Rd. & Putty Hill Ave.) |
410-583-0000
www.ginosgiant.com

"Nostalgia" reigns for those who remember the original Gino's
drive-up, founded by two former Baltimore Colts in the '50s, when
they visit these "popular" sit-down retro revivals in Towson and
Perry Hall; longtime loyalists say the "tasty" burgers and "fantastic"
shakes are "almost as good as the original", the service "lives up to
the food" and the prices are still fairly vintage.

Goldberg's New York Bagels *Bakery/Jewish*

`25` `9` `16` `$11`

Pikesville | 1500 Reisterstown Rd. (Old Court Rd.) | 410-415-7001 |
www.goldbergsbagels.com

You can "skip the trip to NYC" in favor of this "real-deal" Pikesville
bakery/deli that "isn't much to look at" but "sure knows how to bake
bagels", not to mention make all manner of other "kosher Jewish delights" like blintzes and rugalach; "service could be improved" – still,
it's "fast" and the prices are right; P.S. serves breakfast and lunch
only, except Saturdays, when it's dinner only.

Golden West Cafe *Eclectic/New Mexican*

`21` `19` `16` `$21`

Hampden | 1105 W. 36th St. (bet. Falls Rd. & Hickory Ave.) |
410-889-8891 | www.goldenwestcafe.com

"Tasty" New Mexican dishes (including "magical" Frito pie) come in
portions "way too big for one person" at this "funky", "retro" Hampden
"roadhouse", but if that's not your thing it also offers "vegetarian" options and a passel of Eclectic comfort grub and other "hangover" helpers; it's "inexpensive" too, though some say beware the
"too-cool" "hipster" staffers who sometimes "take forever" – the
place is "nicknamed 'Golden Wait' for a reason."

Grace Garden ✍ *Chinese*

∇ `28` `9` `20` `$22`

Odenton | 1690 Annapolis Rd. (Reece Rd.) | 410-672-3581 |
www.gracegardenchinese.com

"Authentic wonders" come from this "unassuming" Odenton
Chinese, where a husband-and-wife team "takes great pride" in
introducing such "un-localized" treats as "flavorful" tea-smoked
duck and noodles "made from ground fish", most at an "unbelievable bargain"; ignore the "hole-in-the-wall" surrounds and
focus on the "rare" fare that'll make you say "we don't need no
stinkin' chop suey" (though they do have a full Westernized
Chinese menu too).

Grace's Fortune *Chinese*

`25` `24` `25` `$30`

Bowie | 15500 Annapolis Rd. (Scarlet Oak Terr.) | 301-805-1108 |
www.gracesrestaurants.com

"Wonderful" Chinese cookery "right down to the soy sauce" is the
way the cookie crumbles at Grace Tang's Bowie bastion that's been
"a family favorite for many years"; it "isn't cheap" exactly, but there's

plenty of value in the "superb" service and "exotic" decor, which features hand-carved wood furnishings and a koi pond.

Grano Emporio *Italian* ▽ 25 | 18 | 22 | $34
(aka Big Grano)

Hampden | 3547 Chestnut Ave. (36th St.) | 443-438-7521 | www.granopastabar.com

The "lovely" owner and "happy" staff "define warmth" at this "cute and cozy" midpriced Italian spot "at the edge of 'hon'-dom", er Hampden, and better yet, the "home-cooked" pasta and such is "outstanding"; add in a wine bar and a "wonderful" deck, and it's a "gem", if somewhat "undiscovered."

Grano Pasta Bar 🗷 *Italian* 25 | 14 | 22 | $22
(aka Little Grano)

Hampden | 1031 W. 36th St. (Hickory Ave.) | 443-869-3429 | www.granopastabar.com

Providing a "laid-back pasta break" in Hampden is this "homey" spot that offers a simple "mix-and-match" menu of "delicious, hearty" pastas and sauces; service is "great", and low prices are abetted by a BYO policy, and though it's "tiny" one can "usually snag" a seat inside or on the sidewalk.

Great Sage Ⓜ *Vegan* 24 | 21 | 24 | $25

Clarksville | Clarksville Square Dr. | 5809 Clarksville Square Dr. (Clarksville Pike) | 443-535-9400 | www.greatsage.com

"Even a carnivore" will feel "satisfied" after a meal at this colorfully decorated vegan bastion in Clarksville, where there's a "creative, delicious" dish for everyone, including "gluten-, soy-, peanut-free" choices and the "occasional raw" option; staff is "accommodating" – "special orders delight them" – and the prices are easy to digest, leaving money for shopping at the other co-owned 'mindful' businesses in the strip (market, pet store, home-goods store).

Greg's Bagels ⊅ *Bakery* 24 | 14 | 22 | $10

York Road Corridor | Belvedere Sq. | 519 E. Belvedere Ave. (York Rd.) | 410-323-9463

"Always there" owner Greg Novik is "the key" to the long-running "success" of this Belvedere Square bakery that weathered the area's decline and rebirth; "friendly" staffers serve "fresh", "interesting" bagels, an "amazing selection of smoked fish" and possibly "the largest choice of spreads in Baltimore", at affordable prices in a no-frills cafe with a checkered floor; P.S. it's cash only and closes by 3 PM weekdays.

Greystone Grill *Steak* 19 | 20 | 19 | $42

Ellicott City | MDG Corporate Ctr. | 8850 Columbia 100 Pkwy. (Centre Park Rd.) | 410-715-4739 | www.greystonegrill.com

Located in an Ellicott City office park, this value-priced steakhouse specializes in "well-prepared, filling" fare fit for a "nice dinner", where "everyone finds something they like"; although some call the whole experience "ho-hum", restaurant-wide WiFi and a private wine vault equipped with audio-visual equipment make the stone-and-wood-accented setting "recommended" for a "business meeting."

Grilled Cheese & Co. *Sandwiches*   22 | 16 | 20 | $12

NEW Federal Hill | 1036 Light St. (bet. E. Cross & Poultney Sts.) | 410-244-6333
Catonsville | 500 Edmondson Ave. (I-695) | 410-747-2610
Eldersburg | 577 Johnsville Rd. (Sykesville Rd.) | 443-920-3238
www.ilovegrilledcheese.com

With an "updated" take on the "comfort classic", this "feel-good" chainlet puts "grilled cheese on steroids", offering "inventive" versions stuffed with everything from crab to crumbled meatballs; though there's "limited seating" in the simple, earth-toned digs, the "fast food"–style counter service is "friendly" and the tabs "reasonable."

Gunning's Seafood *Seafood*   23 | 16 | 21 | $29

Hanover | 7304 Parkway Dr. (Coca-Cola Dr.) | 410-712-9404
NEW Glen Burnie | Burnwood Shopping Plaza |
7089 Baltimore Annapolis Blvd. (Rte. 648) | 410-691-2722
www.gunningsonline.com

"Bring your mallet" to this midpriced seafooder in Hanover (with a newer location in Glen Burnie), where you'll crack open "awesome" steamed Chesapeake Bay crustaceans, gobble "superior" crab cakes and down pitchers of beer "to extinguish the spice"; there's "nothing fancy" about the setting, but with "attentive" servers and specials available "nowhere else", coming here is a "tradition."

Hamilton Tavern *Pub Food*   24 | 21 | 21 | $23

Northeast Baltimore | 5517 Harford Rd. (Hamilton Ave.) | 410-426-1930 |
www.hamiltontavern.com

"Tasty farm-to-table versions of pub standards" make up the "always changing" menu at this affordable Harford Road tavern where folks rave about the "fabulous" burgers (worth a "cross-town" trip) and "thoughtful" microbrew selection; tin ceilings, exposed brick and lots of wood give it a "cozy" vibe, and staffers reinforce the "unpretentious" feel, all the more reason you'll "wish you lived next door."

Harryman House Grill *American*   24 | 23 | 23 | $36

Reisterstown | 340 Main St. (bet. Bond Ave. & Glyndon Dr.) |
410-833-8850 | www.harrymanhouse.com

Fittingly located near "Antiques Row" in Reisterstown, this "quaint" old house has long provided a "cherished" backdrop for well-heeled "family gatherings" and "romantic dates" in its sprawling environs, which include a circa-1791 log cabin room ("dark" and "charming") and a newer high-ceilinged great room and adjacent porch (bright and airy); "creative" New American entrees and more casual "standards like burgers" share the midpriced menu and are served with aplomb.

Havana Road Cuban Café *Cuban*   21 | 18 | 20 | $26

Towson | 8 W. Pennsylvania Ave. (bet. Washington Ave. & York Rd.) |
410-494-8222 | www.havanaroad.com

"Authentic" offerings like pork sandwiches and ropa vieja from Marta Inés Quintana's "Cuban heaven" in Towson are enthusiastically compared to their "South Florida" compadres, and her sauces are so "tasty" they're sold at local stores; BYO mellows already "reasonable" tabs, another reason guests have had "many happy returns" to the "small, attractive spot" decorated with pictures of Old Havana.

NEW Heavy Seas Alehouse ◐ *American* ▽ 19 | 21 | 21 | $41

Harbor East | 1300 Bank St. (Central Ave.) | 410-522-0850 | www.heavyseasalehouse.com

"Stupendous" locally brewed ale gets showcased at this rustic 19th-century tack factory dressed in the "original brick and timber" in Harbor East; "quite tasty" is the early word on the raw bar and American gastropub menu designed by chef/co-owner Matt Seeber (a Tom Colicchio protégé), and of course the able-bodied deckhands can suggest beer pairings as well as high-end rum.

Helmand *Afghan* 27 | 21 | 23 | $32

Mt. Vernon | 806 N. Charles St. (bet. Madison & Read Sts.) | 410-752-0311 | www.helmand.com

Diners make a "culinary expedition" to this midpriced Mt. Vernon "landmark" for "consistently amazing" Afghani fare (baked pumpkin is "especially recommended") served by "gracious" staffers justifiably "proud" of the cuisine; add an "elegant" space enriched with "attractive tapestries" and fans call it a "work of art."

Henninger's Tavern Ⓢ Ⓜ *American* ▽ 25 | 22 | 24 | $35

Fells Point | 1812 Bank St. (bet. Ann & Wolfe Sts.) | 410-342-2172 | www.henningerstavern.com

On a "quiet street" in Fells Point is this "hidden gem" serving "expert" New American fare in an "rustic old pub" whose "every inch" is filled with "kitschy" "photos, paintings and oddities"; tabs are moderate, and the couple who runs it keeps things "friendly" and "always fun."

NEW Hersh's Pizza *Pizza* - | - | - | I

South Baltimore | 1843 Light St. (E. Wells St.) | 443-438-4948 | www.hershspizza.com

The siblings behind this new, inexpensive pizzeria in South Baltimore take pride in their ingredient-driven philosophy, expressed in pie toppings like housemade sausage and house-pickled hot peppers (they also serve Italian small plates) washed down by craft cocktails and microbrews; surreal, larger-than-life photo-realistic grayscale murals are a conversation piece in the speakeasy-feeling digs.

Honey Pig Gooldaegee Korean Grill ◐ *Korean* 23 | 13 | 17 | $24

Ellicott City | Princess Shopping Ctr. | 10045 Baltimore National Pike (Centennial Ln.) | 410-696-2426 | www.eathoneypig.com

See review in the Washington, DC, Directory.

House of India *Indian* 23 | 17 | 20 | $22

Columbia | 9350 Snowden River Pkwy. (Oakland Mills Rd.) | 410-381-3844 | www.houseofindiainc.com

It may be located in a "modest" storefront in a Snowden River Parkway strip mall, but this North Indian option is "worth a second

glance" for "big, bold flavors" and "generous portions" at "low prices",
plus an "excellent" lunch buffet; "very attentive" servers make sure
water glasses are "never empty", much to the relief of its fans (it can
be "very spicy" if so desired).

Hunan Manor *Chinese*
23 | 20 | 21 | $23

Columbia | 7091 Deepage Dr. (Snowden River Pkwy.) | 410-381-1134 |
www.hunanmanorrestaurant.com

For more than 20 years, this "solid" Columbia "standby" has been
serving up "generous" portions of "better-than-average" Chinese
food in a "pleasant" setting surrounded by "large fish tanks"; "many
a work lunch" has been hosted here because there are "tons of tables" (read: "never a wait"), prices are "competitive" and servers
are "so quick" – plus they have "awesome carryout."

Iggies ⓜ *Pizza*
27 | 17 | 19 | $18

Mt. Vernon | 818 N. Calvert St. (Read St.) | 410-528-0818 |
www.iggiespizza.com

"Crisp-crust" pizzas with "inventive toppings" (duck, leeks, squash)
and "creative salads" delight the "highfalutin foodies" who visit
this affordable Mt. Vernon BYO, whether it's "before Centerstage"
or on a "casual" "night out"; the colorful "warehouse-chic" interior is set up "cafeteria style", so "you provide most of the service"; P.S. closed Monday and Tuesday.

Ikaros *Greek*
23 | 17 | 22 | $28

Greektown | 4901 Eastern Ave. (bet. Oldham & S. Ponca Sts.) |
410-633-3750 | www.ikarosrestaurant.com

Building on its decades-long reputation for "solid Greek classics"
that are "reasonably priced" and delivered by staffers who "bend
over backward" to please, this Greektown stalwart recently moved
into new, larger digs nearby, which are more contemporary and
nightclub-esque, thus outdating the Decor rating; all the old menu
favorites remain, but it's adding items from a charcoal rotisserie and
brick oven, plus a late-night taverna menu at a huge square bar.

Iron Bridge
Wine Company *American*
25 | 23 | 23 | $41

Columbia | 10435 State Rte. 108 (Centennial Ln.) | 410-997-3456 |
www.ironbridgewines.com

A "treat to your senses" awaits at this "pricey" but "worth-the-cash"
New American (with locations in the Columbia "farmlands" and
Warrenton, VA) presenting a "seasonal menu" that's "ever evolv-
ing" and "consistently delicious"; however, oenophiles say the real
star is the "amazing wine collection", and the "charming" servers
are "expert at recommending pairings", making for a "jovial" mood
in "cozy, intimate" settings "among the wine racks."

Jack's Bistro ⓜ *Eclectic*
27 | 19 | 24 | $36

Canton | 3123 Elliott St. (S. Robinson St.) | 410-878-6542 |
www.jacksbistro.net

Behold "crazy decadence" at this "quirky" Canton bistro "tucked away
in a row house", in such "outlandish" Eclectic creations as "chocolate

range prices and "helpful" service make this next-door sibling of Kali's Court a good choice for "a cozy date" or group gathering (order the "deliciously fruity" sangria to share).

NEW Kettle Hill 🌑Ⓜ *American* ─ ─ ─ **E**

Downtown | Power Plant Live | 32 Market Pl. (Water St.) | 443-682-8007 | www.kettle-hill.com

This upscale New American tavern, newly landed in Power Plant Live, serves a seasonal menu complemented by fittingly nostalgic cocktails (it's named for a Spanish-American War battle); the cavernous interior sports vintage photos of obscure early 20th-century athletes, custom millwork, reclaimed barn boards and lights crafted from old barrels.

The Kings Contrivance *American* **24 24 25 $50**

Columbia | 10150 Shaker Dr. (bet. Rtes. 29 & 32) | 410-995-0500 | www.thekingscontrivance.com

"Set your GPS" and "step back into the past" to this "tucked-away little treasure" in a "beautiful old mansion" in Columbia; "delightful" service and "consistently excellent" American fare contribute to an "old-fashioned-in-a-good-way" dining experience that "mom would dig", and if it's "slightly expensive", it's "well worth it."

Kloby's Smokehouse *BBQ* **21 16 20 $19**

Laurel | Montpelier Shopping Ctr. | 7500 Montpelier Rd. (Johns Hopkins Rd.) | 301-362-1510 | www.klobysbbq.com

The "mouthwatering" barbecue at this "casual", "rustic" orange-hued joint tucked into a Laurel strip mall includes the curious 'jar-b-que', brainchild of chef/co-owner Steve Klobosits, wherein "all the good stuff" – hand-pulled pork, beans and slaw – is layered in a mason jar; the meats are matched by a "spectacular draft beer selection", "good bourbon too", "friendly people" and easy prices.

Z Kobe Japanese Steak & **27 24 25 $41**
Seafood House *Japanese*

White Marsh | White Marsh Mall | 8165 Honeygo Blvd. (Campbell Blvd.) | 410-931-8900

Largo | 860 Capital Centre Blvd. (Lottsford Rd.) | 301-333-5555 | www.kobejs.com

Chefs "dazzle" diners at this Japanese teppanyaki/sushi palace in Largo (there are also branches in White Marsh and Leesburg, VA, which were not surveyed), with an "intriguing" culinary show featuring fireworks and "games with the food" that provides "entertainment" for diners seated at communal grill tables, watching their "delicious" multicourse meals being prepared; it works well for "group gatherings", when the "amount of food" (doggy bags routinely provided) and the "experience" "make the cost moot."

Z Koco's 🅢Ⓜ *Pub Food* **27 15 24 $28**

Northeast Baltimore | 4301 Harford Rd. (bet. Overland & Weaver Aves.) | 410-426-3519 | www.kocospub.com

Take "a quirky jaunt to the tropics, Baltimore-style", at this Lauraville pub where a "really friendly" staff doles out some of the "best" jumbo lump crab cakes around, plus classic bar food, in "Jimmy Buffett"-esque, "delicious"-margarita-fueled digs; in keeping with the "unpretentious" setting, tabs are "reasonable" – especially on Thursday's crab cake night, when the joint is "humming."

Kooper's Tavern ● *American*   22 | 17 | 21 | $21

Fells Point | 1702 Thames St. (bet. B'way & S. Ann St.) | 410-563-5423 | www.koopers.com

Kooper's Chowhound Food Truck ◪ *Burgers*

Location varies; see website | no phone |
www.koopperschowhound.com

"Fantastic" burgers (Angus, Kobe, lamb, black bean) star on the American "comfort" menu at this "casual, cozy" Fells Point tavern named for the owner's pup; the feel is "always friendly", as are the prices, and hopsheads note an "awesome beer selection" in the bar where "cute dog photos" dot the walls; P.S. its related food truck takes a limited menu out and about (check website for schedule).

La Famiglia *Italian*   22 | 22 | 23 | $43

Homewood | 105 W. 39th St. (University Pkwy.) | 443-449-5555 | www.lafamigliabaltimore.com

"Delicious" "simple Italian dishes" and "attentive" service led by proprietor Dino Zeytinoglu, who "works the crowd", have JHU types and other locals feeling "at home" in this "relaxing", contemporary Homewood space with a "cozy roaring fireplace in winter" (there's a "great" terrace in warmer months); it's costly, but there's "something for everybody" here, even if it's just "drinks and dessert."

Langermann's *Southern*   22 | 21 | 22 | $33

Canton | 2400 Boston St. (Hudson St.) | 410-534-3287 | www.langermanns.com

"Low Country" cuisine is elevated to "haute Southern" at Neal Langermann's "upbeat" "hot spot" set amid warehouse-chic digs in Canton; the staff "aims to please", as do easygoing tabs, which get even easier during the weeknight happy hour and "filling" Sunday brunch (entree charge includes access to a buffet of sides).

La Scala *Italian*   26 | 23 | 25 | $42

Little Italy | 1012 Eastern Ave. (bet. Central Ave. & Exeter St.) | 410-783-9209 | www.lascaladining.com

"Special-occasion" dining and an "indoor bocce ball" court ("no joke") meet with "incredible atmosphere" under one roof at this Little Italy destination where high-end, "delectable" Sicilian fare and an "extensive" wine list are served by a "flawless", "long-tenured" team; upstairs, away from the fray, the mood is "romantic", while for the true sports-minded, an "active bar scene" attracts the "requisite beautiful people."

La Tavola *Italian*   26 | 22 | 25 | $41

Little Italy | 248 Albemarle St. (Fawn St.) | 410-685-1859 | www.la-tavola.com

Still somewhat "undiscovered" despite its longevity (and large exterior mural), this "exquisite" Little Italy ristorante purveys "authentic"

Italian fare with "delicate" sauces that "will knock your socks off" at tabs that are deemed fair for the quality; servers "make dining a pleasurable adventure" in the roomy, toned-down setting.

The Laurrapin Ⓜ *American* ▽ 26 | 24 | 25 | $34

Havre de Grace | 209 N. Washington St. (Pennington Ave.) | 410-939-4956 | www.laurrapin.com

"New York quality" at "half the price" is the hallmark at this "wonderful" Havre de Grace meeting place turning out "excellent" organic, locally sourced California-accented New American fare in a "funky", multicolored and muraled space; in keeping with its "pub-style" aesthetic, "fantastic", "personable" bartenders pour a "nice" selection of drinks, and live local music on weekends further adds to the good times.

Lebanese Taverna ◕ *Lebanese* 23 | 20 | 21 | $29

Harbor East | 719 S. President St. (Lancaster St.) | 410-244-5533 | www.lebanesetaverna.com

See review in the Washington, DC, Directory.

🄲 Ledo Pizza *Pizza* 23 | 15 | 20 | $17

Lanham | 9454 Lanham Severn Rd. (94th Ave.) | 301-577-5550 | www.ledopizza.com

Additional locations throughout the Baltimore area

See review in the Washington, DC, Directory.

Liberatore's *Italian* 24 | 22 | 23 | $33

Bel Air | 562 Baltimore Pike (Rte. 24) | 410-838-9100

Timonium | Timonium Corporate Ctr. | 9515 Deereco Rd. (Padonia Rd.) | 410-561-3300

Perry Hall | Honeygo Village Ctr. | 5005 Honeygo Center Dr. (Honeygo Blvd.) | 410-529-4567

Eldersburg | Freedom Village Shopping Ctr. | 6300 Georgetown Blvd. (Liberty Rd.) | 410-781-4114

Westminster | 140 Village Shopping Ctr. | 521 Jermor Ln. (Rte. 97) | 410-876-2121 Ⓜ

www.liberatores.com

"If you don't feel like going to Little Italy", these extended family-owned ristorantes around Greater Baltimore are "mainstays" for a "low-key" Italian meal, cooking up "old-fashioned", "seriously good grub" in "family-friendly" settings with "upbeat flair" and "solid", "attentive" service; half-price wine specials add to the "value."

Linwoods *American* 27 | 26 | 27 | $56

Owings Mills | 25 Crossroads Dr. (bet. McDonogh & Reisterstown Rds.) | 410-356-3030 | www.linwoods.com

Chef-owner Linwood Dame brings "interesting nuances" to his "impeccable" "modern" American cuisine at this "serene" spot in Owings Mills that's been "charming" "sophisticated" diners for around a quarter-century; a "contemporary, elegant" room with an open grill, patrolled by a "first-rate" staff, enhances an experience that's worthy of a "special occasion" or any time "you're feeling plush."

Little Spice 🖼 *Thai* ▽ 25 | 17 | 24 | $25

Hanover | 1350 Dorsey Rd. (Ridge Rd.) | 410-859-0100 |
www.littlespicethairestaurant.co

Conjuring the "wonderful street food you would find in Thailand" ("upsized" for America "of course"), this Hanover spot between BWI and the Arundel Mills Mall serves "outstanding" Thai fare in "minimalist" digs for a "reasonable" price; "excellent" service comes from a "friendly" staff willing to "adjust the heat level either up or down."

Mama's on the Half Shell *Seafood* 26 | 22 | 23 | $32

Canton | 2901 O'Donnell St. (S. Linwood Ave.) | 410-276-3160 |
www.mamasmd.com

"Butter, cream and deep-fried batter rule the menu" at this "reasonably priced" Canton Square tavern offering "large portions" of "exceptional", "guilty-pleasure seafood", plus an "amazing" oyster selection and "freshly squeezed orange crush"; it's "popular (read: noisy and crowded)", but the service is "timely", and there are plenty of places to perch among the "pictures and artifacts from the city's past" – at the "lively bar downstairs" or "cozy tables upstairs" – or on the sidewalk in the summer.

Mamma Lucia *Italian* 22 | 16 | 21 | $23

Elkridge | Gateway Overlook | 6630 Marie Curie Dr. (Waterloo Rd.) |
410-872-4894 | www.mammaluciarestaurants.com
See review in the Washington, DC, Directory.

M&S Grill *Seafood/Steak* 22 | 21 | 21 | $38

Inner Harbor | Harborplace Pratt Street Pavilion | 201 E. Pratt St. (South St.) | 410-547-9333 | www.mandsgrill.com
See review in the Washington, DC, Directory.

Mango Grove *Indian* ▽ 24 | 20 | 21 | $20

Columbia | 8865 Stanford Blvd. (Dobbin Rd.) | 410-884-3426 |
www.themangogrove.net

Vegetarian and vegan "mouths water just thinking about" the "extensive" buffet at this "friendly" and affordable Indian oasis in Columbia that also throws a few bones to "die-hard meat eaters" with a separate Indo-Chinese menu under the banner Mirchi Wok; followers approve of the new, "larger space" and "snazzier" decor featuring table linens and orange and plum accents.

Manor Tavern *American* 24 | 23 | 23 | $35

Monkton | 15819 Old York Rd. (Manor Rd.) | 410-771-8155 |
www.themanortavern.com

"New ownership has helped" revive this longtime "special-occasion" spot nestled "in the middle of horse country" in Monkton, now featuring a "delightful" menu of midpriced Americana, much of it made from "locally grown and sourced ingredients"; "competent" service and ongoing upgrades to the "pleasant" equine-themed dining room, lounge and banquet facilities add to the consensus that "things are on the upswing."

Marie Louise Bistro *French/Mediterranean*   22 | 21 | 19 | $32

Mt. Vernon | 904 N. Charles St. (Read St.) | 410-385-9946 |
www.marielouisebistrocatering.com

A "relaxing" place to linger near the Walters Art Museum is this
French-Med Mt. Vernonite with an "attractive" European-cafe look
to its tiled floor, marble-topped tables and chandeliers suspended
from the high ceiling (upstairs, there's a bar area); the "reasonably
priced" bistro fare and "gorgeous desserts" are served with aplomb
by a "cheerful" staff, making it a "neighborhood gem."

Mari Luna Latin Grill *Mexican/Pan-Latin*   25 | 22 | 26 | $28

Pikesville | 1010 Reisterstown Rd. (Sherwood Ave.) | 410-653-5151 |
www.mariluna.com

Offering a "nice change of pace" for Pikesville is Jaime Luna's
"popular" Pan-Latin counterpart to his Mexican grill down the
road, where "terrific" eats (including popovers "to die for") are
washed down by gallons of "tasty" sangria in a "beautiful" gold-
and-red setting that features a huge picture-window view of the
kitchen; like its sibling, it boasts "wonderful", "professional" service
and "fair" prices.

Mari Luna Mexican   24 | 16 | 22 | $23
Grill Ⓜ *Mexican/Pan-Latin*

Pikesville | 102 Reisterstown Rd. (Seven Mile Ln.) |
410-486-9910

Mari Luna Bistro Ⓜ *Mexican/Pan-Latin*

Mt. Vernon | 1225 Cathedral St. (Biddle St.) | 410-637-8013
www.mariluna.com

"Unpretentious" but "wonderful" say compadres of chef-owner
Jaime Luna's Pikesville flagship Mexican and its "fantastic", "inexpensive" south-of-the-border classics ported by an "extremely
friendly" staff to a "bustling", "brightly colored" dining space; the
newer Mt. Vernon bistro is a perfect spot to grab some guac or a
drink "before a show at the BSO."

Matsuri *Japanese*   ▽ 24 | 19 | 21 | $25

South Baltimore | 1105 S. Charles St. (Cross St.) | 410-752-8561 |
www.matsuri.us

A "young", "upbeat crowd" claims this Federal Hill sushi spot as
a "local" go-to for "first-rate", "decently" priced raw and cooked
Japanese eats served at a "good tempo"; the "traditional" setting
includes "limited" seating downstairs, supplemented by a more spacious room upstairs (also available for private parties) and sidewalk
tables; P.S. check out the weeknight happy-hour "deals."

Matthew's Pizza *Pizza*   27 | 15 | 23 | $16

Highlandtown | 3131 Eastern Ave. (S. East Ave.) | 410-276-8755 |
www.matthewspizza.com

"Crust, sauce and cheese are in perfect harmony" at this "insanely
good" deep-dish purveyor (they also offer thin crust) in Highlandtown,
which many consider the "birthplace of pizza in Baltimore" because
it opened in 1943; the "friendly" staff, modest tabs and "small"

storefront that's "quirkily" decorated with vivid fauvist murals of Italy all offer a "trip back to simpler times"; P.S. it's "convenient" before or after a show at Creative Alliance.

McCabe's Pub Food
23 | 16 | 22 | $28

Hampden | 3845 Falls Rd. (bet. 40th St. & Kelly Pl.) | 410-467-1000 | www.mccabeshampden.com

"Perfect for a good burger or crab cake", this midpriced Hampden pub is a "true neighborhood place", drawing a "local crowd" with "reliable comfort food" in "quaint" wood-and-brick-accented environs; the "nice folks" who staff it contribute to the overall "charming" vibe.

McCormick & Schmick's Seafood
23 | 22 | 23 | $45

Inner Harbor | Pier 5 Hotel | 711 Eastern Ave. (S. President St.) | 410-234-1300 | www.mccormickandschmicks.com

See review in the Washington, DC, Directory.

Meet 27 American
∇ 21 | 15 | 21 | $24

Charles Village | 127 W. 27th St. (Howard St.) | 410-585-8121 | www.meet27.com

"Picky eaters, wheat-free, vegans" and even carnivores too have no reason to fear at this Charles Village noshery whose "affordable" New American menu, with South Asian and Caribbean influences ,"caters to diet-sensitives" – "and does it well"; reclaimed-wood tables and colorful murals painted by local students provide a modicum of ambiance, and "BYO is a plus."

ⓩ Mekong Delta Cafe ⓜ⌖ Vietnamese
27 | 14 | 22 | $19

Downtown West | 105 W. Saratoga St. (Cathedral St.) | 410-244-8677

For "phenomenal pho" and other "authentic" Vietnamese "delicacies", this "mom-and-pop" "gem" in an "easy-to-miss" location in Downtown West is "worth the occasional wait" for "limited" seating amid "plain-Jane decor"; the family who runs it are "sweet and lovely", and while prices are "low", remember: it's cash only.

Meli Eclectic
23 | 23 | 22 | $41

Fells Point | 1636 Thames St. (S. B'way) | 410-534-6354 | www.kalismeli.com

A "honey of a place", this Fells Point "little brother" to Kali's Court serves pricey, "inventive" New American fare with honey (*meli*, in Greek) as a theme ingredient; diners also buzz about the capable service and the "relaxed yet chic" setting complete with a ceiling ridged with a honeycomb motif; P.S. there's live jazz in the downstairs lounge Friday and Saturday.

Metropolitan Coffeehouse & Wine Bar American
∇ 23 | 18 | 20 | $27

South Baltimore | 902 S. Charles St. (Henrietta St.) | 410-234-0235 | www.metrobalto.com

South Baltimore is home to this "cool, little" multitasker that's "convenient" for "early coffee", "a biz lunch" or "meeting up with friends" to nosh on "beautifully prepared" and moderately priced New

	FOOD	DECOR	SERVICE	COST

American fare; it also boasts a "diverse" wine list and a "good variety of brews", which means the exposed-brick-walled space can get "noisy" (upstairs, which is only open for dinner, is quieter).

Michael's Café ● *American* | 23 | 19 | 22 | $33 |

Timonium | 2119 York Rd. (Timonium Rd.) | 410-252-2022 |
www.michaelscafe.com

Appealing to an "interesting mix of good ol' boys" and "professional types", this sprawling, multipart Timonium American bar and grill is a go-to "meeting spot" for locals, with its seafood-slanted "comfort food at its best" in an "inviting" "modern" space arrayed with sports memorabilia; prices are moderate, service "always smiles" and, no surprise, there's a "vibrant bar scene" too.

Miguel's Cocina y Cantina *Mexican* | ▽ 20 | 24 | 20 | $28 |

Locust Point | Silo Point | 1200 Steuart St. (Clement St.) | 443-438-3139 |
www.miguelsbaltimore.com

Industrial swank meets Día de los Muertos in this "fascinating" room in a "totally awesome" location – Locust Point's luxury Silo Point condo conversion – where floor-to-ceiling windows are offset by colorful skulls and skeletons; like the decor, the "upscale Mexican" eats offer a "fresh take" on "old standards", while solid service adds value to already affordable tabs.

☒ Milton Inn *American* | 28 | 26 | 26 | $59 |

Sparks | 14833 York Rd. (Quaker Bottom Rd.) | 410-771-4366 |
www.miltoninn.com

Dripping with "ambiance", this circa-1740 fieldstone inn is an "enduring treasure" in Sparks, with "cozy fireplaces, oil paintings and white tablecloths" spread over multiple rooms that provide suitably "elegant" backdrops for its "sophisticated" American cuisine; service is "impeccable", and while a typical experience is "pricey", the lounge menu offers "lesser-priced" options.

Minato *Japanese* | ▽ 24 | 22 | 24 | $23 |

Mt. Vernon | 1013 N. Charles St. (Eager St.) | 410-332-0332 |
www.minatosushibar.com

If it's "not the most authentic Japanese in the city", this Mt. Vernon purveyor may be one of the "hippest", with "cute", colorful, contemporary decor and "creative" sushi that attract happy-hour crowds for cocktails and rolls at bargain prices; tempura, rice bowls and noodles (plus Vietnamese pho) are also served, and in a "speedy" manner.

☒ Miss Shirley's *American* | 26 | 21 | 23 | $24 |

Inner Harbor | 750 E. Pratt St. (President St.) | 410-528-5373
Roland Park | 513 W. Cold Spring Ln. (Kittery Ln.) |
410-889-5272
www.missshirleys.com

"Down-home cooking at its best" cheer fans of this "always crowded" daytime mini-chain where the "extensive" menu of "dangerously delish" American fare features many a "Chesapeake" or "Southern" "twist"; yes, there's often "a wait" (no reservations) in "funky", colorful

FOOD DECOR SERVICE COST

digs, but tabs are fair, and staffers are "super", so most ultimately leave "stuffed and happy."

Morton's The Steakhouse *Steak*
26 | 24 | 26 | $71

Inner Harbor | Sheraton Inner Harbor Hotel | 300 S. Charles St. (Conway St.) | 410-547-8255 | www.mortons.com
See review in the Washington, DC, Directory.

Mr. Bill's Terrace Inn Ⓜ *Crab House*
∇ 26 | 13 | 21 | $40

Essex | 200 Eastern Blvd. (Helena Ave.) | 410-687-5996
Hard-shell fans can "wait as long as an hour-plus" to get their mallets on what they claim are "the best steamed crabs in the Baltimore area" at this "quintessential" crab house in Essex ("grab a beer at the bar and be patient"); authenticity comes at a "high cost", but for "laid-back crab pickin'" with a "warm, fuzzy" neighborhood feel, this place is a "little gem."

Mr. Rain's Fun House Ⓜ *New American*
23 | 26 | 23 | $45

South Baltimore | American Visionary Art Museum | 800 Key Hwy. (Covington St.) | 443-524-7379 | www.mrrainsfunhouse.com
The "fun and funky" environs of this "clever", "inventive" New American spot are fitting given its setting within the American Visionary Art Museum, where the "charming and wacky artwork carries into the restaurant"; though a few find it "a little pricey", most consider the "outside-the-box" experience with "lovely" service to be "worth it."

🆕 Museum ● *Eclectic*
- | - | - | M

Mt. Vernon | 924 N. Charles St. (Eager St.) | 410-528-8632 | www.museumrandl.com
The opulent Mt. Vernon townhouse that long housed Brass Elephant has been burnished and updated with sparkling chandeliers and high-backed white tufted banquettes in the upstairs bar and VIP rooms; a midpriced, wide-ranging Eclectic menu attracts diners, while late hours and bottle service aim to keep them long past dessert.

Nacho Mama's ● *Mexican*
22 | 22 | 21 | $22

Canton | 2911 O'Donnell St. (S. Linwood Ave.) | 410-342-2922 | www.nachomamascanton.com
"Hubcap margaritas" (as in four drinks' worth of margarita served in a hubcap) wash down "off-the-hook" grub like "don't-miss" "Mexican meatloaf" and "gold-standard" wings at this "crowded" "cheap-eats" cantina in Canton; the atmosphere is "friendly" and "quirky" (there's an Elvis motif) with a dash of "Bawlmer flair" – Natty Boh served only in a can, Journey "on the juke every night."

Negril 🅼 *Jamaican*
24 | 13 | 20 | $15

Laurel | Laurel Shopping Ctr. | 331 Montrose Ave. (Washington Blvd.) | 301-498-0808
Mitchellville | Mitchellville Plaza | 12116 Central Ave. (Enterprise Rd.) | 301-249-9101
www.negrileats.com
See review in the Washington, DC, Directory.

	FOOD	DECOR	SERVICE	COST

Oceanaire Seafood Room *Seafood* | 24 | 23 | 24 | $58 |

Harbor East | 801 Aliceanna St. (President St.) | 443-872-0000 |
www.theoceanaire.com

See review in the Washington, DC, Directory.

NEW Of Love & Regret 🕊 *American* | - | - | - | M |

Canton | 1028 S. Conkling St. (O'Donnell St.) | 410-327-0760 |
www.ofloveandregret.com

A collaboration between Ted Stelzenmuller (Jack's Bistro) and Brian
Strumke (Stillwater Ales brewery), this Brewers Hill gastropub delivers a midpriced, inventive American menu that appropriately includes beer-laced dishes; thirsts are quenched by a wall of taps
gushing artisanal suds plus wine and iced coffee in the tin-ceilinged
and brick-walled space.

Olive Grove Restaurant *Italian* | 24 | 20 | 22 | $27 |

Linthicum | 705 N. Hammonds Ferry Rd. (bet. Evelyn Ave. & Nursery Rd.) |
410-636-1385 | www.olivegroverestaurant.com

Likened to "Olive Garden" ("endless salad and breadsticks!") but
with a "personal, hometown touch", this Linthicum spot is "well
attended" thanks to its "large portions" of "solid, straightforward
Italian" cooking plus "great, big crab cakes", all at "respectable
prices"; the simple, spacious setting and "professional", "courteous" help make it a lock for "family" outings, and "large parties" note there's a "banquet hall" on-site.

Olive Room *Greek*   ▽ | 24 | 20 | 22 | $44 |

Fells Point | Inn at the Black Olive | 803 S. Caroline St. (Lancaster St.) |
443-681-6316 | www.theblackolive.com

"Small but elegant", this Greek entry perched above the Inn at the
Black Olive in Fells Point offers "high-quality" fare like its big sister
(Black Olive) at slightly "more affordable" tabs; the vibe is "laid-back",
with solid service, and while decor indoors is "sparse", the harbor
view from the rooftop terrace is "fantastic."

One-Eyed Mike's *Pub Food*   ▽ | 23 | 18 | 23 | $27 |

Fells Point | 708 S. Bond St. (Aliceanna St.) | 410-327-0445 |
www.oneeyedmikes.com

Walls lined "with Grand Marnier bottles" (bought by and stored on-
site for "members") set the mood at this "off-the-beaten-path" Fells
Point "neighborhood" tavern, where the "dark and intimate" bar
could be "a setting for a film noir" if the "friendly bartenders" didn't
make it such a "fun and happy place"; "surprisingly good" upscale
pub food at fair prices works for a "casual lunch or dinner."

One World Cafe *Vegetarian* | 22 | 16 | 19 | $19 |

Homewood | 100 W. University Pkwy. (Canterbury Rd.) | 410-235-5777 |
www.one-world-cafe.com

There are some "pleasant culinary surprises" on the "interesting"
vegetarian menu at this affordable Homewood catch-all that's part
cafe, bar, coffeehouse, juice bar and, above all, "hangout for Johns
Hopkins students and professors"; some say the basic decor (local

art on the walls) could use an "upgrade", but it's "comfy" and the staff is "laid-back", making it "conducive to long conversations and unhurried dining."

Open Door Café *American*   24 | 24 | 23 | $19

Bel Air | 528 Baltimore Pike/Rte. 1 (Rte. 24) | 410-838-4393 | www.theopendoorcafe.com

Inside this "charming" Bel Air bistro/coffeehouse "tucked unassumingly" into a strip mall, trompe l'oeil murals ensconce patrons amid a "French country" auberge while they dine on "delicious" American classics with "a bit of a gourmet flair"; other reasons to open the door: "pleasant" service, "value" prices and an "excellent" breakfast menu.

Orchard Market & Café Ⓜ *Persian*   26 | 21 | 26 | $25

Towson | 8815 Orchard Tree Ln. (Joppa Rd.) | 410-339-7700 | www.orchardmarketandcafe.com

"Hidden away" "behind a furniture store" in Towson, this "tiny" Persian prepares a "mouthwatering" blend of "authentic" and "modern flavors"; "artful" decor with a Middle Eastern flavor and "gracious", "warm" service adds up to a "total gem" worthy of "celebrations" that "don't [cost] an arm and a leg" ("BYO helps").

Oregon Grille *Seafood/Steak*   25 | 26 | 25 | $61

Hunt Valley | 1201 Shawan Rd. (Beaver Dam Rd.) | 410-771-0505 | www.theoregongrille.com

Located "nicely away from the city" in Hunt Valley "horse country", this "romantic retreat" is known for its "exquisite" steaks and seafood (at "high-but-worth-it" prices), accompanied by "just-as-it-should-be" service; "proper linens", "equestrian" decor, wood-burning fireplaces and "soft" piano music in the background complete the thoroughbred picture; P.S. jackets required in the main dining room.

NEW Pabu *Japanese*   - | - | - | E

Harbor East | Four Seasons Baltimore | 200 International Dr. (Aliceanna St.) | 410-223-1460 | www.michaelmina.net

Celebrity chef Michael Mina has made a foray into Japanese cuisine (with partner Ken Tominaga) with this high-end izakaya in Harbor East's Four Seasons (but accessed via a separate entrance on Aliceanna Street) that serves classic dishes from a robata grill and a sushi bar, washed down by a world-class sake selection; the rough-wood tables, bamboo ceiling and privacy panels keep things casual even though there's a sleek sheen to everything.

Pappas *American/Seafood*   23 | 16 | 21 | $26

Glen Burnie | 6713 Ritchie Hwy. (Americana Circle) | 410-766-3713

Northeast Baltimore | 1725 Taylor Ave. (Oakleigh Rd.) | 410-661-4357 www.pappascrabcakes.com

A "packed parking lot" and "lots of locals" are a sure sign this "bargain" American seafooder pleases Northeast Baltimore denizens with its signature "primo" crab cakes with "little filler and great flavor" (there's also a newer Glen Burnie branch with a "sports bar atmosphere"); if there's "not much to say" about the decor, diners talk up the merits of the "folksy atmosphere" and "friendly" service from "old-fashioned waitresses."

Pasta Plus Ⓜ Italian   26 | 17 | 24 | $32

Laurel | Center Plaza | 209 Gorman Ave. (bet. Rtes. 1 & 198) | 301-498-5100 | www.pastaplusrestaurant.com

There's "always a line" at this "family-owned" Italian "diamond hidden in the rough" of a "moribund" Laurel strip mall, but carb zealots have no reservations (literally) about standing by for "generous" portions of "perfect" housemade pastas, "great" pizza and other "hearty" fare; folks are "tightly packed" in the simple, white-tablecloth space, but service is "attentive" and the prices "reasonable"; P.S. to avoid a wait, eat in or carry out at the adjacent market, open daily.

Patrick's American   ▽ 22 | 18 | 23 | $28

Cockeysville | 550 Cranbrook Rd. (Ridgland Rd.) | 410-683-0604 | www.patricksrestaurant.com

For "steady", "dependable" American eats (think steaks, fish and crab cakes), this Cockeysville local "favorite" is a "go-to" with a "comfortable atmosphere" and "happy", "pleasant" servers, which adds up to a "great value"; with separate sports bar, martini lounge and fine-dining areas, it's conducive to "everyday" dining or "special occasions."

❷ Pazo Mediterranean   25 | 27 | 24 | $48

Harbor East | 1425 Aliceanna St. (bet. S. Caroline St. & S. Central Ave.) | 410-534-7296 | www.pazorestaurant.com

A former machine shop in Harbor East hosts Tony Foreman and Cindy Wolf's visually "stunning" "industrial-chic" destination for "scrumptious" Mediterranean tapas and entrees delivered by "attentive" pros; a few warn that "small plates equals big bucks", and the noise level on weekend nights can be "deafening" (especially when DJs spin, weekends), but most of the "trendy", "people-watching" crowd is down with the "sizzling-hot scene."

Peerce's Ⓜ American   ▽ 21 | 20 | 20 | $44
(aka The Grille at Peerce's)

Phoenix | 12460 Dulaney Valley Rd. (Loch Raven Dr.) | 410-252-7111 | www.thegrilleatpeerces.com

This "fine old place" in Phoenix offers "really tasty" American tavern fare on a menu that varies from "simple to fancy" amid "pleasant surroundings" that include a "warm fireplace" and horse-and-hound prints; it's expensive, but service is solid, and longtime loyalists say it's "worth" a visit for the "pretty drive" by the Loch Raven Reservoir.

Peppermill American   23 | 18 | 24 | $28

Lutherville | Heaver Bldg. | 1301 York Rd. (bet. I-695 & Seminary Ave.) | 410-583-1107 | www.pepmill.com

"Huge portions" of "consistently excellent" American fare are served by a staff that "knows how to treat guests" at this white-tablecloth Lutherville "institution" with a "low-key feel" and a "very loyal following" among a "lovely, older clientele"; what's more, as "times are changing", "others are discovering" that their elders know a "bang for the buck" when they find it.

Peter's Inn 🅂🅜 *American* | 27 | 17 | 22 | $35 |

Fells Point | 504 S. Ann St. (Eastern Ave.) | 410-675-7313 | www.petersinn.com

"What looks like (and once was) a dive bar is merely a front" for this Fells Point "foodie destination" with a "magic kitchen" plating up "farmer's market–inspired" New American "gourmet" "treats" served by a "friendly", "tattooed" staff; the "almost too hip" scene unfolds in "funky", "cramped quarters", so "go early" or "get in line", because they don't take reservations.

Petit Louis Bistro *French* | 26 | 23 | 25 | $46 |

Roland Park | 4800 Roland Ave. (Upland Rd.) | 410-366-9393 | www.petitlouis.com

Like an "upbeat Paris bistro" set down in Roland Park, this "buzzing little place" delivers "dependably delicious" traditional French "favorites" via "impressively coordinated" service in a "cozy" storefront; it's "pricey", though "more reasonable" at lunch, and one diner's "thrum of happy people" is another's "din" amid "closely arranged" tables, but *c'est la vie*, as this "classique" remains "wildly popular."

🄩 P.F. Chang's China Bistro *Chinese* | 23 | 23 | 22 | $30 |

Inner Harbor | Market Pl. | 600 E. Pratt St. (bet. Gay St. & Market Pl.) | 410-649-2750

White Marsh | White Marsh Mall | 8342 Honeygo Blvd. (White Marsh Blvd.) | 401-931-2433

Columbia | Mall in Columbia | 10300 Little Patuxent Pkwy. (Wincopin Circle) | 410-730-5344

Towson | Towson Town Ctr. | 825 Dulaney Valley Rd. (Fairmount Ave.) | 410-372-5250

www.pfchangs.com

See review in the Washington, DC, Directory.

Phillips *Seafood* | 20 | 19 | 20 | $39 |

Inner Harbor | 601 E. Pratt St. (Pratt St.) | 410-685-6600 | www.phillipsseafood.com

Sure they're "touristy, but who cares?" demand defenders of these tanker-sized seafooders in Baltimore's Inner Harbor and DC – after all, they both sport "spectacular" water views, and their crab cakes are "just about the best"; if a few "serious seafood eaters" judge it a bit "assembly line" for their taste, less picky palates savor the mid-priced tabs and "respectable" service.

Pho Dat Thanh *Vietnamese* | 24 | 14 | 19 | $16 |

Columbia | Columbia Mktpl. | 9400 Snowden River Pkwy. (bet. Carved Stone Way & Rustling Leaf) | 410-381-3839

Towson | 510 York Rd. (Pennsylvania Ave.) | 410-296-9118 www.phodatthanh.com

"For a slurping good time", pho-natics count on this "unfussy" twosome in Columbia and Towson for "huge", "rich" bowls of "excellent"

FOOD
DECOR
SERVICE
COST

broth as well as a "large menu of non-pho options" at attractively "small prices"; less attractive, perhaps, are the "unfussy", "unremarkable" surroundings, leading some to "recommend takeout", though the in-house service is solid.

Pho Nam ⊅ *Vietnamese* ▽ 27 | 14 | 23 | $11

Catonsville | Westview | 6477 Baltimore National Pike (Rolling Rd.) | 410-455-6000

What some claim is the "best pho by far" is ladled out along with a "limited" menu of other Vietnamese fare at this "hole-in-the-wall" noodle shop in a Catonsville strip mall; "super-fast" service "just wants to make you happy", and if decor is "lacking", it doesn't distract from that "aromatic broth" that will "cure what ails you"; P.S. it's cash only, but you won't need much.

Piedigrotta Bakery Ⓜ *Bakery/Italian* ▽ 28 | 20 | 26 | $26

Harbor East | 1300 Bank St. (bet. Central Ave. & Eden St.) | 410-522-6900 | www.piedigrottabakery.com

A few conflicted sorts "hate the calories" but still love the "amazing sweets" ("pastries! pastries! pastries!") as well as "large portions" of gently priced, "home-cooked Italian" fare at this lesser-known Harbor East bakery-plus; the setting is small and no-frills, but a "relaxed atmosphere" and "excellent" service make patrons feel like they've "arrived home."

NEW Plug Ugly's - | - | - | M
Publick House ❶ *Pub Food*

Canton | 2908 O'Donnell St. (S. Linwood Ave.) | 410-563-8459 | www.pluguglyspub.com

Named for a 19th-century Baltimore street gang, this new pub on O'Donnell Square sports a nostalgic, wood-paneled tavern look and trades in midpriced pub classics plus shellfish-packed steam pots and local beers; the two-story space has a outdoor deck, a great place to sip a signature 'pirate juice' – fruit-steeped rum made at the bar.

NEW Poor Boy Steakhouse Ⓜ *Steak* - | - | - | M

Severna Park | 342 Ritchie Hwy. (Whites Rd.) | 410-457-7059 | www.poorboysteaks.com

Dig into premium Black Angus beef and classic sides (plus a po' boy lunch special) at this midpriced Severna Park shopping-strip steakhouse entry from the owner of Breakfast Shoppe; the dimly lit, New Orleans–inspired trappings (red crushed-velvet curtains, rusty antiques) make an apt setting for carnivorous indulgence; P.S. alcohol is served, but BYO is also welcome.

Portalli's *Italian* 22 | 20 | 23 | $38

Ellicott City | 8085 Main St. (Maryland Ave.) | 410-720-2330 | www.portallisec.com

Ellicott City's "historic district" is home to this neighborhood boîte where "well-executed" Italian "standbys" and more "creative" choices share space on an "easy", midpriced menu; service is "attentive but not pushy", and live piano on weekends "sets the mood" in the "relaxing", "romantic" dark-leather and white-tablecloth digs.

Porters *American*

▽ 22 | 19 | 22 | $27

South Baltimore | 1032 Riverside Ave. (Cross St.) | 410-332-7345 | www.portersfederalhill.com

This "comfortable" and "homey" Fed Hill "neighborhood bar" offers "tasty" midpriced New American "gastropub" grub, "great beers on tap" and "plenty of TVs to catch the game" while you munch; the "good" service is in line with the "relaxed atmosphere."

☑ Prime Rib *Steak*

28 | 26 | 28 | $71

Mt. Vernon | 1101 N. Calvert St. (Chase St.) | 410-539-1804 | www.theprimerib.com

Do as they do in *"Mad Men"* – "dress up, have a martini, take it easy and smile" – at these "classic" steakhouses in Baltimore and DC that are still operating at the very "top of their game", delivering "fantastic" "slabs of meat" and "masterful seafood"; from the "sophisticated", "1940s supper-club vibe" to the "sublime" tuxedoed service, it's a "perfect evening out"; P.S. both locations require business-casual dress (with jackets required in DC after 5 PM daily and in Baltimore after 5 PM Saturday only).

R & R Taqueria *Mexican*

27 | 7 | 23 | $10

NEW **White Marsh** | White Marsh Mall | 8200 Perry Hall Blvd. (Honeygo Blvd.) | 410-870-0185

Elkridge | 7894 Washington Blvd. (Waterloo Rd.) | 410-799-0001 www.rrtaqueria.com

Possibly "the best food you'll ever eat in a gas station" is pumped out at this "awesome", "authentic" Mexican fast-fooder in an Elkridge Shell station (there's also a counter in Baltimore's White Marsh Mall) known for its "exemplary selection of tacos" and more, "made fresh in front of you" by folks who "really care"; the "decor is bar stools at a counter", but it's "worth" the *"muy bajo"* prices.

Ra Sushi Bar Restaurant *Japanese*

24 | 24 | 21 | $31

Harbor East | 1390 Lancaster St. (S. Caroline St.) | 410-522-3200 | www.rasushi.com

"Flashy" nightclub-esque decor – and "blaring music" to go with it – make this "trendy" chain link in Harbor East a "favorite happy-hour spot" for "pretty" "young" things; while it may not be a venue for "sushi snobs", admirers assert that the "creative" rolls are equal to the "happening scene", the staff is "helpful" and prices are "affordable."

Red Hot & Blue *BBQ*

22 | 18 | 20 | $21

Laurel | 677 Main St. (Rte. 216) | 301-953-1943 | www.redhotandblue.com

See review in the Washington, DC, Directory.

Red Pearl *Chinese*

26 | 21 | 23 | $23

Columbia | 10215 Wincopin Circle (Little Patuxent Pkwy.) | 410-715-6530 | www.redpearlrestaurant.com

Dim sum "as good as in Hong Kong" is the main draw (especially "on weekends when the carts are rolling") at this "authentic" Chinese spot near Lake Kittamaqundi in Columbia, but "genuine Sichuan" as well as Cantonese dishes round out the budget-friendly menu; the "friendly, smart" staff patrols a "modern" space that feels airy on account of its blond-wood accents, high ceilings and large windows.

Regions ⓜ *Eclectic* ▽ 23 | 19 | 22 | $44

Catonsville | 803 Frederick Rd. (Mellor Ave.) | 410-788-0075 | www.regionsrestaurant.com

"Interesting" Eclectic small and large plates based on different regions – e.g. Maryland, Cajun country, France, Italy, Asia – meet on the "limited but excellent" monthly changing menu of this "upscale" relative of nearby Catonsville Gourmet; exposed brick and earth-toned walls with stenciled accents create a "cozy" yet contemporary space, while solid service and BYO with a small corkage fee bring value to the bill.

Regi's *American* 23 | 19 | 24 | $31

South Baltimore | 1002 Light St. (E. Hamburg St.) | 410-539-7344 | www.regisamericanbistro.com

This "cornerstone" bistro in Federal Hill recently reopened after an earlier fire (outdating the Decor rating), with a new chef who's tweaking the "interesting" American eats (outdating the Food rating), many made with herbs "grown on the roof"; most of the "cozy" interior's details – fireplace, hardwood floors, original bar – remain but have been buffed up, which should ensure it will remain a "neighborhood gem."

Rocket to Venus ❶ *Eclectic* 20 | 19 | 17 | $23

Hampden | 3360 Chestnut Ave. (W. 34th St.) | 410-235-7887 | www.rockettovenus.com

A "hipster crowd" frequents this "quirky" Hampden watering hole, bellying up to the 40-ft. copper horseshoe bar for the "excellent options on tap" or sliding into black-and-teal retro-style booths to chow down on "interesting" Eclectic menu offerings like the deep-fried PB&J; it gets "packed", especially on weekends, but the staff is "nice" enough, and the prices are "definitely right."

Roy's *Hawaiian* 27 | 25 | 26 | $53

Harbor East | 720 Aliceanna St. (President St.) | 410-659-0099 | www.roysrestaurant.com

From the "top-notch", "imaginative" Hawaiian fusion cuisine to the staff that treats each diner like a "big kahuna", "you would never know" this Harbor East spot is part of "a chain" (from celeb chef Roy Yamaguchi); the "upscale"-casual digs feature a lively open kitchen and a bar slinging "potent" drinks, which promotes a "chatty, up-tempo" vibe, and though "fat wallets" are helpful, it's "cheaper than a trip to Hawaii."

Rusty Scupper *Seafood* 22 | 25 | 22 | $47

South Baltimore | 402 Key Hwy. (Covington St.) | 410-727-3678 | www.selectrestaurants.com

The "truly awesome view" of the Inner Harbor has beckoned diners for over 30 years to this South Baltimore seafooder perched right on the water, where "well-prepared" takes on "traditional favorites" are delivered by capable servers in a vast glass box of a room; while some call it "a tourist destination", others say go "if you have someone to impress" – either way, remember that "location, location, location" "comes at a price."

❷ Ruth's Chris Steak House *Steak*   26 | 24 | 26 | $67

Business District | Power Plant Live | 600 Water St. (bet. Gay St. & Market Pl.) | 410-783-0033
Inner Harbor | Pier 5 | 711 Eastern Ave. (S. President St.) | 410-230-0033
Pikesville | 1777 Reisterstown Rd. (Hooks Ln.) | 410-837-0033
www.ruthschris.com
See review in the Washington, DC, Directory.

Sabatino's ● *Italian*   24 | 19 | 24 | $35

Little Italy | 901 Fawn St. (High St.) | 410-727-9414 | www.sabatinos.com
Everything from the 'Bookmaker' salads to the "homemade" pastas is "generously" heaped up in a way that's "more grandmother's kitchen than posh" at this eminently "reliable" "red-sauce" "landmark" in Little Italy; staff with "personality", plus friendly tabs and an "old-fashioned" setting make diners "feel like family", and late hours are nice too.

Salt Ⓜ *American*   27 | 23 | 25 | $46

Fells Point | 2127 E. Pratt St. (Collington St.) | 410-276-5480 | www.salttavern.com
It's "destination-quality" gush adoptees of this "sophisticated" New American eatery on a quiet corner near Patterson Park, thanks to an "original" menu that's full of "surprises" bolstered by "thoughtful" draft beers and a "well-composed" wine list; though it's "on the pricey side", and parking can be a "challenge" ("bring the smallest car you own"), most agree "kind", "knowledgeable" service and "chic"-meets-"relaxed" exposed-brick surrounds work well for a "comfortable night out" or an "occasion."

Sammy's Trattoria *Italian*   21 | 20 | 20 | $42

Mt. Vernon | 1200 N. Charles St. (Biddle St.) | 410-837-9999 | www.sammystrattoria.com
"Skip Little Italy" and head to Mt. Vernon say fans of the "big portions" of "solid" Italian fare at this "reliable" trattoria; it's "on the expensive side", but the high-vaulted-ceilinged space is "tastefully appointed", and the staff is "fast and attentive before shows" at the nearby Meyerhoff or Lyric theaters, taking a more "leisurely" (some say "slow") approach afterward.

❷ Samos Ⓩ⇗ *Greek*   28 | 16 | 24 | $21

Greektown | 600 Oldham St. (Fleet St.) | 410-675-5292 | www.samosrestaurant.com
"As close to the real thing as you can get" say ardent admirers of the "phenomenal" food "like *yia-yia* used to make", at this Greektown elder statesman where even the "salad dressing has a huge following"; the wait is often "long" since there are no reservations and only "limited seating" in the "underwhelming", mural-bedecked space, but it's "stupidly cheap" and "so very worth it"; P.S. it's cash only and BYO.

San Sushi *Japanese*

▽ 26 | 15 | 21 | $29

Cockeysville | 9832 York Rd. (bet. Galloway Ave. & Padonia Rd.) | 410-453-0140 | www.timoniumrestaurant.com

"They don't skimp on the size of the rolls" at this "excellent", mid-priced Japanese BYO in a Cockeysville strip mall, a "locals'" favorite for "tasty" sushi from servers who "learn your name" if you're a regular; "little ones" are entertained by the aquarium in the otherwise simple, traditional digs; P.S. its Canton and Towson siblings also serve Thai food.

San Sushi Too/
Thai One On *Japanese/Thai*

▽ 21 | 16 | 20 | $26

Towson | 10 W. Pennsylvania Ave. (York Rd.) | 410-825-0908 | www.towsonrestaurant.com

Sushi San/Thai Jai Dee *Japanese/Thai*

Canton | 2748 Lighthouse Point (Boston St.) | 410-534-8888 | www.sushisanbaltimore.com

In a stalemate between whether to do Japanese or Thai, these dual-menu "neighborhood staples" in Towson and Canton act as tie-breakers with their "interesting" sushi, cooked Japanese fare and "great pad Thai" and the like; "kind and efficient" service distracts from rather "informal" surroundings, and wallet-watchers note it's "a steal."

Sascha's 527 ⊠ *American*

24 | 24 | 22 | $30

Mt. Vernon | 527 N. Charles St. (bet. Centre & Hamilton Sts.) | 410-539-8880 | www.saschas.com

A "culinary surprise" say diners of this "moderately priced" Mt. Vernon New American offering an "inventive" menu featuring "quality ingredients and a good mix of options"; the "colorful", "gorgeously designed" dining room feels like a "movie set", and service is "attentive without being overbearing", plus it's a "convenient stop" before or after visiting the Walters Art Museum or Peabody Conservatory; P.S. its express cafe at Centerstage operates when there's a show.

Schultz's Crab House *Crab House*

▽ 27 | 20 | 26 | $27

Essex | 1732 Old Eastern Ave. (Walkern Rd.) | 410-687-1020

"Locals who know their Maryland seafood" hit this circa-1969 "Essex tradition" for "flavorful" offerings including "meaty" crabs and what some claim are "the best lump crab cakes"; "old"-time decor (knotty pine walls, trophy fish) make it a "sentimental favorite", while "always accommodating" staffers and "reasonable prices" are more contemporary perks.

Seaside Restaurant &
Crab House *Seafood*

26 | 17 | 24 | $34

Glen Burnie | 224 Crain Hwy. N. (New Jersey Ave.) | 410-760-2200
Pasadena | 8557 Fort Smallwood Rd. (Cottage Grove Dr.) | 410-360-2211
www.theseasiderestaurant.com

"Crabs, crabs, crabs, that's what it's all about" – the "best steamed crabs", "exquisite crab cakes", soft-shell crab sandwiches "that are worth every penny" and a crab dip that's "like a spoonful of heaven" – at these "friendly" crustacean stations in Glen Burnie and Pasadena; the nautically trimmed, sports bar–esque digs have a "down-home feel", and while it "ain't cheap", you won't shell out that much either.

Shin Chon Korean   ∇ 22 | 19 | 19 | $34

Ellicott City | 8801 Baltimore National Pike (Ridge Rd.) | 410-461-3280
"Delicious" Korean BBQ – "how can you go wrong?" ask enthusiasts who roll up their sleeves and grill their own "interesting" vittles right on each table under kitchen-grade vents at this midpriced Ellicott City strip-maller; some report a bit of a "language barrier" and say service is of the "leave you alone unless you ask for something" variety, but to devotees, that's all part of the charm.

Sip & Bite Restaurant ● Diner   19 | 12 | 20 | $14

Fells Point | 2200 Boston St. (Fleet St.) | 410-675-7077
"Classic Bawlmer, hon" servers "get the job done with no fluff" at this "classic" all-nighter in Fells Point, where the "honest diner food" "isn't creative", but "it's exactly what you want", and at a "very good bang for your buck"; the "old-fashioned neighborhood" experience plays out in a remodeled retro setting with red-checked trim and pop art on the walls.

Sofi's Crepes Crêpes   24 | 14 | 21 | $12

Downtown North | 1723 N. Charles St. (Lanvale St.) | 410-727-7732
York Road Corridor | Belvedere Sq. | 5911 York Rd. (bet. E. Belvedere Ave. & Orkney Rd.) | 410-727-5737
NEW **Owings Mills** | Valley Vill. | 9123 Reisterstown Rd. (Craddocks Ln.) | 410-356-4191
www.sofiscrepes.com
"Sweet and savory" crêpes "for every palate", with "quirky names" like "Kevin Bacon", are made "before your eyes" and served "piping hot" at this "cute" chainlet of crêperies that cater to pancake-thin wallets; there's often a "wait" in the "snug" but "friendly" counter-service spaces, so some suggest getting your "yummy" "light lunch or snack" to go.

Sotto Sopra Italian   26 | 25 | 25 | $47

Mt. Vernon | 405 N. Charles St. (bet. Franklin & Mulberry Sts.) | 410-625-0534 | www.sottosopra.us
The "Maserati of Italian restaurants" purr paesani about this "elegant and sexy" Northern Italian in a "tastefully" theatrical room with sweeping curtains and "colorful murals", housed in a Mt. Vernon townhouse, which has remained "steadfast" in providing "divine" cuisine prepared with "an artist's touch"; "attentive" but "not invasive" service and once-monthly Sunday dinners featuring live opera also rev motors.

Spice & Dice Thai   ∇ 29 | 15 | 21 | $18

Towson | 1220 E. Joppa Rd. (bet. Edgeclift Rd. & Mylander Ln.) | 410-494-8777 | www.thaispiceanddice.com
The "authentic" Thai tastes "will set your mouth on fire" in the "first-rate" fare at this Towson BYO sibling of Little Spice, though the spice

averse note with relief that there are five heat levels to choose from; service is "efficient", and if some feel the "quirky", colorful room "resembles a kindergarten classroom" (it's in a comic book/gamer shop), live jazz on Thursday adds a grown-up touch; P.S. extensive gluten-free/vegan options available.

Stanford Grill *American*

24 | 24 | 23 | $41

Columbia | 8900 Stanford Blvd. (Dobbin Rd.) | 410-312-0445 | www.thestanfordgrill.com

"Terrific steaks" hot off the grill and "mouthwatering" rotisserie chicken are standouts on a menu full of "moderately innovative twists" on "typical American fare" at this "upscale-casual" Columbia locals' spot; "responsive" servers cruise the cozy warren of booths, and though it's "a bit pricey", live jazz most nights adds value (even if it's "noisy").

NEW Stang of Siam *Thai*

∇ 23 | 23 | 17 | $27

Mt. Vernon | 200 E. Preston St. (Calvert St.) | 443-453-9142 | www.stangofsiam.com

The owners of The Regent in DC recently brought "much-needed" Thai to Mt. Vernon with this fair-priced "gem" on a "quiet corner", which "displays creativity" with the "ancient cuisine"; "artful decor" – chocolate-brown walls with elaborate teak carvings and Buddha statues – and "pretty" cocktails compensate for "very sweet servers" who a few say can seem "overwhelmed" at peak times.

Stone Mill Bakery & Cafe ☒ *Bakery*

24 | 15 | 19 | $22

Brooklandville | Greenspring Station | 10751 Falls Rd. (Greenspring Valley Rd.) | 410-821-1358 | www.stonemillbakery.com

A "higher-end clientele" (think "ladies who lunch") flocks to this "friendly" bakery/cafe within Brooklandville's posh Greenspring Station for "amazing" "fresh-baked" breads, "lovely" sandwiches and "to-die-for" brownies and other sweets served in a bright, arched-windowed space or on an outdoor patio; true, you may "pay for the privilege", but it "never disappoints."

Suburban House *Deli*

19 | 13 | 17 | $20

Pikesville | 1700 Reisterstown Rd. (Naylors Ln.) | 410-484-7775 | www.suburbanhousedeli.com

"Everything you order is big" at this "classic old-timey Jewish deli" in Pikesville, known for its "tasty" sandwiches, bagels and smoked fish at "reasonable prices"; there's "no real atmosphere" in the simple digs, but the booths are "comfortable", there's "conversation worth overhearing" and the service is "fast"; P.S. it closes at 7 PM.

Sullivan's Steakhouse *Steak*

25 | 25 | 25 | $60

Inner Harbor | 1 E. Pratt St. (Light St.) | 410-962-5503 | www.sullivansteakhouse.com

Satisfy the urge to "splurge" at this "enjoyable" Inner Harbor link in a national chain, a Chicago-style steakhouse known for its chops "done to perfection", "equally good" classic sides and "fancy cocktails" brought by "attentive" servers in a spacious, retro wood-paneled setting; a bar scene at happy hour contributes to a "lively" atmosphere.

	FOOD	DECOR	SERVICE	COST

Sushi Hana *Japanese*
26 | 20 | 23 | $31

Mt. Washington | Lake Falls Shopping Ctr. | 6080 Falls Rd. (Lake Ave.) | 410-377-4228
Timonium | Yorkridge Shopping Ctr. | 6 W. Ridgely Rd. (York Rd.) | 410-560-7090
Towson | 6 E. Pennsylvania Ave. (York Rd.) | 410-823-0372
www.sushihanabaltimore.com

For some of the "best sushi and sashimi around", including an "expansive" selection of "specialty rolls" "filled with melt-in-your-mouth goodness", plus "reliable and tasty" cooked Japanese fare, area raw-fish fans "love" these upscale, "cozy" and "casual" settings in Towson, Mt. Washington and Timonium; bonus: prices are moderate and servers "attentive."

⨯ Sushi King ⓩ *Japanese*
28 | 20 | 24 | $32

Columbia | 6490 Dobbin Rd. (Rte. 175) | 410-997-1269 | www.sushikingmd.com

An "insiders' jewel", this "decently" priced Columbia Japanese "hidden" near the MVA "isn't flashy" but "completely rocks" for "consistently terrific" sushi "masterpieces" created by veritable "artists" and delivered by "prompt and courteous" servers in "traditional garb"; "seating is packed" in the "classic" Japanese dining room, so regulars suggest calling ahead, "even on weekdays."

Sushi Sono ⓩ *Japanese*
27 | 22 | 25 | $38

Columbia | 10215 Wincopin Circle (Little Patuxent Pkwy.) | 410-997-6131 | www.sushisonomd.com

It's easy to become "addicted" to the "first-rate" raw fish (and cooked fare) at this "romantic" yet "casual" Columbia Japanese with "attractive" traditional decor framed by a "scenic view" of Lake Kittamaqundi; "expect a wait at peak hours", "delightful" service and a final bill that's "not that bad" given the "reverence for the art of sushi" on display here.

Szechuan House ⬤ *Chinese*
26 | 16 | 23 | $20

Lutherville | 1427 York Rd. (Seminary Ave.) | 410-825-8181

This Lutherville strip-mall dine-in/carryout is "a cut above" the "typical" with its "extensive" menu offering "delicious" "real" Chinese dishes you don't often see alongside Americanized "standards"; you "don't go there for the decor", but "impossibly fast" service, "ridiculously large portions" and prices "from the '60s" add up to one of the "best values around."

Tabrizi's ⓩ Ⓜ *Mediterranean/Mideastern*
▽ 21 | 24 | 21 | $40

South Baltimore | Harborview | 500 Harborview Dr. (Key Hwy.) | 410-727-3663 | www.tabrizis.com

"Sit outside on a pleasant evening and enjoy" one of the city's "best water views" from this bright, window-lined Med-Mideasterner offering "great" midpriced fare and a "nice, affordable wine list" via "helpful" service; as the setting in South Baltimore's Harborview enclave "can't be beat", Saturdays are often booked for weddings, so call ahead.

Talara ● *Nuevo Latino*

24 | 23 | 22 | $32

Harbor East | 615 S. President St. (Fleet St.) | 410-528-9883 | www.talarabaltimore.com

A "Miami vibe" pulses in Harbor East at this "trendy" Nuevo Latino cantina offering an "amazing selection of ceviche" and "lots of tasty small bites" at "not-too-pricey" tabs; neon and contemporary art add to an "energetic" mood that's all about the "can't-beat" happy hour, though service remains "accommodating" throughout; P.S. Monday night salsa dancing with free lessons is "a plus."

Tapas Adela *Spanish*

23 | 23 | 22 | $35

Fells Point | 814 S. Broadway (bet. Lancaster & Thames Sts.) | 410-534-6262 | www.tapasadela.com

"Stylish" like its elder siblings (Kali's, Meli, Mezze), this Spaniard keeps pace with fairly priced tapas that "burst with flavor", shuttled by "accommodating" servers; a prime location "in the heart of Fells Point" and sexy, Gothic decor pull in "beautiful people" for "date night", or "larger parties" at the communal white-marble table, and in season, the garden has a "great vibe."

Tapas Teatro ●🅼 *Eclectic/Mediterranean*

24 | 21 | 20 | $32

Downtown North | 1711 N. Charles St. (bet. Lafayette Ave. & Lanvale St.) | 410-332-0110 | www.tapasteatro.com

It feels "fun and adventurous" splicing together a meal out of the "innovative", midpriced Eclectic-Med tapas at this "popular", "energetic" Downtown North night spot next to the Charles Theatre; when movie fans "crush" into the dimly lit interior featuring exposed brick and "tiny tables", some say the otherwise-"skilled" service can "suffer", but most love "staying up late discussing" films "over a pitcher" of sangria – and "lovely" outside seating is a quieter option.

Tark's Grill *American*

21 | 21 | 22 | $39

Brooklandville | Greenspring Station | 2360 W. Joppa Rd. (Falls Rd.) | 410-583-8275 | www.tarksgrill.com

With a "classic" menu of "predictably fine" American fare and a "well-trained" staff, this "casual, upscale" "neighborhood gathering spot" for "ladies" who lunch and "business" types alike is a "solid option" in Brooklandville's tony Greenspring Station; vintage photos highlighting the area's sporting history create a clubby feel, and there's a "hopping" bar scene.

Teavolve *American/Tearoom*

23 | 21 | 19 | $21

Harbor East | 1401 Aliceanna St. (Central Ave.) | 410-522-1907 | www.teavolve.com

Leaf-steepers are buzzing over the "best assortment of tea in the city" (plus coffee and cocktails) at this "adorable" Harbor East tearoom/cafe that bolsters its beverage selection with "simply good, light" New American food (served all day); the prices are sweet, service is capable and the mellow lounge vibe and free WiFi make for "a lovely space to linger."

	FOOD	DECOR	SERVICE	COST

NEW Ten Ten *American* ▽ 25 | 26 | 24 | $47

Harbor East | Bagby Bldg. | 1010 Fleet St. (S. Exeter St.) |
410-244-6867 | www.bagbys1010.com

This "secret little place" "nestled" down a pedestrian alley, in Harbor East's Bagby Building, lures a "diverse clientele" with its "remarkable" "farm-to-table" New American dishes and "actually reasonable" wine list; it's expensive, but the "modern" industrial interior – exposed brick, reclaimed wood – is quite "comfortable", and the staff is "well trained", leading guests to gush "wow, what a find."

Z Tersiguel's *French* 28 | 25 | 28 | $59

Ellicott City | 8293 Main St. (Old Columbia Pike) | 410-465-4004 |
www.tersiguels.com

"Exquisite and delectable" French country "creations" comprised of "prime ingredients", including produce from the family farm, plus a "refined but not stuffy" "white-napkin" ambiance and "attentive, unobtrusive" service have Ellicott City diners calling this "romantic" special-occasioner "a favorite for years"; it's "expensive", *oui*, but "a great treat when you want to play grown-up" (and prix fixe menus "help with the cost").

Thai M *Thai* ▽ 24 | 14 | 22 | $25

Charles Village | 3316-18 Greenmount Ave. (bet. 33rd & 34th Sts.) |
410-889-6002

"You really get your money's worth" at this "pleasant little surprise" in Charles Village, a plainly named Thai mainstay known for "excellent", well-priced versions of pad Thai and other standards; the "quiet" setting is "cozy enough for a romantic meal" and still "kitschy enough for a fun gathering", while solid service and parking out back are further pluses.

Thai Arroy M *Thai* 26 | 16 | 23 | $21

South Baltimore | 1019 Light St. (bet. Cross & Hamburg Sts.) |
410-385-8587 | www.thaiarroy.com

Regular waits "speak to the quality and deliciousness" of the "authentic" Thai fare at this small South Baltimore spot; so the "decor could be nicer" – just focus on food that "couldn't be finer" brought by a "fast", "friendly" crew at "bargain" prices, and you'll know why regulars return "again and again"; P.S. BYO is "a welcome treat."

NEW Thames Street Oyster House *Seafood* ▽ 24 | 21 | 23 | $43

Fells Point | 1728 Thames St. (S. Ann St.) | 443-449-7726 |
www.thamesstreetoysterhouse.com

"Just-out-of-the-sea seafood" is reeled into this new brass-and-wood-trimmed oyster house dripping with "tons of charm and character", situated "right off the water" in Fells Point; the menu features "mighty tasty" Eastern coastal fare of every stripe (try a "Baltimore oyster shooter", complete with a splash of Natty Boh), the wine list "pairs perfectly" and service "provides guidance"; P.S. upstairs window seats afford a "harbor view."

13.5% Wine Bar Ⓜ *American*

22	23	22	$31

Hampden | 1117 W. 36th St. (bet. Falls Rd. & Hickory Ave.) | 410-889-1064 | www.13.5winebar.com

NEW Silo.5% Wine Bar ⑤Ⓜ *American*

Locust Point | Silo Point | 1200 Steuart St. (Clement St.) | 443-438- 4044 | www.silo.5winebar.com

"Raise a glass" (or two, or three) say cork dorks who frequent this "hip" Hampden wine bar with a "funky" but "stylish" orange-accented lounge sporting a wall of wine and a long bar; "tasty" pizzas and New American "nibbles" please, but the main draw is vino "at every price point" and a "knowledgeable" staff that "looks great serving it"; P.S. recently opened sibling Silo.5% mimics the "cool" vibe (albeit in a green shade) in Silo Point.

Tidewater Grille *American*

22	23	22	$29

Havre de Grace | 300 Franklin St. (St. John St.) | 410-939-3313 | www.thetidewatergrille.com

You "can't beat the decor" – a "picturesque" view of "water, boats and wildlife" via floor-to-ceiling windows and patio tables – at this "pleasant destination" on the Susquehanna River in Havre de Grace; both "budgets and taste buds" are well served by the variety on the "consistently good" American surf 'n' turf menu brought by a "friendly" team.

Timbuktu *Seafood*

23	15	20	$32

Hanover | 1726 Dorsey Rd. (Coca-Cola Dr./Rte. 100) | 410-796-0733 | www.timbukturestaurant.com

"Crab cakes are the real draw" at this "raucous" and cavernous Hanover seafooder where "an undemanding but hungry" army of eaters goes gaga for "hearty" patties made with "golf-ball-size chunks of crab and very little filler"; the digs are "less than modern" ("don't count on ambiance"), but prices are "reasonable", and the "friendly" service "keeps pace."

Tio Pepe *Continental/Spanish*

26	23	25	$52

Mt. Vernon | 10 E. Franklin St. (bet. Charles & St. Paul Sts.) | 410-539-4675 | www.coloquio.com

If this "immutable" special-occasion "staple" in Mt. Vernon is "favored by people nostalgic for the Nixon administration", well, longtime faithfuls explain it truly is "as great as it was years ago" – from the "outstanding", "authentic" Spanish-Continental fare to the "potent" sangria; a "superb" crew works the "wonderfully cozy", whitewashed subterranean setting (just make sure to bring mucho dinero).

NEW Townhouse Kitchen & Bar ❶ *American*

-	-	-	M

Harbor East | 1350 Lancaster St. (S. Spring St.) | 443-268-0323 | www.townhousebaltimore.com

It's BYOB – as in 'be your own bartender' – at this gastropub entry in Harbor East, where a handful of communal tables are outfitted with personalized beer and vodka taps billed by the ounce (mixers provided); a casual New American menu with international influences complements the beverages within the industrial-chic digs lined with leather sofas and furry pillows.

Towson Diner ❶ *Diner*
21 | 16 | 21 | $18

Towson | 718 York Rd. (Lambourne Rd.) | 410-321-0407

Sporting a menu as thick as a "small-town" "phone book", this "low-priced" 24/7 diner in Towson dishes "huge portions of comfort food", including "breakfast around the clock" and Greek specialties; "pleasant" staffers work the "old-fashioned" room with jukeboxes and a dessert case that makes some "weak in the knees."

Trattoria Alberto ⓢ *Italian*
▽ 28 | 20 | 26 | $63

Glen Burnie | 1660 Crain Hwy. S. (bet. Hospital Dr. & Rte. 100) | 410-761-0922 | www.trattoriaalberto.com

Specials evoking "a trattoria on the Adriatic", and other "delectable" fare are purveyed in this "relaxing", white-tablecloth Northern Italian stalwart consigned to an unlikely storefront setting in Glen Burnie; "personable", "professional" service rounds out the "old-style" experience, though the "steep" tabs should come as no surprise.

Umi Sake *Asian*
▽ 28 | 21 | 25 | $27

Cockeysville | 9726 York Rd. (Padonia Rd.) | 410-667-6586 | www.umisake.com

Considered a "gem amid the clutter of York Road" in Cockeysville's "quintessential suburbia", this "reasonably priced" Pan-Asian "go-to" garners waves of praise for "excellent" offerings, starring "creative" sushi; a team that "makes you feel special" works the simple, "modern" space with separate dining and lounge areas.

Victoria Gastro Pub *Eclectic*
24 | 22 | 22 | $32

Columbia | 8201 Snowden River Pkwy. (Waterloo Rd.) | 410-750-1880 | www.victoriagastropub.com

A "beer-lover's dream", this Columbia "after-office crowd"-pleaser pairs "wonderful" draft selections and an "epic" bottle list with Eclectic "gourmet" gastropub fare (the signature poutine is "decadence in a dish"); "friendly" servers and the "fabulous" "fern bar" setting deliver "first-date classy" at prices that "won't bankrupt you."

Vino Rosina ⓢ *American*
▽ 22 | 24 | 19 | $36

Harbor East | Bagby Bldg. | 507 S. Exeter St. (Eastern Ave.) | 410-528-8600 | www.vinorosina.com

The "modern, sleek and low-key" setting for this Harbor East wine bar in the rehabbed Bagby Building draws in the "almost-40 crowd" for "tasty" midpriced New American eats and a happy hour that delivers "super food and drink specials" plus "ambiance" to boot; service is solid, and if a few wanna-like-its find the experience "uneven", a recent chef change may smooth any rough edges.

NEW Waterfront Kitchen ❶Ⓜ *American*
22 | 24 | 21 | $43

Fells Point | 1417 Thames St. (Block St.) | 443-681-5310 | www.waterfrontkitchen.com

This aptly named Fells Point fledgling is truly a "place to discover", with its "stunning" space featuring "one of the loveliest views of the

those with "more pinch in their pockets", and the mix-and-match "create-your-own pasta" special is "a great option" at lunch.

Main Ingredient Café *American*　　25 | 17 | 22 | $28

Annapolis | 914 Bay Ridge Rd. (Georgetown Rd.) | 410-626-0388 | www.themainingredient.com

With a "deceiving" "strip-mall location" "just outside Annapolis", this New American bakery/cafe wows with "home-cooked fare" exhibiting flashes of "excellence", particularly their "to-die-for" breakfast items and soups; it's "priced right" too, making the earth-toned storefront with "sunny window" booths and a long bar served by a "welcoming staff" "popular with locals"; P.S. check out the "outrageous" desserts.

❷ Miss Shirley's *American*　　26 | 21 | 23 | $24

Annapolis | 1 Park Pl. (West St.) | 410-268-5171 | www.missshirleys.com
See review in the Baltimore Directory.

Nando's Peri-Peri *Chicken*　　22 | 19 | 19 | $17

Annapolis | Annapolis Mall | 2002 Annapolis Mall Rd. (Bestgate Rd.) | 410-224-0585 | www.nandosperiperi.com
See review in the Washington, DC, Directory.

O'Learys Seafood *Seafood*　　26 | 21 | 25 | $52

Eastport | 310 Third St. (Severn Ave.) | 410-263-0884 | www.olearysseafood.com

A "charming house" in Eastport is host to this "long-standing favorite" for what some say is the "best seafood in Annapolis"; the "high-end" fare has a "surprising" "inventiveness", and while it's "not cheap", "superb" service and an "intimate" timber-framed setting, adorned with the owner's colorful abstract artwork, leave diners feeling "pampered."

❷ Osteria 177 *Italian*　　27 | 24 | 25 | $51

Annapolis | 177 Main St. (Conduit St.) | 410-267-7700 | www.osteria177.com

"Outstanding" Northern Italian cuisine paired with "broad-ranging" wines and "delicious" seasonal cocktails are the main attractions at this "delightful surprise in the heart of Annapolis"; "expensive", sì, but the "polished" staff "truly knows the meaning of the word" 'service', making it a lock for "special occasions"; P.S. the $15 set-price lunch menu is "a real steal."

Paladar *Caribbean/Pan-Latin*　　23 | 24 | 23 | $31

Annapolis | Annapolis Town Ctr. | 1905 Town Centre Blvd. (Tower Pl.) | 410-897-1022 | www.paladarlatinkitchen.com

A "vibrant", "whimsical" atmosphere, supported by solid service, is the backdrop for the "flavorful", "extensive" Latin menu with a notable "Caribbean influence" at this midpriced chain link in the Annapolis Town Centre; starring "spectacular" rum-flight options and "devilishly delicious" mojitos that bring out the "inner dancer", happy hour at the "lively" bar is a "great value" and "perfect" for "drinks with coworkers" or "girls' night out."

Paul's Homewood Café *American/Greek*   25 | 19 | 24 | $35

Annapolis | 919 West St. (Taylor Ave.) | 410-267-7891 |
www.paulscafe-annapolis.com

It's "easy to miss" this cafe off the tourist track in Annapolis, but
"the hardest part" after finding it "is deciding what to eat" since everything's "a treat" on its menu of "excellent" American and Greek
"homestyle" cooking; add in "decent" prices, "attentive" service
and a "relaxed", "attractive", "modern" setting, and no wonder it's
a "local favorite."

☒ P.F. Chang's China Bistro *Chinese*   23 | 23 | 22 | $30

Annapolis | Annapolis Town Ctr. | 307 Sail Pl. (Forest Dr.) |
410-573-2990 | www.pfchangs.com
See review in the Washington, DC, Directory.

Red Hot & Blue *BBQ*   22 | 18 | 20 | $21

Annapolis | 200 Old Mill Bottom Rd. S. (Rte. 50, exit 28) |
410-626-7427 | www.redhotandblue.com
See review in the Washington, DC, Directory.

Reynolds Tavern   23 | 25 | 23 | $35
Restaurant *American/British*

Annapolis | Reynolds Tavern | 7 Church Circle (West St.) |
410-295-9555 | www.reynoldstavern.org

"Step back in time" to "Colonial Annapolis" at this "historic" inn serving a "varied" American menu, though it's perhaps better known for
its "unmatched" "British-style afternoon tea" (make reservations);
the "warm and friendly owners" and "refined" atmosphere that pervades the "quaint", "cozy" rooms allow patrons "to pause, reflect"
and "recover from life's vicissitudes"; P.S. the basement tavern, Sly
Fox Pub, is "quite good too."

The Rockfish ● *American*   ▽ 20 | 22 | 22 | $44

Eastport | 400 Sixth St. (Severn Ave.) | 410-267-1800 |
www.rockfishmd.com

A "welcoming" stop "after sailing on the bay", this Eastport eatery across the bridge from the Annapolis City Dock offers solid if
pricey seafood-centric American fare along with "a bit of local flavor"; the airy, open space is enhanced by a "knowledgeable" staff,
live music Tuesday–Saturday and "outgoing patrons" fishing for
dates at the "popular bar."

☒ Ruth's Chris Steak House *Steak*   26 | 24 | 26 | $67

Eastport | 301 Severn Ave. (3rd St.) | 410-990-0033 | www.ruthschris.com
See review in the Washington, DC, Directory.

Severn Inn *American*   22 | 25 | 22 | $44

Annapolis | 1993 Baltimore Annapolis Blvd. (Baltimore Blvd.) |
410-349-4000 | www.severninn.com

"The view is the big attraction" at this American seafood specialist
with plenty of deck seating overlooking the Severn River and the Naval
Academy, though the "delicious" fare (including "one of the best"
Sunday brunches in Annapolis) is also available inside, where there's a

"nice nautical" feel; service is "attentive", but tabs can get "pricey", so frugal locals suggest "go for a drink with out-of-town guests."

Sofi's Crepes *Crêpes*
24 | 14 | 21 | $12

Annapolis | 1 Craig St. (Prince George St.) | 410-990-0929 | www.sofiscrepes.com
See review in the Baltimore Directory.

Tsunami ● *Asian*
25 | 22 | 23 | $36

Annapolis | 51 West St. (bet. Calvert St. & Church Circle) | 410-990-9868 | www.kapowgroup.com
Take a seat at the window for a "great view" of "hipsters inside and out" of this "trendy" Annapolis Asian fusion drink-and-eatery plating "fantastic" midpriced sushi and the like in a "modern" milieu, supported by "personable" service and "creative bartending"; just "don't go for a quiet romantic dinner" on the "very crowded" weekends.

🄼 Vin 909 🅼 *American*
28 | 25 | 26 | $32

Annapolis | 909 Bay Ridge Ave. (Chesapeake Ave.) | 410-990-1846 | www.vin909.com
"Off the beaten path" in Annapolis, this "local walk-to" for Eastporters appeals to visitors as well with its "great-value" offering of "fabulous", "refined" New American fare and an "outstanding" wine selection; "exceptional" service and an "intimate", contemporary "cottage" setting create a "calming" backdrop "suitable for quiet conversation."

Wild Orchid Café *American*
23 | 21 | 23 | $42

Annapolis | 200 Westgate Circle (Spa Rd.) | 410-268-8009 | www.thewildorchidcafe.com
A "modern", "minimalist" setting is the backdrop at this New American on Westgate Circle, where "ingenuity" is evident in the "unique" seasonal menu focusing on local produce, meat and seafood ("which shows clearly in the prices"); factor in "personable" service, and it's "where Annapolis adults go for peaceful fine dining."

Yellowfin *American*
23 | 22 | 21 | $36

Edgewater | 2840 Solomons Island Rd. (Old S. River Rd.) | 410-573-1371 | www.yellowfinrestaurant.com
"Come by land or by sea, dressed up or down" for "lovely sunsets over the South River" at this midpriced, seafood-leaning American in Edgewater; the extensive menu offers many "good" options (even sushi), but what this place is really known for is its "worst-kept secret" of a happy hour (from 11:30 AM to 7 PM daily) and "can't-be-beat" Sunday brunch.

Eastern Shore

Ava's *Italian/Pizza*
27 | 20 | 24 | $28

St. Michaels | 409 S. Talbot St. (bet. Grace & Thompson Sts.) | 410-745-3081 | www.avaspizzeria.com

"High-end pizzas" and other "inspiring", "always delicious" choices (e.g. wasabi oysters, meatball sliders) pair with "serious wine" at this "reasonably priced" Italian "jewel" in St. Michaels; "personable" service is another asset, and if the brick-walled quarters get a bit "cozy" for some, a fireplace-enhanced patio provides a "pleasant" alternative.

Banning's Tavern *American*
▽ 22 | 20 | 23 | $29

Easton | Avalon Theatre | 42 E. Dover St. (Harrison St.) | 410-822-1733 | www.banningstavern.com

An "old-fashioned pub" ambiance, "great beer deals" and a "friendly" staff endow this Easton tavern with a convivial glow; and "hearty portions" of "good, honest" American eats at moderate prices also make it a "perfect" fueling spot when attending a show at the adjacent Avalon Theatre.

⊠ Bartlett Pear Inn Restaurant *American*
28 | 25 | 27 | $58

Easton | Bartlett Pear Inn | 28 S. Harrison St. (bet. E. Dover & South Sts.) | 410-770-3300 | www.bartlettpearinn.com

"Extraordinary doesn't begin to describe this culinary temple" rave pear-amours of the "beautifully prepared" New American dishes presented by "superb" staff at this "charming" and "gorgeous" Easton inn that dates to the late 18th century; prices place it "high on the romance and special-occasion scale", though the chef's tasting menu is a "relative bargain", and the bar offers a more casual approach.

Big Pickle Food Bar *American*
▽ 21 | 21 | 20 | $27

St. Michaels | 209 S. Talbot St. (bet. Carpenter & Willow Sts.) | 410-745-8011 | www.bigpicklefoodbar.com

"In the heart of historic St. Michaels", this "happy place" has a new chef (possibly outdating its Food rating) and a new emphasis on locally sourced ingredients in the "expertly prepared" New American dishes, many of them upscale riffs on deli fare; the moderate prices, "vibrant" decor and "inventive" cocktails remain, along with "very friendly" service and a courtyard dining area scented by an on-site meat smoker.

Bistro Poplar *French*
▽ 28 | 25 | 28 | $41

Cambridge | 535 Poplar St. (High St.) | 410-228-4884 | www.bistropoplar.com

"Every flavor is spot-on" at this "pleasantly authentic" French bistro "surprise" in Cambridge that offers "a refreshing" breath of "fine dining" on the Eastern Shore; with über-"friendly" service and a "lovely" Gallic atmosphere (buttery yellow walls, zinc bar), it's a "great value"; P.S. closed Tuesday and Wednesday.

	FOOD	DECOR	SERVICE	COST

Brasserie Brightwell *American/French* | 21 | 23 | 18 | $34 |

Easton | 206 N. Washington St. (Harisson St.) | 410-819-3838 | www.brasseriebrightwell.com

French and American "food with flair" – including "a wide variety of *petits plats*" plus selections from a raw bar and wood-fire grill – is served up at this "friendly" Easton brasserie whose "garage-chic" setting gets a lot of adaptive reuse out of its bay doors that open to a "sprawling patio" and outside bar; the "joie de vivre" is further expressed by an "ample" selection of wine and beer, all "reasonably" priced.

Crab Claw *Crab House* | 21 | 18 | 20 | $36 |

St. Michaels | 304 Burns St. (Talbot St.) | 410-745-2900 | www.thecrabclaw.com

"Hammering claws with a wooden mallet" while sipping a cold beer is "a must" on a summer day at this "friendly", "casual" St. Michaels "landmark" crab shack with views of the "boats" on the "beautiful" Miles River; "be prepared to claw your way" to an "outdoor waterfront table", as the place is "touristy for a reason"; P.S. open seasonally, March–November; Chesapeake Bay Maritime Museum is next door.

Harris Crab House *Crab House* | 24 | 18 | 21 | $33 |

Grasonville | 433 Kent Narrows Way N. (Rte. 50, exit 42) | 410-827-9500 | www.harriscrabhouse.com

"Amazing" crabs, "oysters galore" and other "excellent" catch are ferried by an "honest", hard-working staff, an ample "reward for driving" by land or sea to this moderately priced "old-time crab house" in Grasonville; the huge, "shabby-chic" setting may feel like a "cafeteria" to some, but on a nice day there's "nothing better" than a brown-papered picnic table with a "commanding view of Kent Narrows."

Kentmorr *Crab House*   ∇ | 25 | 18 | 22 | $33 |

Stevensville | 910 Kentmorr Rd. (Lane Ave.) | 410-643-2263 | www.kentmorr.com

An "extensive" menu of "fantastic" seafood-focused American fare draws crab-lovers and others "off the beaten path", by car and boat, to this "casual", midpriced Kent Island "bay-front spot" that recalls the Eastern Shore "years ago"; the service is "warm and friendly", and its "cool" Tiki bar, with hammocks on the beach, gives new meaning to "relaxing" "by the water."

Mason's ⓩ *American* | 26 | 24 | 25 | $49 |

Easton | 22 S. Harrison St. (South Ln.) | 410-822-3204 | www.masonsgourmet.com

As a purveyor of "delectable" New American edibles, this "classic" in an old home in Easton's "historic district" has foodies "dreaming"; a staff that goes the "extra mile" patrols the multitude of rooms that leavens their "traditional character" with "an upbeat contemporary atmosphere", and though the experience can be pricey, "they never skimp on the portions"; P.S. "alfresco dining is a plus" in fine weather.

FOOD | DECOR | SERVICE | COST

The Narrows *Seafood* `25` `21` `23` `$42`

Grasonville | 3023 Kent Narrows Way S. (Rte. 50, exit 41/42) | 410-827-8113 | www.thenarrowsrestaurant.com

"Those delicious creatures that inhabit the bay" take the form of "buttery" crab cakes "full of giant lumps" and "to-die-for" crab soup at this "expensive" "touch of fine dining" in Kent Narrows; the other seafood offerings are "fabulous" too, and "spectacular" waterfront views are supported by "impeccable" servers who work the "open and airy", nautically themed space.

▣ Out of the Fire 🅂Ⓜ *American/Eclectic* `28` `24` `26` `$42`

Easton | 22 Goldsborough St. (Washington St.) | 410-770-4777 | www.outofthefire.com

"Sit at the bar and watch the action" in the kitchen at this "superb" Easton American-Eclectic where "amazing chefs" who really "get the magic of fresh, local ingredients" "artfully plate" "great things" cooked via the showpiece open hearth; it's not cheap for such an "informal" vibe, but service is "attentive" and the space is "inviting" with a "warm" "Tuscan" palette.

Pope's Tavern *American* ▽ `27` `25` `28` `$44`

Oxford | Oxford Inn | 504 S. Morris St. (Oxford Rd.) | 410-226-5220 | www.oxfordinn.net

A circa-1880 Oxford inn is the romantic setting for this high-end "Eastern shore favorite" offering "superbly prepared" New American selections in a best-of-both-worlds setting: "cozy in winter, airy in summer"; a mix of "locals" and "visitors" appreciates the "first-rate" service and complimentary "Popemobile" (i.e. a British cab) that shuttles diners from the dock or other locales within town; P.S. closed Tuesday and Wednesday.

Rustico *Italian* ▽ `25` `23` `23` `$37`

Stevensville | 401 Love Point Rd. (Rte. 8) | 410-643-9444 | www.rusticoonline.com

This "terrific" "little gem" in Stevensville "does not disappoint" Eastern Shore residents with its "delicious", midpriced menu of "awesome pasta" and other traditional Southern Italian fare served in "huge portions" indoors or "alfresco on a summer's day"; a "comfy" rustico atmosphere, capable service and an "excellent wine list" are also inducements, and the four-course prix fixe dinner gets special mention.

▣ Ruth's Chris Steak House *Steak* `26` `24` `26` `$67`

Berlin | GlenRiddle Golf Clubhse. | 11501 Maid at Arms Ln. (off Rte. 50) | 888-632-4747 | www.ruthschris.com

See review in the Washington, DC, Directory.

Salter's Tavern *American/Seafood* `25` `23` `23` `$54`

Oxford | Robert Morris Inn | 314 N. Morris St. (Strand) | 410-226-5111 | www.robertmorrisinn.com

"Every meal hits the mark" at this Oxfordian in a "picturesque" circa-1710 inn, where chef Mark Salter brings a British sensibility to crab cakes and other Chesapeake classics, which are "smoothly" served by a "dedicated" staff; the "dark" and "cozy" space, with its open-hearth fireplace, has the "quaint elegance of Colonial times", while the patio and porch, with a view of the ferry, are "bliss on a summer's eve"; P.S. the casual tap room is significantly cheaper.

Scossa *Italian*   `28` `26` `27` `$52`

Easton | 8 N. Washington St. (Dover St.) | 410-822-2202 | www.scossarestaurant.com

This "sophisticated" "surprise for the Eastern Shore" in Easton comprises "exceptional", "authentic" Northern Italian fare "you'll dream about for weeks" with "a great wine list to support it", a "delightful, chic" interior (plus "lovely" terrace) and "superb" service; it can be "expensive", yes, but it's an all-around "fabulous dining experience."

NEW **Theo's Steakhouse** Ⓜ *Steak*   `-` `-` `-` `E`

St. Michaels | 407 S. Talbot St. (Grace St.) | www.theossteakhouse.com

The lean, meat-focused menu at this rookie St. Michaels steakhouse may not be big, but it includes all the usual suspects plus a few pricey, limited-availability prime cuts (sourced from a butcher shop two blocks away); classic and not-so-classic apps and sides round out the offerings in the sleek, caramel-hued space; P.S. closed Monday and Tuesday.

NEW **208 Talbot** Ⓜ *American*   `-` `-` `-` `E`

St. Michaels | 208 N. Talbot St. (North St.) | 410-745-3838 | www.208talbot.com

Shore star chef David Clark gathers fellow veterans from his sous-chef days at this newly resurrected, reinvigorated sequel to what was once a foodie and weekender destination on St. Michaels' main drag; well-heeled types may recognize some edgy New American-Chesapeake items from his erstwhile restaurant Julia's in Centerville while dining in the redecorated tavern setting that's dressed in exposed bricks and dove-gray walls; P.S. closed Monday and Tuesday.

Wine Vintage Chart

This chart is based on a 30-point scale. The ratings (by U. of South Carolina law professor **Howard Stravitz**) reflect vintage quality and the wine's readiness to drink. A dash means the wine is past its peak or too young to rate. Loire ratings are for dry whites.

Whites	95	96	97	98	99	00	01	02	03	04	05	06	07	08	09	10
France:																
Alsace	24	23	23	25	23	25	26	22	21	22	23	21	26	26	23	26
Burgundy	27	26	22	21	24	24	23	27	23	26	26	25	26	25	25	-
Loire Valley	-	-	-	-	-	-	-	25	20	22	27	23	24	24	24	25
Champagne	26	27	24	25	25	25	21	26	21	-	-	-	-	-	-	-
Sauternes	21	23	25	23	24	24	29	24	26	21	26	25	27	24	27	-
California:																
Chardonnay	-	-	-	-	22	21	24	25	22	26	29	24	27	23	27	-
Sauvignon Blanc	-	-	-	-	-	-	-	-	-	25	24	27	25	24	25	-
Austria:																
Grüner V./Riesl.	22	-	25	22	26	22	23	25	25	24	23	26	25	24	25	-
Germany:	22	26	22	25	24	-	29	25	26	27	28	26	26	26	26	-

Reds	95	96	97	98	99	00	01	02	03	04	05	06	07	08	09	
France:																
Bordeaux	25	25	24	25	24	29	26	24	26	25	28	24	24	25	27	-
Burgundy	26	27	25	24	27	22	23	25	25	23	28	24	24	25	27	-
Rhône	26	22	23	27	26	27	26	-	26	25	27	25	26	23	27	-
Beaujolais	-	-	-	-	-	-	-	-	-	-	27	25	24	23	28	25
California:																
Cab./Merlot	27	24	28	23	25	-	27	26	25	24	26	24	27	26	25	-
Pinot Noir	-	-	-	-	-	-	26	25	24	25	26	24	27	24	26	-
Zinfandel	-	-	-	-	-	-	25	24	26	24	23	21	26	23	25	-
Oregon:																
Pinot Noir	-	-	-	-	-	-	-	26	24	25	24	25	24	27	24	-
Italy:																
Tuscany	25	24	29	24	27	24	27	-	24	27	25	26	25	24	-	-
Piedmont	21	27	26	25	26	28	27	-	24	27	26	26	27	26	-	-
Spain:																
Rioja	26	24	25	22	25	24	28	-	23	27	26	24	24	25	26	-
Ribera del Duero/Priorat	25	26	24	25	25	24	27	-	24	27	26	24	25	27	-	-
Australia:																
Shiraz/Cab.	23	25	24	26	24	24	26	26	25	25	26	21	23	26	24	-
Chile:	-	-	-	-	24	22	25	23	24	24	27	25	24	26	24	-
Argentina:																
Malbec	-	-	-	-	-	-	-	-	-	25	26	27	26	26	25	-

Latest openings, menus, photos and more on plus.google.com/local